PLATO
DICTIONARY

Books by Morris Stockhammer

Platons Weltanschauung

Kants Zurechnungsidee und Freiheitsantinomie

PLATO DICTIONARY

Edited by
MORRIS STOCKHAMMER

PHILOSOPHICAL LIBRARY
New York

Copyright, 1963, by
Philosophical Library, Inc.
15 East 40 Street, New York 16, N.Y.
All rights reserved
Library of Congress Catalog Card Number: 63-11488

Printed in the United States of America

To my grandchildren

PREFACE

It is generally agreed that Plato was born in Athens or Aegina about 428/7 and died in Athens in 348/7. But like so many accounts of the life and deeds of ancient heroes we find that the history of Plato is deeply entwined in myth and legend. Greek heroes were produced and protected by the gods so it was fitting to trace Plato's paternal lineage back to the ancient kings of Athens and even to Poseidon. On his mother's side the facts relate him to distinguished historical figures active in the establishment of the rule of the Thirty and from their influence arose his earliest interests in a political career. We may conjecture that he was educated along the usual lines of Grecian paidaia, a prerequisite for one so well endowed with natural talent and one who had achieved such extraordinary knowledge as evidenced in the Dialogues. That he chose the career of a "college professor" rather than that of a politician may have been due to his early disillusionment with the political activities of his relatives and, especially, the horrors associated with the fate of Socrates. After Socrates' death Plato seems to have concentrated on the quest for wisdom as a means of furthering the noble aspirations of such an impressive friend.

There are fascinating legends about Plato's trips to Italy, Egypt, Palestine and Sicily, where he is supposed to have acquired a knowledge of Pythagorean philosophy, Egyptian mathematics, art and games and Jewish beliefs as well as an opportunity to employ a statesman's hand in practical politics. Most people agree that he did visit Syracuse several times in an attempt to educate Dionysius II in the art of governing. However, the Platonic ideal had scant chance of practical success. The impetuous ruler resented beginning with an education in the humanities and sciences before putting into execution the effective powers of the State.

For several years he had been writing dramatic dialogues in which he not only perpetuated the delightful memory of Socrates but also applied his penetrating dialectical inquiry into the definable essence of the various virtues required for living the good life in society. It was about the year 388/7 that he founded the Academy, a school dedicated to the education of youths in the way of wisdom. Literature and the sciences, especially mathematics, were pre-requisites to excursions into the realm of Metaphysics. His ideas about a university curriculum and about the nature and function of the disciplines which constitute it appear throughout the Dialogues he had already written and would continue to write while head of the University. For the next forty years he spent most of his time educating the young adults in the pursuit of truth on all possible levels. In 367 Aristotle came under his influence and later developed into one of the Academy's greatest graduates. The curriculum itself became a model for education in the Middle Ages and even today it is followed, in its general pattern, by some liberal arts colleges.

The ideas discussed in the Platonic Dialogues have had a far-reaching influence. In fact, someone has remarked that the subsequent development of philosophy was in part merely footnotes to Plato. Perhaps the greatest influence has been felt in the philosophy and speculative theology of the Christian Church. One of the earliest Christian scholars labeled as a "philosopher" was Justin, the Martyr (d. 167) who, after investigating all the schools of his day, decided that the Platonic was the one best adapted to lead him to wisdom. The general philosophical method of enquiry and the organic unity of Platonic thought appealed more than any other to the medieval Christians. Clement of Alexandria, Origen, Minucius Felix, Arnobius, Gregory of Nyssa and Maximus the Confessor drew copiously from the Platonic well. Most everyone is aware of the Christian Platonist, Augustine of Hippo, who did more than any other to make the ideas of Plato popular in the West. His version of Platonism was the basic philosophy in the Christian Church up to the time of the formal "approval" of the philosophy of St. Thomas Aquinas in the fourteenth century. In spite of this formal acceptance the philosophy of Plato continued to influence the majority of Christian thinkers and, actually, even the philosophy of St. Thomas owes more to Plato than a lot of Thomists will admit. Of the two outstanding Greek philosophical developments, Plato's has influenced more people and delighted more students engaged in the pursuit of truth than any other even down to our own day.

Plato's emphasis on the need for truth and its possibility of attainment, on the necessity of following truth wherever it led, on the presence of order and intelligence in the universe as an indication of the providential interest of a supreme being and as a basis of scientific progress, on the spiritual character and immortal destiny of the human soul, on the role of Ideal-Forms in the logical, metaphysical and ethical realms, on the need for living the good life publicly and privately, on virtue, self-control and intelligence as elements of happiness, all have been accepted, developed and integrated into the Christian way of life. Platonic ascesis formed a background for the principles of the Christian combat and Platonic mysticism was accepted as a natural preliminary for the way of supernatural union.

Theodore E. James

Manhattan College

INTRODUCTION

> "Henceforward I shall begin
> to think about justice"
> (Alcibiades, 135)

I

The Platonic dialogues reveal with excellent artistry that the two-fold role of the philosopher is to be an acute discoverer of truth and a wise guide to righteousness. Plato starts his inquiries with virtue and not with freedom, which must be subordinated to it: "Wealth, freedom and tranquillity are neither good nor bad; nothing but statesmanship makes us wise" (Euthydemus, 292). Since freedom is not, as many assume, an incontestable ideal, being neither absolutely good nor absolutely bad, it is a mistake to regard freedom as a separate value, existing beside justice, and being good even when abused by totalitarian conspirators. Wise righteousness is the only ideal, reigning supreme. Since freedom is not an end but only a means, one must make sure that the person to whom one grants freedom is a worthy character. Plato does not share the widespread opinion that freedom must be accorded to everybody alike. Wealth, freedom and tranquillity are only profitable if they serve good purposes. Democratic freedom means restricted liberty, i.e., limited freedom. Only a man who cherishes democratic ideals deserves the privilege of freedom in general and the right of freedom of speech in particular. Only a qualified freedom servicing humanity is in the interest of democracy. Daniel Webster said: "Liberty belongs (only) to those who deserve it," that is, to champions of brotherhood and not to advocates of hate. Democracy must be, like life itself, realistic or militant: "gentle with friends but fierce with enemies" (Republic, II, 375).

II

Plato seeks intelligently a proper balance between order and freedom. An excess of freedom is just as objectionable as an excess of authority. Democracy has no chance to survive if it does not effectively parry the dictatorial menace by rejecting absolute freedom of speech, press and assembly. Exaggerated freedom invites tyranny.

Plato has often been considered as a fascist. He critisizes, however, only deteriorating democracy, as he excludes degenerated poetry and music from his ideal state. But he admires sound democracy as well as healthy poetry and music. "We philosophers belong to a brotherhood of the free" (Theaetetus, 173). Democrats as well as Plato advocate the spiritual aristocracy of wisdom, which is still a rare commodity.

By the way, Plato's proposal that rulers should be philosophers is not a queer dream, for Plato understands, in this context, by a philosopher not only an academic professor but also a wise, noble and gentle person. Don't we wish that our statesmen should be endowed with wisdom? Call the ruler philosopher, king or president, he ought to be wise. Had Plato expressed this familiar thought that wise men should be rulers in a prosaic fashion he would have gone unnoticed by the reader; but giving the truism an unusual formulation, he caught the attention of the centuries. Plato's original diction is one of the secret weapons of his style.

III

As can be seen, Plato reaches theoretically and emotionally into the heart of our present-day problems. He asks and answers eternal questions, not confined to any particular time period. Far from being antiquated and abstruse, Plato's *philosophia perennis* vividly deals with practical issues such as democracy and dictatorship, peace and war, righteousness and happiness, idealism and materialism. Plato belongs to us for he reminds us tirelessly, with prophetic fervor, that man does not live on bread alone but also strives for spiritual nourishment. Man possesses a soul which, like the body, requires attentive care. Plato compassionately admonishes the preachers of materialism that man is an intelligent being having a soul, moral character, a reasonable vocation. "No one can argue that pleasure is not pleasant" (Philebus, 13), but *homo sapiens* must be mindful of responsibility and duty as well as enjoyment. Man is a political or civilized animal who aspires to the attainment of certain ideals or valuable goals. Without the moral aspect man would be doomed to a mere bestial existence. Gifted with reason man ought not to rant against reason.

IV

Plato's basic assumption of two sorts of conditions has far-reaching implications. For two different conditions (reasons and causes) are responsible for the generation of two separate orders: the world of prescriptive or normative ideas and the world of non-prescriptive or mechanical (amoral) facts. The natural phenomena or effects ("becoming") originate in causes which are void of intelligence, but the spiritual phenomena of merit and guilt ("being") are derived from "rational grounds on which we praise or blame" (Statesman, 283). "Here are two principles (existences, conditions) — one is generation (nature, cause) and the other is essence (spirit, ground)" (Philebus, 54). The dichotomy of amoral causes and moral reasons is a manifestation of the dualism of matter and spirit. Spiritual science must simply be established because there are, besides apprehensible facts, also spiritual or moral ideas which require comprehension, too. Natural science consists of "reasoning combined with sensation" (Republic, VIII, 546), spiritual science of intuitive reasoning. Reasoning is in both cases an essential source of knowledge, although being discredited by the empiricists who tolerate only sensation. Plato, therefore, glorifies the capacity of pure thinking or "dialectic" without overlooking observation, the other fountain of knowledge.

To the materialists reason and wisdom appear to be empty shells but spiritual value-ideas — in Plato's condensed phrase: "ideas" — exist and Plato defended them against the materialists. He is thus the Greek Kant advocating the dualism between spirit and matter, intelligent idea and unintelligent fact, moral value and amoral event, noumena and phenomena. Spiritual essence is the positive quality behind the negative attributes of "immortality, invisibility, immovability and unchangeability." Plato, a philosopher's philosopher, believes with Anaxagoras "that the moral mind or soul is the ordering and containing principle of all things" (Cratylus, 400). Spiritual morality or moral spirit exists and human conduct is pervaded by reason. This anti-materialism is his main contribution to occidental philosophy.

Plato's teachings are well known: "A higher order is the reality of objects . . . at the heart of things there is intelligence at work, endeavoring to fulfill itself everywhere . . . the visible world is a copy or image of the invisible . . . an incorporeal law holds rule over a living body . . . man beholds the universal light of reason . . . the soul is superior to the body and makes us what we are . . . God is the creating demiurgos and the world is his product. . . ." The assumption of the two worlds, the one visible and the other invisible, is the guiding thread through Plato's labyrinthian system.

V

The key to unlock Plato's philosophy is his concept of the idea. Properly understood, Plato 'ideas" disclose the mystery surrounding them. His "ideas" are moral-ideas, value-ideas. Modern translators substitute the term "form" for the "idea." One should, however, return to the older translation and even use the explicatory phrase "moral idea." Be it justice, goodness or morality it is always a normative idea which Plato distinguishes from non-moral matter. He is a "worshipper of virtue" (Epinomis, 989): "The sum of all noble thoughts shall be that the life which is by the gods deemed to be the happiest is the holiest; we shall affirm this to be a most certain purpose" (Laws, II, 664). Being the Greek conscience of mankind, Plato is due for a renaissance.

But enough of the praise. Let Plato speak for himself, in his own inimitable words. It should turn out to be a rewarding reading.

VI

A new look at Plato's ethics of moral ideas has occasioned this book which is written in a non-technical language — as philosophy should be written. For philosophy is only a general science which can be expressed in generally understandable terms; only the particular science of an expert must use *termini technici*.

* *

This text of Plato is based on: The Dialogues of Plato, in Four Volumes, translated in English with Analyses and Introduction by B. Jowett, M. A., The Jefferson Press, Boston & New York, 1871, and on: Werke, by F. Schleiermacher, Realschulbuchhandlung, Berlin, 1804/05.

References are given thus: 'Republic, VII, 521', which means 'Plato's Dialogue Republic, edited by Henry Estienne (Stephanus), Book VII, Page 521'.

M. S.

A

Ability. You have already admitted that he who is false must have the ability to be false: you said that he who is unable to be false will not be false. — Lesser Hippias, 367.

Above and Below. If a person were to go round the universe in a circle, he would often, when standing at the antipodes, speak of the same point as above and below; but to speak of the whole which is in the form of a globe as having one part above and another below is not like a sensible man. — Timaeus, 63.

Absolute. There is an absolute beauty and an absolute good, and of other things to which the term "many" is applied there is an absolute; for they may be brought under a single idea, which is called the essence of each. — Republic, VI, 507.

Tell me, whether there is or is not any absolute beauty or good or any other absolute existence? — Cratylus, 439.

Those who see the many beautiful, and who yet neither see absolute beauty, nor can follow any guide who points the way thither; who see the many just, and not absolute justice, and the like — such persons may be said to have concrete, but no abstract knowledge. — Republic, VI, 479.

Abstention. They are willing to abstain from the pleasures of love for the sake of a victory in wrestling, running, and the like; and shall our young men be incapable of a similar endurance for the sake of a much nobler — moral — victory, which is the noblest of all? Will not the fear of impiety enable them to master that which inferior people have mastered? — Laws, VIII, 840.

Abstract Art. I do not mean by the beauty of form such beauty as that of animals or pictures, which the many would suppose to be my meaning; but understand me to mean straight lines and circles, and the plane and solid figures which are formed out of them by turning lathes and rulers and measures of angles; for these I affirm to be not only relatively beautiful, like other works of art, but they are eternally and abstractly beautiful. — Philebus, 51.

Abstraction. Such abstraction [thinking of the spiritual apart from the material] is the lifelong study of the soul. — Phaedo, 80.

Abuse. The abuse of a thing brings discredit on its lawful use. — Symposium, 182.

Accounting. He who transgresses the laws is to be called to account, which is a term used not only in your country, but also in many others. — Protagoras, 326.

Accurate. To learn all these things accurately would be very tiresome. — Euthyphro, 14.

Accusers. The hardest of all — the names of my accusers I do not know and cannot tell. — Apology, 18.

Acheron. In the opposite direction flows Acheron, which passes under the earth through desert places. — Phaedo, 112.

Achilles. I cannot allow our citizens to believe that Achilles, the son of a goddess [Thetis] and of Leleus who was the gentlest of men and third in descent from Zeus, was so disordered in his wits as to have been at one time affected with overweening contempt of gods and men. — Republic, III, 391.

Achilles was quite aware, for he had been told by his mother, that he might avoid death and return home, and live to a good old age, if he abstained from slaying Hector. Nevertheless he gave his life to revenge his lover Patroclus. — Symposium, 180.

Acquisitive. Next follows the whole class of learning and cognition, together with trade, fighting, hunting; since none of these produces anything, but is only engaged in conquering by word and deed, or in preventing others from conquering, things which exist and have been already produced — in each and all of these branches there appears to be an art which may be called acquisitive. — Sophist, 219.

Acquittal. The law says that when a man is acquitted he is free from guilt, and what holds at law may hold in argument. — Republic, V, 451.

Action. I suppose that we begin to act when we think that we know what we are doing? — First Alcibiades, 117.

There is the kind of actions done by violence and in the light of day, and another kind of actions which are done in darkness and with secret deceit, or sometimes both with violence and deceit. — Laws, IX, 864.

All his actions should be with a view to justice. — Gorgias, 527.

All our actions are to be done for the sake of the good. — Gorgias, 500.

Our actions have life, and there is much virtue in them and much vice. — Laws, X, 904.

Actions vary according to the manner of their performance. Take, for instance, that which we are now doing, drinking, singing, and talking; these actions are not in themselves either good or evil, but turn out in this or that way according to the mode of performing them; and when well done they are good, and when wrongly done they are evil; and in like manner not every love, but only that which has a noble purpose, is noble and worthy of praise. — Symposium, 181.

Are not actions also a class of being? — Yes, actions are real as well as things. — Cratylus, 386.

Actor. The same men cannot be actors for tragedies and comedies. — Republic, III, 395.

Actual. We are to look at the ideals of absolute justice and the character of the perfectly just in order that we might judge of our own happiness according to the standard which they exhibit and the degree in which we resemble them, but not with any view of showing that they could be realized in fact. Must not the actual always fall short of the ideal? Then you must not insist on my proving that the actual state will in every respect coincide with the ideal: if we are only able to discover how a city may be governed nearly as we proposed, you will admit that we have discovered the possibility which you demand;

and will be contented. — Republic, V, 472, 473.

Administration. In the administration of the state, man will benefit his friends and damage his enemies. — Meno, 71.

Admission. Such an open admission appears to me to be a better sort of precaution than concealment. — Protagoras, 317.

Admonition. There is the time-honored mode which our fathers commonly practiced towards their sons, and which is still adopted by many — either of roughly reproving their errors, or of gently advising them, which may be called by the general term of admonition. — Sophist, 230.

Adoption. If any citizen is willing to adopt a son who is put away, no law shall hinder him. — Laws, XI, 929.

Adultery. Do you believe that he who bribes his neighbor's wife and commits adultery with her, acts justly or unjustly? — Unjustly. — Eryxias, 396.

Adulterers are generally of the lascivious breed. — Symposium, 191.

Advance. Unless we can protect our retreat, we shall pay the penalty of our advance. — Theaetetus, 181.

Advantage. If they give everything and we give nothing, that must be an affair of business in which we have very greatly the advantage of them. — Euthyphro, 15.

We do not simply kill a man or exile him or expropriate him for the sake of these acts, but because they are conducive to our advantage. — Gorgias, 468.

Advice. My advice is simple in appearance but difficult to understand. — Letter XI, 359.

I will not give advice to a man who either does not ask for it, or demonstrates distinctly that there is not the least probability of his taking it. — Letter VII, 331.

I do advise a man with all my heart if he will probably listen to my counsel, or if he has at least fairly well regulated his daily habits. — Letter VII, 331.

Adviser. There are not many advisers of the young. — Letter V, 321.

I consider an adviser as a coward, who gives counsel to men who have relinquished the right path of governments, and tolerate only such an adviser who caters to their wishes by showing them the quickest and easiest way to satisfy them. — Letter VII, 331.

Some laugh at the very notion of advising others, and when they are asked for counsel will not say what they think. They guess at the wishes of the person who asks them, and answer according to the inquirer's, and not according to their own, opinion. — Laches, 178.

Advocate of Justice. There are many noble things in human life, but to most of them attach evils which corrupt and spoil them. Has not justice been the civilizer of humanity, and is not that noble? And must not the advocate of justice be also noble? And yet upon this has come an evil reputation, shielded under the fair name of art. — Laws, XI, 937.

Aesop. If Aesop had noticed them, he would have made a fable. — Phaedo, 60.

Affairs. The fact that attending to one's own affairs is most pleasant in life, is obvious almost to anyone. — Letter IX, 358.

Affirmation. We know that in discourse there is affirmation and denial. — Sophist, 263.

Agamemnon. Agamemnon chose the life of an eagle, because he hated human nature by reason of his sufferings. — Republic, X, 620.

Age. When a man has reached old age he ought not to be repining at the prospect of death. — Crito, 43.

At our age, there should be no feeling of irritation. — Laws, I, 634.

At his age, he can hardly be expected to understand. — Charmides, 162.

The middle age of man is a breathing spell in the miseries of life. — Epinomis, 974.

He arrived at middle age, the adjusted period of life. — Letter III, 316.

He is just of an age at which he will like to talk. — Charmides, 154.

The truth is that these regrets, and also the complaints about relations, are to be attributed to the same cause, which is not old age, but men's characters and tempers; for he who is of a calm and happy nature will hardly feel the pressure of age, but to him who is of an opposite disposition youth and age are equally a burden. — Republic, I, 329.

There is nothing which I like better than conversing with aged men; for I regard them as travelers who have made a journey which I too may have to make, and of whom I ought to inquire whether the way is smooth and easy, or rugged and difficult. — Republic, I, 328.

The young men in the state often give honors to the aged. — Laws, IV, 721.

Is life hard towards the end? — Republic, I, 328.

Agent. The agent is the same as the cause, and the same may be said of the patient or effect. — Philebus, 26, 27.

Agility. In all bodily actions, not quietness, but the greatest agility and quickness, is noblest and best. — Charmides, 159.

Aggravation. I do but aggravate a disorder which I am seeking to cure. — Protagoras, 340.

Agitation. When someone applies external agitation to affectations of anxiety, the rocking motion coming from without gets the better of the terrible and violent internal one, and produces a peace and calm in the soul, and quiets the restless palpitation of the heart, which is a thing much to be desired, sending some to sleep, and making others who are awake to dance to the pipe, and producing in them a sound mind, which takes the place of their former agitation. And in this is a considerable degree of sense. — Laws, VII, 790, 791.

Agreement. If my opponent says anything which is convincing, I shall be the first to agree with him. — Gorgias, 506.

You cannot have been led to agree with me, either from lack of knowledge or from superfluity of modesty, nor from a desire to deceive me, for you are my friend. — Gorgias, 487.

Everyone is aware that about some things we agree, whereas about other things we differ. When one speaks of iron or silver, is not the same thing present in the minds of all? But when one speaks of justice and goodness, there is every sort of disagreement, and we are at odds with one another and with ourselves. — Phaedrus, 263.

If you ask anyone about the nature of wood and stone are the many not agreed? But are the many agreed with themselves, or with one another, about the justice or injustice of men? — First Alcibiades, 111, 112.

Ought a man fulfill his agreement he admits to be right, or ought he to break it? — Crito, 49.

Agriculture. After this they came together in greater numbers, and increased the size of their cities, and betook themselves to agriculture, first of all at the foot of the mountains, and made enclosures of loose walls and works of defense, in order to keep off wild beasts; thus creating a single large and common habitation. — Laws, III, 681.

The production of barley and wheat and the preparing of food from them, excellent crafts though they are, will not make a man fully wise — why, the very word *produce* might tend to cause a certain repugnance to the product — and the same thing is true of all farming. — Epinomis, 975.

Air. There are differences in the air, of which the brightest part is called ether, as the most turbid sort of air is called mist. — Timaeus, 58.

Ajax. Ajax could not be wounded by steel. — Symposium, 219.

The soul which obtained the twentieth lot chose the life of a lion, and this was the soul of Ajax the son of Telamon, who would not be a man, remembering the injustice which was done him in the judgment about the arms. — Republic, X, 620.

Alcestis. Love will make men dare to die for their beloved; and women as well as men. Of this, Alcestis the daughter of Pelias is a monument to all Hellas; for she was willing to lay down her life on behalf of her husband, when no one else would, although he had a father and mother; but the tenderness of her love so far exceeded theirs, that they seemed to be as strangers to their own son, having no concern with him; and so noble did this action of hers appear, not only to men but also to the gods, that among the many who have done virtuously she was one of the very few to whom the gods have granted the privilege of returning to earth, in admiration of her virtue; such exceeding honor is paid by them to the devotion and virtue of love. — Symposium, 179.

Alcibiades. I know that you have been in chase of the fair Alcibiades. — Protagoras, 309.

Alien. Any alien who likes may come and be resident on certain conditions; a foreigner, if he likes, and is able to settle, may dwell in the land, but he must practice a craft, and not abide more than twenty years from the time at which he has registered himself. And he shall pay no sojourner's tax however small, except good conduct, nor any other tax for buying and selling. — Laws, VII, 850.

Alike. Things which are alike in some particular ought not to be called alike, nor things which are unlike in some particular, however slight, unlike. — Protagoras, 331.

There is always some point of veiw in which everything is like every other thing; white is in a certain way like black, and hard is like soft, and the most extreme opposites have some qualities in common. — Protagoras, 331.

Have I not heard someone say that the like is the greatest enemy of the like, the good of the good? — and in fact he quoted the authority of Hesiod, who says, "That potter quarrels with potter, bard with bard, beggar with beggar"; and of all other things he also says, "That of necessity the most like are most full of envy, strife, and hatred of one another, and the most unlike of friendship. For the poor man is compelled to be the friend of the rich, and the weak requires the aid of the strong, and the sick man of the physician; everyone who knows not has to love and court him who knows." — Lysis, 215.

Allegory. The narrative of Hephaestus binding Hera his mother, or how on another occasion Zeus sent him flying for taking her part when she was being beaten, and all the battles of the gods in Homer — these tales must not be admitted into our state, either wrought in allegory or without allegory. For a young person cannot judge what is allegorical and what is literal; anything that he receives into his mind at that age is likely to become indelible and unalterable; and therefore it is most important that the stories which the young first hear should be models of virtuous thoughts. — Republic, II, 378.

Alliances. In what sort of actions is the just man most able to do his friends good? — In making alliances with them. — Republic, I, 332.

Amateurs. Musical amateurs run about at the Dionysiac festivals as if their ears were under an engagement to hear every chorus; whether the performance is in town or country — that makes no difference — they are there. — Republic, V, 475.

Amatory Art. To lavish gifts on those we hunt is the amatory art. — Sophist, 222.

Ambassador. If any herald or ambassador carry a false message to any other city, or bring back a false message, let him be indicted for having offended the laws, and let there be a penalty fixed, which he shall suffer or pay if he be convicted. — Laws, XII, 941.

Ambiguity. Ambiguity of words causes difficulty and obscurity. — Laws, VIII, 837.

I thought that I must be plain with him and have no more ambiguity. — Symposium, 218.

Ambition. When his ambition is once fired, he will go on to learn. — Laches, 182.

If they leave philosophy and lead the lower life of ambition, then, probably in the dark or in some other careless hour, the two wanton animals take the two souls when off their guard and bring them together, and they accomplish that desire of their hearts which to the many is bliss; and this having once enjoyed they continue to enjoy, yet rarely because they have not the approval of the whole soul. — Phaedrus, 256.

Amending. I will amend the definition. — Euthyphro, 9.

Amoral. Wood, stones, and the like — these are things which are neither good nor evil; they are morally indifferent or amoral things. — Gorgias, 468.

There are some things which are amoral: neither good nor evil. — Protagoras, 351.

Amphibious. He is one of an amphibious class — one of those whom Prodicus describes as on the border ground between philosophers and statesmen — they think that they are the wisest of all men. Nothing but the rivalry of the philosophers stands in their way. They are of the opinion that if they can prove the philosophers to be good for nothing, no one will dispute their title to the palm of wisdom. . . . The amphibious class of thinkers have a certain amount of philosophy, and a certain amount of political wisdom; there is reason in what they say, for they argue that they have just enough of both, while they keep out of the way of all risks and conflicts (of true philosophy). — Euthydemus, 305.

Amusement. Persons should put forth problems to one another, passing their time in an amusement far more agreeable and worthy of elderly men than the game of draughts. — Laws, VII, 820.

Anacreon. Anacreon the wise! — Phaedrus, 235.

Anarchy. From youth upwards we ought to practice this habit of commanding others; anarchy should have no place in the life of man or of the beasts who are subject to man. — Laws, XII, 942.

Anaxagoras. I heard someone who had a book of Anaxagoras, out of which he read that mind was the disposer and cause of all, and I was quite delighted at the notion of this, which appeared admirable. — Phaedo, 97.

Ancestor. Truly, the figure of an ancestor is a wonderful thing. For when they are honored by us, they join in our prayers, and when they are dishonored, they utter imprecations against us. And so the man who conducts himself as he ought to father and grandfather and other aged relations, will have the best of all images which can procure him the favor of the gods. — Laws, XI, 931.

Having such ancestors you ought to be first in all things. — Charmides, 158.

Ancients. The ancients were our betters and nearer the gods than we are. — Philebus, 16.

Anger. Anger differs from desires, and is sometimes at war with them. — Republic, IV, 440.

Nursing up his wrath by the entertainment of evil thoughts, and exacerbating that part of his soul which was formerly civilized by education, he lives now in a state of savageness and moroseness, and pays thus a bitter penalty for his anger. And in such a case almost all men have a way of saying something ridiculous about their opponent. — Laws, XI, 935.

An angry man turns all kinds of color. — Letter VII, 349.

Angler. The angler is familiar to all of us, and not a very interesting or important person. — Sophist, 218.

Animal, Political. An idiot may know that the political animal is a pedestrian — you will allow that? — Certainly. — Statesman, 264.

Animals. All animals are divided into tame and wild. — Statesman, 264.

There are two species of animals; man being one, and all other animals making up the other. — Statesman, 263.

The wild pedestrian animals originated from those men who had no philosophy in all their thoughts, and never meditated at all about the nature of the heavens, because they had ceased to use the courses of the head, and followed the guidance of those parts of the soul which surround the breast. — Timaeus, 91.

Answer. I gave him a true answer. And if my questioner were a philosopher of the quarrelsome and antagonistic sort, I should say to him: "You have my answer, and if I am wrong, it is your business to take up the argument and refute me." But if he were a friendly person, my answer should be in a milder strain and more explanatory; that is to say, I should not only speak the truth, but I should also make use of premises which the questioner would be willing to admit. — Meno, 75.

I remark with surprise that you have not answered what I asked. — Euthyphro, 8.

How am I to shorten my answers? Shall I make them too short? — Protagoras, 334.

If you will not answer for yourself I must answer for you. — Gorgias, 515.

That is very like a true, but not a sufficient answer. — Protagoras, 312.

His approving answers reassured me. — Charmides, 156.

Answer like a man what you think. — Theaetetus, 157.

He is at home in answering. — Euthydemus, 275.

He has taught you the habit of answering questions in a grand and bold style. — Meno, 70.

Anticipation. There is an anticipatory pleasure or pain, and this has to do with the future. — Philebus, 39.

Antiquity. The legislator must somehow find a way of implanting reverence for antiquity. — Laws, VII, 798.

Antiquity, Inquiry Into. They themselves and their children were for many generations in want of the necessaries of life; they therefore directed their attention to the supply of their wants, and of that they discoursed, to the neglect of events that had happened in times long passed; mythology and the inquiry into antiquity are introduced into cities when they have leisure, and when they see the necessaries of life already beginning to be provided, but not before. — Critias, 109, 110.

Anxiety, Parental. There is a sort of madness in many of our anxieties about our children: in the first place, about marrying a wife of good family to be the mother of them, and then about heaping up money for them — and yet taking no care about their education. — Euthydemus, 306.

Anytus. Anytus has a quarrel with me [Socrates] on behalf of the craftsmen and politicians. — Apology, 23.

Aphrodite. There are two goddesses. The elder one, having no mother, who is called the heavenly Aphrodite — she is the daughter of Uranus; the younger, who is the daughter of Zeus and Dione, whom we call the earthly Aphrodite. — Symposium, 180. Vide Eros, Love.

Apparel. Care should be taken not to destroy the natural qualities of the head and the feet by covering them with extraneous apparel, and so hindering their natural growth of hair and soles. — Laws, XII, 942.

Appeal, Divine. One should always appeal to the gods when one starts to reflect. — Letter VIII, 353.

Appeal, Legal. He who goes to law with another, should go first of all to his neighbors and friends who know best the question at issue. And if he be unable to obtain from them a satisfactory decision, let him make an appeal to another court. — Laws, 767.

Appearance. Would the art of measuring be the saving principle, or would the power of appearance? Is not the latter that deceiving art which makes us wander up and down and take the things at one time of which we repent at another? But the art of measurement is that which would do away with the effect of appearances, and, showing the truth, would fain teach the soul at last to find rest in the truth, and would thus save our life. — Protagoras, 356.

In all these cases the theory of the truth of deceiving perception is unmistakably refuted, as in dreams and illusions we certainly have false perceptions; and far from saying that everything is which appears, we must rather say that nothing is which only appears. — Theaetetus, 157, 158.

To the sick man his food appears to be and is bitter, and to the man in health the opposite. — Theaetetus, 166.

Are you certain that the colors appear to every animal — say to a dog — as they appear to you? Or that anything appears the same to you as to another man? Would you not rather question whether you yourself see the same thing at different times, because you are never exactly the same? — Theaetetus, 154.

Appeasement. The appeasing class are always ready to lead a peaceful life, and do their own business; this is their way of living with all men at home, and they are equally ready to keep the peace with foreign states. And on account of this fondness of theirs for peace, which is often out of season where their influence prevails, they become by degrees unwarlike, and bring up their young men to be like themselves; they are at the mercy of their adversaries; and hence in a few years they and their children and the whole city often pass imperceptibly from the condition of freemen into that of slaves. That is a hard, cruel fate. — Statesman, 307.

Appetite. I had been overcome by a sort of wild beast appetite. — Charmides, 155.

Applause. I observed that in the theatre the actors are spurred on by the children, to say nothing of their friends, whenever they believe that they are being applauded with serious benevolence. — Letter IV 321.

Appropriate. Do we describe the appropriate as that which by its presence causes things to appear or to be beautiful, or neither? — Greater Hippias, 293, 294.

Ivory and gold beautify a thing when they are appropriate; otherwise they uglify it. — Greater Hippias, 290.

Archer. You cannot say of the archer that his hands push and pull the bow at the same time, but what you say is that one hand pushes and the other pulls. — Republic, IV, 439.

Architecture. Architecture is the art of building houses. —Charmides, 165.

Argument. Come out, children of my soul [arguments], and convince Phaedrus, who is the father of similar beauties. — Phaedrus, 261.

The majority of mankind are so ignorant of the pretended value of your arguments, that they would be more ashamed of employing them in the refutation of others than of being refuted by them. — Euthydemus, 303.

The argument is to be yours as well as ours. — Protagoras, 357.

You have no better argument than numbers. — Gorgias, 474.

Answer and fear not; for you will come to no harm if you nobly give yourself to the healing power of the argument, which is a sort of physician; and either say "Yes" or "No" to me — Gorgias, 475.

I perceive that you are dainty, and dislike the taste of an argument which you have heard before. — First Alcibiades, 114.

Attend only of the argument, and see what will come of the refutation. —Charmides, 166.

Somehow or other our arguments,

on whatever ground we rest them, seem to turn round and walk away. — Euthyphro, 11.

Arguments, like men, are often pretenders. — Lysis, 218.

I really do not know as yet, but whither the wind carries the argument, thither we go. — Republic, III, 394.

An argument, like a horse, ought to be pulled up from time to time, and not to be allowed to run away, but held with bit and bridle; and then we shall not, as the proverb says, fall off our ass, which is the argument. — Laws, III, 701.

I am not discoursing only for the pleasure of talking, but for the argument's sake. — Laws, III, 699.

Come then, Nicias, and do what you can to help your friends, who are tossing on the waves of argument, and at the last gasp: you see our extremity, and may save us. — Laches, 194.

That which proceeds by rules of art to dispute about justice and injustice, and about things in general, we are accustomed to call argumentation. — Sophist, 225.

One sort of argumentation wastes money, and the other makes money. — Sophist, 225.

This is my argument, which you may overthrow by an opposite argument, or if you like you may put questions. But I must beg you to put fair questions: for there is great inconsistency in saying that you have a zeal for virtue, and then always behaving unfairly in argument. The unfairness of which I complain is that you never distinguish between mere disputation and dialectic: the sophist may trip up his opponent as often as he likes, and make fun; but the dialectician will be in earnest, and only correct his adversary when necessary. If you do this, he will blame his confusion on himself, and not on you. He will follow and love you, and escape from himself into philosophy. But the other mode of arguing will have just the opposite effect upon him: he will learn to hate philosophy. — Theaetetus, 167, 168.

When a simple man believes an argument to be true which he afterward finds to be false, and when this experience repeats itself often, he loses any faith in the soundness of arguments. — Phaedo, 90.

Until a man knows the truth of the several particulars of which he is writing or speaking, and is able to define them as they are, and having defined them again to divide them until they can be no longer divided, and until he is able to discover the different modes of discourse which are adapted to different natures — until he has accomplished all this, he will not be competent to handle arguments scientifically. — Phaedrus, 277.

Aristocracy. The man corresponding to aristocracy of the government of the best we rightly call just and good. — Republic, VIII, 544, 545.

Our government was an aristocracy — a form of government which receives various names, according to the fancies of men, and is sometimes called democracy, being really an aristocracy or government of the best with the consent of the many. — Menexenus, 238.

Aristophanes. Why are you lying here, not by a professor or lover of jokes, like Aristophanes? — Symposium, 213.

You have seen yourselves the accusation in the comedy of Aristophanes, who has introduced a man whom he calls Socrates, going about and saying that he can walk in the air, and talking a deal of nonsense concerning matters of which I do not pretend to know either much or little. — Apology, 19.

Do you expect to shoot your shafts of ridicule and escape, Aristophanes? — Symposium, 189.

Arithmetic. All arithmetic and calculation have to do with number and lead, in a very remarkable manner, the mind towards truth. — Republic, VII, 525.

Arithmetic has a very great and elevating effect, compelling the soul to reason about abstract number, and rebelling against the introduction of visible or tangible objects into the argument. You know how steadily the masters of this art repel and ridicule anyone who attempts to (distract them by examples). And those who have a natural talent for calculation are generally quick at every other kind of knowledge. — Republic, VII, 525, 526.

They must carry on the study of arithmetic until they see the nature of numbers; not in the spirit of merchants and hucksters, with a view to buying and selling, but for the sake of military use. — Republic, VII, 525.

We must endeavor to persuade those who are to be the principal guardians of our state to go and learn arithmetic, not as amateurs, but they must carry on the study until they see the nature of numbers with the mind only. — Republic, VII, 525.

How ingenious this science [arithmetic]! The very mention of it suggests that: and how conducive to our desired goal [justice], if pursued in the spirit of a philosopher, and not of a shopkeeper. — Republic, VII, 525.

Arithmetician. The philosopher must be an arithmetician. — Republic, VII, 525.

Art. All the higher arts require much discussion and lofty contemplation of nature; this is the source of sublimity and perfect comprehensive power. — Phaedrus, 269.

All arts are either acquisitive or productive. — Sophist, 219.

Surely the art of the painter and every other creative and constructive art are full of graces and harmonies; in all of them there is grace or the absence of grace. And ugliness and discord and disharmony are nearly allied to ill words and ill nature, as grace and harmony are the twin sisters of goodness and virtue. — Republic, III, 401.

That which we know with one art we do not know with the other. — Ion, 537.

The soul and body, being two, have two arts corresponding to them: there is the art of politics attending on the soul; and another art attending on the body, of which I know no specific name. — Gorgias, 464.

Art, Rules of. Many are the noble words in which poets speak of actions; but they do not speak of them by any rules of art. — Ion, 534.

Art and Nature. They say that the greatest and fairest things are done by nature and chance, and the lesser by art, which receives from nature all the greater and primeval creations, and fashions them in detail; and these lesser works are generally termed artificial. — Laws, X, 889.

Artist. As to the artists, do we not know that he only of them whom love inspires has the light of fame? He whom love touches not walks in darkness. — Symposium, 197.

Are the poets only to be required by us to express the image of the good in their works? Or is the same control to be extended to other artists, and are they also to be prohibited from exhibiting the forms of vice and intemperance and meanness and indecency in sculpture and building and the other creative arts? We would not have our guardians grow up amid images of moral deformity, as in some noxious pasture, and there browse and feed upon many a baneful herb and flower day by day, little by little, until they silently gather a festering mass of corruption in their own soul — Republic, III, 401.

We are satisfied with the artist who is able in any degree to imitate the earth and its mountains, and the rivers, and the woods, and the universe, and the things that are and move therein. — Critias, 107. *Vide* Abstract Art.

Asclepius. Asclepius was the creator of the art of Medicine. — Symposium, 186.

Asking. The asker of a question is necessarily dependent on the answerer. Euthyphro, 14.

Speak and ask anything which you like, while the magistrates of Athens allow. — Phaedo, 85.

Aspirations. The principle of piety, the love of honor, and the desire of beauty, not in the body but in the soul — these are, perhaps, romantic aspirations; but they are the noblest of aspirations, if they could only be realized in any state, and God willing, in the matter of love we may be able to enforce one of two things — either that no one shall venture to touch any person of the freeborn or noble class except his wedded wife, or sow the unconsecrated and bastard seed among harlots, or in barren and unnatural lusts. — Laws, VIII, 841.

Assimilation. Some substances are assimilated when others are present within them; and there are some which are not assimilated; take, for instance, the case of an ointment or color which is put on another substance. — Lysis, 217.

Assistants. What I mean to say is that besides doctors there are doctors' assistants, who are also styled doctors. — Laws, IV, 720.

Association. Whenever from seeing one thing you conceived another, whether like or unlike, there must surely have been an act of associative recollection. — Phaedo, 74.

From the picture of Simmias, you may by association be led to remember Cebes. — Phaedo, 73.

Astronomy. Knowledge in relation to the revolutions of the heavenly bodies and the seasons of the year is termed astronomy. — Symposium, 188.

The words of astronomy are about the motions of the stars and sun and moon, and their relative swiftness. — Gorgias, 451.

The absence of clouds and rains in Egypt and Syria permits a full view of the stars almost all year round. This clear and dry climate was conducive to the astronomical observations in these countries, which are, indeed, among the first ones. — Epinomis, 987.

Everyone, as I think, must feel that astronomy compels the soul to look upwards, and leads us from this world to another. — Republic, VII, 529.

Atheist. Some of us deny the very existence of the gods, while others are of opinion that they do not care about us; and others that they are turned from their course by gifts. — Laws, X, 885.

Do you contend that I believe in some gods, though they are not the same gods which the city recognizes, or do you mean that I do not believe in gods at all? — I mean the latter — you are a complete atheist. — Apology, 26.

As to the class of monstrous atheists who not only believe that there are no gods, or that they are negligent, or to be propitiated, but conjure the souls of the living, and say they can conjure the dead, and promise to charm the gods with sacrifices and prayers, and will utterly overthrow whole houses and states for the sake of money — let him who is guilty of any of these things be condemned by the judge. — Laws, X, 909.

Who can preserve calmness, having to speak of the existence of the gods to atheists? For he must hate and abhor these men who will not believe. . . . Yet the attempt must be made; for it would be unseemly that one half of mankind should go mad with lust, and the other half in righteous indignation at them. Let us suppose ourselves to select some one of them, and gently reason with him, repressing our anger: O my son, we say to him, you are young, and the advance of time will make you reverse many of the opinions which you now hold. Do not attempt to judge of high matters at present. You and your friends are not the first who have held this disparaging opinion about the gods. There have always been persons who have had the same disorder. But no one who had taken up this opinion, that the gods do not exist, ever continued in the same until he was old. — Laws, X, 888.

Athenians. The Athenians were renowned all over Europe and Asia for the beauty of their persons and for the many virtues of their souls, and were more famous than any of their contemporaries. — Critias, 112.

I say that the Athenians are an understanding people, as indeed they are esteemed by the other Greeks. — Protagoras, 319.

I feel at this moment that I like to hear the Athenian tongue spoken; the common saying is quite true, that a good Athenian is more than ordinarily good, for he is the only man who is freely and genuinely good by the inspiration of nature, and is not manufactured by the law. — Laws, I, 642.

A man may be thought wise; but the Athenians, I suspect, do not care much about this, until he begins to make other men wise; and then for some reason or other they are angry. — Euthyphro, 3.

Athens. Here at Athens there is a dearth of the commodity — all wisdom seems to have emigrated from us to you. — Meno, 71.

Is not the road to Athens made for conversation? — Symposium, 173.

How great would be the disgrace, if we, who know the nature of things, and are the wisest of the Greeks, and as such are met together in Athens, which is the metropolis of wisdom, should have nothing to show worthy of this height of dignity, but should only quarrel with one another like the meanest of mankind. — Protagoras, 337.

Have there not been many good men in this city? And many good statesmen also there always have been, and there are still, in the city of Athens. — Meno, 93.

Athletes. I am afraid that a habit of body such as the athletes have is but a drowsy sort of thing, and rather perilous to health. Do you not observe that these athletes sleep away their lives, and are liable to most dangerous illness if they depart, in ever so slight a degree, from their customary regimen? — Republic, III, 404.

Have we not heard of Iccus of Tarentum, who, with a view to the Olympic and other contests, in his passion for victory, never had any connection with a woman during the whole time of his training? And the same is said of Crison and Astylus and Diopompus and many others, and yet they were far worse educated in their minds than yours and my fellow citizens, and in their bodies far more lusty. This has been often affirmed as a matter of fact by the ancients about these athletes. — Laws, III, 839, 840.

Atlantic, Ocean. From Atlas (son of Poseidon) the whole island and the ocean received the name of Atlantic. — Critias, 114.

Atlantis. The islands of Atlantis once had an extent greater than that of Lybia and Asia; and when afterwards sunk by an earthquake, became an impassable barrier of mud to travelers sailing from hence to the ocean. — Critias, 108.

Atlas. They expect to find another Atlas of the world who is stronger and more everlasting and more containing than the good is. — Phaedo, 99.

Attachment. A hasty attachment is held to be dishonorable, because time is the true test of things. — Symposium, 184.

Attention. What is the meaning of "attention"? For attention can hardly be used in the same sense when applied to the gods as when applied to other things. — Euthyphro, 13.

All men of action succeed when they pay attention to what they are doing, otherwise they fail. — Laws, VI, 783.

We will give you our best attention; and that is the way in which a gentleman expresses his approval. — Laws, III, 688.

Is not attention always designed for the benefit of that to which the attention is given? — Euthyphro, 13.

Attentive. When I am talking with a wise man, I am very attentive to what he says. — Lesser Hippias, 369.

Attributes. You appear to me to offer an attribute only, and not the essence. — Euthyphro, 11.

I assume three attributes: the good, the bad, and that which is neither good nor bad. — Lysis, 216.

When I do not know the essence of something I cannot know its attributes. — Meno, 71.

Audience. The authority which determined and gave judgment, and punished the disobedient, was not expressed in a hiss, nor in the most unmusical shouts of the audience, as in our days; nor in applause and clappings of the hands. But the directors of public instruction insisted that the spectators should listen in silence to the end. Such was the good order which the multitude were willing to observe; they would not have dared to give judgment by noisy cries. — Laws, III, 700.

To seem to speak well of the gods to men is far easier than to speak well of mortals to them: for the inexperience and sheer ignorance of the audience about such matters is a see the beauty of institutions and laws, and understand that all this is of one kindred, and that personal beauty is only a trifle; and after laws and institutions he will lead on to sciences, that he may see their beauty . . . looking at the abundance of beauty and drawing towards the sea of beauty; and at last the vision is revealed to him of a single science, which is the science of beauty everywhere. — Symposium, 210.

Let our artists rather be those who are gifted to discern the true nature of the beautiful and graceful; then will our youth dwell in a land of health, amid fair sights and sounds, and receive the good of everything; and beauty, the effluence of fair works, shall flow into the eye and ear, like a health-giving breeze from a purer region, and insensibly draw the soul from earliest years into likeness and sympathy with the beauty of reason. — Republic, III, 401.

Beauty gives a beautiful being to everything to which it is added. — Greater Hippias, 292.

Becoming and Being. They say that everything is becoming and in relation; and being has to be altogether abolished, although custom may compel us to retain the use of the word. — Theaetetus, 157.

What is that which always is and has no becoming; and what is that which is always becoming and has never any being? That which is apprehended by reflection and reason always is, and is the same; that, on the other hand, which is perceived by opinion with the help of sensation and without reason, is in a process of becoming and perishing, but never really is. — Timaeus, 27, 28.

Bee. Leaving the sting the bee dies. — Phaedo, 91.

Suppose that I ask of you, What is the nature of the bee? — and you answer that there are many kinds of bees, then I would have to say: Tell me that quality in which they do not differ, but are all alike. — Meno, 72.

Beggar. Let there be no beggars in our state; and if anybody begs, seeking to collect the means of life by perpetual entreaties, let the wardens of the agora turn him out of the agora, and the wardens of the city out of the city, and the wardens of the country send him out of any other part of the country over the border, that so the country be cleared of this sort of creature. — Laws, 936.

Beginning. The proverb says, "Well begun is half done," and in my opinion the beginning is a great deal more than half the business. — Laws, VI, 753.

Beginning and End. A city which is aristocratically constituted can hardly be shaken; but seeing that everything which has a beginning has also an end, even a constitution such as yours will not last forever, but will in time be dissolved. And this is the dissolution: In plants that grow in the earth, as well as in animals that move on the earth's surface, fertility and sterility of soul and body occur when the revolutions of their orbs come full circle, which in short-lived existences pass over a short space, and in long-lived ones over a long space. — Republic, VIII, 546.

Behavior. The parents enjoin the teachers to see to the child's behavior even more than to his reading and music. — Protagoras, 325.

Being. The nature of being is quite as difficult to comprehend as that of non-being. — Sophist, 246.

First of all I wish that you would say whether, in your opinion, "being" is the same as "becoming." — Not the same, certainly. — Protagoras, 340.

They say that being is one and many, which are held together by enmity and friendship, ever parting, ever meeting, as the more potent masters of harmony assert, while the gentler ones do not insist on perpetual strife and peace, but admit a relaxation and alternation of them; peace and friendship sometimes prevailing under the sway of Aphrodite, and then again diversity and war, by reason of a principle of strife. — Sophist, 242.

The not-beautiful is the contrast of being to being. Upon this view, the beautiful is not a more real and the not-beautiful a less real existence. — Sophist, 257.

Spiritual being is not a combination of rest and motion, but something different from them. Spiritual being, according to its own essence, is neither moving nor resting, but spaceless or intelligible. — Sophist, 250.

We maintain that there are two sorts of being, spirit being one and matter the other; that there is no tertium quid common to both; that spirit is more excellent than matter. The first we presuppose to be intelligent, the second unintelligent. — Epinomis, 983.

Being is not, as well as it is, and all other things in many respects are, and in many respects are not. — Sophist, 259.

Nothing can be incorporeal, save only being of the spiritual kind: soul — whose proper and exclusive function is to mold and make. To body it pertains to be molded, be made, be seen, but to the spiritual being — we may repeat it, because it needs to be emphasized more than once — to be unseen, to know, to be apprehended by mind, and to have its part in memory and computation of the interrelations of odd and even. — Epinomis, 981.

Two classes of being were sufficient for our former discussion: one assumed by us to be spiritual, and a second which was physical. The third kind we did not distinguish at the time, conceiving that the two would be enough. But now the argument seems to require that we should make clear another kind of being, which is difficult of explanation and only dimly seen. — Timaeus, 48, 49.

We must acknowledge that there is one kind of being, which is always the same, uncreated and indestructible, never receiving anything itself from without, nor itself going out to any other, but invisible and imperceptible by any sense, and of which the understanding is granted to intelligence only. And there is another existence of the same name "being" with it, and unlike to it, perceived by sense, generated, always in motion, becoming in place and vanishing out of place, which is apprehended by opinion jointly with sense. — Timaeus, 52.

The opposition of the other [spirit], and of being, to one another is as truly essence as being itself, and signifies not the opposite of being, but only another being. — Sophist, 258.

My suggestion would be, that anything which possesses any sort of power to affect another, or to be affected by another, has real existence; I hold that the definition of being is simply power. — Sophist, 247.

To which class would you refer being or essence; for this, of all our notions, is the most universal? — Theaetetus, 186.

Belief. Knowledge and belief are not the same. . . . There is belief without knowledge. . . . Belief, not knowledge, can be simultaneously right and wrong. — Gorgias, 454.

Beneficial. Is not the beneficial that which creates the good? — Greater Hippias, 303.

Benefit. So various and changeable is the nature of the benefit that which is the greatest good to the outward parts of a man, is a very great evil to his inward parts. — Protagoras, 344.

Best. We must at least endeavor and do our best. — Laws, VI, 770.

Betrothal. The betrothal by a father shall be valid in the first degree, that by a grandfather in the second degree, and in the third degree, bethrothal by brothers who have the same father; but if there are none of these alive, the betrothal by a mother shall be valid in like manner; in cases of unexampled fatality, the next of kin and the guardians shall have authority. — Laws, VI, 774.

Betterment. Would you say that when you do a holy act you make any of the gods better? — No. — Euthyphro, 13.

Birds. No bird sings when cold, or hungry, or in pain, not even the nightingale, nor the swallow, nor yet the hoopee; which are said indeed to tune a lay of sorrow, although I do not believe this to be true of them any more than of the swans. — Phaedo, 85.

Birds fight for their young against any fierce animal, and die or undergo any danger. — Laws, VII, 814.

There he saw the soul that was once Orpheus choosing the life of a swan out of enmity to the race of women, hating to be born of a woman because they had been his murderers; he saw also the soul of Thamyris choosing the life of a nightingale; birds, on the other hand, like the swan and other musicians, choosing to be men. — Republic, X, 620.

The race of birds was created out of innocent light-minded men who, although their thoughts were directed towards heaven, imagined, in their simplicity, that the clearest demonstration of the things above was to be obtained by sight; these were transformed into birds, and they grew feathers instead of hair. — Timaeus, 91.

Let not the insidious practice of catching birds, which is hardly worthy of freemen, come into the head of any youth. — Laws, VII, 824.

Birth. Birth is a sort of eternity and immortality. — Symposium, 206.

Birth itself is an aching experience for any creature which comes into the world. One has first to get acquainted with life as a fetus, then to be factually born, and then to be brought up and educated, all processes, as must be admitted, involving untold pains. — Epinomis, 973.

Blame. If anything goes wrong, man, not god, ought to be blamed for the fault. — Epinomis, 979.

A man often thinks that others are to be blamed, and not himself, for the errors which he has committed, and the many evils which befell him in consequence, and is fancying himself to be exempt and innocent. — Laws, V, 727.

We blame our fathers for letting us be spoiled in the days of our youth. — Laches, 179.

When man had time to reflect, he began to beat his breast and lament over his choice; and, instead of throwing the blame of his misfortune on himself, he accused chance and the gods, and everything rather than himself. — Republic, X, 619.

Some things are not matters of reward and punishment, but of praise and blame only. — Laws, V, 730.

Blasphemy. If when a sacrifice is going on, and the victims are being burnt according to law — if anyone who may be a son or brother, standing by another at the altar and sacred rites, horribly blasphemes, will he not inspire despondency, and evil omens and forebodings, in the mind of his father and of his other kinsmen? — Laws, VII, 800.

What can be more dreadful than blasphemy? — Phaedrus, 242.

Blind. A blind man, as they say, might see that. — Sophist, 241.

We may be truly described as the blind leading the blind. — Theaetetus, 209.

Bliss. My thesis is that attainment of bliss and happiness is impossible for men, with the exception of a chosen few. — Epinomis, 973.

Blood. The red color for the most part predominates; and hence the liquid which circulates in the body has such a color, which we call blood, being the nurturing principle of the flesh and of the whole body, whence all parts are watered and the empty places filled. — Timaeus, 80.

Bloom. They are like faces which were never really beautiful, but only blooming; and now the bloom of youth has passed away from them. — Reblic, X, 601.

Blush. The blush heightened his beauty. — Charmides, 158.

Body. We are enshrined in that living tomb which we carry about, now that we are imprisoned in the body, as in an oyster shell. — Phaedrus, 250.

Excessive care of the body, when carried beyond the rules of gymnastic, is most inimical to the practice of virtue. And equally incompatible with the management of a house, an army, or an office of state; and, what is most important of all, irreconcilable with any kind of study or thought or self-reflection. — Republic, III, 407.

The body should have the most exercise when growing most. — Laws, VII, 789.

A healthy body gets spoiled by inactivity and idleness, and is well preserved by motion and exercise. — Theaetetus, 153.

One has a body which is a good servant to his mind, while the body of the other is a hindrance to his mind. — Republic, V, 455.

Could we live, having a corrupted body? — Certainly not. — Crito, 48.

Even in decay, still there are some parts, such as the bones and ligaments, which are practically indestructible. — Phaedo, 80.

The body is a source of endless trouble to us by reason of the mere requirement of food; and also is liable to diseases which overtake and impede us in the search after truth: and by filling us so full of loves, and lusts, and fears, and fancies, and idols, and every sort of folly, prevents our ever having, as people say, so much as a thought. — Phaedo, 66. (Ed. Note: But this is only half the story of the body.)

We have to consider, which of the honors given to the body are genuine, and which are counterfeit. — Laws, V, 728.

There is no profit in a man's life if his body is in an evil plight, for in that case his life also is evil. — Gorgias, 505.

Body and Soul. When in man there is an impassioned soul more powerful than the body, that soul convulses and disorders the whole inner nature of man; and when too eager in pursuit of knowledge, causes wasting. And when a body large and too much for the soul is united to a small and weak intelligence, then the motions of the stronger principal getting the better and increasing their own power, but making the soul dull, and stupid, and forgetful, engender ignorance. — Timaeus, 88.

Boldness. Foolish boldness and endurance appeared to be base and hurtful. — Laches, 193.

Bone. Bones are lifted at their joints by the contraction or relaxation of the muscles. — Phaedo, 98.

Books. What greater achievement could there be in my life than to write a book beneficial to mankind, and to elucidate the essence of things to all men? — Letter VII, 341.

Like books, they can neither ask nor answer. — Protagoras, 329.

Boxing. If we were training boxers, or pancratians, or any other sort of athletes, would they never meet until the hour of contest arrived? Surely, if we were boxers, we should have been learning to fight for many days before, and exercising ourselves by imitating all those blows and wards which we were intending to execute in the hour of conflict; and in order that we might come as near to reality as possible, instead of cestuses we should have our arms bound round with boxing gloves, that the blows and the wards be practiced by us to the utmost of our power. And if there should be a deficiency of competitors, without fearing the laughter of fools, should we not have ventured to hang up a lifeless image and practice at that? Or should we, in the dearth of antagonists, not spar with ourselves? And shall the warriors of our city, who are destined to enter the greatest of all contests, be worse prepared than combatants of this sort? — Laws, VII, 830.

Boy. Of all animals, the boy is the most unmanageable, inasmuch as he has the fountain of reason in him not yet regulated; he is the most insidious, sharp-witted, and insubordinate of animals. Wherefore he must be bound with many bridles. — Laws, VII, 808.

Brain. The brain may be the originating power of the perceptions of hearing and sight and smell. — Phaedo, 96.

The word of command issues from the citadel [brain]. — Timaeus, 70.

The creator fashioned a globe made of bone, which he placed around the brain, and in this globe he left a narrow opening. — Timaeus, 74.

Bravery. When you speak of brave men, do you mean the confident, or another sort of nature? — Protagoras, 349.

Bravery is not concerned with the fearful and hopeful, but with the good and evil. — Laches, 199.

Cowards go where there is safety, and the brave where there is danger. — Protagoras, 359.

Is he likely to be brave who has no spirit? Have you never observed how invincible and unconquerable is spirit and how the presence of it makes the soul of any creature to be absolutely fearless and indomitable? — Republic, II, 375.

Breeding. If care is not taken in

the breeding, dogs and birds deteriorate. — Republic, V, 459.

The shepherd or herdsman, or breeder of horses or the like, when he has received his animals will not begin to train them until he has first purified them in a manner which befits the community of animals; he will divide the healthy and unhealthy, and the good breed and the bad breed, and will send away the unhealthy and badly bred to other herds, and tend the rest, reflecting that his labors will be vain and without effect . . . if he neglects to purge them away. — Laws, V, 735.

The bride and bridegroom should consider that they are to produce for the state the best and fairest specimens of children which they can. — Laws, VI, 783.

How can marriages be made most beneficial? — that is a question which I put to you, because I observe in your house hunting dogs, and of the nobler sort of birds not a few. Now, do tell me, did you ever attend to their pairing and breeding? . . . Do you breed from them all indifferently, or do you take care to breed from the best only? . . . The same principle holds of the human species. — Republic, V, 459.

Brevity. I am explaining that this Lacedaemonian brevity was the style of primitive philosophy. — Protagoras, 343.

Bribery. We must not let our men be accepters of bribes or greedy for money. Neither must we sing to them of "gifts persuading gods, and persuading reverend kings." — Republic, III, 390.

Those who serve their country ought to serve without receiving bribes, and there ought to be no excusing or approving the saying, "Men should receive gifts as the reward of good, but not of evil deeds"; for to know what is good and to persevere in what we know is no easy matter. The safest course is to obey the law which says, "Do not service for a bribe." — Laws, XII, 955.

Charioteers are often bribed to give up the victory to other chariots. — Laws, X, 906.

Bricklayer. In the laying of bricks and stones, is the just man a more useful or better partner than the bricklayer? — Quite the reverse. — Republic, I, 333.

Broker. The broker of an unreliable seller who is not able to make good a loss shall himself be responsible; the agent and the principal shall be equally liable. — Laws, XII, 954.

Brothers. In a family there may be several brothers, who are the offspring of a single pair; very possibly the majority of them may be unjust, and the just may be in a minority. — Laws, I, 627.

Builder. The art of the builder, which has a number of measures and instruments, attains from them a greater degree of accuracy than the other arts. — Philebus, 56.

Burial. After the death of the examiners, the manner of laying and carrying them out, and their sepulchres, shall be different from the burial of the other citizens: they shall be decked in a robe all of white, and there shall be no cryings or lamentations over them; but a chorus shall stand around the bier on either side, hymning the praises of the dead in alternate responses. — Laws, XII, 947.

Business. Business is not disposed to wait upon the leisure of the businessman, but the businessman must make his business his main object and attend to it diligently. — Republic, II, 370.

He would make a bad business worse. — Euthydemus, 297.

What is the meaning of a man doing his own business? — Charmides, 162.

Busybody. Men who mind their own business in the city are called simpletons, and held in no esteem, while the busybodies who mind other people's affairs are honored and applauded. — Republic, VIII, 550.

Butcher. A natural classification does not divide things like a clumsy butcher. — Phaedrus, 266.

Buying. There is a greater risk in buying knowledge than in buying meat and drink: the one you purchase and carry them away in other vessels, and before you receive them into the body as food, you may call in any experienced friend who knows what is good to be eaten or drunken, and how much and when. But when you buy the wares of knowledge you cannot carry them away in another vessel; they have been sold to you, and you must take them into your soul and go your way, either greatly harmed or greatly benefited by the lesson: and therefore we should think about this. — Protagoras, 314.

C

Calamity. To rob us of philosophy would be the greatest of calamities. — Sophist, 260.

The most extraordinary of all their sayings is about virtue and the gods: they say that the gods apportion calamity and evil to many good men, and good and happiness to the evil. — Republic, II, 364.

Calculation. The art of calculation considers the quantities of odd and even numbers, in their relation to one another as well as in themselves. — Gorgias, 451.

When I consider that all these creatures are constantly making calculations in their dealings with one another, I imagine it was for some deeper purpose, as well as for this, that human creatures began to have an insight into the relations of number with number. — Epinomis, 979.

In Egypt, systems of calculation have been actually invented for the use of children, which they learn as a pleasure and amusement. — Laws, VII, 819.

If you had no power of calculation you would not be able to calculate on future pleasure, and your life would be the life, not of a man, but of a kind of oyster or "pulmo marinus." — Philebus, 21.

Calculation is one of the theoretical sciences; it knows the differences of numbers, and forms a judgment on them, and has no other function. — Statesman, 259.

Here are three fingers — a little finger, a second finger, and a middle finger. Each of them equally appears a finger, whether observed in the middle or at the extremity; a finger is a finger all the time. In these simple cases a man is not compelled to ask of thought the question what is a finger? for the sight never suggests to the mind that a finger is other than a finger. There is nothing here which provokes or excites intelligence. In complicated cases the soul first summons to her aid calculation and reflection. — Republic, VII, 523, 524.

Calf. If, contrary to nature, a horse have a calf, then I should not call that a foal but a calf; nor do I call any inhuman birth a man, but only a natural birth. Cratylus, 393.

Calm. The breathless calm and stillness are wasting and impairing, and wind and storm preserving. — Theaetetus, 153.

I have always thought you happy in the calmness of your temperament. — Crito, 43.

Calumniators. I was defeated in the struggle against the calumniators. — Letter VII, 333.

Capital punishment. Capital punishment is the only remedy for souls whose web of life is morally finished. — Laws, XII, 957.

[26]

Captains. Captains of ships are guilty of numberless evil deeds. They play false and run away at the moment of sailing, and they wreck their vessels and cast away freight and lives; not to speak of other rogueries. — Statesman, 298.

Career, Public. At first I eagerly strived for a public career; but at last I got dizzy when I noticed the maze of public life and its incessant metamorphoses. — Letter VII, 325.

Carelessness. You are careless when you ought to be careful. — Gorgias, 485.

Do we imagine carelessness and idleness and luxury to be virtues? — Certainly not. — Laws, X, 900.

Caricature. I shall praise Socrates in a figure which will appear to him to be a caricature. — Symposium, 215.

Catamite. Is not the life of a catamite terrible, foul, and miserable? Or would you venture to say, that they too are happy, if they only get enough of what they want? — Gorgias, 494.

Cause. One must include the variable [cause besides the unchangeable ground, and vice versa]. — Timaeus, 48.

These are the works of the causes which God uses as his tools when executing his grounds or moral ideas. The causes are thought by most men to be the sole conditions of all things. But this is not true; causes are void of reason or intellect, and there are also intelligible grounds. — Timaeus, 46. *Vide* Cause; Ground.

Cause and Effect. The cause and that of which it is the cause are different, for the cause cannot be the cause of the cause. — Greater Hippias, 297.

The cause is not the cause of the cause, but of that which is coming into existence through it. The father is not his son, nor the son his father. The cause is not that which it brings into being, nor vice versa. — Greater Hippias, 297.

Everything that becomes or is created must of necessity be created by some cause, for nothing can be created without a cause. — Timaeus, 28.

How can there be anything which has no cause? . . . The agent or cause always naturally leads, and the patient or effect naturally follows. — Philebus, 26, 27.

The effect cannot remain when the cause is destroyed. — Lysis, 221.

Any event presupposes a previous event; an effect does not effect itself, but follows a cause; an event is not effected because it occurs, but it occurs because it is effected. — Euthyphro, 10.

Cause and Reason. There is surely a strange confusion of causes and reasons in all this. I wonder that they cannot distinguish the cause from the reason, which the many, feeling about in the dark, are always mistaking and misnaming. As I have failed to learn of anyone else the nature of the reason, I will exhibit to you what I have found to be the second best mode of inquiring into the reason. I want to show you the nature of that condition which has occupied my thoughts. — Phaedo, 99, 100.

The lover of intellect and knowledge ought to explore conditions of intelligent nature first of all, and, secondly, those which are moved by others and of necessity move others. And this is what we also must do. Both kinds of conditions should be considered by us, and a distinction should be made of those conditions which are endowed with mind and those conditions which are deprived of intelligence. Of the second conditions, enough has been said. I will therefore proceed to speak of the higher conditions. — Timaeus, 46.

He attributes my actions to ten thousand causes, forgetting to mention their reason, which is that I thought it right to remain here. For these muscles and bones of mine would have gone off to Megara or Boeotia, if they had been guided by a bad reason, and if I had not chosen a noble reason. — Phaedo, 99.

Caution. At this point I thought that Protagoras was getting ruffled and excited; he seemed to be setting himself in an attitude of war. Seeing this I became more cautious and asked my question gently. — Protagoras, 333.

My caution occasioned my investigations. — Letter XIII, 360.

Cave, Parable of the. Let me show in a figure how far our nature is enlightened or unenlightened: Behold! human beings living in a cave, which has a mouth open towards the light; here they have been from their childhood, and have their legs and necks chained so that they cannot move, and can only see before them, being prevented by the chains from turning round their heads. Above and behind them a fire is blazing at a distance. — Republic, VII, 514.

Cebes. Cebes is a man who is always inquiring, and is not to be convinced all in a moment, nor by every argument. — Phaedo, 63.

Censorship. The poet shall compose nothing contrary to the ideas of the lawful, or just, or beautiful, or good, which are allowed in the state; nor shall he be permitted to show his compositions to any private individuals, until he shall have shown them to the appointed censors and the guardians of the law, and they are satisfied with them. — Laws, VII, 801.

The beginning is the most important part of any work, especially in the case of a young and tender thing; for that is the time at which the character is being formed and the desired impression is more readily taken. Shall we, then, just carelessly allow children to hear any casual tales which may be devised by casual teachers? Then the first thing will be to establish a censorship of the writers of fiction, and let the censors receive any tale of fiction which is good, and reject the bad; and we will induce mothers and nurses to tell their children the authorized ones only. Let them fashion the mind with such stories, even more fondly than they mold the body with their hands; but most of those tales which are now in use must be discarded. — Republic, II, 377.

Censure. He likes and approves rather than dislikes, and only censures playfully as if he had a suspicion of his own badness. — Laws, II, 656.

Certainty. "I believe" is not the proper word, but I would say, rather, that "I am certain." — Laws, II, 656.

What formerly seemed most uncertain, now appears to them quite certain, while what appeared certain then, seems now uncertain. — Letter II, 314.

How can there be any certainty to us about that which has no fixedness? — Philebus, 59.

The attainment of any certainty about questions such as these is very hard or almost impossible. — Phaedo, 85.

I am certain about Dion, as far as

one can have certainty about another man. — Letter VII, 335.

Chalk. I am simply such a measure as a white line is of chalk. — Charmides, 154.

Chance. I was going to say that man never legislates, but that destinies and accidents happening in all sorts of ways, legislative in all sorts of ways. Either the violence of war has overthrown governments, and changed laws, or the hard necessity of poverty. And the power of disease has often caused innovations in the state. Anyone who sees all this, naturally rushes to the conclusion, that no mortal legislates in anything, but that in human affairs chance is almost everything. And yet there is another thing which may be said with equal truth: that God governs all things, and that chance and opportunity cooperate with him in the government of human affairs. — Laws, IV, 709.

Change. Let me show what is the least change which will enable a state to pass into the truer form; and let the change, if possible, be of one thing only, or, if not, of two; at any rate, let the changes be as few and slight as possible. . . . There might be a reform of the state if only one change were made, which is not a slight or easy though still a possible one. — Republic, V, 473.

If you change your mind, change openly, and let there be no deception. — Republic, I, 345.

All things which have a soul change, and possess in themselves a principle of change, and in changing move according to law and the order of destiny: lesser changes of character move on level ground, but greater crimes sink into the abyss, that is to say, into Hades and other places in the world below, of which the very names terrify men. And when the soul changes greatly, either for the better or worse, when she has communion with divine virtue, she is carried into another and better place, which is also divine; and when she has communion with evil, then she also changes the place of her life. — Laws, X, 904.

A thing which changes becomes different from its previous state; it perishes and passes into another state. But that which does not change can neither come into being nor perish. — Parmenides, 163.

Any change but the change of the bad is the most dangerous of all things; this is true in the case of the seasons and of the winds, in the management of our bodies and the habits of our minds. — Laws, VII, 797.

All living beings feel the strain intensely and can hardly stand it, when great changes of many different kinds occur at once. — Statesman, 270.

Chaos. The primal nature was a chaos or disorder, until attaining to the present cosmos or order. — Statesman, 273.

Charges. In order that they may not appear at a loss, they repeat the ready-made charges which are used against all philosophers. — Apology, 23.

Charm. The charm will do more than only cure the headache. — Charmides, 156.

Charmer. Seek for the good charmer of your fears among the good men, far and wide, sparing neither pains nor money; for there is no better way of using your money. — Phaedo, 78.

Chastising. Injustice is punished, whereas no one would instruct, or rebuke, or be angry at those whose calamities they suppose to come to them either by nature or chance; they do not try to alter them, they do but pity them. Who would be so foolish as to chastise or instruct the ugly, or the diminutive, or the feeble? — Protagoras, 323.

Cheerful. A cheerful temper may be regarded as having much to do with courage. — Laws, VII, 791.

Children. Children have certain natural modes of amusement which they find out for themselves when they meet.—Laws, VII, 794. *Vide* offspring.

The younger children are, the more they will need moving about by day and night; infants should live, if that were possible, as if they were always rocking at sea. When mothers want their restless children to go to sleep they do not employ rest, but, on the contrary, motion — rocking them in their arms; nor do they give them silence, but they sing to them and lap them in sweet strains; and the Bacchic women are cured of their frenzy in the same manner by the use of the dance and of music. — Laws, VII, 790.

He was remarkable even then when he was still a child. — Charmides, 154.

Children would like to have "both." — Sophist, 249.

Children are your riches; and upon their turning out well or ill will depend the whole order of their father's house. — Laches, 185.

I maintain that pleasure and pain are the first experiences of children, and that these are the forms under which virtue and vice are originally present to them. — Laws, II, 653.

Let children, if they avoid the evil ways of their father, have glory, and let honorable mention be made of them, as having nobly and manfully escaped out of evil into good. — Laws, IX, 855.

They say that the children of the faithful and just shall survive to the third and fourth generation. — Republic, II, 363.

I need hardly repeat what he said concerning young children dying almost as soon as they were born. — Republic, X, 615.

We begin by telling children fables which, though not wholly destitute of truth, are in the main fictitious; and these fables are told them when they are not of an age to learn gymnastics. — Republic, II, 377.

And this is clearly seen to be the intention of the law, which is the ally of the whole city; and is seen also in the authority which we exercise over children, and the refusal to let them be free until we have established in them a principle analogous to the constitution of a state, and by cultivation of this higher element have set up in their hearts a guardian and ruler like our own, and when this is done they may go their ways. — Republic, IX, 590, 591.

We should not run the risk of spoiling the children of friends, which is the most formidable accusation that can be brought against anyone. — Laches, 186.

The proper officers will take the children of the good parents to the pen or fold, and there they will deposit them with certain nurses who dwell in a separate quarter; but the offspring of the inferior, or of the better when they chance to be deformed, will be put away in some mysterious, unknown place, as they should be. — Republic, V, 460.

The colony which we are about to

found has no father or mother, except the colonizing people themselves. And I know that many colonies have been, and will be, at enmity with their parents. But in early days the child, as in a family, loves and is beloved; even if there come a time later, when the tie is broken, still, while he is in want of education, he naturally loves the parents and is beloved by them, and flies to them for protection. — Laws, VI, 754.

Children, Bearing of. A woman at twenty years of age may begin to bear children to the state, and continue to bear them until forty; a man may begin at twenty-five, when he has passed the point at which the pulse of life beats quickest, and continue to beget children until he be fifty-five. Both in men and women those years are the prime of physical as well as of intellectual vigor. Anyone above or below the prescribed ages who takes parts in the public hymeneals shall be said to have done an unholy and unrighteous thing; the child will be the offspring of darkness and strange lust. The same law will apply to anyone of those within the prescribed age who forms a connection with any woman in the prime of life without the sanction of the rulers; for we shall say that he is raising up a bastard to the state, uncertified and unconsecrated. — Republic, V, 460, 461.

Choice, Moral. This was what the prophet said at the time: "Even for the last comer, if he chooses wisely and will live diligently, there is appointed a happy and not undesirable existence. Let not him who chooses first be careless, and let not the last despair." And when he had spoken, he who had the first choice came forward and in a moment chose the greatest tyranny; his mind having been darkened by folly and sensuality, he had not thought out the whole matter before he chose. — Republic, X, 619.

Choosing. If I must choose between them — I would rather suffer than do injustice. — Gorgias, 469.

Chorus. The chorus is made up of two parts, dance and song. — Laws, II, 654.

At these words the followers of Euthydemus, like a chorus at the bidding of their director, laughed and cheered. — Euthydemus, 276.

There is something strange, on first hearing, in a Dionysiac chorus of old men. —Laws, II, 665.

Circle. There are descriptions which are composed of words and expressions. For instance, the description of a circle would run as follows: a closed curve whose points are equally distant from its center. — Letter VII, 342.

Circumstances. A man cannot help being bad when the force of circumstances overpowers him. — Protagoras, 344.

I must make the best of bad circumstances. — Gorgias, 499.

Citizens. Our state like every other has rulers and subjects. All of whom will call one another citizens. — Republic, V, 463.

City. Cities, if they are to be happy, do not want walls, or triremes, or docks, or numbers, or size, if they have no virtue. — First Alcibiades, 134.

A city should be free, should be at unity with herself, and should have understanding. — Laws, III, 701.

Do you imagine that a city can subsist and not be overthrown, in which the decisions of law have no power, but are set aside and nullified by individuals? — Crito, 50.

Our city among existing cities has indeed no fellow, either in respect of leisure or command of the necessaries of life, and like an individual she also ought to live happily. — Laws, VIII, 828, 829.

No city ought to be easily able to imitate its enemies in what is mischievous. — Laws, IV, 705.

There are conflicts which all cities undergo. — Timaeus, 19.

Cities cannot exist, if a few only share in the virtues, as in the arts. — Protagoras, 322.

Mankind at first lived dispersed, and there were no cities. — Protagoras, 322.

City-State. While they act according to the rules of wisdom and justice, whether with or without laws, if they use their power in order as far as possible to make their city better, then the city over which they rule, and which has these characteristics, may be described as the only true state. All other governments are not genuine or real, but only imitations of this government. — Statesman, 293.

Civil War. Will he who organizes a state order its life with a view to external war, or rather to civil or internal war, which no one, if he could prevent, would like to have occurring in his own state; and when occurring, everyone would wish to get rid of as soon as possible? — Laws, I, 628.

Would one prefer that a civil war should be terminated by the destruction of one of the parties, or that peace and friendship should be reestablished among them; in which case, they would be able to give undivided attention to their foreign enemies? — Laws, I, 628.

Claiming. May not the wolf claim a hearing? — Phaedrus, 272.

Clarity. Men have more or less difficulty in gaining final clarity; the difficulty is almost never minor. — Letter II, 313.

There is a wonderful difference in the clearness of different validities of knowledge. — Philebus, 57.

Class. I wish that this distinction between a part and a class could still be made somewhat clearer. — Statesman, 263.

Classes. Citizens, you are brothers, yet God has framed you differently. Some of you have the power of command, and these he has composed of gold; others of silver, to be auxiliaries; others again who are to be farmers and craftsmen he has made of brass and iron. And God proclaimed to the rulers that they should watch over their offspring. If the son of a golden or silver parent has an admixture of brass and iron, then nature orders a transposition of classes . . . just as there may be others sprung from the artisan class who become guardians and auxiliaries. For an oracle says that when a man of brass or iron guards the state, it will then be destroyed. Such is the tale. Is there any possibility of making our citizens believe in it? — Republic, III, 415.

Ignorance is not the reason why we do not allow our potters to repose on couches, while their wheel is conveniently at hand, and working at pottery as much as they like, and no more; or, why we do not make every class happy in this way — and then, as you imagine, the whole state would be happy. But do not suggest this; for, if we listen to you, the potter will cease to be a potter, and nobody will have any distinct character. — Republic, IV, 420, 421.

Classification. You would make a much better and more natural classification of numbers, if you divided them into odd and even; or of the human species, if you divided them into male and female. — Statesman, 262.

These persons, from not being accustomed to distinguish classes according to their essential differences, jumble together widely different things, under the idea that they are the same, and fall into the converse error of dividing other things according to immaterial differences. — Statesman, 285.

Clay. Clay is moistened earth. — Theaetetus, 147.

Clemency. Clemency is an infraction of the strict rule of justice. — Laws, VI, 757.

Cleverness. Reliability and loyalty and sincerity denote genuine wisdom. Other kinds of intelligence and cleverness I believe I term correctly mere embellishments. — Letter X, 358c.

Climate. There have been all sorts of changes of the climate in which animals may be expected to have undergone innumerable modifications. — Laws, VI, 782.

Coat, Parable of the. A tailor, having made and worn out many coats, though he outlived several of them, is himself outlived by the last; but this is surely very far from proving that a man is slighter and weaker than a coat. — Phaedo, 87.

Cock. Socrates said (these were his last words): Crito, we ought to offer a cock to Asclepius; will you remember to pay the debt? — Phaedo, 118.

Cockfighting. Not only boys, but not unfrequently older persons, are in the habit of training young birds for the purpose of cockfighting. And they are far from thinking that the contest in which they stir them up to fight with one another are sufficient exercise; for, in addition to this, they carry them about — the big birds tucked beneath their armpits, and the smaller in their hands, and go for a walk of a great many miles for the sake of health, that is to say, not their own health but the health of the birds. — Laws, VII, 789.

Cogency. I can teach you to answer with such cogency that nobody would be able to disprove you. — Greater Hippias, 287.

Coinciding. All things cannot coincide as they are wanted. — Laws, V, 745.

Colonization. Cities find colonization in some respects easier when the colonists are of one race, which like a swarm of bees goes from a single country, friends from friends, owing to some pressure of population, or other similar necessity; or because a portion of a state is driven by factions to emigrate. And there have been cities which have taken flight, when utterly conquered by a superior power in war. — Laws, IV, 708.

When men who have nothing, and are in want of food, show a disposition to follow their leaders in an attack on the property of the rich — they are sent away by the legislator in a friendly spirit as far as he is able; and this dismissal of them is euphemistically termed colonization. — Laws, V, 735, 736.

Color. Must not pleasure be of all things most absolutely like pleasure, just as color is like color? As far as they are colors, there is no difference between them. — Philebus, 12.

Comedy. Older children will be advocates of comedy; educated women, and young men, and people in general, will favor tragedy. — Laws, II, 658.

Comic Writers. Do we not admit in our state the comic writers who are so fond of making mankind ridiculous, if they attempt in a good-humored manner to turn the laugh against our citizens? — Laws, XI, 935.

Commander. Thus a very fair distinction has been attained between the man who gives his own commands, and him who gives another's. — Statesman, 261.

He is a miserable fellow, who is only fit to be a commander of old women. — Laws, I, 639.

What would you say of the commander of an army? Will he be able to command merely because he has military skill if he be a coward, who when danger comes, is sick and drunk with fear? — Laws, I, 639.

Commensurability. A man who is good for anything ought to be able to distinguish the natures of commensurable and incommensurable things in their relation to one another.... As regards line and surface when compared with volume, or surface and line when compared with one another, are not all the Greeks agreed that these things are commensurable with one another in some way? ... But if some things are commensurable and others wholly incommensurable, and you think that all things are commensurable, you do not stand very well. — Laws, VII, 820.

Length is naturally commensurable with length, and breadth with breadth, and depth in like manner with depth. — Laws, VII, 819.

Commerce. Most of the Greeks obtain their food from sea and land, but our citizens from land only. And this makes the task of the legislator less difficult. For he has nothing to do with laws about commerce, waterborne or land-borne, retailers, innkeepers, tax collectors, mines, money lending, compound interests, and innumerable other things; he gives laws to farmers, shepherds, bee-keepers, and the guardians and superintendents of their implements. — Laws, VIII, 842.

Common Opinion. I should be absurd indeed, if while I am still in ignorance of myself I were to be curious about that which is not my business. And therefore I say farewell to all extraneous speculation; the common opinion is enough for me. — Phaedrus, 299, 230.

Communication. Suppose that we had no voice or tongue, and wanted to communicate with one another, should we not, like the deaf and dumb, make signs with the hands and head and the rest of the body? The running of a horse, for instance, would be expressed by the most nearly similar gestures of our own frame. — Cratylus, 422, 423.

Communion. He who is incapable of communion is also incapable of friendship. — Gorgias, 507.

Communism. The highest form of government is that in which there prevails most widely the ancient saying, that "Friends have all things in common." Whether there is now, or ever will be, this community of women and children and of the property, in which the private and individual is altogether banished from life, and things which are by nature private, such as eyes and ears and hands, have become common, and in some way see and hear and act in common, and all men express praise and blame, and feel joy and sorrow, on the same occasions — whether all this is possible or not, I say that no man, acting upon any other principle, will ever constitute a state better than this. — Laws, V, 739.

And so we have arrived at the conclusion that in the perfect state wives and children are to be in common; and that all education and the pursuits of war and peace are also to be common. — Republic, VIII, 534.

Companions. Loyal companions could not be created anew with ease. — Letter, VII, 325.

He who is joined to bad companions must do and suffer what such men by nature do and say to one another. — Laws, V, 728.

He who takes pleasure in bad companions will surely become like them, even though he be ashamed to praise them. — Laws, II, 656.

Comparatives. Your word "strongly" suggests to me that such expressions as "strongly" and "slightly" imply comparatives of more or less, for whenever they occur they do not allow of the existence of definite quantity; they are always introducing degrees into actions, instituting a comparison of the more or less violent or more or less gentle, and at each creation of more or less, definite quantity disappears. — Philebus, 24.

Comparatives, such as the hotter and the colder, are to be ranked in the class of the infinite. — Philebus, 24.

Comparison. The most beautiful of apes, when compared to a man, is ugly. Does not Heraclitus say, "The wisest of men, when compared to a god, seems to be but an ape in wisdom?" — Greater Hippias, 289.

This comparison is a most just one. — Laws, X, 901.

Compassion. Athens was too compassionate and too much inclined to favor the weak. And in this instance she was not able to hold out or keep her resolution of refusing aid to her injurers when they were being enslaved, but she was softened, and delivered the Greeks from slavery, and they were free until they afterwards enslaved themselves. — Menexenus, 244, 245.

Compensation, Punishment as. When compensation is meted out, the law must always seek to convert the enmity between doers and sufferers of misdeeds into friendship. — Laws, IX, 862.

Complaint. The character of the son begins to develop when he hears his mother complaining that her husband has no governmental position and that she is for this reason slighted among other women. Further, when she sees her husband not very concerned about money, and instead of battling and railing in the law courts or assembly, taking whatever happens to him easily; and when she observes that his thoughts always center in himself, while he treats her with very considerable indifference, she is annoyed, and says to her son that his father is far too slack and only half a man: adding all the other complaints about her own ill-treatment which women are so fond of rehearsing. — Republic, VIII, 549.

Complete. It is a great thing to be a complete man. — Greater Hippias, 281.

Complexity. There complexity engendered license, and here disease. — Republic, III, 404.

Compliments. Compliments are sometimes insincere, but we will show that we really prize your words. — Laws, III, 688.

Compound. The compound or composite may be supposed to be naturally capable of being dissolved in like manner as of being compounded; but that which is uncompounded must be indissoluble. And the uncompounded may be assumed to be the same and unchanging, whereas the compound is always changing and never the same. — Phaedo, 78.

Comprehensive. The comprehensive mind is always the dialectical. — Republic, VII, 537.

Compromise. Since you are neither fully victorious nor completely beaten, the middle road of compromise would be most advantageous for you and your adversary. — Letter, VIII, 355.

Compulsion. Suppose that a skillfull physician had a patient, whom he compels against his will to do something which is contrary to the written rules, what is this compulsion to be called? Would you ever dream of calling it a violation of the art, or breach of the laws of health? — Statesman, 296. *Vide* Statesman.

Computation. The art of computation has to do with odd and even numbers. — Charmides, 166.

Conceit. There is a conceit of knowledge, which is a disgraceful sort of ignorance. — Apology, 29.

No one who thinks himself wise is willing to learn any of those things, in which he is conceited of his cleverness. — Sophist, 230.

One of the two types of conceited persons is a simple-minded person, who thinks that he knows that which he only fancies; the other sort has knocked about among arguments, until he suspects and fears that he is ignorant of that which to the many he pretends to know. — Sophist, 268.

Let us examine the conceited person, and see whether his metal is sound, or whether there is any crack left in it. — Sophist, 267.

Conception. The woman in her conception and generation is but the imitation of the earth, and not the earth of the woman. — Menexenus, 238.

When the hour of conception arrives, and the teeming nature is full, there is such a flutter and ecstasy about beauty whose approach is the alleviation of pain. — Symposium, 206.

Conciliation. A person will listen with more gentleness and good-will to the laws addressed to him by the legislator, when his soul is not altogether uncivilized. Even a little done is the way of conciliation gains his ear, and is always worth having. For there is no great inclination or readiness on the part of men to be made as good, or as quickly good, as possible. — Laws, IV, 718.

Conclusion. A conclusion, being a statement, is likewise true or false. — Sophist, 264.

Let us endeavor to add on a suitable conclusion to the beginning of our tale. — Timaeus, 69.

Condemned. I have seen men of reputation, when they have been condemned, behaving in the strangest manner: they seemed to fancy that they were going to suffer something dreadful if they died, and that they could be immortal if you only allowed them to live; and I think that they were a dishonor to the state. — Apology, 35.

Conduct in Office. Every judge and ruler shall be liable to give an account of his conduct in office, except those who have the final decision. — Laws, VI, 761.

Confessing. I am not ashamed to confess that I was mistaken. — Charmides, 164.

Confidence. Confidence and courage are not the same; and I argue that the courageous are confident, but not all the confident courageous. For confidence may be given to men by art, and also by anger and madness; but courage comes to them from nature and the healthy state of the soul. — Protagoras, 351.

Those who are thus confident without knowledge are really not courageous but mad; and in the other case the wisest are also the most confident, and being the most confident are also the bravest, and upon that view again wisdom will be courage. . . . I certainly did say that the courageous are the confident; but I was not asked whether the confident are the courageous. . . . Have you not seen persons utterly ignorant, and yet confident? — Protagoras, 350.

We should not be confident that we can say anything certain all in a moment. — Laws, VII, 799.

Confiscation. If there are sacred treasures in the city, the tyrant will confiscate and spend them. — Republic, VIII, 568.

Conflagration. A great conflagration of things upon the earth recurs at long intervals of time; when this happens, those who live upon the mountains and in dry and lofty places are more liable to destruction than those who dwell by rivers or on the seashore. — Timaeus, 22.

Conflict. As we acknowledge the heaven to be full of many gods and also of evils, there is an eternal conflict going on among us, which requires wondrous watchfulness; and in that conflict the gods and demigods are our allies, and we are their property. — Laws, X, 906.

Conformity. When a man consorts with the many, and exhibits to them his poem or other work of art or the service which he has done the state, making them his judges when he is not obliged, the so-called necessity of Diomede will oblige him to produce in conformity whatever they praise. — Republic, VI, 493.

Congenial. Love and desire, and friendship would appear to be of the natural or congenial. — Lysis, 221.

Conqueror. All the good things of the conquered pass into the hands of the conquerors. — Laws, I, 626.

If the conqueror abides by the law as the conquered, there will prevail everywhere a climate of happiness, continuity, and deliverance from all troubles. — Letter, VII, 337.

Conscience. The good man is, as he ought to be, a willing servant to the conscience, of which the meaner sort of man is independent and fearless. — Laws, III, 699.

All these causes created in them the spirit of friendship; there was the immediate fear of the occasion, and that reverent fear, which sprang out of the habit of obeying their traditional laws: conscience. — Laws, III, 699.

I thought that I should be safer if I cleared my conscience by writing, in obedience to my dream, some poetry before I departed. — Phaedo, 61.

The sign is a voice which comes to me and always forbids me to do something which I am going to do, but never commands me to do anything. — Apology, 31.

[37]

This is the voice which I seem to hear murmuring in my ears, like the sound of the flute in the ears of a mystic; that voice, I say, is humming in my ears, and prevents me from hearing any other. — Crito, 54. *Vide* Daimonion.

Consciousness. Are we living beings always conscious of what happens to us, for instance, of growth; or are we not almost wholly unconscious of this and similar phenomena? — Philebus, 43.

Consecrating. And women especially, and men too, when they are sick or in danger, or in any sort of difficulty, or again on their receiving any good fortune, have a way of consecrating the occasion, offering up prayers and sacrifices, and promising statues to the gods. — Laws, X, 910.

Consent. Tyrannical contenders should rather endeavor to enjoy high honors by the consent of voluntary subjects and of impartial laws. — Letter VIII, 354.

Conservatism, Linguistic. Our forefathers liked the sounds *i* and *d*, especially the women, who are most conservative of the ancient language, but now they change *i* into *e*, and *d* into *z*; this is supposed to increase the grandeur of the sound. — Cratylus, 418.

Consideration. Those philosophers showed little consideration for plain people like ourselves, talking over our heads; they did not care whether they took us with them, or left us behind them. — Sophist, 243.

The time for consideration has passed when violence is employed. — Charmides, 176.

Conspirator. The political conspirator calls property owners foes. — Letter, VII, 351.

Constitution. There are two prototypes of constitutions from which all others may be truly said to be derived; and the one of them may be called monarchy and the other democracy; the Persians have the highest form of the one, and we of the other; almost all the rest are variously made up of these. Now, if you are to have liberty and the combination of friendship with wisdom (wise authority), you must have both of these forms of constitution in a measure; no city can be well governed which is not made up of both. The state which has become exclusively and excessively attached to monarchy or to freedom has not effected a proper balance between them. — Laws, III, 693.

I cannot offhand say what kind of constitutions we Lacedaemonians have, for it seems to me to be like a tyranny; the power of our ephors is amazingly tyrannical; and sometimes it appears to me to be of all cities the most democratical; and who can reasonably deny that it is an aristocracy? We have also a monarchy which is held for life; and, therefore, when asked on a sudden, I cannot precisely say which form of constitution the Spartan is. — Laws, IV, 712.

Thousands and thousands of cities have come into being, and no less a number have perished. And has not each of them had every form of constitution many times over, now growing larger, now smaller, and again improving or declining? — Laws, III, 676.

The (proposed) form of constitution being unusual, may excite wonder when mentioned for the first time; but upon reflection and trial, will appear to us, if not the best, to be the second best. Some persons may not approve this form; but the truth is, that there are three forms of government, the best, the second and the third best. — Laws, V, 739.

Constraint. Constraint I will not use, even though it be my own son. A slave I would counsel and also constrain, if he refused to obey. It is sinful to constrain father or mother, unless they are suffering from mental disease. — Letter, VII, 331.

Consultation. If you were going to commit the body to someone, and there was a risk of your getting good or harm from him, would you not carefully consider and ask the counsel of your friends and relatives, and deliberate many days as to whether you should give him the care of your body? But when the soul is in question, which you hold to be of far more value than the body — about this you never consult either with your father or with your brother or with anyone of us who are your companions. — Protagoras, 313.

Contact. Two objects are the smallest number which make a contact. And every additional term makes one additional contact, whence it follows that the contacts are one less in number than the terms. And if there is only a one, not a pair of things, there is no contact. — Parmenides, 149.

Contamination. Wearing such a beautiful suit and such nice shoes you ought not to be contaminated by such vulgar language. — Greater Hippias, 291.

Contest. If anyone hinders by force a competitor in gymnastic or music, or some other sort of contest, from being present at the contest, any person who may please shall inform the judges of the contest, and they shall liberate him who is desirous of contending. — Laws, XII, 955.

Take part in the great contest between good and evil, which is the contest of life, and greater than every other earthly conflict. — Gorgias, 526.

Contest, Gymnastic. We must remember, about all gymnastic contests, that only the warlike sort of them are to be practiced and to have prizes of victory; and those which are not military are to be given up. — Laws, VIII, 832.

Contract. When a man does not fulfill an admitted contract, unless the contract be of a nature which the law or a vote of the assembly does not allow, or which he has made under the influence of some unjust compulsion, or which he is prevented from executing against his will by some unexpected chance, the other party may go to law with him in courts of the tribe, for non-fulfillment of contract, if the parties are not able previously to come to terms before arbiters or before their neighbors. — Laws, XL, 920.

If a law prescribed that everyone shall enter into voluntary contracts at his own risk, there would be less of this scandalous money-making. — Republic, VIII, 556.

Contradicting. How can he who speaks contradict him who speaks not? — Euthydemus, 286.

O my father, did you not wish me to live as happily as possible? And yet you also never ceased telling me that I should live as justly as possible. Are you not contradicting yourself? — Laws, II, 662.

Contradiction, Law of. The same thing cannot at the same time with the same part of itself act in contrary ways about the same. — Republic, IV, 439.

The same thing clearly cannot act or be acted upon in the same part in the same relation, at the same time, in contrary ways; and therefore whenever this occurs in things apparently the same, we shall know that they are not really the same, but different. — Republic, IV, 436.

Were we not saying that such a contradiction is impossible — the same faculty cannot have contrary opinions at the same time about the same thing? — Republic, X, 602, 603.

Contraries. If friendship goes by contraries, the contraries must be friends. — Lysis, 216.

There is an idea of likeness, and another of unlikeness, which is the contrary of likeness, and in these two, you and I and all other things to which we apply the term "many," participate; and the things which participate in likeness are in that degree like; and those which participate in unlikeness are in that degree unlike. And all things may partake of both contraries, and be like and unlike to themselves, by reason of this participation. In that there is nothing surprising. — Parmenides, 129.

Controversy. When the war is one of words, that may be termed controversy. — Sophist, 225.

Conversation. Our conversation should be, not a dispute, but a discussion. A dispute is between adversaries and enemies, but a discussion is carried on among friends with good faith. — Protagoras, 337.

The more the pleasures of the body fade away, the more grows the love of conversation in me. — Republic, I, 328.

You and I are conversing with one another, soul to soul. — First Alcibiades, 130.

Conversion. The process is not the spinning round of an oyster shell, but the conversion of a soul out of darkness (sin) to the day (virtue). — Republic, VII, 521.

The good judge ought to make himself and the city stand upright, procuring for the good the continuance and increase of justice, and for the bad, on the other hand, a conversion from ignorance and intemperance, and in general from all unrighteousness, as far as their minds can be healed. — Laws, XII, 957.

And this is the way in which the study of the one has a power of drawing and converting the mind to the contemplation of true being. — Republic, VII, 524, 525.

Conviction. When the conviction of the best idea gets the upper hand, and orders the soul, even though sometimes in error, yet what is done in accordance with and in obedience of this rule, is best for the whole life of man, and is to be called justice; although the action, done in error, is thought by the multitude to be involuntary injustice. — Laws, IX, 864.

Convinced. Somehow or other your words, Socrates, always appear to me to be right words; and yet, like the rest of the world, I am not quite convinced by you. — Gorgias, 513.

Cookery. The cook will be a better judge than the guest, who is not a cook, of the pleasure to be derived from the dinner which is in preparation. — Theaetetus, 178.

Cookery is flattery. — Gorgias, 465.

Cookery is not an art, but only a routine. — Gorgias, 501.

Copper. This, which is denser than gold, and contains but a small and fine portion of earth, and is therefore harder, and yet because of the great interstices within is lighter, is a sort of bright and condensed fluid, and when made into a mass is called copper. — Timaeus, 59.

Corpse, Robbing a. Ought the conquerors take anything of the slain but their armor? Does not the practice of despoiling the corpses of the enemy afford an excuse for not facing the battle? They skulk about the dead, pretending to be executing a duty, and many an army before now has been lost from this love of plunder. And is there not illiberality and avarice, and a degree of meanness, in robbing a corpse, and making the dead body an enemy when the real enemy has walked away? — Republic, V, 469.

Corrupter. He who is a corrupter of the laws is more than likely to be a corrupter of the young and foolish portion of mankind. — Crito, 53.

What do they say? Something of this sort: That Socrates is a doer of evil, and corrupter of the youth. — Apology, 24.

A mender of old shoes who made the shoes worse than he received them, could not remain undetected, and would very soon have to starve. But corrupters of souls go undetected for many decades. — Meno, 91.

Corruption. It is not of much consequence, when the corruption of society, and pretension to be what you are not, extends only to cobblers; but when the guardians of the laws and of the government are only seemingly (and not really) guardians, that is the utter ruin of the state: for they alone are the authors of order in a state. — Republic, IV, 421.

What numberless causes may tend to destroy these rare philosophical natures! In the first place there are their own virtues, their courage, temperance, and the rest of them, every one of which praiseworthy qualities (and this is a most singular circumstance) destroys and distracts from philosophy the soul which is the possessor of them. Then there are all the ordinary goods of life — beauty, wealth, strength, rank, and great connections in the state — on which I need not enlarge, having given a general outline of them; these also have the effect of corrupting and distracting them. — Republic, VI, 491.

We have to consider the corruptions of the philosophic nature, why so many are spoiled and so few escape spoiling — I am speaking of those who were said to be useless but not wicked — and, when we have done with them, we will speak of the imitators of philosophy, who aspire after a profession which is above them and of which they are unworthy, and then, by their manifold inconsistencies, bring upon philosophy, and upon all philosophers, that universal disrepute of which we speak. — Republic, VI, 490, 491.

Counting. How did we learn to count? How have we come to apprehend the concepts of *one* and *two*, the scheme of the world endowing us with an inborn capacity for there concepts? There are many creatures whose innate equipment does not extend to the faculty to learn from our heavenly Father how to count. But in our own case, God bestowed on us the capacity of understanding. Now Uranus never ceases to teach men the notions of *one* and *two* until even the dullest scholar has sufficiently comprehended the lesson of counting. — Epinomis, 978.

Country. We are born partly for

our country, partly for our parents, partly for our friends. These various contingencies which catch up with our lives make many demands upon us. When our country herself calls us to public office, it would probably be odd not to comply, since we would thus give a chance to unworthy men who do not enter public life for the best motives. — Letter IX, 358.

Has a philosopher like you [Socrates] failed to discover that our country is more to be valued and higher and holier far than mother or father or any ancestor, and more to be regarded in the eyes of the gods and of men of understanding? Also to be soothed, and gently and reverently entreated when angry, even more than a father, and if not persuaded, obeyed? And when you are punished by it, the punishment is to be endured in silence; and if it leads you to wounds or death in battle, thither you follow as is right; neither may anyone yield or retreat or leave his rank, but whether in battle or in court of law, he must do what his country orders him; or he must change its view of what is just: and if he may do no violence to his father or mother, much less may he do violence to his country. — Crito, 51.

The country which brought them up is not like other countries, a stepmother to her children, but their own true mother; she bore them and nourished them and received them, and in her bosom they now repose. — Menexenus, 237.

Countryman. Simonides is a countryman of yours, and you ought to come to his rescue. — Protagoras, 340.

Courage. Is courage to be regarded only as a combat against fears and pains, or also against desires and pleasures, and against flatteries? — Laws, I, 633.

Courage, when untempered by the gentler nature during many generations, may at first bloom and strengthen, but at last bursts forth into every sort of madness. — Statesman, 310.

Courage is the knowledge of the grounds of hope and fear. — Laches, 196.

Courage is a sort of endurance of the soul. — Laches, 192.

If a man is a physician, and his patient has inflammation of the lungs, and begs that he may be allowed to eat or drink something, and the other refuses; is that courage? — Laches, 192.

Surely the lawgivers of Crete and Lacedaemon have not legislated for a courage whis is lame of one leg, able only to meet attacks of a cunning enemy, but impotent against the insidious flatteries of desire. — Laws, I, 633, 634.

Not even such a big pig as the Crommyonian sow would be called by you courageous. And this I say not as a joke, but because I think that he who assents to your doctrine, that courage is the knowledge of the grounds of fear and hope, cannot allow that any wild beast is courageous, unless he admits that a lion, or a leopard, or perhaps a boar, or any other animal, has a degree of wisdom which but a few human beings, and these only with difficulty, attain. He who takes your view of courage must affirm that a lion, and a stag, and a bull, and a monkey, have equally little pretensions to courage.—Laches, 196.

Courage which has no prudence is

only a sort of confidence. — Meno, 88.

You may observe that many men are utterly unrighteous, unholy, intemperate, ignorant, who are nevertheless remarkable for their courage. — Protagoras, 349.

What now is the case with the more courageous natures? Are they not always inciting their country to go to war, owing to their excessive love of the military life? Their enemies are many and mighty; and if they do not ruin their cities, they enslave and subject them to their enemies. — Statesman, 308.

If they are to be courageous, must they not learn lessons such as will have the effect of taking away the fear of death? Can any man be courageous who has the fear of death in him? — Republic, III, 386.

A courageous temper is a gift of nature and not of reason. — Laws, XII, 963.

Do not courageous men endure death because they are afraid of yet greater evils? All but the philosophers are courageous only from fear; and yet that a man should be courageous from fear, and because he is a coward, is surely a paradoxical thing. — Phaedo, 68.

I don't call animals or any other creatures courageous, which have no fear of dangers, because they are ignorant of them, but fearless and senseless only. Do you think that I should call little children courageous, which fear no dangers because they know none? — Laches, 197.

This sort of universal preserving power of true conviction in conformity with law about real and false dangers, I call and maintain to be courage. — Republic, IV, 430.

There is a difference between fearlessness and courage. Now I am of opinion that thoughtful courage is a quality possessed by very few, but that rashness, and boldness, and fearlessness, which has no forethought, are very common qualities possessed by many men, many women, many children, many animals. And you, and men in general, call by the term "courageous" actions which I call rash, and my courageous actions are wise actions. — Laches, 197.

Court of Appeals. If the two courts cannot settle the matter, let the third [court of appeals] put an end to the suit. — Laws, VI, 767.

Court of Law. There shall be a court of law in every ward, and the judges shall be chosen by lot; they shall give their decisions at once, and shall be inaccessible to entreaties. — Laws, VI, 768.

A city which has no regular courts of law ceases to be a city; and again, if a judge is silent and says no more than the litigants in preliminary trials and in private arbitrations, he will never be able to decide justly. — Laws, VI, 766.

The court of law is a place, not of instruction, but of punishment. — Apology, 26.

Courts. Men who from their youth upwards have been knocking about in the courts and such like places, compared with others who have received a philosophical education, are slaves, and the others are freemen. — Theaetetus, 172.

They can teach a man how to use the weapons of the courts. — Euthydemus, 273.

Courtesan. You may say that a courtesan is hurtful, and disapprove of such creatures and their practices, and yet for the time they are very pleasant. — Phaedrus, 240.

If a man is to keep his health, would you allow him to have a Corinthian courtesan? — Republic, III, 404.

Covetous. Of course you know that to be covetous of honour and covetous of money is said to be, as indeed it is, a disgrace? — Republic, I, 347.

Cowardice. Of the men who came into the world, those who were cowards or have led unjust lives may be fairly supposed to change into the nature of women in the second generation. — Timaeus, 90.

If a professor of this art is a coward, he will be likely to become rash. — Laches, 184.

What the cowards make for is exactly the opposite of what the brave men make for. The brave, for instance, are ready to go to battle, and the others are not ready. — Protagoras, 359.

The soldier who leaves his rank or throws away his arms, or is guilty of any other act of cowardice, should be degraded into the rank of a farmer or artisan. — Republic, V, 468.

He who loves his life too dearly, shall live forever under the stigma of cowardice. — Laws, XII, 944.

The cowardly and mean nature has no part in true philosophy. — Republic, VI, 486.

Craft. The legislator will unintentionally create in the souls of the disciples, instead of wisdom, the habit of craft, which evil tendency may be observed in the Egyptians and Phoenicians, and many other races, through the general illiberality of their pursuits and possessions. — Laws, V, 747.

Craftsmen. The man who is versed in crafts used to be counted wise in ancient times, but has not such reputation today; his knowledge of those things is rather looked upon as a reproach to him. — Epinomis, 974.

More than four citizens will be required; for the farmer will not make his own plough or mattock, or other implements of agriculture, if they are to be good for anything. Neither will the builder make his tools — and he, too, needs many; and the same may be said of the weaver and shoemaker. Then carpenters, and smiths, and other craftsmen, will be sharers in our little state, which is already beginning to grow. — Republic, II, 370.

The craftsman of all men will seldom misuse his expert knowledge, in itself a straightforward and honest thing, and take advantage of the layman by the tricks of his trade. — Laws, XI, 921.

At last I went to the craftsmen, for I was conscious that I knew nothing at all, as I may say. They did know many things of which I was ignorant, and in this they certainly were wiser than I was. But I observed that even the perfect craftsmen fell into the same error as the poets; because they were excellent workmen they thought that they also knew all sorts of high matters, and this defect in them overshadowed their wisdom. — Apology, 22.

Crane. Suppose that some wise and understanding creature, such as a crane appears to be, were to make a classification, and set up cranes against all other animals to their own special glorification, at the same time jumbling together all the others, including man, under the appellation of "beasts" — that would be a sort of error which we must try to avoid. — Statesman, 263.

Creation. All that is created may be dissolved. — Timaeus, 41.

God made the creation as good as possible, out of things which were neither good nor bad. — Timaeus, 53.

There is an opinion that nature creates natural things by unintelligent causes. Shall we agree with this, or say that they are created by divine reasons? — Sophist, 265.

Was the world always in existence and without beginning or created and having a beginning? — Created, being always in process of creation and created. — Timaeus, 28.

Shall we say that they [animals, and plants, and inanimate substances] come into existence in any way but by the creation of God, or shall we agree with the popular opinion about them? — Sophist, 265.

Creature, Living. The name "living creature" is most properly applied in the case when a complex of soul and body gives birth to a being. — Epinomis, 981.

Credit. He who gives credit, whether he obtain his money or not, must be satisfied, for in such exchanges he will not be protected by law. — Laws, VIII, 850.

Crime. Will you determine what are voluntary and what are involuntary crimes, and shall we make the punishments greater for voluntary errors and crimes and less for the involuntary; or shall we make the punishment of all to be alike, under the idea that there is no such thing as voluntary crime? — Laws, IX, 860.

If any freeman eat or drink, or have dealings with a criminal, or only has voluntarily touched him, he shall not enter into any temple, nor into the agora, nor into the city, until he be purified; for he should consider that he has become a partaker of a fatal crime. — Laws, IX, 881.

Crime, Causes of. Let us speak, as far as we are able, of the causes of crime. The greatest is lust, which gets the mastery of the soul maddened by passion; and this is most commonly found to exist where the obsession reigns, which is strongest and most prevalent among the mass of mankind: I mean where the power of wealth breeds endless desires for never to be satisfied acquisition, originating in natural disposition, and a miserable want of education. — Laws, IX, 869, 870.

We may speak to the criminal whom some tormenting passion by night and by day tempts to go and rob a temple, in words of exhortation: Poor soul, the impulse which moves you to rob temples comes neither from man nor from god, but is a sort of madness which is begotten in men from ancient and unexpiated crimes, the curse of which revolves in a cycle: against this you must guard as well as you can. — Laws, IX, 854.

Criminals. Criminals released from Tartarus lift up their voices and call upon the victims whom they have slain or wronged, to have pity on them, and to receive them, and let them come out of the river into the lake. — Phaedo, 114.

A cunning and suspicious criminal, when he is among men who are like himself, is resourceful in his precautions against others, because he judges of them by himself: but when he gets into the company of virtuous men, who have the experience of age, he appears to be foolish again, owing to his unreasonable suspicion: he cannot recognize an honest man, because he has no honesty in himself to judge from. — Republic, III, 409.

There is no rudeness in maintaining that some one of our citizens is a tough bean which cannot be softened by the heat of the fire. Among our citizens there may be some criminal elements who cannot be subdued by all the strength of the law. — Laws, IX, 853.

We may speak to the potential criminal in words of admonition: When any evil thought comes into your mind, hasten and perform expiations, hasten as suppliant to the temples of the gods who avert evil, hasten to the society of those who are called good men among you; hear them tell, and yourself try to repeat after them, that every man should honor the noble and the just. Fly from the company of the wicked — fly, and turn not back; and if thy disorder is lightened sensibly by the use of these remedies, well and good, but if not, then acknowledge death to be nobler than life, and depart hence. — Laws, IX, 854.

Those criminals who appear to be incurable by reason of the greatness of their crimes are hurled into Tartarus, from whence they never come out. Those again who have committed crimes, which, although great, are curable, are temporarily plunged into Tartarus. — Phaedo, 113.

Criminal, Plea of the. A man may very likely commit some crime, either in a state of madness or when affected by disease, or under the influence of extreme old age, or in a fit of childish wantonness, himself no better than a child. And if this be made evident to one of the judges elected to try the cause, on the plea of the criminal or his advocate, and he be judged to have been in this state when he committed the offense, he shall simply pay for the hurt which he may have done to another; but he shall be exempt from other penalties, unless he have slain someone, and have on his hands the stain of blood. — Laws, IX, 864.

Criterion. I never asked which was the greatest or best or usefulest of arts or sciences, but which had clearness and accuracy, and the greatest degree of truth, however humble and however little useful a science or art; that was the criterion I was asking. — Philebus, 58.

Criticism. You may be as free as you like in your criticism of our laws, for there is no harm in knowing what is wrong; that is the first step to improvement, if a man receives criticism in no resenting or hostile spirit. — Laws, I, 635.

Crito. A great many of them I [Socrates] see in the court — first Crito over there, who is of the same age and of the same town with myself. — Apology, 33.

Crito closed the eyes and mouth [of the deceased Socrates]. — Phaedo, 118.

Cronos, Days of. In those (utopian) days God himself was their shepherd, and ruled over them, just as man, who is by comparison a divine being, still rules over the animals, under him there were no governments or separate possessions of women and children. For all men rose again from the earth, having no memory of any past events; and they had no property or families, but the earth gave them abundance of fruits, which grew on trees and shrubs unbidden, and were not planted by the hand of man. And they dwelt naked, and mostly in the open air, for the temperature of their seasons was mild; and they had no beds, but lay on soft couches of grass, which grew plentifully out of the earth. Such was the life of man in the days of Cronos; the character of our present life you know from your own experience. Can you, and will you determine which of them you deem the happier? — Statesman, 271, 272.

Cross-Questioning. Young men like to hear persons cross-questioned, and they often cross-question others themselves. — Apology, 23.

Crowd. The rhetorician will have greater powers of persuasion than the physician even in matters of health — before a crowd. — Gorgias, 459.

How little does the crowd know of the nature of justice and truth. — Euthyphro, 4.

Cry. Every creature when born is wont to utter some cry, and this is especially the case with man, and he, moreover, is affected with the inclination to cry more than any other animal. — Laws, VII, 791.

Cultivation. He is not a man of cultivation. — Republic, VIII, 554.

Culture. What should be the end of culture if not the love of beauty? — Republic, III, 403.

Curators. Let them, in the first place, be the curators of the law; and, secondly, of the registers in which each one registers before the magistrate the amount of his property. — Laws, VI, 754.

Curing. As to unjust hurts or unjust gains — of these evildoers we may cure as many as are capable of being cured. — Laws, IX, 862.

As you ought not to attempt to cure the eyes without the head, or the head without the eyes, so neither ought you to attempt to cure the body without the soul. — Charmides, 156.

Curiosity. If curiosity alone makes a philosopher, you will find many a strange being claiming the name. For all the lovers of sights have a delight in learning, and will therefore have to be included. Musical amateurs, too, are a folk wonderfully out of place among philosophers, as they are the last persons in the world who would come to anything like a philosophical discussion, if they could help. — Republic, V, 475.

I should be absurd indeed, if while I am still in ignorance of myself I were to be curious about that which is not my business. — Phaedrus, 230.

Currency. The law enjoins that no private man shall be allowed to possess gold and silver, but only currency for daily use. Our citizens should have a currency among themselves, but not allowed among the rest of mankind; with a view, however, to expeditions and journeys to other lands — for embassies the state must also possess a common Greek currency. — Laws, V, 742.

Currents. The currents in the Euripus are going up and down in never-ceasing ebb and flow. — Phaedo, 90.

Curriculum, Man's. This is man's curriculum: he is born and brought up and begets and brings up own children, and has his share of dealings with other men, and suffers if he has done wrong to anyone, and receives satisfaction if the has been wronged, and so at the appointed time, under the dominion of the laws, he grows old, and meets his end in the order of nature. — Laws, XII, 958.

Curses, Parental. Oedipus, when dishonored by his sons, invoked on them the fulfillment of those curses from the Gods which everyone declares to have been heard and ratified by the gods; and Amyntor in his wrath invoked curses on his son Phoenix, and Theseus upon Hippolytus, and innumerable others have also called down wrath upon their children; and the curses of a parent are, as they ought to be, mighty against his children, as no others. — Laws, XI, 931.

Custom. When a stranger expresses wonder at the singularity of what he sees, any inhabitant will naturally answer him: Wonder not, O stranger; this is our custom, and you may very likely have some other custom about the same things. — Laws, I, 637.

They could hardly have wanted lawgivers as yet; no written law was likely to have existed in those ancient days, for they had no letters at this early stage; they lived according to custom and the so-called traditionary law of their fathers. — Laws, III, 680.

These customs would incline them to order, when the parents had the element of order in them; and to courage, when they had the element of courage in them. And they would naturally stamp upon their children, and upon their children's children, their own institutions. — Laws, III, 681.

The truth is, Socrates, that you, who pretends to be engaged in the pursuit of truth, are appealing now to the vulgar notions of right, which are not natural, but only conventional. Custom and nature are generally at variance with one another: and hence, if a person is too modest to say what he thinks naturally, he is compelled to contradict himself. — Gorgias, 482.

Many apparently trifling customs and usages overflow their barriers and extend the domain of law. — Laws, VII, 793.

There is an element of friendship in the community of races and language, and laws, and in common sacrifices, and all that; but inasmuch as such colonies kick against any laws which are other than they had at home, although they have been undone by the badness of them, yet because of the force of habit they would fain preserve the very customs which were their ruin. — Laws, IV, 708.

Perhaps your ears may fail to catch their answer, which I recognize because I am accustomed to them. — Sophist, 248.

Cyclical Destruction. There are legends about cyclical destructions of mankind which have been occasioned by deluges and diseases, and in many other ways. — Laws, III, 677.

Cyclops. Dynasty is the government which is declared by Homer to have prevailed among the Cyclops. — Laws, III, 680.

Cyrus. The first king of Persia, Cyrus, by his valor freed the Persians, who were his countrymen, and subjected the Medes, who were their rulers, and he ruled over the rest of Asia, as of Egypt. — Menexenus, 239.

I imagine that Cyrus, though a great and patriotic general, never had any real education. — Laws, III, 694.

From his youth upwards Cyrus was a soldier, and intrusted the bringing up of his children to the women; and they brought them up from their childhood as the favorites of fortune, who were blessed already, and needed no more blessings. They thought that they were happy enough, and that no one should be allowed to reprove them in any way, and they compelled everyone to praise all that they said or did. — Laws, 694.

Cyrus did not observe that his sons were being educated in the corrupt Median fashion by women and eunuchs, which led to their becoming such as people do become when they are brought up unreproved. — Laws, II, 695.

D

Daedalus. The beauty of the starry heavens is like the beauty of the diagrams drawn with exquisite care by Daedalus. — Republic, VII, 529.

Daedalus would look a bungler if he were to be born today and produce his works of art, which made him famous. — Greater Hippias, 282.

Daimonion. The familiar daimonion [voice of conscience] within me has constantly been in the habit of opposing me even about trifles, if I was going to make a slip or error about anything. — Apology, 40.

Damage. It is difficult to damage somebody else without being damaged, too. — Letter, VIII, 352.

Dancing. The peaceful dances may be divided into two classes, one in which there is an escape from daily toils and dangers to good, and this has greater pleasures; the other which is celebrated on account of preservation and increase of former good, and in which the pleasure is less exciting. — Laws, VII, 815.

All dances ought to be performed with a view to military excellence, and agility and ease should be cultivated for the same object; and also endurance of the want of meats and drinks, and winter cold and summer heat, and hard couches. — Laws, XII, 942.

If we know what is good in song and dance, then we know also who is rightly educated and who is uneducated; but if we do not know this, then we certainly shall not know wherein lies the safeguard of education, and whether there is any or not. — Laws, II, 654.

One sort of dancing imitates musical recitation, and aims at preserving dignity and freedom. — Laws, VII, 795.

Movement of the body may be called dancing, and includes two kinds: one of the nobler figures, imitating the honorable, the other of the more ignoble figures, imitating the mean; and of the serious there are two further divisions. One kind is of those engaged in war and vehement action; the other exhibits a temperate soul, and may be truly called, and is, the dance of peace. — Laws, VII, 814.

If a dancer is more orderly and disciplined in courage he moves less; but if he is a coward, and has no training or self-control, he makes greater and more violent movements. — Laws, VII, 815.

Darius. Darius was not the son of a king, and had not received a luxurious education. He made laws upon the principle of introducing a sort of universal equality in the order of the state, thus creating a feeling of friendship and community among all Persians. Hence his armies cheerfully acquired for him countries as large as those which Cyrus had left behind him. — Laws, III, 695.

Day. The view of day is one of the most beautiful spectacles for man. — Epinomis, 978.

Daydreaming. Let me feast my mind as daydreamers are in the habit of feasting themselves with their own dreams when they are walking alone; for before they have discovered any means of effecting their wishes — that is a matter which never troubles them — they would rather not tire themselves by thinking about possibilities; but assuming that what they desire is already theirs, they pursue their plan, and delight in detailing what they are going to do when their wish has come true; that is a way which they have of not doing much good to a capacity which was never good for much. And I too am beginning to lose heart, and would wish to reserve the question of possibility. — Republic, V, 458.

Deaf. If I had been deaf, and you were going to converse with me, you would have had to raise your voice. — Protagoras, 334.

Dear. What is beloved may be dear, whether loving or hating: for example, very young children, too young to love, or even hating their father or mother when they are punished by them, are never dearer to them than at the time when they are hating them. — Lysis, 212, 213.

They too are dear, but not so dear to one another as the others, either at the time of their love or afterwards. — Phaedrus, 256.

That which is only dear to us for the sake of something else is improperly said to be dear; the truly dear is that in which all these so-called friendships terminate. — Lysis, 220.

Death. Death is regarded by men in general as a great evil. — Phaedo, 68.

Do we believe that there is such a thing as death? — Phaedo, 64.

Death is not the worst that can happen to men; far worse are punishments. — Laws, IX, 881.

The philosopher will not assume death to be terrible. — Republic, VI, 486.

Real death would be destruction, not of the body, but of the soul; for in the body the work of destruction is ever going on. — Phaedo, 91.

Can he be fearless of death, or will he choose death in battle rather than defeat and slavery, who believes in terror of the world below? — Impossible. — Republic, III, 386.

Death, if caused by disease or produced by wounds, is painful and difficult; but that sort of death which comes of old age and fulfills the debt of nature is the least painful of deaths, and is accompanied with pleasure rather than with pain. — Timaeus, 81.

When a man thinks himself to be near death he has fears and cares which never entered into his mind before; the tales of a life below and the punishment which is exacted there of deeds done here were a laughing matter to him once, but now he is haunted with the thought that they may be true: either because of the feebleness of age, or from the nearness of the prospect, he seems to have a clearer view of the other world. — Republic, I, 330.

Death is good, for one of two things: either death is a state of nothingness and utter unconsciousness, or, as men say, there is a migration of the soul from this world to another. Now if you suppose that there is no consciousness, but an undisturbed sleep, death will be an unspeakable gain. But if death is the journey to another place, what good can be greater than this? — Apology, 40.

You must argue us out of our fears — and yet, strictly speaking, they are not our fears, but there is a child within us to whom death is a sort of bogey; him too we must persuade not to be afraid when he is alone with him in the dark. — Phaedo, 77.

Those of us who think that death is an evil are in error. — Apology, 40.

Is not for some people death better than life? — Phaedo, 62.

Not much can be done in the way of helping a man after he is dead. — Laws, XII, 959.

The laying out of the dead shall not continue for a longer time than is sufficient to distinguish between him who is in a trance only and him who is really dead. — Laws, XII, 959.

Being dead is the attainment of the separation of soul and body when the soul exists in herself, and is parted from the body and the body is parted from the soul. — Phaedo, 64.

This fear of death is indeed the pretense of wisdom, and not real wisdom, being the appearance of knowing the unknown; since no one knows whether death, which they in their fear apprehend to be the greatest evil, may not be the greatest good. — Apology, 29.

When a man is dead his soul does not die with him. — Phaedo, 88.

There is nothing ignoble in the death of a man who becomes the victim of his ideals. — Letter, VII, 334.

As the true philosophers are always occupied in the practice of dying, to them least of all men is death terrible. — Phaedo, 67.

Death is the separation from one another of two things, soul and body; this, and nothing else. And after they are separated they retain their several characteristics, which are much the same as in life. The body has the same nature and ways and affections, all clearly discernible; and I should infer that this is equally true of the soul. — Georgias 524.

Neither on the battlefield nor in the court of law ought any man to use any means of escaping death. — Apology 39.

I should like to know whether you think that life is always better than death. May not death often be the better of the two? — Laches, 195.

What is generated from life? — Death. — And what from death? — I can only say in answer — life. — Phaedo, 71.

Any man, who is not devoid of natural feeling, has reason to fear death, if he has no knowledge or proof of the soul's immortality. — Phaedo, 95.

Death, Foreknowledge of. I will deprive men of the foreknowledge of death, which they at present possess. — Gorgias, 523.

Death Penalty. Every citizen should regard the friend and enemy of the state as his own friend or enemy; and if one makes peace or war with any on his own account, and without the authority of the state, he shall undergo the penalty of death. And if any fraction of the city declare war or peace against any, the generals shall indict the authors of this proceeding, and if they are convicted death shall be the penalty. — Laws, XII, 955.

Debating. The first presupposition of good debating is that the mind of the speaker should know the truth of what he is going to say. — Phaedrus, 259.

Debauchery. When the lusts, amid clouds of incense and perfumes and garlands and wines, and all the debauchery of social life are buzzing around him and flattering him to the utmost, there is implanted in him the sting of desire, and then this master of the soul is in a frenzy — madness becoming the captain of the guard — and if he discerns in his soul any opinions or appetites which may be regarded as good, and which have any sense of shame remaining, he puts an end to them, and casts them forth until he has purged away temperance and brought in madness to the full. — Republic, IX, 573.

Debt. Debts are always a source of dangerous contention. — Laws, V, 736.

Very good — you have paid me the debt. — Statesman, 266.

Deceit. They endeavor to eradicate the spirit of deceit: they cross-examine a man as to what he is saying when he thinks that he is saying something and is really saying nothing; he is easily convicted of inconsistency in his opinions; these they collect, and placing them side by side, show that they contradict one another about the same things, in relation to the same things, and in the same respect. He seeing this is angry with himself, and grows gentle towards others, and thus is entirely delivered from great prejudices and harsh notions. — Sophist, 230.

There is no greater good in a state than that the citizens should become acquainted with one another. When darkness, and not light, reigns in the daily intercourse of social life, no man will receive the honor he deserves, or the power or the justice to which he is fairly entitled: wherefore, in every state, above all other things, every man ought to take heed of this — that he have no deceit in him, but that he is always right and simple, and that no other deceitful person takes any advantage of him. — Laws, V, 738.

Decency. Decency will be respected. — Republic, V, 460.

Deception. No primitive man had the wit to suspect another of deception, as men do now; but what they heard about gods and men they believed to be true, and lived accordingly. — Laws, III, 679.

He is not to be trusted who loves voluntary deception, and he who loves involuntary deception is a fool. — Laws, V, 730.

The same object appears straight when looked at out of the water, and crooked when in the water; and the convex becomes concave, owing to the illusion about colors to which the sight is liable. There is no end to this sort of confusion in the mind; and there is a similar deception about painting in light and shade, and juggling, and other ingenious devices, which have quite a magical power of imposing upon our weakness. — Republic, X, 602.

Gods do not deceive mankind in word or deed. — Republic, II, 383.

They ought not to deceive in such matters, out of respect to the gods. — Laws, XI, 921.

Is there any impossibility in stealing the hearts of youths through their ears, when they are still at a distance from the truth, by showing them fictitious arguments, and making them think, that they are true, and that the speaker is the wisest of men in all things? — Sophist, 234.

You certainly treat me as if I were a child, sometimes saying one thing, and then another, as if you were meaning to deceive me. — Gorgias, 499.

Do the false deceive by reason of their simplicity and folly, or by reason of their cunning and a certain sort of prudence? — Greater Hippias, 365.

I hate him like the gates of death, who thinks one thing and says another. — Lesser Hippias, 365.

In works either of sculpture or of painting, which are of any magnitude, there is a certain degree of deception; for if the true proportions were given, the upper part, which is farther off, would appear to be out of proportion in comparison with the lower, which is nearer; and so our artists give up the truth in their images and make only the proportions which appear to be beautiful, disregarding the real ones. — Sophist, 236.

Decision. A good decision is based on knowledge and not on numbers. — Laches, 184.

Decking Out. Should a man deck himself out with vain words at a meeting of friends? — Laches, 196.

Decorum. Silence and decorum of speech are to be observed by the judges. — Laws, XII, 957.

Decrees. We are always inquiring which of our decrees tends to virtue and which not. — Laws, VIII, 836.

Deeds. You value deeds more than words. — Apology, 32.

His deeds show that free and noble sentiments may be expected from him. — Laches, 189.

Defamation. When he will understand, which he does not at present, what is the meaning of defamation, he will forgive me my criticism of it. — Meno, 95.

No one shall use defamatory words of another; and when a man disputes with another he shall teach and learn from the disputant and the company, but he shall abstain from evil speaking; for out of the imprecations which men utter against one another, and the feminine habit of casting aspersions on one another, and using foul names, beginning in words light as air, they proceed to deeds, and the greatest enmities and hatreds spring up. For the speaker gratifies his anger, which is an ungracious element of his nature. — Laws, XI, 934, 935.

Defeat. The defeat which came upon us was our own doing. — Menexenus, 243.

Defects. Natural or inherent defects of the beloved enhance the delight of the lover; and his acquired defects are created by the lover who otherwise would be deprived of his fleeting joy. The lover cannot help being jealous, and will debar the beloved from the advantages of society which would make a perfect man of him, and especially from that society which would have given him wisdom. — Phaedrus, 239.

Defense. What is left to be done proves to be defense, defense of a lot of clients by a lot of means. — Epinomis, 975.

Let everything have a guard as far as this is possible; and let the defense of the city be committed to the generals and taxiarchs, and hipparchs, and phylarchs, and prytans, and the wardens of the city. The defense of the country shall be provided for as follows. . . . — Laws, VI, 760.

Deficiency. The reason for this is

not any deficiency of years, but a deficiency of knowledge. — Lysis, 209.

Definition. We may both of us have the thing in our minds, but we ought always to come to an understanding about the thing in terms of a definition, and not merely about the name minus the definition. — Sophist, 218.

This is a naive sort of definition. — Meno, 75.

Let us first of all agree upon a definition of love which shows its nature and power. — Phaedrus, 237.

In searching after one virtue we have found many virtues; but we have been unable to find the common element which runs through all of them. . . . Ever and anon we are landed in particulars, but this is not what I want. . . . I am looking for the *"simile in multis."* — Meno, 74, 75.

There are virtues numberless, and no lack of definitions of them. . . . But they have all a common nature which makes them virtues; and on this he who would answer the question, "What is virtue?" would do well to have his eye fixed. — Meno, 72.

Sometimes a person may give the name and ask the definition; or he may give the definition and ask the name. — Laws, X, 895.

I did not ask you to give me two or three examples of piety, but to explain the general idea which makes all pious things to be pious. Do you not recollect that there was one idea which made the impious impious, and the pious pious? — Euthyphro, 6.

For intelligent persons a living creature is better described by a definition than by a drawing or model, which suits other persons. — Statesman, 277.

There is the comprehension of scattered particulars in one idea: the speaker defines his several notions in order that he may make his meaning clear, as in our definition of love, which whether true or false certainly gave lucidity and consistency to the discourse. — Phaedrus, 265.

Deformity. We ought to consider the state of ignorance, which has many kinds, to be deformity. — Sophist, 228.

Degeneration. Under the influence either of poverty or of wealth, artisans and their work are equally liable to degenerate. Here, then, is a discovery of new evils: wealth and poverty. The one is the parent of luxury and indolence, and the other of meanness and viciousness, and both of discontent. — Republic, IV, 421.

Delicacies. Would you approve of the delicacies, as they are esteemed, of Athenian confectionary? — I should not. — Republic, III, 404.

Delight. Great delight was felt at the prospect of hearing wise men talk. — Protagoras, 317.

Delphi. I will refer you to an unimpeachable authority as my witness, who will tell you about my wisdom: to the god of Delphi. — Apology, 20.

I agree with him who dedicated the inscription, "Know thyself," at Delphi. That word is put there as a sort of salutation which the god addresses to those who enter the temple; as much as to say that the ordinary salutation of "Hail" is not right, and that the exhortation, "Be temperate," would be a far better way of saluting one another. — Charmides, 164.

Deluge. The fact is that a single night of excessive rain washed away the earth and laid bare the rock; at the same time there were earthquakes, and then occurred the third extraordinary deluge, which immediately preceded the great destruction of Deucalion. — Critias, 112.

When the gods purge the earth with a deluge of water, herdsmen and shepherds on the mountains are the survivors, whereas those who live in cities are carried by the rivers into the sea. — Timaeus, 22.

I mention the great destruction of mankind which was caused by a deluge. I mean to say that those who then escaped would only be hill shepherds, — small sparks of the human race preserved on the tops of mountains. — Laws, III, 677.

The fewness of the survivors of the deluge would make them desirous of intercourse with one another. — Laws, III, 678.

Demagogue. There is the dissembler, who harangues a multitude in public in a long speech. Is he the statesman or the demagogue? — The demagogue. — Sophist, 268.

Demeter. Wines appeared, which had previously no existence, and also olives, and the gifts of Demeter and her daughter. — Laws, VI 782.

Demigods. Can a man believe in spiritual and divine ideas, and not in spirits or demigods? Now what are spirits or demigods? Are they not either gods or the sons of gods? — Apology, 27.

That what is created from water is a demigod, which is sometimes to be seen, but anon veils itself and becomes invisible, thus perplexing us by its indeterminate appearance. — Epinomis, 985.

Democratic. Democratic authority is mostly in the hands of the people, who dispense offices and power to those who appear to be most deserving of them. Neither is a man rejected from weakness or poverty or obscurity of origin, nor honored by reason of the opposite, but there is one principle — he who appears to be wise and good is a governor and ruler. — Menexenus, 238.

Democracy. There being no necessity for you to govern in this state, even if you have the capacity, or to be governed, unless you like, or to go to war, or to be at peace when others are at peace, unless you are so disposed — is not this a way of life which for the *moment* is delightful? And is not their humanity to the condemned in some cases quite charming? Have you not observed how, in a democracy, many persons, although they have been sentenced to death or exile, just stay where they are and walk about the world — the gentleman parades like a hero, and nobody sees or cares? Democracy is a charming form of government, full of disorder, and dispensing a sort of equality to equals and unequals alike. — Republic, VIII, 557, 558.

Modesty, which they call silliness, is ignominiously thrust into exile by them, and temperance, which they nickname unmanliness, is trampled in the mire and cast forth; they persuade men that moderation and orderly expenditure are vulgarity and meanness. Insolence they euphemistically term breeding, and anarchy liberty, and waste magnificence, and impudence courage. And so the young man passes out of his original nature, which was trained in the school of orderly necessity, into the freedom and libertinism of useless and unnecessary pleasures. Neither does he receive or let pass into the fortress any true word of advice. His life has neither law nor order; and this distracted existence he terms joy and bliss and freedom. And democracy has her own good, of which the *insatiable* desire brings her to dissolution: freedom, which, as they tell you in a democracy, is the glory of the state. When a democracy which is thirsting for freedom has evil cupbearers presiding over the feast, and has drunk too deeply the strong wine of freedom, then [she disintegrates]. — Ibid., VIII, 559-562.

Loyal citizens are insultingly termed by her slaves who hug their chains; she would have subjects who are like subjects. Now, in such a state, can liberty have any limit? By degrees the anarchy finds a way into private houses. I mean that the father grows accustomed to descend to the level of his sons and to fear them, and the son is on a level with his father, he having no respect or reverence for either of his parents; and this is his freedom. In such a state of society the master fears and flatters his scholars, and the scholars despise their masters and tutors, young and old are alike; and the young man is on the level with the old, and is ready to compete with him in words and deeds; and old men condescend to the young and are full of pleasantry and gaiety; they are loath to be thought morose and authoritative, and therefore they adopt the manners of the young. — Ibid., VIII, 562, 563.

And the horses and asses have a way of marching along with all the rights and dignities of freemen; and they will run at anybody who comes in their way if he does not leave the road clear for them: and all things are just ready to burst with liberty. See how sensitive the citizens become; they chafe impatiently at the least touch of authority and at length they cease to care even for the laws; they will have no one over them. Such is the fair and glorious beginning out of which tyranny springs — the truth being that the excessive increase of anything often causes a reaction in the opposite direction. The *excess* of liberty seems only to pass into the excess of slavery. — Ibid., VIII, 563, 564.

See to the forgiving spirit of democracy, and the "don't care" about trifles, and the disregard which she shows of all the fine principles which we solemnly laid down at the foundation of the city — how grandly does she trample all these fine notions of ours under her feet, never giving a thought to the pursuits which make a statesman, and promoting to honor anyone who pretends to be the people's friend. — Republic, VIII, 558.

Freedom creates rather more drones in the democratic than there were in the oligarchical state. In a democracy they are almost the entire ruling power, and while the keener sort speak and act, the rest keep buzzing about the beam and do not suffer a word to be said on the other side; hence in democracies almost everything is managed by the drones. — Republic, VIII, 564.

Democracy is likely to be the fairest of states, and may be compared to an embroidered robe which is spangled with flowers; and being in like manner spangled with the manners and characters of mankind will appear to be the fairest of them all. And just as women and children think men who will deem this the fairest of states. — Republic, VIII, 557.

Then democracy comes into being after the poor have conquered their opponents, killing some and banishing some, while to the remainder they give an equal share of freedom and power; and this is the form of government in which the magistrates are commonly elected by lot. That is the nature of democracy, whether the revolution has been effected by arms, or whether fear has caused the opposite party to withdraw. — Republic, VIII, 557.

If democracy had only consisted of educated people, there would have been no fatal harm done. — Laws, III, 701.

The rule of the multitude is called by the name of democracy. — Statesman, 291.

Democracy is unable to do either any great good or any great evil, when compared with the other governments, because the officers are too much subdivided and too many hold them. — Statesman, 303.

Because of the liberty which reigns in democracy: they have a complete assortment of constitutions; and if a man intends to establish a state, he must go to a democracy as he would go to a bazaar, where they sell them, and pick out one that suits him. — Republic, VIII, 557.

Demonstration. Would you like me to give you a demonstration of the notion of reason? — Phaedo, 99.

Departed, the. I am going to men departed who are better than the living whom I leave behind. — Phaedo, 63.

Desertion. The soldier who deserts his post or throws away his arms, or is guilty of any other act of cowardice, should be degraded into the class of a farmer or artisan. — Republic, V, 468.

If anyone goes on an expedition, and returns home before the appointed time, when the generals have not withdrawn the army, he shall be indicted for desertion before the same persons who took cognizance of his failure of service. — Laws, XII, 943.

Deserving. He deserves praise for paying the money cheerfully. — Letter XIII, 362.

Desire. There is no such thing as desire of the body. — Philebus, 35.

There are two desires natural to man — one of food for the sake of the body, and one of wisdom for the sake of the diviner part of us. — Timaeus, 88.

Desires, pleasures, and flatteries exercise such a tremendous power, that they make the hearts even of respectable citizens to melt like wax. — Laws, I, 633.

This sort of man will be at war with himself; he will be two men, and not one; but, in general, his better desires will be found to prevail over his inferior ones. — Republic, VIII, 554.

Despotic Power. If the despotic power has since that time horridly misused the gifts of the state, for this the penalty has partly been paid, and is partly still to be paid. — Letter VIII, 353.

Destiny. Let him who draws the first lot have the first choice of life, which shall be his destiny. — Republic, X, 617.

Destruction. There is something unreasonable in supposing that anything can perish from without through external affection of evil, which could not be destroyed from within by any internal corruption. — Republic, X, 609.

Destruction of Mankind. There have been, and will be again, many destructions of mankind arising out of many causes; the greatest have been brought about by the agencies of fire and water, and other lesser ones by innumerable other causes. — Timaeus, 22.

Detail. You must acquaint yourself with all details as far as you can. — Letter XIII, 362.

Deterioration. There seem to be two causes of the deterioration of the crafts, wealth and poverty. — Republic, IV, 421.

The good man may become deteriorated by time, or toil, or disease, or other accident. — Protagoras, 345.

Detraction. All things are liable to detraction. — Republic, VI, 500.

Detriment. The legislator must fix his eye on the distinction between injustice and detriment. . . . Favor me by stating the difference between detriment and injustice. — Laws, IX, 862, 863.

Devour. Man did not at first sight perceive that he was fated, among other evils, to devour his own children. — Republic, X, 619.

Diagnosis. If a doctor were trying to judge, by external examination, of a patient's health or some physical defect, he might look at his face and hands, and then remark, "Let me also see your chest and back, so that I may make a more satisfactory diagnosis." — Protagoras, 352.

Dialect. Let us ask Prodicus, for he ought to be able to answer questions about the dialect of Simonides. — Protagoras, 341.

He is twitting Pittacus with ignorance of the use of terms, which in a Lesbian, who has been accustomed to speak a barbarous dialect, is natural. — Protagoras, 341.

Dialectic. We have at last arrived at the hymn of dialectic. This is that strain of cognition which is of the spiritual only. Sight was described by us to behold the living things and stars, and last of all the sun himself. [Not] so with dialectic; when a person starts on the discovery of the spiritual by the help of understanding only, and without any assistance of sense, and perseveres until by mere thinking he arrives at the knowledge of the absolute good, he at last finds himself at the end of the intellectual world, as in the case of sight at the end of the visible world. — Republic, VII, 532.

Dialectic is the coping-stone of the sciences. — Republic, VII, 534.

You will have to prove them by the help of dialectic, in order to learn which of them is able to abstain from the use of sight and other senses, and in company with mere understanding to attain knowledge of being. — Republic, VII, 537.

This faculty of reasoning is given. . . . It may be hard to believe it, yet, from another point of view, it is harder still to deny it. — Republic, VII, 532, 533.

Dialectic, and dialectic alone, goes directly to the first principle and is the only science which does away with hypotheses in order to make her ground secure; the eye of the soul, which is literally buried in an outlandish slough, is by her gentle aid lifted upwards; and she uses as handmaids and helpers in the work of conversation the sciences. — Republic, VII, 533.

That your feelings may not be

moved to pity about our thirty-years-old disciples, every care must be taken in introducing them to dialectic. They must not be allowed to taste the dear delight of dialectic too early. — Republic, VII, 539.

Do you not remark, how great the evil is which dialectic has introduced? — Republic, VII, 537.

Dialectician. The dialectician is one who attains a conception of the essence of each thing. — Republic, VII, 534.

The dialectician knows how to ask and answer. — Cratylus, 390.

Diet. When men are sick and ailing in their bodies, their attendants give them wholesome diet in pleasant meats and drinks, but unwholesome diet in disagreeable things, in order that they may learn to like the one, and to dislike the other. And in like manner the true legislator will persuade, and, if he cannot persuade, will compel the poet to express, by fair and noble words, in his rhythms, the figures, and in his melodies, the music of temperate, and brave, and in every way good men. — Laws, II, 659, 660.

Of course, they will have a relish to their meals — salt, and olives, and cheese, and onions, and cabbages or other country herbs which are fit for boiling; and we shall give them a dessert of figs, and peas, and beans, and myrtle berries, and beechnuts, which they will roast at the fire, drinking in moderation. And with such a diet they may be expected to live in peace to a good old age, and bequeath a similar life to their children after them. — Republic, II, 372.

Homer feeds his heroes when they are campaigning on a soldier's fare; they have no fish, although they are on the shores of the Hellespont, and they are allowed nothing but roast meat — which only requires fire, and is therefore the most convenient diet for soldiers — and not boiled, as this would involve a carrying about of pots and pans. — Republic, III, 404.

Differentia Specifica. There is the popular notion of telling the differentia specifica which distinguishes the thing in question from all other things. — Theaetetus, 208.

Suppose that I know Theaetetus to be a man who has nose, eyes, mouth, and every member complete. This does not enable me to distinguish Theaetetus from Theodorus.... Surely I cannot have a conception of Theaetetus until his differentia specifica is stamped on my mind. — Theaetetus, 209.

Dilettante. He lives through the day indulging the appetite of the hour; and sometimes he is lapped in drinks and strains of the flute; then he drinks only water, and tries to get lean; then, again, he is at gymnastics; sometimes idling and neglecting everything, then once more living the life of a philosopher; often he is at politics, and starts to his feet and says and does anything that may turn up; and, if he is emulous of anyone who is a warrior, off he is in that direction, or of man in business, once more in that. — Republic, VIII, 561.

Dimensions. After the second dimension the third, which is concerned with cubes and dimensions of depth, ought to follow. — Republic, VII, 528.

Dion. Dion who was very quick of apprehension, responded to my advice more eagerly and more intensely than any other young man, and was determined to live for his whole life differently from most of the Greeks in Sicily and Italy, estimating virtue higher than *forbidden* pleasure and luxury. — Letter VII, 327.

Dion stumbled over his enemies, whom he almost had conquered. And this is not surprising. For a good man, who has no illusions about the wicked character of his adversaries, is still often caught napping like a good helmsman, who might not altogether overlook the approaching storm, but might underrate the unexpected and extraordinary magnitude. Dion made such a mistake. — Letter VII, 351.

Dion chose to be the victim of crimes rather than commit them, though he took precautions against such perils. — Letter VII, 351.

Dionysius. Dionysius, who united all Sicily into a single state, still met with disaster, because in his wisdom he trusted nobody. He was in want of tried and devoted friends. — Letter VII, 332.

Dionysius II. Though son of a tyrant, Dionysius II is, by voluntarily granting freedom to his citizens, acquiring honorable immortality for himself and for his lineage instead of transitory and dishonest tyranny. — Letter VIII, 356.

Dionysus. There is a tradition or story, which has somehow gone about the world, that Dionysus was robbed of his wits by his stepmother Hera, and that in revenge for this he inspired Bacchic furies and dancing madness in others; for which reason he gave men wine. — Laws, II, 672.

Diotima. Diotima of Mantineia was a wise woman. She was the same who deferred the plague of Athens ten years by a sacrifice, and was my instructress in the philosophy of love. — Symposium, 201.

Dirge. It would be monstrous to command any man to weep or abstain from weeping over the dead, but it shall be forbidden to utter dirges over him. — Laws, XII, 959.

Disbeliever. A man who believes in god, is not a disbeliever. — Apology, 28.

Discernment. The power of discernment always springs from memory and perception. — Philebus, 38.

Disciple. Some disciples are hearers of many things and learn nothing. — Phaedrus, 275.

I will be the disciple, and you shall be my master. — First Alcibiades, 135.

Discord. Perhaps you have never reflected that disease and discord are the same. — Sophist, 228.

Can there be any greater evil than discord and distraction where unity ought to reign? — Republic, V, 462.

Discourse. Without rational discourse men will never become wise. — Epinomis, 977.

If we were deprived of discourse we should be deprived of philosophy. — Sophist, 260.

I should like to wash down the bitter taste in my mouth with a wholesome draught of discourse. — Phaedrus, 243.

Every discourse ought to be a living creature, having its own body and head and feet; there ought to be a middle, beginning, and end, which are in a manner agreeable to one another and to the whole. — Phaedrus, 264.

The whole life is the only limit which wise men assign to the hearing of such great discourses. — Republic, V, 450.

What a tiresome creature is a man who is fond of discourse! I am disheartened at my own stupidity and tiresome garrulity; for what other term will describe the habit of a man who is always arguing on all sides of a question; whose dullness cannot be convinced, and yet he will not leave off? — Theaetetus, 195.

Reason should say to him who censures the length of discourses, that he should not at once lay them aside or censure them as tedious, but he should also prove that they could have been shorter, though expressing the truth. — Statesman, 286, 287.

Discovery. If things had always continued their old way, how could any discovery have ever been made even in the least particular? — Laws, III, 677.

Is not the discovery of things as they truly are a common good to all mankind? — Charmides, 166.

Only a few are, under a light guidance, capable of discovering the truth by themselves. — Letter VII, 341.

Discussion. No tedious or irrelevant discussion can be allowed; that which is said must be pertinent. — Philebus, 36.

The discussion of our actions does not cease with our death. — Letter II, 311.

They do not appreciate the words of fair and free discussion, which men use when they are earnestly and in every way seeking after truth, for the sake of knowledge; they look coldly on the subtleties of controversy, the end of which is but arbitrary opinion and strife in courtroom and in private talk. — Republic, VI, 499.

This makes all the difference between a contentious and a philosophical discussion. — Philebus, 17.

All those who praise or censure instantly any practice which should be a matter of discussion, seem to me to proceed in a wrong way. — Laws, I, 638.

Disease. Every form of disease is in a form akin to the living being. — Timaeus, 89.

The creation of disease is the production of a state of things at variance with the natural order. — Republic, IV, 444. *Vide* Procreation.

In disease the pain exceeds the pleasure. — Laws, V, 734.

Everything has a good and also an evil; as ophthalmia is the sickness of the eyes, and disease of the whole body; as mildew is of corn, and rot of timber, or rust of iron and steel: in everything, or almost everything, there is an inherent evil and disease. — Republic, X, 609.

The body is compelled by reason of disease to court and make friends of the art of medicine. — Lysis, 217.

If anyone regardless of his appointed time attempts to subdue diseases by medicine, he only increases and multiplies them. — Timaeus, 89.

The disorder of the mind will be acknowledged to be folly; but there are two kinds of folly — one madness, and the other ignorance; and whatever affection gives rise to either of them may be called disease. — Timaeus, 86.

Disease ensues. For when the flesh becomes decomposed and sends back the wasting substance into the veins, then there is a great deal of blood of different kinds as well as of air in the veins: and also from its acid and salt qualities it generates all sorts of bile and lymph and phlegm. For all things go the wrong way and are corrupted, and first of all destroy the blood, and then ceasing to give nourishment to the body are carried along the veins in all sorts of ways, no longer preserving the order of their natural courses, but at war with themselves, because they receive no good one from another, and are hostile to the abiding constitution of the body, which they dissolve and corrupt. The oldest part of the flesh wastes away, refusing to assimilate. — Timaeus, 82, 83.

Disgrace. Sons, the event proves that you are the sons of brave men; for we might have lived dishonorably, but preferred to die honorably rather than bring you and your children in disgrace, and rather than dishonor our fathers and forefathers; considering that life is not life to one who is a disgrace to his race, either while he is on the earth or after death. — Menexenus, 246.

Can there be a worse disgrace than this — that I should be thought to value money more than the life of a friend? — Crito, 44.

He who is gracious to his lover under the impression that he is rich, and is disappointed of his gains because he turns out to be poor, is disgraced all the same. — Symposium, 185.

The greater disgrace is the greater evil. — Gorgias, 474.

Disobedience. There are cases in which a man is compelled to disobey the law, if he is required, for example, to marry a woman who is insane, or has some other terrible sickness of soul or body, such as makes marriage intolerable. — Laws, XI, 926.

Disparagement. Disparagement and envy have brought death to many good men. — Apology, 28.

Display. A great man never saw fit to give displays of his wisdom. — Greater Hippias, 282.

Disputation. Youngsters, as you may have observed, when they first get the taste of disputation in their mouths, argue for amusement, and are always contradicting and refuting others in imitation of those who refute them; like puppy dogs, they rejoice in pulling and tearing at all who come near them. And when they have made many conquests and receive many defeats, they violently get into a way of not believing anything which they believed before, and hence, not only they, but philosophy is apt to become discredited. But when a man grows older, he will no longer be guilty of such insanity; he will imitate the dialectician who is seeking for truth, and not the eristic, who is contradicting for the sake of amusement. — Republic, VII, 539.

Glorious is the power of the art of contradiction! Because I think that many a man falls into this practice against his will. When he thinks that he is reasoning he is really disputing, just because he is unable to define and divide that of which he is speaking; and he will pursue a merely verbal opposition in the spirit of contention and not of fair discussion. — Republic, V, 454.

You must have observed that disputants do not always terminate their subjects to their mutual improvement; disagreements are apt to arise, and one party will often deny that the other has spoken sincerely and clearly. And then they leave off arguing and begin to quarrel, both parties imagining that their opponents are anxious for verbal victory rather than for truth. And sometimes they will go on abusing one another until the company at last are quite annoyed at their own condescension in listening to such fellows. — Gorgias, 457.

Dissension. There we have discovered a fountainhead of dissensions; it is yours to remedy them. — Laws, III, 690.

Dissolution. There are many elements of dissolution in a state, as there are also in a ship, or in an animal; they all have their cords, and girders, and sinews — one nature diffused in many places, and called by many names; and the office of examiner is a most important element in the preservation and dissolution of states. — Laws, XII, 945.

Distribution. It would be superhuman folly and depravity that the founders of a new state should create themselves enmities, by reason of their mode of distribution of land and houses. — Laws, V, 737.

Dithyrambic Poetry. What do you say of dithyrambic poetry? — does it not seek only pleasure? — Gorgias, 501.

Diversity. We are not all alike; there are diversities of natures among us which are adapted to different occupations. — Republic, II, 370.

Divination. God has given the art of divination to the foolishness of man. — Timaeus, 71.

The business of divination is to guide the intemperate loves and to heal them, and divination is the source of harmony between gods and men, working by a knowledge of the religious and irreligious tendencies which exist in human loves. — Symposium, 188.

Divine. May we not truly call those men divine who, not having technical knowledge, yet succeed by wisdom in many a grand deed and word? — Meno, 99.

In my opinion, he is not a god at all; but I do call him divine, for of all philosophers I should affirm this. — Sophist, 216.

There is something divine in being able to argue as you have done for the superiority of injustice, and remaining uninfluenced by your own arguments. — Republic, II, 368.

The divine dwells afar from the realm of pleasure and pain. — Letter III, 315.

The women, too, call good men divine. — Meno, 99.

Diviner. The priest and the diviner are full of pride and prerogative — this is due to the greatness of their employments. — Statesman, 290.

Division. There is the faculty of division of things according to natural criteria. — Phaedrus, 265.

Let us see if we can proceed to a division of the realm of knowledge. — Statesman, 259.

Division of Labor. Shall each man bring the result of his labor into a common stock — the farmer, for instance, producing for four, and laboring four times as long and as much as he need in the provision of food for himself only; or shall he not be at the trouble of producing for them, but provide for himself alone a fourth of the food in a fourth of the time, and in the remaining three-fourths of his time be employed in making a house or a coat or a pair of shoes, having no exchange with others? Adeimantus thought that he should aim at producing food only and not at producing everything. That would be the better way. There are diversities of natures among us which are adapted to different occupations. . . .

All things are produced more plentifully and easily and of a better quality when one man does one thing which is natural to him and does it at the right time, and leaves other things to other people. — Republic, II, 369, 370.

The division of labor which required the carpenter and the shoemaker and the rest of the citizens to be doing only a specialized job, and nothing else, is a kind of shadow of justice. — Republic, IV, 443.

Do you think that a state would be well ordered by a law which compelled every man to weave and wash his own coat, and make his own shoes, and his own flask and strigil, and other implements, on this principle of everyone doing and performing his own, and abstaining from what is not his own? — I think not. — Charmides, 161, 162.

Hardly any human being is capable of pursuing two professions or two arts rightly, or of practicing one art himself, and superintending another. Let this, then, be our first work principle in the state: No one who is a smith shall be a carpenter. — Laws, VIII, 846.

Divorce. If any continue without children, let them take counsel with their kindred and with the women holding office, and be divorced for their mutual benefit. — Laws, VI, 784.

If a man and his wife have an unfortunate incompatibility of temper, ten of the guardians of the law, who are impartial, and ten of the women who regulate marriages shall look to the matter, and if they are able to reconcile them they shall be formally reconciled; but if their souls are too much tossed with passion, they shall endeavor to find other partners. Now, they are not likely to have very gentle tempers; and, therefore, we must endeavor to associate with them deeper and softer natures. — Laws, XI, 930.

Doctors. The doctor of slaves never talks to his patients individually, or lets them talk about their own individual complaints. He only prescribes what he thinks good with an air of perfect knowledge which cannot be questioned; and when he has given his orders, like a dictator, he rushes off with equal assurance to some other servant who is ill. — Laws, IV, 720.

The doctor of freemen studies the history and nature of a disease; he discusses it with the patient and his friends, and is at once getting information from the sick man, and also instructing him as far as he is able, and he will not prescribe for him until he has first convinced him; at last, when he has brought the patient more and more under his persuasive influences and set him on the road to health, he attempts to effect a cure. — Laws, IV, 720.

Let us remember that there are two sorts of doctors, a gentler and a ruder, who cure in different ways. — Laws, IV, 720.

When intemperance and diseases multiply in a luxurious state, halls of justice and medicine are always being opened; and the arts of the doctor and the lawyer begin to give themselves airs, finding how keen is the interest which the very freemen of a city take about them. — Republic, III, 405.

The two doctors disagree, and someone is needed to decide between them. — Laches, 184.

Doctrine. This doctrine may be

true, but it also very likely to be untrue; and therefore I would have you reflect well, and not allow yourself to be too easily persuaded. — Cratylus, 440.

Doctrine is contained in the very briefest statements. — Letter VII, 344.

Dog. In a democracy, the she-dogs, as the proverb says, are as good as their she-mistresses. — Republic, VIII, 563.

Dogs are often being silenced by wolves. — Laws, X, 906.

The dog is the gentlest of animals. — Sophist, 231.

The trait of which I am speaking, may be also seen in the dog, and is very remarkable in the animal. For a dog, whenever he sees a stranger, is angry; when an acquaintance, he welcomes him, although the one has never done him any harm, nor the other any good. Did this instinct never strike you as marvelous? — Republic, II, 376.

. . . like a dog who cannot get at his assailant, quarreling with the stones which strike him instead. — Republic, V, 469.

Not everyone is qualified to attend dogs, but only the huntsman. — Euthyphro, 13.

Well-bred dogs are perfectly gentle to their familiars and acquaintances, and the reverse to strangers. — Republic, II, 375.

Surely this instinct of the dog is very charming — your dog is a true philosopher. — Republic, II, 376.

Doing. Men do, not what they wish, but what they can. — Greater Hippias, 301.

In some of the arts a great deal is done and nothing or very little said. — Gorgias, 450.

Domestics. My domestics became on some occasions my masters. — Symposium, 175.

Dorian. We are not attuned to the Dorian mode, which is a harmony of words and deeds; for our deeds are not in accordance with our words. — Laches, 193.

Dotard. Are you such an old dotard, that you bring up now what I said at first — and if I had said anything last year, I suppose that you would bring that up — but are nonplused at the words I have just uttered? — Euthydemus, 287.

Double. The double nature we call the living being. — Timaeus, 87.

May not the many which are doubles be also halves — doubles, that is, of one thing, and halves of another? — Republic, V, 479.

Doubt. There is no difficulty in raising a doubt, since there may even be a doubt whether we are awake or in a dream. — Theaetetus, 158.

The wise are doubtful, and if, like them, I also doubted, there would be nothing strange in that. — Phaedrus, 229.

Dowry. In marrying and giving in marriage, no one shall give or receive any dowry at all. — Laws, V, 742.

Poor men should be taught that he who neither gives nor receives a dowry on account of poverty, will reach an old age. Wives will be less likely to be insolent, and husbands to be mean and subservient to them on account of property. — Laws, VI, 774.

Draught Player. Is the just man or the skillful player a more useful or better partner at a game of draughts? — The skillful player. — Republic, I, 333.

There could not be found fifty draught players in a city of a thousand men, and there would certainly not be as many rulers. — Statesman, 292.

Dreadful. Prodicus corrects me when I use the word "dreadful" as a term of praise. If I say that Protagoras is a dreadfully wise man, he asks me if I am not ashamed of calling that which is good dreadful; and then he explains me that the term "dreadful" is always taken in a bad sense, and that no one speaks of being dreadfully healthy or wealthy or wise, but of dreadful war, dreadful poverty, dreadful disease, meaning by the term "dreadful," evil. — Protagoras, 341.

Dream. In a dream man believes in things which he abandons when he awakes. — Statesman, 277.

I suppose that someone of them divined the truth in his dream or in waking trance. — Laws, VII, 800.

He who would understand what he remembers to have been said, whether in dream or when he was awake, by the prophetic and enthusiastic nature, or what he has seen, must recover his wits; and then he will be able to explain rationally what all such words and apparitions mean. — Timaeus, 72.

He who fancies to have a sense for beautiful things, but really has none, or, if another lead him to a knowledge of them, is unable to follow — is he awake or in a dream only? — Republic, V, 476.

When people are awakened by terrible apparitions, and have dreams or remember visions, they find in altars and temples the remedies of them. — Laws, X, 910.

I started to write poetry in order to find out the meaning of certain dreams, and to clear my conscience which seemed to suggest this art. — Phaedo, 60.

When the rest is profound, sleep comes with but few dreams; but when the greater motions remain, whatever may be their nature and locality, they engender corresponding visions in dreams within us, which are remembered by us when we awake to the external reality. — Timaeus, 45, 46.

You must often have heard persons ask: "How can you prove whether at this moment we are sleeping, and all our thoughts are dreams; or whether we are awake, and talking to one another in the waking state? For all the phenomena correspond; and there is no difficulty in supposing that we have now been talking to one another in our sleep; and when in a dream we seem to be telling thoughts which are only dreams, the resemblance of the two states is quite astonishing." — Theaetetus, 158.

When a man's pulse is healthy and temperate, and he goes to sleep cool and rational, after having supped on a feast of reason and meditation, and comes to a knowledge of himself, having indulged his appetites neither too much nor too little, but just enough to lay them to sleep, and prevent them and their enjoyment from interfering with the better part of his self: when, again, before going to sleep he has allayed his passionate anger, if he has had a quarrel against anyone — I say, when, after pacifying the two irrational elements, he rouses up the third or rational element before he takes his rest, then he attains truth most nearly, and is least likely to be the sport of fanciful and lawless dreams. — Republic, IX, 571, 572.

Dreamer. Is not the dreamer, sleeping or waking, one who likens dissimilar things, who puts the copy in the place of the real object? — Republic, V, 476.

I certainly cannot undertake to argue that madmen and dreamers think truly, when they imagine; some of them that they are gods, and others that they can fly, and are flying in their sleep. — Theaetetus, 158.

Drinking. Perception and memory, and judgment and prudence entirely desert a man if he becomes saturated with drink. — Laws, I, 645.

I may be forgiven for saying, as a physician, that drinking is a bad practice, which I never, if I can help, follow, and certainly do not recommend to another, least of all to anyone who still feels the effects of yesterday's carouse. — Symposium, 176.

I am afraid of appearing to elicit a very long discourse out of very small materials. For drinking may indeed appear to be a slight matter, and yet is one which cannot be rightly ordered according to nature, without correct principles of music. — Laws, I, 642.

When a man drinks, he at first becomes more cheerful than he was before, and the more he drinks the more he is filled full of brave hopes, and the fancy of his power, and at last the string of his tongue is loosened, and imagining himself wise, he is brimming over with lawlessness, and has no more fear or respect, and is ready to do or say anything. — Laws, I, 649.

Does not the drinker return to the state of the soul in which he was when a young child? Then at that time he will have the least control over himself. — Laws, I, 645.

During the whole year and all his life long, and especially while he is begetting children, the drinker ought to take care and not intentionally do what is injurious to health, or what involves insolence and wrong; for it needs must be that the souls and bodies of the children receive the impress which is stamped upon them at birth, and he begets children in every way inferior. And especially on the day and night of marriage should a man abstain from such things. . . . Drunkenness is always improper, except at the festivals of the god who gave wine; and peculiarly dangerous, when a man is engaged in the business of marriage; for at such a crisis of their lives a bride and bridegroom ought to have all their wits about them, and they ought to take care that their offspring may be born of reasonable beings; you cannot tell on what day or night Heaven will give them increase. Moreover, they ought not to be begetting children when their bodies are dissipated by intoxication, but their offspring should be compact and solid; whereas the drunkard is all abroad in all his actions, and is beside himself both in body and soul. The drunken man is bad and unsteady in sowing the seed of increase, and is likely to beget offspring who are unstable and untrustworthy, and cannot be expected to walk straight either in body or mind. — Laws, VI, 775.

The weak heads like myself and others who never can drink, are fortunate in finding that the stronger ones are not in a drinking mood. — Symposium, 176.

Drinkers who are not able to converse or amuse one another with the sound of their own voices and conversation by reason of their stupidity, raise the price of flute girls in the market, hiring for a great sum the voice of a flute instead of their own breath, to be the medium of intercourse among them: but where the company are real gentlemen and men of education, you will see no flute girls, nor dancing girls, nor harp girls; and they have no nonsense or games, but are contented with one another's conversation, of which their own voices are the medium. — Protagoras, 347.

They appeared to us to have been drinking rather too much, which made them difficult to manage. — Lysis, 223.

On such occasions the souls of the drinkers become like iron heated in the fire, and grow softer and younger. — Laws, II, 671.

I am disposed rather to the law of the Carthaginians, that no one while he is on a campaign should be allowed to taste wine at all; but I would say that he should drink water during all that time. — Laws, II, 674.

Drinking Party. Did anyone ever see a drinking party rightly ordered? I have come across many of them in many different places, and moreover I have made inquiries about them wherever I went, and never did I see or hear of anything of the sort which was carried on altogether rightly; in some few particulars they might be right, but in general they were utterly wrong. — Laws, I, 639.

I should imagine that a drinking party is likely to become more and more tumultuous as the drinking goes on. — Laws, II, 671.

A gathering attended by drinking will probably not be free from excitement. — Laws, I, 640.

No state can be free from unrest under the best laws, if its citizens indulge in excesses, while making it a rule to dodge all industry except that of attending drinking parties and of gratifying coveted lust. — Letter VII, 326.

Drone. You will find that the natural desires of the drone commonly exist in him all the same, whenever he has to spend what is not his own. — Republic, VIII, 554.

The drone is the man who overindulges in pleasures and desires, and is governed by unnecessary appetites. — Republic, VIII, 559.

As soon as these dire magicians and tyrant-makers discover that they are losing their hold on the shifting youth, they contrive to implant in him a master passion, to be the lord over his idle and spendthrift lusts — like a monster drone having wings. That is the only image that will adequately depict him. — Republic, IX, 572, 573.

God has made the flying drones all without stings, whereas of the walking drones he has made some without stings and others with dreadful stings: of the stingless class are those who in their old age end by dying paupers; of the stingers come all the criminal class, as they are termed. — Republic, VIII, 552.

The luxurious and heedless and idle qualities the poet compares to stingless drones. — Laws, X, 901.

May we not say that this is the drone in the house who is like the drone in the honeycomb, and that one is the plague of the city as the other is of the hive? — Republic, VIII, 552.

Drunkard. The drunkard is in a most wretched plight. And not only an old man but also a drunkard becomes a second time a child. — Laws, I, 646.

Drunkards and children tell the truth. — Symposium, 217.

Has not a drunken man the spirit of a tyrant? — Republic, IX, 573.

Do you not see that a drunken pilot or a drunken ruler of any sort will ruin ship, chariot, army — anything, in short, of which he has direction? — Laws, I, 640.

Anyone who meets a drunken or disorderly person, will immediately have him punished, and will not let him off on any pretense, not even at the time of a Dionysiac festival. — Laws, I, 637.

Dualists and Monists. With those [dualists] who make being to consist in ideas, there will be less difficulty [in discussing existence] for they are civil people enough; but there will be very great difficulty, or rather an absolute impossibility, in arguing with those [materialistic monists] who drag everything down to matter. — Sophist, 246.

Due. If a man has any feeling of what is due to himself, he cannot let the thought which comes into his mind pass away unheeded and unexamined. — Charmides, 173.

Duty. Our first duty will be to take care of the soul. — Alcibiades, 132.

It is more our duty to speak of the good than of the evil. — Timaeus, 87.

Does not he who does his duty act temperately or wisely? — Charmides, 164.

Dye. We would like to prepare our soldiers to take the dye of the laws in perfection, so that the color of their opinions was to be indelibly fixed by their nurture and training, and not to be washed away by such potent a lye as pleasure. — Republic, IV, 430.

Dyeing. The dyers, when they want to dye wool for making the true sea purple, begin by selecting their white color first, in order that the white ground may take the purple hue in full perfection. The dyeing then proceeds; and whatever is dyed in this manner becomes a fast color, and no washing with lyes or without lyes can take away the bloom of the color. — Republic, IV, 429.

Dying. Like children, you are haunted with fear that when the soul leaves the body, the wind may really blow her away and scatter her; especially if a man should happen to die in stormy weather and not when the sky is calm. — Phaedo, 77.

A man when he is about to die is a fearful thing, and may cause a great deal of anxiety and trouble. — Laws, XI, 922.

I have heard that a man should die in peace. — Phaedo, 117.

Dysentery. If the bile is driven out of the body like an exile out of an insurgent state, it causes diarrheas and dysenteries, and all sorts of similar disorders. — Timaeus, 86.

E

Earnest. You are truly in earnest; and yet most of your hearers are likely to be still more in earnest in their opposition to you. — Republic, VI, 498.

Earth. There are diverse regions in the hollows on the face of the earth everywhere, some of them deeper and also wider than those which we inhabit; all have numerous holes, and passages broad and narrow in the interior of the earth, connecting them with one another; and there flows into and out of them, as into basins, a vast tide of water, and huge subterranean streams of perennial rivers, and springs hot and cold, and a great fire, and great rivers of fire, and streams of liquid mud, thin or thick (like the rivers of mud in Sicily, and the lava streams which follow them), and the regions about which they happen to flow are filled with them. And there is a sort of swing in the interior of the earth which moves all this up and down. — Phaedo, 111.

The earth is our nurse. — Timaeus, 40.

The earth conceives and yields her harvest, and thus procures food for all the creatures, if rains and winds are propitious and not excessive. — Epinomis, 979.

The earth, when looked at from above, is like one of those balls which have leather coverings in twelve pieces. — Phaedo, 110.

Easy. Nothing great is easy. — Republic, II, 365.

Eating. The desires of eating and drinking begin at birth. — Laws, VI, 782.

Echo. The echo leaps from the smooth rocks and rebounds to them again. — Phaedrus, 255.

The echo of the rocks and the place in which they are assembled redoubles the sound. — Republic, VI, 492.

Eclipse. People may injure their bodily eyes by observing and gazing on the sun during an eclipse, unless they take the precaution of only looking at its image reflected in the water, or in some similar medium. — Phaedo, 99.

Education. If this is your first attempt at education, there is a danger that you may be trying the experiment, not on worthless Carian slaves, but on your own sons. — Laches, 187.

Let us make the education of the youths our own education. — Laches, 201.

In education, a change of state has to be effected. — Theaetetus, 167.

Am I not right in maintaining that a good education is that which tends to the improvement of mind and body? — Laws, VII, 788.

A man of true nurture and education attains the fullness and health of the perfect man; but if he neglects education he walks lame throughout existence in his life. — Timaeus, 44.

Education and admonition commence in the first year of childhood, and last to the very end of life. Mother and nurse and father and tutor are quarreling about the improvement of the child as soon as ever he is able to understand them: he cannot say or do anything without their setting forth to him that this is just and that is unjust; this is honorable, that is dishonorable; this is holy, that is unholy; do this and abstain from that. And if he obeys, well and good; if not, he is straightened by threats and blows, like a piece of warped wood. — Protagoras, 325.

All elements of instruction should be presented to the mind in childhood; not, however, under any notion of forcing our system of education. For a freeman ought not to be a slave in the acquisition of any kind. Bodily exercise, when compulsory, does no harm to the body; but knowledge which is acquired under compulsion obtains no hold on the mind. Do not, then, use compulsion, but let early education be a sort of amusement; you will then be better able to find out the natural bent. — Republic, VII, 536.

The first shoot of any plant rightly tending to the perfection of its own nature, has the greatest effect on its maturity; and this is not only true of plants, but of animals wild and also of men. Man is a tame or civilized animal; nevertheless, he requires proper instruction and fortunate nature, and then of all animals he becomes the most divine and most civilized; but if he be insufficiently or ill-educated he is the savagest of earthly creatures. Wherefore the legislator ought not to allow the education of children to become a secondary or accidental matter. — Laws, VI, 765, 766.

There shall be compulsory education, as far as this is possible. And such law would apply to girls as well as to boys; they shall both go through the same exercises. — Laws, VII, 804.

According to my view he who would be good at any thing must practice that thing from early childhood, both in sport and earnest. For instance, he who is to be a good builder, should play at building children's houses; the future carpenter should learn to measure or apply the line in play. The teacher should endeavor to direct the children's inclinations and pleasures by the help of amusements, to their final aim in life. The sum of education is right training in the nursery. The soul of the child in his play should be trained to that sort of exellence in which, when he grows up to manhood, he will have to be perfected. — Laws, I, 643.

What greater proof can there be of a disgraceful state of education than this, that not only the meaner classes but also the claimants of a liberal education are in need of the high skill of physicians and judges? It is a lack of education that a man should have to go to others for his law and physic because he has none of his own, and must therefore surrender himself into the hands of others. — Republic, III, 405.

Let us not leave the meaning of education ambiguous or ill-defined. When we speak in terms of praise or blame about the bringing up of a person, we generally call one man educated and another uneducated in reference to the calling of a retail trader, or of a captain of a ship, and the like. But at present we are not speaking of education in this sense of the word, but of education in virtue from youth upwards, which makes a man eagerly pursue the ideal perfection of citizenship, and teaches him how rightly to rule and how to obey. This is the only training which would be characterized as education; that other sort of training, which aims at the acquisition of wealth or bodily strength, or mere cleverness apart from intelligence and righteousness, is mean and illiberal, and is not worthy to be called education at all. — Laws, I, 643, 644.

Our youth should be educated from the first in a stricter system, for if amusements become lawless, and the youths themselves become lawless, they can never grow up into well-conducted and virtuous citizens. — Republic, IV, 424.

May we not say that the most gifted minds, when they are ill-educated, become pre-eminently bad? Do not great crimes and the spirit of pure evil spring out of a fullness of nature ruined by education rather than from any inferiority, whereas weak natures are scarcely capable of any great good or very great evil? And our philosopher follows the same analogy — he is like a plant which, having proper nurture, must necessarily grow and mature into all virtue, but, if sown and planted in alien soil, becomes the most noxious of all weeds, unless he be preserved by some divine power. — Republic, VI, 492.

We must not cast a slight upon education, which is the first and fairest thing that the best of men can ever have, and which, though liable to take a wrong direction, is capable of correction. And this work of correction is the great business of every man while he lives. — Laws, I, 644. *Vide* Victory.

Education of Girls. After the age of six years the time is arrived for the separation of the sexes — let boys live with boys, and girls in like manner with girls. Now they must begin to learn — the boys going to teachers of horsemanship and the use of the bow, the javelin, and sling; and if they do not object, let girls go too to learn if not to practice; above all, they ought to know the use of arms; for these are matters which are almost entirely misunderstood at present. — Laws, VII, 794.

I have no sort of fear of saying that gymnastic and horsemanship are as suitable to girls as to boys. — Laws, VII, 804.

While they are yet girls they should have practiced dancing in arms and the art of fighting — when they are grown-up women, applying themselves to evolutions and tactics, and the mode of grounding and taking up arms. — Laws, VII, 813.

Educators. Educators must be mistaken in saying that they can put a knowledge into the soul which was not there before, like giving eyes to the blind. — Republic, VII, 518.

Efficiency. A work is more efficiently done when the workman has only one occupation. — Republic, II, 370.

Elders. Our young men break forth into dancing and singing, and we who are their elders deem that we are fulfilling our part in life when we look on at them. Having lost the agility of youth, we delight in their plays and merriment; because we love to think of our former selves, and gladly institute contests for those who are able to awaken in us the memory of what we once were. — Laws, II, 657.

Election. The mode of election which has been described, is in a mean between monarchy and democracy, and such a mean the state ought always to observe; for servants and masters never can be friends, merely because they are said to have equal privileges. — Laws, VI, 756, 757.

Elements. There are four elements out of which the body is compacted, earth and fire and water and air, and the unnatural excess or defect of these, or the change of any of them from its own natural place into another, or — since there are more kinds than one of fire and of the other elements — the assumption by any of these of a wrong kind produces disorders and diseases. — Timaeus, 82.

That which we are now calling water, when congealed becomes stone and earth, as our sight seems to show us; and this same element, when melted and dispersed, passes into vapor and air. Air, again, when burnt up, becomes fire; and again fire, when condensed and extinguished, passes once more into the form of air; and once more, air, when collected and condensed, produces cloud and vapor; and from these, when still more compressed, comes flowing water, and from water comes earth and stones once more; and thus generation appears to be transmitted from one to the other in a circle. How can anyone have the assurance to maintain positively that any of the elements is one thing rather than another? No one can. — Timaeus, 49.

Fire above all things penetrates everywhere, and air next, as being next in rarity of the elements; and the rest in like manner penetrate according to their degrees of rarity. For those things which are composed of the largest particles have the largest void left in their compositions, and those which are composed of the smallest particles have the least. And the tendency towards condensation thrusts the smaller particles into the interstices of the larger. — Timaeus, 58.

We see the elements which enter into the nature of the bodies of all animals, fire, water, air, and, as the storm-tossed sailor cries, "land" (i.e., earth), in the constitution of the world. — Philebus, 29.

Among elements which are similar and uniform, none can change or be changed by another of the same class and in the same state. — Timaeus, 57.

When the small parts are placed side by side with the larger, and the lesser divide the greater and the greater unite the lesser, all the elements are borne up and down and every way towards their own places; for the change in the size of each changes its position in space. And these causes generate an inequality which is always maintained, and is continually creating a perpetual motion of the elements in all time. — Timaeus, 58.

Fire and water, and earth and air, all exist by nature, absolutely inanimate existences . . . and all the seasons come from these elements, not by the action of mind, or any god, but by nature only. — Laws, X, 889.

Elenchus. This is a new sort of elenchus — when anyone says anything, instead of refuting him to laugh at him. — Gorgias, 473.

Elephant. There were a great number of elephants in the island of Atlantis, and there was provision for animals of every kind, both for those which live in lakes and marshes and rivers, and also for those which live in mountains and on plains, and therefore for the animal which is the largest and most voracious of them. — Critias, 115.

Eloquence. If by the force of eloquence they mean the force of truth, then I do indeed admit that I am eloquent. — Apology, 17.

Embalming. The body when embalmed, as is the custom in Egypt, may remain almost intact through infinite ages. — Phaedo, 80.

Empedocles. Does not Empedocles say that there are certain effluences of existence? — Meno, 76.

Employment. We had given to each one that single employment and particular art which were suited to his nature. — Timaeus, 17.

Emptiness. Hunger, thirst, and the like, are emptinesses of the bodily state. — Republic, IX, 585.

Enchanter. The art of the enchanter is a mode of charming snakes and spiders and scorpions, and other monsters and pests. — Euthydemus, 290.

End. All things have ends. — Republic, I, 353.

When he considers anything for the sake of another thing, he thinks of the end and not of the means. — Laches, 185.

If a man does something for the sake of something else, he wills not always that which he does, but that for the sake of which he does it. — Gorgias, 467.

Endowment. Natural endowments should not be spoiled by bad habits in so far as this can be avoided. — Laws, VII, 795.

Endurance. Any deeds of endurance attributed to famous men ought to be noticed by our youth. — Republic, III, 390.

The Spartans frequently practice the endurance of pain, exhibited in certain hand-to-hand fights, also in stealing with the prospect of getting a beating; there is, too, the so-called Crypteia or secret service, in which wonderful endurance is shown. Those who are employed in this, wander over the whole country by day and by night, and even in winter have not any shoes on their feet, and are without beds to lie upon, and have no one to attend them. Marvelous, too, is the endurance which the Spartans show in their gymnastic exercises, contending against the violent summer heat. — Laws, I, 633.

A wise endurance is also good and noble. — Laches, 192.

I cannot say that every kind of endurance is to be deemed courage. . . . Only the wise endurance is courage. — Laches, 192.

Enemies. Many are enemies to those who love them, and friends to those who hate them. — Lysis, 213.

We must abstain from plundering the enemies' dead or hindering their burial. — Republic, V, 469.

Did you write your enemies' names as well as your friends'? — Charmides, 161.

The right attitude in any situation is to do the most damage to the enemy and the most good to your own part. — Letter VIII, 352.

Dion was well aware of the dishonesty of his enemies. But he underrated the depth of their hostility, wickedness, and greediness. As a result, he succumbed. — Letter VII, 351.

Engineers. If the engineer who is not usually conceited were to speak in a bombastic style, he would bury us under a mountain of words, declaring and insisting that we ought all of us to be engineers, since the other professions are worthless. Nevertheless we often despise him and his art, and sneeringly call him an "engineer," and would not allow our daughter to marry his son, or marry our son to his daughter. And yet, what right have we to despise the engineers? — Gorgias, 512.

Enjoyment. Enjoyment results from acquiring wisdom and knowledge, but pleasure arises from eating or experiencing some other bodily delight. — Protagoras, 377.

I would not bid a human being, still less a god, to enjoy himself. — Letter III, 315.

Enlightening. Shall we enlighten him instead of abusing him? — Laches, 195.

Enmity, Causes of. What differences are those which, because they cannot be decided by weighing and measuring, make us angry and set us at enmity with one another? I dare say that this happens when the matters of difference are the just and unjust, good and evil, honorable and dishonorable. Are not these the points about which, when differing, and unable satisfactorily to decide our differences, we quarrel? — Euthyphro, 7.

In order to put to the test the metal of your different races, which, like Hesiod's, are of gold and silver, and brass, and iron, iron will be mingled with silver, and brass with gold, and hence there will arise inequality and irregularity, which always and in all places are causes of enmity and war. — Republic, VIII, 546, 547.

Enslavement. The enslavement of others is altogether terrible, and attempted by mean and slavish men, who have no idea of the good and just. — Letter VII, 334.

You would not deny that a state may unjustly attempt to enslave other states, or may have already enslaved them, and may be holding many of them in subjection? — True; and I will add that the best and most perfectly unjust state will be most likely to do this. — Republic, I, 351.

Entertainer. When enjoyment is to be the order of the day, the entertainer ought to be honored most, and bear the palm for superior ingenuity, who gives most enjoyment to the greatest number. — Laws, II, 657.

Envy. The envious man finds something in the misfortunes of his neighbors at which he is pleased. — Philebus, 48.

Let every man freely compete for the prize of virtue, and let there be no envy. For the unenvious nature increases the greatness of states — he himself contends in the race and defames no man; but the envious, who thinks that he ought to get the better by censuring others, is less energetic himself in the pursuit of true virtue, and reduces his rivals to despair by his unjust slanders of them. And thus he deprives the whole city of the proper training for the contest of virtue, and diminishes her glory as far as in him lies. — Laws, V, 731.

Ephesians. In accordance with their textbooks, the Ephesians are always in motion; but as for dwelling upon an argument or a question, and quietly asking and answering in turn, they are absolutely without the power of doing this. If you ask any of them a question, he will produce, as from a quiver, sayings brief and dark, and shoot them at you; and if you inquire the reason of what he has said, you will be hit by some other newfangled word; for their great care is, not to allow of any settled principle either in their arguments or in their minds, conceiving, as I imagine, that this would be stationary; and they are at war with the stationary. Disciples, my good sir, they have none; men of this sort are not one another's disciples, but they grow up anyhow and get their inspiration anywhere, each of them saying of his neighbor that he knows nothing. From these men, then, you will never get a reason; we must take the question out of their hands, and make the analysis ourselves. — Theaetetus, 179, 180.

Epicure. I may liken myself to an epicure who snatches a taste of every dish which is successively brought to table before he has fairly enjoyed the one before. — Republic, I, 354.

Epilepsy. When the phlegm is mingled with black bile and dispersed about the courses of the head, which are the divinest part of us, and disturbs them in sleep, the attack is not severe; but when assailing those who are awake it is hard to be got rid of, and, being an affection of a sacred part, is most justly called sacred. — Timaeus, 85.

Epimenides. The ingenuity of Epimenides does indeed far overleap the heads of all your great men; what Hesiod had theorized about long before, he converted into a fact. — Laws, III, 677.

Epimetheus, Tale of. Epimetheus made the distribution [of animal qualities]. There were some creatures to whom he gave strength without swiftness, or again swiftness without strength; some he armed, and others he left unarmed; and devised for the latter some other means of preservation, making some large, and having their size as a protection, and others small, whose nature was to fly in the air or burrow in the ground; this was to be their way of escape. Thus did he compensate them with the view of preventing any race from becoming extinct. He contrived also means of protecting them against the seasons; clothing them with close hair and thick skins sufficient to defend them against the winter cold and summer heat, and for a natural bed of their own when they wanted to rest; also he furnished them with hoofs and hair and hard and callous skins under their feet. Then he gave them varieties of food — to some herbs of the soil, to others fruits of trees, and to others roots, and to some again he gave other animals as food. — Protagoras, 320, 321. *Vide* Prometheus.

Epistemology. Epistemology alone is a science of other sciences, and of itself. — Charmides, 166.

Equality. Equals delight in equals; equality of years inclines them to the same pleasures, and similarity begets friendship, and yet you may have more than enough even of this, and compulsion is always said to be grievous. — Phaedrus, 240.

He who is our equal will do as we do. — Protagoras, 338.

In my opinion the makers of laws are the many weak; and they make laws and distribute praises and censures with a view to themselves and to their own interests: and they terrify the mightier man, in order that he may not get the better of them. And they say, that dishonesty is shameful and unjust; meaning, when they speak of injustice, the desire to have more than their neighbor. Knowing their own inferiority they are only too glad of equality. — Gorgias, 483.

The legislators of that day, when they equalized property, escaped the great accusation which generally arises in legislation, if a person attempts to redistribute the possession of land, or to abolish debts, because he sees that with this there can never be any real equality. — Laws, III, 684.

Equal treatment of unequals causes inequality when not harmonized by proper proportion; and both by reason of equality, and by reason of inequality, cities are filled with seditions. The old saying, that "equality makes friendship," is witty and also true; but there is obscurity and confusion as to what sort of equality is meant. For there are two different equalities. One of them is the rule of measure, weight, and number; the other is the judgment of Zeus, which gives to the greater more, and to the inferior less. With a view to this latter equality, we ought to order the new state. — Laws, VI, 757.

It would have been well that every man should come to the colony having all things equal; but seeing that this is impossible, for the sake of equal opportunity, qualifications of property must be unequal. . . . And so by a law of inequality, which will be in proportion to the citizen's wealth, he will receive honors and offices as equally as possible. — Laws, V, 744.

Let all that apply equally to men and women who have been distinguished in virtue. — Laws, VII, 802.

I must not forget to tell of the liberty and equality of the two sexes in relation to one another. — Republic, VIII, 563.

That which has greatness and smallness also has equality which lies between them. — Parmenides, 161.

Equality and not excess is justice. — Gorgias, 489.

We affirm that there is such a thing as equality, not of wood with wood, or of stone with stone, but that, over and above this, there is absolute equality. — Phaedo, 74.

The basis of this our government is equality of birth; for other states are made up of all sorts and unequal conditions; there are tyrannies and there are oligarchies, in which the one party are slaves and the others masters. But we and our citizens are brethren, the children all of one mother, and we do not claim to be one another's masters or servants; but the natural equality of birth compels us to seek for legal equality, and to recognize no superiority except in the reputation of virtue and wisdom. — Menexenus, 238, 239.

The regulations about war, and about liberty of speech in poetry, ought to apply equally to men and women. — Laws, VIII, 829.

Equilibrium. Any thing which, being in equilibrium, is in the center of a uniformly diffused medium, will not incline any way in any degree, but will always remain in the same state and not deviate. — Phaedo, 109.

Erect. God gave men the soul as a genius, which was to dwell at the extremity of the body, and to raise us like plants, not of an earthly but of a heavenly growth, from earth to our kindred which is in heaven. And this must be true; for the deity suspended the head and root of us from that place where the generation of the soul first began, and thus made erect the whole body. — Timaeus, 90.

Eristics. If the Eristic sees a phony puzzle, his pleasure is to drag words this way and that; but the argument will prove to him that he is not making a worthy use of his faculties. For there is no charm in such puzzles, and there is no real difficulty in them; but we can tell him of something else in the pursuit of which there is great charm and also a difficulty. — Sophist, 259.

You would not confuse the principle and the consequences in your reasoning, like the Eristics. — Phaedo, 101.

Eros. Is not Eros the son of Aphrodite a mighty god? — Phaedrus, 242.

Erring. Is it better to possess the mind of an archer who voluntarily or involuntarily misses the mark? — Of him who voluntarily misses. — Then the mind which voluntarily errs is better than that which involuntarily errs. — Lesser Hippias, 375.

No craftsman or sage or ruler errs at the time when he is what he is called, though he is commonly said to err. But the more precise expression is that the ruler, as ruler, is unerring. — Republic, I, 340.

Error. If he begins in error, he may force the remainder [of the proof] into agreement with the original error; there would be nothing strange in this, any more than in geometrical diagrams, which often have a slight and invisible flaw in the first part of the demonstration, and are consistently mistaken in the long deductions which follow. — Cratylus, 436.

We must not be guilty of the error which we condemn in others. — Phaedrus, 237.

This is not the only point about which mankind are in error. — Protagoras, 352.

Men devise evil by reason of some error. — Greater Hippias, 296.

Escape. When every way is blocked, there is no escape. — Sophist, 231.

Essence. We have discovered two kinds of essence: the one immortal the other mortal. Epinomis, 984.

Would you say that the things differ as the names differ, and are they relative to individuals, as Protagoras tells us? For he says that man is the measure of all things, and that things are to me as they appear to me, and that they are to you as they appear to you. Do you agree with him, or would you say that things have a permanent essence of their own? — Cratylus, 385, 386.

Let us now go to the friends of ideas. To them we say, You would distinguish essence from generation. And you say that we perceive generation by means of the body through sense; but we conceive essence by means of the soul through reflection. — Sophist, 248.

Things must be supposed to have their own proper and permanent essence: they are not in relation to us, or influenced by us, fluctuating according to our fancy, but they are independent, and maintain their essence. — Cratylus, 386.

We unconsciously but wrongly transfer species of time to the spiritual essence. We say that intelligible being was, is, and will be, but the truth is that "is" alone truly expresses it, and that "was" and "will be" are only to be spoken of physical things; for they are motions, but the spiritual, which is immovable cannot become older or younger by time which is attached to material things only. — Timaeus, 37, 38.

Is there not a notion or essence of each thing just as there is color, or figure, or sound? And is there not an essence of color and sound as well as of anything else which may be said to have essence? — Cratylus, 423.

Are ideas or essences liable at times to some degree of change? or are they each of them always what they are, having the same simple, self-existent and unchanging forms, and not admitting of variation at all, or in any way, or at any time? — Phaedo, 78.

There appears to be a sort of war of Giants and gods going on amongst them; they are fighting about the nature of essence. Some of them are dragging down all things from heaven and from the unseen to earth, and are determined to grasp in their hands rocks and oaks only; of these they lay hold, and are obstinate in maintaining, that the things only which can be touched or handled have being or essence, because they define being as body only, and if anyone says that also incorporeal spirit exists they altogether despise him, and will hear of nothing but body. I have often met with such men, and terrible fellows they are. And that is the reason why their opponents cautiously defend themselves from above, out of an unseen world, mightily contending that true essence also consists of certain intelligible and incorporeal value ideas. . . . There is an endless war raging between these two armies on this issue. — Sophist, 246.

Essential. Why, if bald men are shoemakers, forbid the hairy men, or if the hairy men are shoemakers, forbid the bald men to be shoemakers? The absurdity only arises from mistaking the accidental as essential. A man or a woman, having the soul of a physician, is essentially the same: a human being. — Republic, V, 454.

There are — this is most important — two things: the essential and the accidental quality. And when the mind seeks after the essential, it is often confronted with the unsought accidental. — Letter VII, 343.

Esteem. Esteem is a sincere conviction of the hearers' souls, but praise is often an insincere expression of men uttering words contrary to their conviction. — Protagoras, 377.

Eternal. Let us suppose that philosophical minds always love knowledge of a sort which shows them the eternal nature not varying from generation and corruption. — Republic, V, 485.

Eternity. Could there be a great thing in a little time? The whole period of three score years and ten is surely but a small thing in comparison with eternity. — Republic, X, 608.

Ethics. The ethical inquiry into good and bad is one and the same science. — Ion, 532.

Etymology. This is a very shabby etymology. Original names are always being buried and bedizened by people sticking on and stripping off letters for the sake of euphony, and twisting and turning them in all sorts of ways. One cares nothing about the truth, but thinks only of putting the mouth into shape. And the changes are often such that at last no human being can possibly make out the original meaning of the word. — Cratylus, 414.

Eugenics. The best of either sex should cohabit with the best as often as possible, and the inferior with the inferior; and they are to rear the offspring of the one sort of union, but not of the other; for this is the only way of keeping the flock in prime condition. Now these eugenic goings on must be a secret which the rulers only know, or there will be a further danger of our herd breaking out in rebellion. — Republic, V, 459.

Eulogies. Citizens who have been obedient to the laws, should receive eulogies; this will be very fitting. — Laws, VII, 801.

Euphemism. People in general use the term Pluto as a euphemism for Hades. — Cratylus, 403.

Euphony. They alter her name Pherepaphe into Pherephatta nowadays, because the present generation cares for euphony more than truth. — Cratylus, 404.

Euripides. Tragedy is a wise thing and Euripides a great tragedian, because he is the author of the ill-reputed saying, "Tyrants are wise by living with wise men," and he clearly meant to say that the associates of a tyrant are wise. And therefore we object to having him in our state. — Republic, VIII, 568.

Europe. The children of Europe, who were our fathers, held back the Persians. — Menexenus, 239.

Evasion. Did I not tell you that he would try irony or another evasion in order that he might avoid answering? — Republic, I, 337.

Even Number. The even number represents a figure having two equal sides. — Euthyphro, 12.

Evidence. If a man refuses to give evidence, he who wants him shall summon him. And he who is summoned to give evidence and does not answer to his summoner, shall be liable for the harm which ensues according to law. And if a judge is summoned to give evidence, he shall give evidence, but not afterwards vote in the case. — Laws, XI, 937.

Evil. Only an evil being would wish to dissolve that which is harmonious and happy. — Timaeus, 41.

We ought to consider it a lesser evil to be sufferers of great wrongs and crimes than to be doers of them. — Letter VII, 335.

Each evil enlarges the burden which the sinner must shoulder. — Letter VII, 355.

Men commit from their youth evil more abundantly than good. — Greater Hippias, 296.

No evil thing is honorable. — Laws V, 727.

As if there were any who did evil voluntarily; all who do evil and dishonorable things do them against their will. — Protagoras, 345.

Is there any reason why, because evil perishes, that which is not evil should also perish? — Lysis, 221.

Evil cannot be the friend of the good. — Lysis, 217.

Do you really imagine that a man knows evils to be evils and desires them notwithstanding? — Meno, 77.

Meletus and Anytus will not injure me morally: they cannot; for it is not possible that a bad man should injure morally a better than himself. I do not deny that he may, perhaps, kill him, or drive him into exile, or deprive him of civil rights; and he may imagine, and others may imagine, that he is doing him a great moral injury: but in that I do not agree with him; for the evil of doing as Anytus is doing — of unjustly taking away another man's life — is [physical, but not moral injury]. — Apology, 30.

Can anything be clearer than that those who are ignorant of the evils do not desire them, but they desire what they suppose to be good when they are really evils, and they who do not know them to be evils, and suppose them to be good, desire good? — Meno, 77.

The heaven is full of more evils than goods. — Laws, X, 906.

The evil of the soul is the most disgraceful of all evils. — Gorgias, 477.

Are there some who desire evil? — Yes. — Meno, 77.

To prefer evil to good is not in human nature. — Protagoras, 358.

Most things which are evil may be accidentally good. — Phaedo, 62.

Evils can never perish; for there must always remain something which is antagonistic to good. — Theaetetus, 176.

No evil can happen to a good man. — Apology, 41.

As to actions of curable evil, let us remember that the unjust man is not unjust of his own free will. For no man chooses voluntarily to possess the greatest of evils, and least of all in the most honorable part of himself. For the soul is deemed by all men the most honorable. — Laws, V, 731.

Evils are only evils to the just and so-called goods to the unjust; and goods are truly goods to the good, but evils to the evil. — Law, II, 661.

People seldom reflect that some of the evil of other men is communicated to themselves. — Republic, X, 606.

We must endeavor to divide to the utmost of our power the greater and more serious evil from the lesser. And language admits of a distinction in the use of the opprobrious terms. A man does not always deserve to be called the thrower away of his shield; he may be only the loser of his arms. For there is a great difference between him who is deprived of his arms by a sufficient force, and him who voluntarily lets his shield go. — Laws, XII, 944.

It is not to be supposed that the soul, or anything else which is not destroyed by an internal evil, can be destroyed by an external one. — Republic, X, 610.

When any seed or plant fails to meet with proper nutriment or climate or soil, the greater the vigor, the greater the need also of suitable conditions, because evil is a greater enemy to the good than to the not-good. — Republic, VI, 491.

I say that all men do evil involuntarily. — Laws, IX, 860.

There are two kinds of evil in the soul — the one may be compared to disease in the body, the other to deformity. — Sophist, 227, 228.

Evildoer. The legislator knows quite well that to incurable evildoers themselves there is no profit in the continuance of their lives, and that they would do a double good to the rest of mankind if they would take their departure, inasmuch as they would be an example to other men not to offend, and they would relieve the city of bad citizens. In such cases, and in such cases only, the legislator ought to inflict death as the punishment of offenses. — Laws, IX, 862, 863.

The evildoer is miserable in any case — more miserable, however, if he be not punished and does not meet with retribution, and less miserable if he be punished and meets with retribution. — Gorgias, 472, 473.

Evildoing. Nobody ever considers the greatest penalty of evildoing — namely, to grow into the likeness of bad men, and growing like them to fly from the conversation of the good. — Laws, V, 728.

The fortunes of evil men, who, though not morally blessed, are wrongly counted blessed in the judgment of men, draw you aside from your original piety. — Laws, X, 899.

Exactness. I hope that you will be as exact as you can. — Phaedo, 58.

I speak generally, and not with any pretension to exactness. — Republic, III, 414.

Example. My example requires the assistance of another example. — Statesman, 277.

Excellent. There always are in the world a few excellent men whose acquaintance is beyond price, and who spring up quite as much in ill-ordered as in well-ordered states. — Laws, XII, 951.

Excelling. While certain persons excel in swiftness, vigor, and courage, others are expected to excel in veracity, righteousness, and generosity. — Letter IV, 320.

Excess. When desire devoid of reason rules in us and drags us to pleasure, that power of misrule is called excess. — Phaedrus, 237.

A man should refrain from excess either of laughter or tears, and should exhort his neighbor to do the same; he should veil his immoderate sorrow or joy. — Laws, V, 732.

All great things are great by excess. — Greater Hippias, 294.

Excess of money, property, and distinction is apt to be a source of hatred and division among states and individuals. — Laws, V, 729.

Let us begin by considering the whole nature of excess and defect, and then we shall have a rational ground on which we may praise or blame the too great length or conciseness of discussions. — Statesman, 283.

The ruin of oligarchy is the ruin of democracy; the same disorder intensified by freedom dominates over democracy, the truth being that the excessive increase of anything often causes a reaction in the opposite direction; and this is the case not only in the seasons and in vegetable and animal forms, but above all in forms of government. The excess of liberty seems only to pass into an excess of slavery. The most aggravated form of tyranny arises out of the most extreme form of liberty. — Republic, VIII, 564.

Exchange. They shall exchange money for goods, and goods for money. — Laws, VIII, 849.

They exchange goods with one another, and one gives, and another receives, under the idea that such exchange will be for their good. — Republic, II, 369.

The exchange of one fear or pleasure or pain for another, measured like coins, the greater with the less, is not the exchange of virtue. — Phaedo, 69.

Excuses. The time for excuses is long passed. — Laws, VI, 751.

When it comes to excuses, two heads are better than one. — Symposium, 174.

All these are not reasons but only ingenious excuses for having no reasons. — Cratylus, 426.

If you think that by killing a man you can avoid the accuser censuring your lives, you are mistaken; that is not a way of excuse which is either possible or honorable; the easiest and the noblest way is not to be crushing others, but to be improving yourselves. — Apology, 39.

Executioner. If a slave slay a freeman voluntarily, let the public executioner inflict upon him stripes, and if he survives, let him put him to death. — Laws, IX, 872.

Exercise. Is not rapid growth without proper and abundant exercise the source of endless evils in the body? — Laws, VII, 788.

The youth will undertake exercises in order to stimulate the spirited element of his nature, rather than with a view of increasing his strength; he will not, like common athletes, use exercise and regimen to develop his muscles. — Republic, III, 410.

Exercise and motion in the earliest years of life have a great tendency to create a part of virtue in the soul. — Laws, VII, 791.

The most ridiculous thing of all will be the sight of naked women in the palaestra, exercising with the men, especially when they get old; they certainly will not be a vision of beauty any more than the wrinkled old men, who have anything but an agreeable appearance when they take to gymnastics; this, however, does not deter them. — Republic, V, 452.

Exhortation. As long as they are leading an orderly life that pleases them, though it does not me, I would not estrange them by useless exhortations or play the subservient flatterer and procure them means to satisfy their desires that I myself had rather die than be addicted to. — Letter VII, 331.

Existence. All things which are or have been or will be, exist either by nature, or by art, or by chance. — Laws, X, 888.

I am very far from admitting that he who contemplates spiritual existences through the medium of moral ideas, sees them only "through a glass darkly," any more than he who sees physical phenomena in their working and effects. — Phaedo, 100.

Has not the body less of existence than the spirit? — Republic, IX, 585.

Surely, that which exists must always exist somewhere? — Parmenides, 151.

We have not only shown that moral ideas which are not matter exist, but we have also shown what kind of being not-being is; for we have shown that the other exists. — Sophist, 258.

All existence must of necessity be in some place and occupy a space; and that what is neither in the sky nor on earth has no existence. — Timaeus, 52.

Which classes of things have a greater share in existence — those of which food and drink and condiments are examples, or the class which contains true opinion and mind and, in general, all virtue? — Republic, IX, 585.

It seems to be the truth that, whether one is or is not one and the others in relation to themselves and one another, all of them, in every way, exist and do not exist, and appear and do not appear. — Parmenides, 166.

Not-being: this is the very existence which the materialistic Sophist compelled us to examine. And has not this as real an existence as any other class? May I not say with confidence that so-called not-being or spirit has an assured essence of its own . . .

and is to be reckoned one among many classes of being? — Sophist, 258.

Let us suppose that there are *two* sorts of existences, one physical, and the other spiritual. — Phaedo, 79.

Justice, wisdom, and goodness are spiritually existent things (normative ideas). — Greater Hippias, 287.

If he sees something, it must exist. Do you suppose that "something" can be found among non-existing things? — Theaetetus, 188.

Existence, Partaking of. The one must surely partake of existence. — Parmenides, 161. . . . Was this your own distinction between normative ideas and the physical things which partake of them? — Ibid., 130. . . . They had agreed about the spiritual existence of normative ideas and the participation in them of the physical things. — Phaedo, 102.

Existential Question. Are spiritual things of which we speak self-existent? Or are only those things which we see, or in some way perceive through the bodily organs, truly existent, and no others besides them? And is all that which we call intelligible essence nothing at all and only a word? Here is a question which we must not leave unexamined or undetermined, or affirm too confidently that there can be no decision. — Timaeus, 51.

Existential Separation. The attempt to separate *all* existences from one another is not only tasteless but also illiterate and unphilosophical. The attempt at universal separation of everything from everything else is the final annihilation of all reasoning; for only by the union of conceptions with one another do we attain to discourse of reason. — Sophist, 259.

Expectation. There are opinions about the future, which have the general name of expectations; and the specific name of fear, when the expectation is of pain; and of hope, when of pleasure. — Laws, I, 644.

Expediency. Whatever name he gives to the thing, he would allow that the good or expedient is the aim of legislation, and that the state as far as possible imposes all laws with a view to the greatest expediency; can legislation have any other aim? — Theaetetus, 177.

Is the good that which is expedient for man? — Yes, indeed; and there are some things which may be inexpedient, and yet I call them good. — Protagoras, 333.

You surely do not suppose that you know what is expedient for mankind, or why a thing is expedient? — First Alcibiades, 113.

Expenditure. A prompt expenditure is gainful when important interests are at stake. — Letter XIII, 362.

Experience. The experience of the stricken is of the same nature as the act of the striker. — Gorgias, 476.

He will have to fight against and conquer his own cowardice, and in this way become perfected in courage — since if he be unpracticed and inexperienced in such conflict, he will not be half the man which he might have been in respect of virtue. Are we to suppose, that perfect temperance will be attained by him who has no experience of this sort? — Laws, I, 647.

His experience will enable him to judge better than anyone. — Republic, IX, 582.

Experience proves. — Republic, VII, 527.

When youths advance in years, and come more into contact with realities, and have learned by sad experience to see and feel the truth of things, they change many opinions which they had, and the great appears small to them, and the easy difficult, and all their seeming speculations are overturned by the facts of life. — Sophist, 234.

That my advice is correct you will find out by experience if you put to test my words about laws. Experience appears to be the best touchstone, in any respect. — Letter VIII, 355.

He possesses practical wisdom by nature, and he has improved it by experience. — Letter VI, 323.

They lack experience because they have passed a long portion of their lives only with us, who are honest, not unrighteous; they have to be acquainted with other people, as well. — Letter VI, 322.

There are many arts among mankind which are experimental, and have their origin in experience, for experience makes the days of men to proceed according to art, and inexperience according to chance. — Gorgias, 448.

Experiences come to men in diseases, or in war or poverty, or the opposite of these. — Laws, I, 632.

There must be something in what you say because you have great experience, and learning, and invention. — Protagoras, 320.

Experiment. The experiment will show. — Theaetetus, 201.

Expert. When the assembly meets to elect a physician or a shipwright or any other craftsman, will the rhetorician be taken into counsel? Surely not. For at each such election he ought to be chosen who is an expert. — Gorgias, 455.

Explanation. What I mean I may explain by an illustration of what I do not mean. — Euthyphro, 12.

I have said the truth; but I must give a clarifying explanation. — Timaeus, 49.

Do you not see that you are yourself repeating words and explaining nothing? — Gorgias, 489.

Export. No one should export anything which is needed in the country. — Laws, VIII, 847. *Vide* perfume.

Expression. When anyone has any good idea which is for the advantage of the state, he cannot abstain from expressing it. — Laws, VII, 821.

When a manly soul is in trouble, and when a cowardly soul is in the same or similar straits, they are not likely to express themselves in equal postures and gestures, or give utterance to the same sounds. — Laws, II, 654, 655.

Expropriation. And the persons who have been expropriated are compelled to defend themselves before the people as they best can. When they see the people, not of their own initiative, but through ignorance, and because they are deceived by informers, seeking to do them additional wrong, then at last they are forced to become oligarchs in reality; they do not wish to be, but the sting of the drones torments them and breeds counterrevolution in them. — Republic, VIII, 565.

Extracting. You have extracted a good deal more out of me than ever was in me. — Theaetetus, 210.

Extremes. Few are the extremes, but many are in the mean between them. — Phaedo, 90.

In a state which is desirous of being saved from the greatest of all plagues — not faction, but rather distraction — there should exist among the citizens neither extreme poverty, nor excessive wealth, for both are productive of both these evils. — Laws, V, 744.

Extremities. Whether the extremities of the body, among all parts of it, are taken care of or not is of the greatest consequence for man. — Laws, XII, 942.

Eye. The eyes are the most beautiful parts of the body. — Republic, IV, 420.

The duller eye may often see a thing sooner than the keener. — Republic, X, 596.

The eye of the soul is more precious by far than ten thousand bodily ones, for it alone beholds the vision of truth. — Republic, VII, 527.

Of all the organs of sense the eye is likest the sun. — Republic, VI, 508.

The eyes are the natural doors and windows of the soul. — Phaedrus, 255.

Is there not something of the nature of a mirror in our own eyes? — First Alcibiades, 132.

The eye is not like the ear, and has not the same functions. — Protagoras, 330.

Any one who has common sense will remember that the bewilderments of the eyes are of two kinds, and arise from two causes, either from coming out of the light or from going into the light, which is true of the mind's eye, quite as much as of the bodily eye. — Republic, VII, 518.

We ought not to beautify the eyes to such a degree that they no longer look like eyes. — Republic, IV, 420.

Anyone will remember that the disturbances of the eyes arise from two causes, either from changing from light to darkness or from darkness to light; this is true of the mind's eye, quite as much as of the bodily eye. And he who remembers this when he sees the soul of anyone whose vision is perplexed and weak, will not be too ready to laugh. If he still has an urge to laugh, he would laugh at the soul which comes from darkness more reasonably than at that which comes from the light.—Republic, VII, 518.

Did you ever observe that the face of the person looking into the eye of another is reflected in the visual organ which is over against him, and which is called the pupil, as in a mirror? — First Alcibiades, 133.

Eyelid. The gods invented the eyelids for the preservation of sight. — Timaeus, 45.

F

Face. The parts of a face are related to the whole face. — Protagoras, 329.

Facility. Facility in learning is learning quickly. — Charmides, 159.

Fact. It is equally impossible to allow courts of law to determine all things, or not to determine any of them. There is indeed one particular which they must determine in all cases — the question of fact. — Laws, IX, 875.

Faction. Cities torn by faction breed still more faction. — Letter, VII, 337.

In a weak state, faction arises even without an external cause. — Republic, VIII, 556.

There are times in which a state is compelled slightly to change the use of its standards, in the hope of escaping in some degree from factions. — Laws, VI, 757.

Faculties. We may fairly infer that there are two faculties, and that they differ from one another; the one with which a man reasons, we may call the rational faculty of the soul, the other, with which he loves and hungers and thirsts and feels the emotions of desire, may be rightly termed the irrational or appetitive. — Republic, IV, 439.

Might a man be thirsty, and yet unwilling to drink? Would you not say that there is one faculty in the soul bidding a man to drink, and a second forbidding him, which is other and stronger than that which bids him? And the forbidding faculty is derived from reason, and the bidding and attracting faculties are the effects of passion and disorder. — Republic, IV, 439.

I will begin by placing faculties in a class by themselves: they are powers in us, by which we do as we do. Sight and hearing, for example, I should call faculties. Have I clearly explained the class which I mean? — Republic, V, 477.

We are satisfied to have four subdivisions, two for understanding and two for judgment; and to call the first subdivision certain understanding, the second uncertain understanding, the third certain belief, and the fourth uncertain belief. — Republic, VII, 533.

Corresponding to the four subdivisions, let there be four faculties in the soul — certain understanding answering to the highest, uncertain understanding to the second, certain faith to the third, and uncertain faith to the last. — Republic, VI, 511.

Faint. Such a faint heart will never take a city. — Sophist, 261.

A faint heart never yet raised a trophy. — Critias, 108.

As I have put on the lion's skin, I must not be faint of heart. — Cratylus, 411.

Fair. I understand you to say that the fair is not the same as the good. — Gorgias, 474.

Does not the fair exist? And is not the foul its contrary? — Protagoras, 332.

False. Hesiod and Homer and many other poets have, it seems to me, invited false stories which they narrated and still narrate to mankind. — Republic, II, 377.

False thinking assumes the things in an other or opposite way than they are. — Sophist, 240.

If he cannot speak falsely, may he not think falsely? — Euthydemus, 286.

We have discovered the essence of false judgment and false statement sooner than we expected. — Sophist, 264.

Falsehood. Falsehood is naturally hateful to modesty and justice. — Laws, XII, 943.

Is not falsehood saying the thing which is not? — Cratylus, 429.

To think or to say what is not — that is falsehood, which thus arises in the region of thought and in speech. — Sophist, 260.

Our rulers will have to practice upon society with medicines. . . . They will find a considerable dose of falsehood and deception necessary for the benefit of their subjects: they might be used with advantage as medicines. — Republic, V, 459.

Falsification. Many are too fond of saying, that at proper times the practice of falsification may often be right. But they leave the time and place and occasion undefined and unregulated, and from this want of definiteness in their language they do a great deal of harm to themselves and to others. Now, a legislator ought not to leave the matter uncertain; he ought to prescribe some limit. — Laws, XI, 916.

Fame. Think only of the ambition of men, and you will marvel at their senselessness, unless you consider how they are stirred by the love of an immorality of fame. They are ready to run risks greater far than they would have run for their children, and to spend money and undergo any amount of toil, and even to die for the sake of leaving behind them a name which shall be eternal. I am persuaded that all men do all things for the sake of the glorious fame of immortal virtue, and the better they are the more they desire this; for they are ravished with the desire of the immortal. — Symposium, 208.

Those who are really righteous men should justly obtain the fame that they deserve. — Letter, IV, 320.

Famous men of antiquity should be reverenced, and not be liable to wanton insinuations. — Sophist, 243.

Family. Many family men seek their ease, and receive with open arms those who are like themselves, and hate those who are unlike them; and are wholly under the influence of their feelings of dislike. — Statesmen, 310.

In order that the distribution of land may always remain, they ought to consider that the present number of families should be always retained, and neither increased nor diminished. — Laws, V, 740.

Greater family differences than there ought to be sometimes arise between fathers and sons. — Laws, XI, 928.

I know that you will say, "I am a better man and of better family." But if the better is not genuine righteousness, and virtue consists only in a man saving himself and his relations, regardless of his moral character, then your claim is ridiculous. — Gorgias, 512.

When they sing the praises of family, and say that someone is a gentleman because he has had seven generations of wealthy ancestors, the philosopher thinks that their sentiments only betray the dullness and narrowness of vision of those who utter them, and who are not educated enough to look at the whole, nor to consider that every man has had thousands of progenitors, and among them have been rich and poor, kings and slaves. And when someone boasts of a catalogue of twenty-five ancestors, and goes back to Amphitryon, he cannot understand his poverty of ideas. Why is he unable to calculate that Amphitryon had a twenty-fifth ancestor, who had a fiftieth, and so on? Now, in all these cases our philosopher is derided vulgar, partly because he is above them, and also because he is always at a loss in matters of daily life. — Theaetetus, 174, 175.

We devised means that no one should ever be able to know his own child, but that all should imagine themselves to be of one family. — Timaeus, 18.

Will you give them [who are not a family] only the names of family ties, or are they in all their actions to conform to these names? For example, in the use of the word "father," would the care of a father be implied and filial reverence? — Republic, V, 463.

Fancying. Men fancied that they knew what they did not know. — Laws, III, 701.

Men in general often fancy that they see some beautiful thing which might have effected wonders if they had only made the right use of it; and yet this mode of looking at things may turn out after all to be a mistake. — Laws, III, 686.

Fantastic Art. We may fairly call that sort of art, which produces an appearance and not an image, fantastic art. — Sophist, 236.

Farmer. Many are the works of the farmer; but his chief occupation is the production of food from the earth. — Euthyphro, 14.

The good farmer takes care of the shoots first. — Euthyphro, 3.

Fate. A fate stronger than man wrought havoc with our intentions. — Letter, VII, 337.

The same fate which brings terror and shame to Tantalus and Zethus and Dardanus is benevolent for Pelops and kindred heroes. — Greater Hippias, 293.

A triple fate watchfully secures the achievements of all gods who act with accomplished judgment. — Epinomis, 982.

Father. Is this dog the father of the puppies? — Yes, I certainly saw him and the mother of the puppies come together.... The dog is a father, and he is yours; ergo, he is your father, and his puppies are your brothers. — Euthydemus, 298.

Fatherland. There can be no more important kind of information than the exact knowledge of a man's own fatherland. — Laws, VI, 763.

Fattening. Shall a man live fattening like a stalled ox? — Laws, VII, 807.

Fault. I am not given to finding fault. — Protagoras, 346.

Faultless. I will not throw away my life in searching after the impossible, hoping in vain to find a perfectly faultless man. — Protagoras, 345. *Vide* Great Man.

Favor. Grant me this favor, which will also be a kindness to yourself. — Laws, III, 702.

Favorite. Some persons have one favorite, and some another. — Lysis, 204.

Fawn. Don't bring the fawn in sight of the lion lest he devour him. — Charmides, 155.

Fear. I should not say that where there is fear there is also reverence; for I am sure that many persons fear poverty and disease, but I do not perceive that they reverence these objects of their fear. — Euthyphro, 12.

I cared not a straw for death; my only fear was the fear of doing an unrighteous thing. — Apology, 32.

Fear is not of the present, nor of the past, but is of future and expected evil. — Laches, 198.

They had no longer any fear, and the absence of fear begets shamelessness. For what is shamelessness but the insolent refusal to regard the opinion of the better by reason of an excessive liberty. — Laws, III, 701.

If fear has such a power we ought to consider further, that every soul which from youth upward has been subject to fear, will be rendered more timorous by being accustomed to fear, and everyone will admit that this is the way to form a habit of cowardice rather than of courage. And, on the other hand, the habit of overcoming, from our youth upwards, the fears and terrors which beset us, may be said to be an exercise of courage. — Laws, VII, 791.

Fear is to be found in animals and in infants. — Laws, XII, 963.

The affection of the children is an emotion of fear; and fear springs from an evil habit of the soul. And when someone applies external agitation to affections of this sort, the motion coming from without produces a peace and calm in the soul, and quiets the restless palpitation of the heart, which is a thing much to be desired, sending some to sleep, and making others who are awake to dance. — Laws, VII, 791.

No man but an utter fool and coward is afraid of death itself, but he is afraid of doing wrong. — Gorgias, 522.

Feast. When you make a feast, invite not your friend, but the beggar and empty soul, for they will love you, and attend you, and come about your doors, and will be best pleased, and the most grateful, and will invoke blessings on your head. — Phaedrus, 233.

Feelings. The feelings of the body are derived from the feelings of the soul. — Philebus, 41.

The good man dissembles his feelings. — Protagoras, 346.

Feeling, Community of. If there were not some community of feeling among mankind, however varying in different persons — I mean to say, if every individual had a private feeling which was not shared by the rest of his species — I do not see how we could ever communicate our impressions to one another. — Gorgias, 481.

Feelings, Mixed. The argument implies that pleasure is mixed with pain, not only in tragedies and comedies, but also in the entire tragicomedy of life. — Philebus, 50.

Fellowship. One should not teach the soul or accustom her to know or understand how to do anything apart from one's fellows. Of all soldiers the life should be common and together; there neither is nor ever will be a higher, or better, or more scientific principle for the attainment of safety and victory than this. — Laws, XII, 942.

Female. The female sex is by nature prone to secrecy and stealth on account of their weakness. — Laws, VI, 781.

Fencing. None of these masters of fencing has ever been distinguished in war. — Laches, 183.

There is an advantage in their being employed during their leisure hours in fencing which tends to improve their bodily constitution, and not in the way which young men are too apt to be employed. — Laches, 181, 182.

They are masters of legal fence, and are ready to do battle in the courts. — Euthydemus, 272.

Festivals. I am speaking of the arrangements of days in periods of months, and of months in years, which are to be observed, in order that times and sacrifices and festivals may proceed in regular and natural order, and keep the city alive and awake, and pay to the gods the honors due to them, and cause men to have a better understanding of them. — Laws, VII, 809.

The gods, pitying the toils which our race is born to undergo, have appointed holy festivals, in which men alternate rest with labor. — Laws, II, 653.

Festivities. Festivities are praiseworthy where there is a spirit of endurance, but are very senseless when they are under no regulation. — Laws, I, 637.

Festivities occasion friendship and acquaintance. — Laws, V, 738.

Feudal Order. In a feudal order of things, there will not be much opportunity for making a fortune; no man either ought, or indeed will be allowed to exercise any ignoble occupation, of which the vulgarity deters a freeman, and disinclines him to acquire riches by any such means. — Laws, V, 741.

Fever. Do not people who have fever, feel cold or thirst or other bodily affection more intensely? — Philebus, 45.

The quartan fever can only with difficulty be taken off. — Timaeus, 86.

Few. Few are the good and few are the evil, and the great majority are in the interval between them. — Phaedo, 90.

Fiction. Let no one be deluded by the fictions of the poets and mythologers. — Laws, XII, 941.

We must assume control over this class of fiction, and beg the authors not simply to revile, but rather to commend the world. — Republic, III, 386.

Listen to a tale which you may be disposed to regard as fiction only, but which, as I believe, is a true tale. — Gorgias, 523.

Fiend. Fiends disguised as guests prevented my plan. — Letter, VIII, 357.

Fight. To fight against two opponents is a difficult thing. — Laws, XI, 919.

Few to fight and few to rule. — Republic, VIII, 551.

Figure. I define figure to be that in which the solid ends; or, more concisely, as the limit of solid. — Meno, 76.

Figure is like figure, there is one species of all of them; and yet some figures are opposed to one another, and there is an infinite diversity of them. — Philebus, 12.

Financial. It is disadvantageous to you and your reputation to be considered inferior in your financial dealings. — Letter, XIII, 362.

Fine. When a man appears to have done anything which deserves a fine, he shall pay the fine. — Laws, IX, 855.

Finery. I have put on my finery

because he is a fine creature. — Symposium, 174.

Finite. All things which do not admit of more or less, may be rightly reckoned in the class of the limited or finite. — Philebus, 25.

Fire. There is a fire within us, and in the universe. And is not our fire small and weak and mean, but the fire in the universe is wonderful in quantity and beauty, and in every power that fire has. — Philebus, 29.

Fire and warmth, which are supposed to be the parent and nurse of all other things, are born of friction only. — Theaetetus, 153.

Of all elements fire has the smallest parts, and therefore penetrates through earth and water and air and their compounds, nor can anything hold it. — Timaeus, 78.

Nothing is visible when there is no fire. — Timaeus, 31.

Fish. Fishes and oysters, and other aquatic animals, received the most remote habitations as a punishment of their extreme ignorance. — Timaeus, 92.

If any man could arrive at the exterior limit, or take the wings of a bird and fly upward, he would see a world beyond, just as fishes see our world when they put up their heads out of the water. — Phaedo, 109.

Fishing. May no desire or love of fishing in the sea, or of angling or of catching the creatures in the sea, ever take possession of you. — Laws, VII, 823.

Fitness. He says that there is a fitness of names, but he never explains what this fitness is, so that I cannot tell whether his obscurity is intended or not. — Cratylus, 427.

Flame. There are, first, flame; and secondly, those emanations of flame which do not burn but only give light to the eyes; thirdly, the remains of fire, which are seen in things red-hot after the flame has been extinguished. — Timaeus, 58.

Flatterers. There are some sort of animals, such as flatterers, which are dangerous and mischievous, and yet nature has mingled a temporary pleasure and grace in their composition. — Phaedrus, 240.

Flattery. Man is reproached for flattery and meanness because he subordinates his spirited element to the unruly monster, and, for the sake of money, habituates him in the days of his youth to be trampled in the mud, and from being a lion to become a monkey. — Republic, IX, 590.

This is the sort of thing which I term flattery, whether concerned with the body or the soul, and always employed with a view to pleasure, and without any consideration to good and evil. — Gorgias, 501.

That sort of hireling whose conversation is pleasing and who baits his hook with pleasure and only exacts his maintenance as the price, we should describe as possessing flattery. — Sophist, 222.

Man should avoid all flattery of himself as well as of others, of the few as of the many. — Gorgias, 527.

Flavor. In all things which have an accompanying charm, this very charm is of important value; for example, I should say that there is a gusto which accompanies eating and drinking, and the use of food in general, and this we call flavor. — Laws, II, 667.

Flaw. I am mistaken if I don't find a flaw in him. — Euthyphro, 5.

Flute Playing. Does not flute playing appear to be an art which seeks only pleasure, and thinks of nothing else? — Gorgias, 501.

Follower. I can count on the loyalty of one follower, namely myself. — Letter, II, 310.

Folly. Do you admit the existence of folly? — Protagoras, 332.

Folly and ignorance are a sort of emptiness of the soul. — Republic, IX, 585.

When the soul of an individual is opposed to reason, that I call folly, just as in the state, when the mass of the people refuses to obey the laws. — Laws, III, 689.

Folly is the opposite of moderation and temperance. — Protagoras, 332.

The greatest folly is when a man hates that which he nevertheless thinks to be good and noble, and loves and embraces that which he knows to be unrighteous and evil. This dissonance between the sense of pleasure and the judgment of reason in the soul is the worst folly; and the greatest too, because affecting the greatest part of the human soul, for the faculty which feels pleasure and pain in the individual, is like the multitude in a state. — Laws, III, 689.

The probability is that folly will be a more prevalent disorder among kings, because they lead a proud and luxurious life. — Laws, III, 691.

Food. Persons get accustomed to all sorts of foods and drinks by which they were at first disturbed; as time goes on, they even learn to like the new habits. — Laws, VII, 797.

The first and greatest of necessities is food, which is the condition of life and existence. — Republic, II, 369.

You want to know what is the meaning of food for the soul; the other kind you understand. — Sophist, 223.

This exchange of the merchant is partly an exchange of food for the use of the body, and partly of the food of the soul which is bartered and received in exchange for money. — Sophist, 223.

God planted the fruits of the earth to be our daily food. — Timaeus, 80.

Wheat and barley are the best and noblest sustenance for man. — Menexenus, 238.

Foolishness. What proof of foolishness can be greater than to differ from wise men? — Lesser Hippias, 372.

Foot. The foot is the best servant of the body. — Laws, XII, 942.

Force. Open force may be called fighting, and secret force may have the general name of hunting. — Sophist, 219.

If a wise man believes that the constitution of his state is imperfect, he should say so, unless such action will either be useless or will lead to his own death; but he must not apply force to his country by revolutionary methods. When it is impossible to make the constitution perfect except by sentencing men to exile or death, he must refrain from action and pray for the best for himself and for his fatherland. — Letter, VII, 331.

Foreigners. Let the wardens of the city take the foreign offender and examine him, not forgetting their duty to the God of foreigners. — Laws, IX, 879.

Forgetfulness. Are there not pains of forgetfulness, if a man is full of knowledge and his knowledge is lost? — Philebus, 52.

Forgetfulness is the exit of memory. — Philebus, 33.

If the philosopher is forgetful and retains nothing of what he learns, he will be an empty vessel. Then the forgetful soul cannot be ranked among philosophers; a philosopher ought to have a good memory. — Republic, VI, 486.

Is not forgetting just the losing of knowledge? — Phaedo, 75.

Form. The form must be the same, but the material may vary. — Cratylus, 389.

Formulation. The precise and perfect formulation of a thesis is an additional difficulty. — Epinomis, 979.

Fortitude. If a few men should die, others as good as they will be born; but if fortitude is dead, then the citizens will never find a test of superior and inferior in desert, which is a far greater evil to the state than the other. — Laws, VIII, 831.

Fortunate. You are fortunate to know the way of life a man has to follow. — Greater Hippias, 304.

It is most fortunate for every one to be healthy, rich, respected by the Greeks, maturing in age and, after having buried his parents decently, himself to be carried to the grave with solemnity by his own children. — Greater Hippias, 291.

You compel your poets to say that the good man, if he be temperate and just, is fortunate and happy; and this whether he be rich or poor; and that, on the other hand, if he have a wealth passing that of Cinyras or Midas, and be unjust, he is miserable and lives in pain. — Laws, II, 660.

To act with a wise man is more fortunate than to act with an ignorant one. — Euthydemus, 279.

We should be happy and fortunate if many good things were present with us. — Euthydemus, 280.

Fortune. All, even the most foolish, admit that good fortune is the greatest of goods. — Euthydemus, 279.

No man could have good and evil fortune at the same time. — Gorgias, 497.

Foundation. Let us be very careful in laying the foundation. — Philebus, 23.

It is ridiculous, after a great deal of labor has been spent, to place a thing at last on an insecure foundation. — Laws, XII, 960.

Fountain. They used fountains both of cold and hot springs; these were very abundant, and both kinds wonderfully adapted to use by reason of the sweetness and excellence of their waters. — Critias, 117.

Here are two fountains which are flowing at our side: one, which is pleasure, may be likened to a fountain of honey; the other, which is a sober draught in which no wine mingles, is of water pure and healthful; out of these we must seek to make the fairest of all possible mixtures. — Philebus, 61.

Fowler. The fowler in the mountains and in waste places shall be permitted, but on cultivated ground and on consecrated wilds he shall not be permitted. — Laws, VII, 824.

Frankness. There is a noble frankness in your way of approaching the argument; for what you say is what the hypocritical rest of the world think, but are unwilling to say. — Gorgias, 492.

Fraud. Fraud and violence are not the delight and practice of the sons of Zeus. — Laws, XII, 941.

Free Speech. Only to think that having come on a visit to Athens, which enjoys the utmost freedom of speech in Greece, you alone should be deprived of it — that is hard indeed. — Gorgias, 461.

Free Will. The formation of character qualifies the king of the world. For every one of us is made pretty much what he is by the bent of his desires and the nature of his soul. — Laws, X, 904.

Freedom. Freedom is the natural enemy of the barbarians. —Menexenus, 245.

Consequent upon excessive freedom in the arts comes the freedom of disobedience to rulers; and then the attempt to escape the control and exhortation of father, mother, elders, and when near the end, the control of the laws also; and at the very end there is the contempt of oaths and pledges, and no regard at all for the gods — herein they exhibit and imitate the old Titanic nature; and thus they return again to the old, and lead an evil life, and there is no cessation of ills. — Laws, III, 701.

The party desiring freedom should obtain freedom under a king.—Letter, VIII, 355.

Where freedom is, the individual is clearly able to order for himself his own life as he pleases. — Republic, VIII, 557.

Their and our fathers, and these, too, our brethren, having been brought up in all freedom, and nobly born, performed many noble deeds famous over the whole world. They were the deeds of men who thought that they ought to fight for the sake of Greeks and on behalf of freedom. — Menexenus, 239.

As you never think of controlling yourself, but only of controlling him who is your slave, and this is your notion of freedom, I must yield to your irresistibility, for I cannot help. — Meno, 86.

Absolute and unqualified freedom is by no means so good as a limited government. — Laws, III, 698.

Freedom and servitude are utterly destructive, if exaggerated extremely, but highly beneficial in proper measure. — Letter, VIII, 354.

They lived extravagantly and ruled their rulers; they would not be subject to anyone, lawful ruler or reign of law, but wanted to be absolutely or entirely free. But by this way they got their tyrants. — Letter, VIII, 354.

Are they not free? And their city is full of freedom and frankness — there a man may do as he likes. — Republic, VIII, 557.

The insatiable desire of licentious freedom introduces a change in orderly democracy, and occasions a demand for tyranny. — Republic, VII, 562.

Let us speak of the laws of ancient music, in order that we may trace the growth of the excess of political freedom from the beginning. — Laws, III, 700.

Freedom in Persia. There was a time when the Persians followed a middle course between slavery and freedom. Under the reign of Cyrus, the rulers gave a share of freedom to the subjects, and being treated as equals, the soldiers were on better terms with their generals, and showed themselves more ready in the hour of danger. And a wise councilor could impart his wisdom to the public; for the king allowed him full liberty of speech. And the nation waxed in all respects, because there was freedom and friendship and communion of the soul among the citizens. — Laws, III, 694.

Freedom of Virtue. A prophet, having mounted a high pulpit, spoke as follows: "Hear the word of Lachsis, the daughter of Necessity. Mortal souls, behold a new circle of life and mortality. Your genius will not be allotted to you, but you will choose your genius. Virtue is free, and as a man honors or dishonors her he will have more or less of her." — Republic, X, 617.

Fresh. While we are fresh, we shall get on better. — Statesman, 265.

Friction. The friction of two things when rubbed together may possibly strike a light. — Republic, IV, 434.

Friend. Friends were not easily to be found immediately. — Letter, VII, 325.

The only friend worth mentioning, whom the tyrant can have, will be one who is of the same character, and has the same likes and dislikes, and is at the same time willing to be subject and subservient to him; he is the man who will have the power in the state, and no one will injure him with impunity. — Gorgias, 510.

Like cannot be the friend of like. — Lysis, 216.

We had better correct an error into which we have fallen in the use of the words "friend" and "enemy." — Republic, I, 334.

Is not even a ridiculous friend better than a dangerous enemy? — Phaedrus, 260.

Whom are we to call friends to one another? Do any remain? — Indeed, I cannot find any. — Lysis, 213.

Surely, nothing can be accomplished without loyal friends and companions. — Letter, VII, 325.

Is a just man the friend of the unjust, or the temperate of the intemperate, or the good of the bad? — Neither. — Lysis, 216.

Many are the friends of their enemies, and the enemies of their friends. — Lysis, 213.

God himself, as they say, makes friends and draws them to one another. — Lysis, 214.

He is a friend who is, as well as seems, good. — Republic, I, 335.

To me every man appears to be most the friend of him who is most like him — like to like, as ancient sages say. — Gorgias, 510.

No one is a friend to anything that does not love him in return. People are not friends to horses, whom the horses do not love in return; nor to quails, nor to dogs, nor to wine, nor to gymnastic exercises, who have no return of love; no, nor to wisdom, unless wisdom loves them in return. — Lysis, 212.

Loyal friends will strengthen him more than an increase of his military resources and gold reserves. — Letter, VI, 322.

Friends have all things in common, so that one of you can be no richer than the other, if you say truly that you are friends. — Lysis, 207.

There is no truer sign of man's character than this, whether he is or is not lacking loyal friends. — Letter, VII, 332.

I have from my childhood upward set my heart upon a certain thing. All people have their fancies; some desire horses, and others dogs; and some are fond of gold, and others of honor. Now, I have no violent desire of any of these things; but I have a passion for friends. — Lysis, 211.

Neither like and like nor unlike and unlike are friends. — Lysis, 216.

Friendship. His friendship was not founded on philosophy but on social hospitality. — Letter, VII, 333.

Those who say that the like is friendly to the like mean to intimate, if I do not misapprehend, that the good man is a friend to the good man only, but that the bad man never attains to any real friendship either with a good or a bad man. — Lysis, 214.

The idea of friendship existing between similars is not the truth, the most opposed are the most friendly; for everything desires not like but unlike: for instance, the dry desires the moist, the cold the hot, the bitter the sweet, the sharp the blunt, the void the full, the full the void, and so of all other things (the sin desires the virtue, and vice versa); for the opposite is the food of the opposite, whereas like receives nothing from like. — Lysis, 215.

Fugitive of Justice. May not the fugitive of justice be compared to a person who is afflicted with the worst of diseases and yet contrives not to pay the penalty to the physician for his sins against his constitution, and will not be cured because, like a child, he is afraid of the pain of being burned or cut — is not that a parallel case? — Gorgias, 479.

Funeral. Of three kinds of funerals, there is one which is too extravagant, another is too niggardly, the third is a mean; and you choose and approve and order the last without qualification. But if I had an extremely rich wife, and she bade me bury her, and I were to describe her burial in poetry, I should praise the extravagant one; and a poor miserly man, who had not much to spend, would approve of the niggardly one; and the man of moderate means, who was himself moderate, would praise a moderate funeral. — Laws, IV, 719.

Death in battle is certainly in many respects a noble thing. The dead man gets a fine and costly funeral, although he may have been poor, and a speech is made over him by a wise man who weighs his words, although he who is praised may not have been good for much. The speakers praise him for what he has done and for what he has not done; and they praise all our ancestors who went before us; and they praise ourselves also who are still alive, until I feel quite elevated by their laudations, and all of a sudden I imagine myself to have grown up into a greater and nobler and finer man than I was before. — Menexenus, 234.

Future. Let us not be discouraged about the future. — Sophist, 264.

G

Gadfly. I [Socrates] am that gadfly which God has given to the state, and all day long and in all places am always fastening upon you, arousing and persuading and reproaching you. — Apology, 30.

Game. People must be acquainted with those into whose families and to whom they marry and are given in marriage; in such matters as far as possible to avoid mistakes is all important, and with this serious purpose let games be instituted in which boys and girls shall dance together, seeing and being seen undressed, at a proper age, and on a suitable occasion, not transgressing the rules of modesty. The masters of choruses will be the superintendents and regulators of these games. — Laws, VI, 771, 772.

Whoever misses shall sit down, as at a game of ball, and be donkey, as the boys say, to the rest of the company; he who lasts out his competitors in the game without missing, shall be our king. — Theaetetus, 146.

Gem. And there are hills, and stones in them in a like degree smoother, and more transparent, and fairer in color than our highly valued emeralds and sardonyxes and jaspers, and other gems, which are but minute fragments of them. — Phaedo, 110.

Genealogy. They rejoice in the genealogies of men and of cities, in short, of all kinds of antiquarian stories. For this reason I have acquired a complete knowledge of that branch of learning. — Greater Hippias, 285.

As for those genealogies of yours which you have recounted to us, they are no better than the tales of children. — Timaeus, 23.

General. The art of the general is only ministerial, and therefore not political. —Statesman, 305.

We must not forget to speak of generals and other tacticians, who are the experts of our art of safety, which is war. — Laws, XI, 921.

The general claims to be, not the servant of the soothsayer, but his master, because he knows better what is happening or is likely to happen in war: and accordingly the law places the soothsayer under the general, and not the general under the soothsayer. — Laches, 198, 199.

The art of the general is assigned to courage rather than to wisdom. — Epinomis, 975.

When generals have taken a city or camp, they hand over the new acquisition to the statesmen, for they do not know how to use their captures, just as quail hunters transfer the quails to the keepers of them. — Euthydemus, 290.

General Concept. All things have a general concept. Suppose that someone asked you, what is a figure? And if you answered "roundness," he would ask you whether you would say that roundness is "figure" or "a figure";

and you would answer "a figure," for there are also other figures. — Meno, 74.

How can a general concept, being of generation or of destruction, but retaining a permanent essence, be conceived either as dispersed and multiplied in the many things of generation, or as still entire and yet contained in particular things? — Philebus, 15.

Tell me the general concept of virtue — do not make a singular into a plural. — Meno, 77.

Generation. If generation were in a straight line only, and there were no compensation or circle in nature, no cyclic turn and return of opposites into one another, then all things would at last have the same cooled down form and pass into the same state of inertia, and there would be no more generation of them. — Phaedo, 72.

The gods created in us the desire of generation, contriving in man one animated substance, and in woman another. — Timaeus, 91.

Generations. The great reason why we provide ourselves with friends and children is, that when we get old and stumble, a younger generation may be at hand, and set us on our legs again in our words and in our actions. — Gorgias, 461.

Genesis. Once upon a time there were gods only, and no mortal creatures. But when the time of genesis came, the gods fashioned them out of earth and fire and various mixtures of both elements in the inward parts of the earth. — Protagoras, 320.

Genius. The poets write poetry, not by wisdom, but by a sort of genius or inspiration; they are like diviners or soothsayers who also say many fine things, but do not understand the meaning of them. — Apology, 22.

Gentlemen. You say that gentlemen speak of things as they are? — Yes. — Euthydemus, 284.

Gentleness. Gentleness, if too much relaxed, will turn to softness, but, if educated, will be modest. — Republic, III, 410.

Every man should be spirited, but he should also be gentle. — Laws, V, 731.

Genus. When I have only your genus, I do not have your differentia specifica. The genus does no more belong to you than to another person. — Theaetetus, 209.

Geographer. The earth is indeed in nature and extent very unlike the notions of our geographers, as I believe on the authority of one who shall not be mentioned. — Phaedo, 108.

Geometer. The good and wise geometer has the double power of speaking truly and falsely in the highest degree; and if there be a man who is false about diagrams the good man will be the man, for he is able to be false; whereas the bad man is not able, and for this reason cannot be false. — Lesser Hippias, 367.

Geometrician. Is not the same person best able to speak falsely or to speak truly about diagrams, and he is the geometrician? — Lesser Hippias, 367.

Geometry. The knowledge at which geometry aims is of the a priori, and not of the a posteriori. — Republic, VII, 527.

The science of geometry has indirect effects, which are not small. There are the military advantages; and in all departments of study, any one who has studied geometry is infinitely quicker of apprehension. — Republic, VII, 527.

Geometry will draw the soul towards truth, and create the mind of philosophy, and raise up that which is so unhappily allowed to fall down. — Republic, VII, 527.

Ghost. In the neighborhood of tombs and sepulchres are seen ghosts of souls which have not departed pure, and therefore retain some visibility. — Phaedo, 81.

Giants. I am even more pugnacious than the giants of old. — Theaetetus, 169.

Those stories are not fit to be repeated. Far be it from us to tell of the battles of the giants. — Republic, II, 378.

The gods annihilated the giants with thunderbolts. — Symposium, 190.

Gift. A good man would be wrong in receiving gifts from a polluted man. — Laws, IV, 716.

Gifts, Natural. When you say that one man has natural gifts and another not, was this your meaning — that the former will acquire a thing easily which the latter will have a difficulty in acquiring; a little learning will lead the one to discover a great deal whereas the other, after a great deal of learning and application, will only forget what he has learned? — Republic, V, 455.

Giving. The right way of giving is to give them what they want of us. There would be no meaning in an art which gives to anyone that which he does not want. — Euthyphro, 14.

Globe. The creator made the world in the form of a globe, round as from a lathe, in every direction equally distant from the center to the extremes, the most perfect and the most like itself of all figures. — Timaeus, 33.

Gluttony. Insatiable gluttony . . . an enemy to philosophy and music. — Timaeus, 73.

The authors of our race were aware that we should be intemperate in eating and drinking, and take a good deal more than was necessary or proper, by reason of gluttony. — Timaeus, 72.

The desire of eating, which gets the better of the higher reason and the other desires, is called gluttony. — Phaedrus, 238.

Goal. No goal is ever attained — each apparent end is just a beginning. — Letter, VIII, 353.

Goat. Suppose a person to praise the keeping of goats, and then someone who had seen goats feeding without a goatherd in cultivated spots, and doing mischief, was to censure a goat who has no keeper, would there be any sense at all in such censure? — Certainly not. — Laws, I, 639.

Falsehood dwells in the lower world, and is rough like the goat of tragedy; for falsehoods have generally to do with the tragic or goatish life, and tragedy is the place of them. — Cratylus, 408.

God. The word of god, I thought, ought to be considered first. — Apology, 21.

God (spirit) does not mingle with man (matter). — Symposium, 203.

God desires that all things should be good and nothing bad as far as this could be accomplished. — Timaeus, 30.

God who enjoys the fullness of divine spirituality is clearly above both pleasure and pain, though possessed of universal wisdom. — Epinomis, 985.

God, as the old tradition declares, holding in his hand the beginning, middle, and end of all that is, moves according to his nature in a straight line towards the accomplishment of his end. — Laws, IV, 715.

God is perfectly simple and true both in word and deed. — Republic, II, 382.

God, if he be good, is not the author of all things, as the many assert, but he is the cause of a few things only, and not of most things that occur to men. For few are the goods of human life, and many are the evils, and the good alone is to be attributed to God; of the evils the causes are to be sought elsewhere, and not in him. — Republic, II, 379.

Even God is said not to be able to fight against necessity. — Laws, V, 741.

Surely God must not be supposed to have a nature which he himself hates. — Laws, X, 901.

God, and not man, is the measure of all things. — Laws, IV, 716.

God is the creator of the bed and of all other things. — Republic, X, 597.

God takes away the minds of poets, and uses them as his ministers, as he also uses diviners and holy prophets, in order that we who hear them may know that they speak not of themselves who utter these priceless words in a state of unconsciousness, but that God is the speaker, and that through them he is conversing with us. —Ion, 534.

I would not have you ignorant that, in the present evil state of governments, whatever is saved and comes to good is saved by the power of God. — Republic, VI, 492.

If such is the will of God, I am willing. — Crito, 44.

Then let me follow the intimations of the will of God. — Crito, 54.

A man should be serious about serious, and not about unserious, matters. And God is the proper and worthy object of a man's most serious endeavor. — Laws, VII, 803.

Men have the faculty to attain a certain knowledge of God. — Letter VI, 323.

They say that we ought not to inquire into the supreme God, and that theology is impious; but the very contrary of this is the truth. — Laws, VII, 821.

How can we found out the father and maker of all this universe? Or when we have found him how shall we be able to speak of him to all men? — Timaeus, 28.

He who should attempt to test the truth of mixing colors by experiment, would forget the difference of the human and divine nature. For God only has the knowledge and also the power which are able to combine many things into one and again dissolve the one into many. But no man is or ever will be able to accomplish either of these operations. — Timaeus, 68.

Gods, the. Serious letters I introduce with "God," otherwise with "the gods." — Letter XIII, 363.

Gods and temples are not easily established, and to establish them rightly is the work of a mighty intellect. — Laws, X, 909.

Will anyone who admits all this venture to deny that all spiritual things are full of gods? — Laws, X, 899.

I do believe that there are gods, and in a far higher sense than that in which any of my accusers believe in them. — Apology, 35.

All the gods, and especially the god

of strangers, are companions of the meek and just. — Sophist, 216.

The gods care about the small as well as about the great. — Laws, X, 900.

Who are they, and what is their nature? Must not the gods be at least rulers? — Laws, X, 905.

Gods cannot be supposed to have either joy or sorrow. — Philebus, 33.

The gods are our spiritual masters. — Laws, V, 727.

We will not have the poets trying to persuade our youth that the gods are the authors of evil, and that heroes are no better than men — sentiments which are neither pious nor true, for we have already proved that evil cannot come from the gods. And further they are likely to have a bad effect on those who hear them; for everybody will begin to excuse his own vices when he is convinced that similar wickednesses are always being perpetrated by "the kindred of the gods." And therefore let us put an end to such tales, lest they engender laxity of morals among the young. — Republic, III, 391.

Now a certain portion of mankind do not believe at all in the existence of the gods, and others imagine that they take no care of us, and the opinion of most men and of the worst men is that in return for a small sacrifice and flattering words they will aid them in their misdeeds, and deliver them from great and divers penalties. — Laws, XII, 948.

I wish that you would tell me what benefit accrues to the gods from our gifts. — Euthyphro, 14.

The gods do not know things of men. — Yet, surely, to deprive God of knowledge is monstrous. — Parmenides, 134.

The divine authority cannot rule us; gods are not our masters. — Parmenides, 134.

How would you prove the existence of gods? — How? The earth and the sun, and the stars and the universe, and the fair order of the seasons, and the division of them into years and months, furnish proofs of their existence; and also there are value ideas or normative laws in which all Greeks and non-Greeks believe. — Laws, X, 885, 886.

When you and I argue that there are gods, and produce the sun, moon, and stars as gods or divine beings, the philosophers say that these celestial bodies are earth and stone only, and that all this is a cooking up of words and a make-believe. What shall we answer? — Laws, X, 886.

I think that we have sufficiently proved the existence of the gods, and that they take care of man: that they are appeased by wicked men, and take gifts is what I will not allow, and what every man should disprove to the utmost of his power. — Laws, X, 905.

If impious discourses were not scattered, as I may say, throughout the world, there would have been no need of the argument in support of the existence of the gods — but seeing that they are spread far and wide, such arguments are needed; and who should come to the rescue of the normative laws, when they are being undermined by bad men, but the legislator himself? — Laws, X, 891.

If ever we are to call upon the gods, let us call upon them now in all seriousness to come to the demonstration of their own existence. And so holding fast to the rope of a prayer we will plunge into the deep waters of the argument. — Laws, X, 893.

Many other tales about the gods would quite amaze you. — Euthyphro, 6.

That which is hateful to the gods has been shown to be also dear to them. — Euthyphro, 9.

Every man ought to make up his mind that he will be one of the followers of the gods; there can be no doubt of that. — Laws, IV, 716.

The friend of the gods may be supposed to receive from them all things at their best, excepting only such evil as is the necessary consequence of former sins. — Republic, X, 613.

Gold. Anything will by the adornment of gold become beautiful even though it was ugly before. — Greater Hippias, 289.

All the gold which is under or upon the earth is no adequate exchange for virtue. — Laws, V, 728.

Do you believe that we have come here to look for gold or to hear a discourse? — Republic, V, 450.

We wouldn't be better off, even if without trouble and digging all the gold that there is in the earth were ours. For if we knew how to convert stones into gold, the knowledge would be of no value to us, unless we also knew how to use the gold. — Euthydemus, 288, 289.

We will tell them that they have in their souls gold and silver of divine quality and, therefore, do not need that secular gold. They ought not to pollute their heavenly possession by an earthly admixture; for that commoner metal has been the source of many unholy deeds, while their own is undefiled. — Republic, III, 416, 417.

Although we may often say that gold and silver are highly valued by us, that is not the truth; for the truth is that there is a further object, which we value most of all, and for the sake of which gold and all other possessions are acquired by us. — Lysis, 220.

Golden. I suppose that he means by the golden men, not men literally made of gold, but good and noble; and I am convinced of this, because he further says that we are the iron race. — Cratylus, 398.

Golden Rule. May I, being of sound mind, do to others as I would that they should do to me. — Laws, XI, 913.

Good. There is a difficulty in becoming good; and yet this is possible. — Protagoras, 344.

You surely wouldn't say that unqualified pleasure is the good? — God forbid. — Republic, VI, 509.

We ought to repeat not twice but thrice that which is good. — Philebus, 59.

The good are a law in themselves. — Symposium, 181.

The theory that the good is necessarily beautiful, is in fact wrong. — Greater Hippias, 297.

The goods of which the many speak are not really good. — Laws, II 661.

The matter is not merely whether it is black or white, light or heavy, but whether it is good or evil. — Eryxias, 396.

I used to imagine that no human care could make men good; but I know better now. — Protagoras, 328.

Can that be good which does not make men good? — Charmides, 160.

He would provide the good, as he would know how to deal with gods or men. — Laches, 199.

He who is moderately good, and does no evil, is good enough for me. — Protagoras, 346.

[104]

He may put me into the pot, like Medea the Colchian, kill me, pickle me, eat me, if he will make me good. — Euthydemus, 285.

You can make a good man only of him who is convinced that he ought to learn of you. — Euthydemus, 274.

The good are not unjust. — Euthydemus, 296.

A good man might often compel himself to love and praise another and there might be an involuntary love, such as a man might feel for an ungainly father or mother, or for his country. — Protagoras, 346.

Although there is a difficulty in becoming good, yet this is possible for a time, and only for a time. — Protagoras, 344.

Every man is good in that in which he is wise, and bad in that in which he is unwise. — Laches, 194.

Hard is the knowledge of the good. — Cratylus, 384.

How can you know whether a thing is good or bad of which you are wholly ignorant? — Meno, 92.

All things are good with which evil is unmingled. — Protagoras, 346.

You are not only good yourself, but also the cause of goodness in others. — Protagoras, 348.

Whether the better is ever really conquered by the worse, is a question which requires much discussion. — Laws, I, 627.

The good are not by nature [but by reason] good. — Meno, 89.

What should be done to a good man? Doubtless some good thing. — Apology, 36.

I will never fear or avoid a possible good rather than a certain evil. — Apology, 29.

You surely do not think that two men are morally better than one, or that your slaves are better than you because they are stronger? — Gorgias, 489.

Not life, but a good life, is to be chiefly valued. — Crito, 48.

There are two kinds of goods, physical and spiritual goods, and the latter hang upon the former. Of the physical goods the first is health, the second beauty, the third strength, and the fourth wealth; wisdom is chief and leader of the spiritual class of goods. — Laws, i, 631.

The infliction of death, and exile, and the deprivation of property are sometimes a good and sometimes not a good. — Gorgias, 470.

The good is not the same as the pleasant, or the evil the same as the painful. — Gorgias, 497.

All good things are morally advantageous. — Meno, 87.

He is good whose soul is good. — Republic, III, 409.

If we are not able to hunt the good with one idea only, with three we may catch our prey: Beauty, Symmetry, Truth, are the three, and these when united we may regard as the cause of the mixture, and the mixture as being good by reason of the admixture of them. — Philebus, 65.

They are fond of denying that a man is good; but man, they insist, is man and good is good. I dare say that you have met with persons who take an interest in such matters — they are often elderly men, whose meager sense is thrown into amazement by these discoveries of theirs, which they regard as the highest form of wisdom. — Sophist, 251.

Good he pronounces to be what pleases the beast, and evil what it dislikes; and he can give no other account of these moral concepts. — Republic, VI, 493.

A physician who cures a patient may do good to himself and good to another also. — Charmides, 164.

There is nothing which to my mind is so evident as that the good has a most real existence. — Phaedo, 77.

If there would be no disease, there would be no remedy. Is not this the nature of the good — to be loved by us because of the evil? There is no use in the good for its own sake. — Lysis, 220.

The good is the author of essence, and yet the good is not essence, but far exceeds essence in dignity. — Republic, VI, 509.

We are always repeating that there is a goodness. — Phaedo, 76.

I think that doing good things is a work of human agency. — Eryxias, 398.

By goodness things become good. — Greater Hippias, 287.

Things are not to be regarded as goods in themselves, but the degree of good and evil in them depends on whether they are or are not under the guidance of wisdom and virtue. — Euthydemus, 281.

Great is the issue at stake, greater than appears, whether a man is to be good or bad. And what will anyone profit if under the influence of honor or money or power, aye, or under the excitement of poetry, he neglect justice and virtue? — Republic, X, 608.

They are clearly of opinion that the obligatory and containing power of the good is as nothing; and yet this is the principle which I would fain learn if anyone would teach me. — Phaedo, 99.

A just and pious and good man is the friend of the gods; is he not? And the unjust and utterly bad man is the reverse. — Philebus, 39.

A man cannot be continuously good, but he may become good and may also become bad. — Protagoras, 345.

Governing. They do not wish to be directly paid for governing and so get the name of hirelings, nor by indirectly helping themselves out of the public revenues to get the name of thieves. — Republic, I, 347.

Anyone who means to govern, not only himself, but also the state, must in the first place acquire virtue. — First Alcibiades, 134.

Neither the uneducated and uninformed of the truth, nor yet those who never make an end of their education, will be able to govern the state: not the former, because they have no single aim of duty; nor the latter, because they will not act at all except upon compulsion, fancying that they are already in the islands of the blest. — Republic, VII, 519.

To what wrongs are you referring? — To those which we were examining when we spoke of who ought to govern whom. Did we not arrive at the conclusion that parents ought to govern their children, and the elder the younger, and the noble the ignoble? — Laws, IV, 714.

Government. Mankind will not see better government until either wise men acquire political power, or statesmen by divine grace gain wisdom. — Letter, VII, 326.

I observed that when we are met together in the assembly, and the matter in hand relates to building, the builders are summoned as advisers; when the question is one of ship-building, then the ship-builders. And if some person offers to give them advice who is not supposed by them to have any skill in the art, even though he be good-looking, and rich, and noble, they don't listen to him, but laugh at him, and hoot him. When, however, the question concerns government, then everybody is free to have a say — carpenter, tinker, cobbler, sailor, passenger; rich and poor, high and low — anyone who likes gets up, and no one reproaches him, as in the former case, with not having learned, and yet giving advice. — Protagoras, 319.

The government of good men is good, and of bad men bad. — Menexenus, 238.

As I examined the kind of men who dominated the political life, the more I considered them and the more I grew older, the more difficult it seemed to me to govern the state correctly. — Letter VII, 325.

A government cannot be well organized without the existence of some authority. — Letter XI, 359.

A trustworthy government is composed of loyal friends. — Letter VII, 331.

At last I realized that the governmental system of all existing states was not good. — Letter VII, 326.

As the government is, such will be the man. — Republic, VIII, 557.

Government, Forms of. Each form of government has a sort of voice as if it were a kind of animal. There is one of democracy, another of oligarchy, and a third of monarchy. Many persons will contend that they understand the science of these voices, but, except for some few, they are far from a profound understanding of them. Any form of government which utters its own voice, is always flourishing and endures. But when it copies another it disintegrates.—Letter V, 321c.

Monarchy divides into royalty and tyranny; the rule of the few into aristocracy, which has an auspicious name, and oligarchy; and democracy or the rule of the many, which before was one, must now be divided. — Statesman, 302.

Democracy, oligarchy and tyranny are not governments, for none of them exercises a voluntary rule over voluntary subjects; they may be truly called states of discord, in which the government is voluntary, and the subjects always obey against their will, and have to be coerced. — Laws, XIII, 832.

The several forms of government cannot be judged by the words few or many, voluntary or compulsory, poverty or riches; but some notion of [justice] must enter in. — Statesman, 292.

We selected two forms of government, the one the most despotic, and the other the most free; and now we are considering which of them is the right form: we took a mean in both cases, of despotism in the one, and of liberty in the other, and we saw that in a mean they attained their perfection; but that when they were carried to the extreme of either, slavery or license, neither party were the gainers. — Laws, III, 701.

Government, Principle of. May not any man, rich or poor, with or without written laws, with the will of the citizens or against the will of the citizens, do what is for their interest? Is not this the true principle of government, in accordance with which the wise and good man will order the affairs of his subjects? — Statesman, 296.

Governor. Whether the government

is in the hands of one or many, if the governors have been trained in the manner which we have described, the fundamental laws of the state will not be subverted. — Republic, IV, 445.

Grace. You have no difficulty in discerning that grace or the absence of grace is the effect of good or bad rhythm. — Republic, III, 400.

Grammar. Observing that none of us could learn any one of the alphabetical letters and not learn them all, and in consideration of this common bond, which in a manner unites them, an ancient god or prophet assigned to them all a single art, and this he called the art of grammar. — Philebus, 18.

Grandeur. How can he who has grandeur of mind, contemplating all time and all existence, think only in terms of human life? — Republic, VI, 486.

Grasshoppers. I can fancy that the grasshoppers who are chirruping in the sun over our heads are talking to one another and looking at us. What would they say if they saw that we are not talking but slumbering at midday, lulled by their voices, too indolent to think? They would have a right to laugh at us, and might imagine that we are slaves coming to our place of resort, who lie asleep at noon. But if they see us discoursing, they may perhaps, out of respect, give us of the gifts which they receive of the gods. — Phaedrus, 259.

When the Muses came and song appeared men were ravished with delight; and singing always, never thought of eating and drinking, until at last they forgot and died. And now they live again in the grasshoppers; and this is the return which the Muses make to them — they hunger no more, neither thirst any more, but are always singing from the moment that they are born. — Phaedrus, 259.

Grateful. They were rightly grateful to their saviors. — Letter VIII, 353.

Gratification. He lives happily in the gratification of his desires. — Gorgias, 494.

As you are so fond of gratifying others, will you gratify me to a small extent? — Gorgias, 462.

Grave. You attempted to utter grave thoughts on a grave subject. — Epinomis, 979.

Great. Things certainly are great if they exceed though they do not appear to. — Greater Hippias, 294.

Greatness. If greatness and smallness had no existence they could not be opposed to one another. — Parmenides, 149.

Great Man. In general, great men are also bad. — Gorgias, 526. *Vide* Faultless.

He who would be a great man, ought to regard justice, and not himself or his interests, whether in his own actions, or those of others. — Laws, V, 732.

A great man never saw fit to charge money for his wisdom. — Greater Hippias, 282.

Greedy. One, seeing another grow wealthy, tries to rival him — and thus the whole body of the citizens acquires a greedy character. — Republic, VIII, 550.

We will not believe Achilles himself to have been so greedy that he took gifts from Agamemnon. — Republic, III, 390.

The greedy is the oligarchical youth. — Republic, VIII, 553.

Greece. Grece is a large place, and has many good men. — Phaedo, 78.

Greeks. The Greeks enjoy a geographical situation which is extraordinarily conducive to the attainment of perfection. For Greece lies midway between summer and winter. —Epinomis, 987.

Whenever Greeks borrow anything from non-Greeks, they ultimately develop it to a higher perfection. — Epinomis, 987.

Training and wisdom — these are the things which Greeks value. — First Alcibiades, 123.

Greeks ought not to enslave, but to spare Greeks, considering the danger that the whole Greek race may one day fall under the yoke of the barbarians. No Greek should be owned by a Greek as a slave. That is the way to unite them against barbarians, and make them keep their hands off one another. — Republic, V, 469.

The Greek race is all united together by ties of blood and friendship, and alien and strange to the barbarians. And therefore when Greeks fight with barbarians and barbarians with Greeks, they will be described by us as being by nature enemies, and this kind of antagonism should be called war; but when Greeks fight with one another we shall say that they are by nature friends; and such enmity is to be called discord. — Republic, V, 470.

You Greeks are but children, and there is never an old man who is a Greek. I mean to say that in mind you are all young; there is no old opinion handed down among you by ancient tradition; nor any science which is hoary with age. — Timaeus, 22.

We are not like many others, who are by nature barbarians, and yet pass for Greeks, and dwell among us; but we are pure Greeks, having no admixture of foreigners, and therefore the hatred of the foreigners has passed unadulterated into the lifeblood of the city. — Menexenus, 245.

In this part of the world they make a division into Greeks and barbarians. — Statesman, 262.

Grief. Grief stands in the way of that which at the moment is most required. — Republic, X, 604.

Some of us have fathers and mothers still living, and we would urge them, if our death is to be the event, to bear the calamity as lightly as possible, and not to commiserate one another; for they have sorrows enough, and will not need anyone to stimulate them. While we gently heal their wounds, let us remind them that the gods have heard the chief part of their prayers; for they prayed, not that their children might live forever, but that they might be famous and brave. And this which is the greatest good, they have attained. — Menexenus, 247.

Ground. This is the ground of his indictment. — Euthyphro, 3.

Growth. The growth of every living creature is by far the greatest and fullest in its initial years; many will even contend that a man at twenty-five does not grow to twice the height which he attained at five. — Laws, VII, 788.

Is the growth of animals the result of some decay which that hot and cold principle contracts, as some have said? — Phaedo, 96.

Grudging. I cannot imagine that parents grudge their own children the attainment of the highest virtue. Greater Hippias, 283.

Guard. The nocturnal assembly of the magistrates shall be a guard set according to law for the salvation of the state. — Laws, XII, 968.

Guardians. The continuous practice of virtue is to be the sole pursuit of the guardians. — Timaeus, 18.

Let me dare to say that the perfect guardian must be a philosopher. — Republic, VI, 503.

Do not compel us to assign to the guardians a sort of happiness which will make them anything but guardians ... but the guardians and auxiliaries, and all others equally with them, must be compelled or induced to do their own work in the best way. And thus the whole state will grow up in a noble order. — Republic, IV, 420, 421.

Our guardian is both warrior and philosopher. — Republic, VII, 525.

Of all persons a guardian should be the last to get drunk and not to know where in the world he is. That a guardian should require another to guard him is ridiculous indeed. — Republic, III, 403.

Guardians ought to be dangerous to their enemies, and gentle to their friends; if not, they will destroy themselves without waiting for their enemies to destroy them. — Republic, II, 375.

The guardians are only fed, and not paid, in addition to their food, like other men; and therefore they cannot make a journey of pleasure, they have no money to spend on a mistress or any other luxurious fancy, which, as the world goes, is thought to be happiness. — Republic, IV, 420.

The guardians alone of all the citizens may not touch or handle silver or gold, or wear them, or drink them. And this will be their salvation, and the salvation of the state. But should they ever acquire homes or lands or moneys of their own, they will become householders and farmers instead of guardians, enemies and tyrants instead of allies of the other citizens; hating and being hated, plotting and being plotted against, they will pass through life in much greater terror of internal than of external enemies, and the hour of ruin, both to themselves and to the rest of the state, will be at hand. — Republic, III, 417.

Both the community of property and the community of families tend to make more truly guardians; they will not tear the city in pieces by differing about "mine" and "not mine"; each man dragging any acquisition which he has made into a separate house of his own, where he has a separate wife and children and private pleasures and pains. ... And as they have nothing but their persons which they can call their own, suits and complaints will have no existence among them; they will be delivered from all those quarrels of which money or children or relations are the occasion. — Republic, V, 464.

Our guardians are to be released from every other art, but to be the special artificers of freedom. — Republic, III, 395.

Trials for assault or insult cannot be expected to occur among the guardians. For that equals should defend themselves against equals we shall surely maintain to be fair and right; and in this way we shall oblige them to keep themselves protected. — Republic, V, 464.

One ought to take the utmost pains with the selection of the guardians of the law, who must be chosen with the greatest care; the other officials are of less importance. — Laws, VI, 752.

The aspiring guardian must be

tested in those labors and dangers and pleasures which we mentioned before; and there is another kind of probation which we did not mention — he must be exercised also in many kinds of knowledge, to see whether his soul will be able to endure the highest of all, or will faint under them, as many do in trials and contests of the body. — Republic, VI, 503, 504.

Guide. The only right guides are science and wisdom — these are the guides of man; for things which happen by chance are not under the guidance of man: but the guides of man are wisdom and science. — Meno, 99.

Guilt. Rhetoric is of no use in helping to excuse one's own guilt, or that of his parents or friends or children, or his country. — Gorgias, 480.

Guilty. The guilty, whoever he may be, ought not to go unpunished. — Euthyphro, 5.

They do not venture to argue that the guilty are to be unpunished, but they deny their guilt. — Euthyphro, 8.

Gyges. When Gyges turned the collet of his ring inwards he became invisible, when outwards he reappeared. — Republic, II, 360.

Gymnasium. Gymnasia and common meals do a great deal of good, and yet they are a source of evil in civil troubles. These institutions seem always to have a tendency to degrade natural love in man below the level of the beasts. — Laws, I, 636.

Gymnastic. Did you never observe the effect on the mind of exclusive devotion to gymnastic, or the opposite effect of an exclusive devotion to music? — Republic, III, 410.

Then they send the youths to the master of gymnastic, in order that their bodies may better minister to the virtuous mind, and that the weakness of their bodies may not compel them to play the coward in war or on any other occasion. — Protagoras, 326.

Simple gymnastic will incline the youth to have as little as possible to do with medicine. — Republic, III, 410.

Gymnastics. As man advances to mature intelligence, he should increase the gymnastics of the soul. — Republic, VI, 498.

H

Habit. His virtue was a matter of habit only. — Republic, X, 619.

The other qualities seem to be akin to the body, being infused by habit and exercise and not originally innate. — Republic, VII, 518.

In infancy more than at any other time the character is ingrained by habit. — Laws, VII, 792.

There is no difference to be found in the use of the feet and the lower limbs; but in the use of the left hand we are in a manner lame, by reason of the folly of nurses and mothers. For although our limbs are by nature balanced, we created a difference in them by bad habit. — Laws, VII, 794.

There are persons, whose natures are right and their habits wrong, or whose habits are right and their natures wrong. — Laws, II, 655.

Hail. Water compressed above the earth is called hail. — Timaeus, 59.

Hair. The part about the brain needs hair to be a light covering or guard, which gives shade in summer and shelter in winter, and at the same time does not impede our quickness of perception. — Timaeus, 76.

Half. The half is relative to the double. — Charmides, 168.

Hesiod said that the half is often greater than the whole. His meaning was, that when the whole was injurious and the half moderate, then the moderate was more and better than the immoderate. — Laws, III, 690.

Half-truths. Some persons were crammed with philosophical half-truths. — Letter, VII, 338.

Handbook. He has written a handbook, claiming that its ideas in which I instructed him were his own. — Letter, VII, 341.

Handsome. You are handsome, Theaetetus; for he who utters the handsome is himself handsome and good. — Theaetetus, 185.

A blindfolded man has only to hear you talking, and he would know that you are a handsome youth. For you always speak in imperatives: like all beauties when they are in their prime, you are tyrannical. — Meno, 76.

Happiness. Do not all men desire happiness? And yet, perhaps, this is one of those ridiculous questions which I am afraid to ask, and which ought not to be asked by a sensible man: for what human being is there who does not desire happiness? — Euthydemus, 278.

The several classes will have to receive the proportion of happiness which nature assigns to them. — Republic, IV, 421.

He has not caught the accent of speech which praises the true life of happiness. — Theaetetus, 176.

I should say that happiness is the most precious of human possessions. — Eryxias, 393.

State and individual can attain happiness only through just conduct, whether one be guided by his own sense of justice or by just habits acquired under the rule of righteous men. — Letter VII, 335.

Happiness consists in never having known evils rather than in being delivered from them. — Gorgias, 478.

He whose happiness rests with himself, has his life ordered for the best. — Menexenus, 247.

The matters at issue between us are not trifling; to know or not to know happiness and misery — that is the sum of them. And what knowledge can be nobler than this? or what ignorance more disgraceful? — Gorgias, 472.

Happiness consists in education and justice. Then men and women who are noble and good are also happy, and the unjust and evil are also miserable. — Gorgias, 470.

Let us place the most just by the side of the most unjust, and then we shall be able to compare the relative happiness or unhappiness of pure justice and pure injustice; this will complete the inquiry. — Republic, VIII, 545.

The lover of the good is longing for happiness. For men are made happy by the acquisition of the good. And there is no need to ask why a man desires happiness; the answer is already final. — Symposium, 204, 205.

You say that pleasure, and I say that intelligence, is a state of happiness. — Philebus, 11.

We have not yet discovered whether by acting according to wisdom we shall be happy. — Charmides, 173.

The more wise and temperate you are, the happier you will be. — Charmides, 176.

Shall we not be happy if we have many good things? — Euthydemus, 279.

Should we be happy by reason of the presence of good things, if they profited us not, or if they profited us? — Euthydemus, 280.

Happy indeed would be the condition of youth if they had one corrupter only, and all the rest of the world were their improvers. — Apology, 25.

You cannot tell at once, and without having an acquaintance with him, whether a man is happy. — Gorgias, 470.

The just is happy, and the unjust miserable. — Republic, I, 354.

Many men who do wrong are happy. — Gorgias, 470.

They are quite ready to call wicked men happy. — Republic, II, 364.

Some say without any qualification that all who feel pleasure are happy, whatever may be the moral character of their pleasure. — Gorgias, 494.

If pleasant, then also happy? — Gorgias, 494.

If we are looking for that art which is to make us happy, and which is able to use that which it makes or takes, the art of the general is not the one, and some other must be found. — Euthydemus, 290.

A man who would be happy must not only have the good things, but he must also use them; there is no advantage in merely having them. — Euthydemus, 280.

He who lives well will be blessed and happy, and he who lives ill unhappy. — Republic, I, 354.

Women and children foolishly apply the term "happy" to the rich. Such usage makes those who apply it envious. — Letter VIII, 355.

Those who want nothing are not truly said to be happy. — No, indeed, for then stones and the dead would be the happiest of all. — Gorgias, 492.

How can a man be happy who is the servant of anything? On the contrary, I plainly assert, that he who would truly live should have courage and intelligence to minister to his desires and to satisfy all his longings. — Gorgias, 492.

Which are the happier? Those who lead the justest, or those who lead the pleasantest life? — Laws, II, 662.

He who is not wise and good cannot be happy. — First Alcibiades, 134.

Hard. Simonides in using the word "hard" meant what all of us mean, not evil, but that which is not easy — that which takes a great deal of trouble. — Protagoras, 341.

That is called hard to which our flesh yields, and soft which yields to our flesh; and things are also termed hard and soft relatively to one another. — Timaeus, 62.

Hardness. The sense which is concerned with the quality of hardness is necessarily concerned also with the quality of softness, and only intimates to the soul that the same thing is felt to be hard and soft. — Republic, VII, 524.

Harm. They have done me no harm, although neither of them meant to do me any good. — Apology, 41.

Any man may easily do harm, but not every man can do good to another. — Laws, VIII, 843.

I know many things which are partly beneficial for men, and partly harmful; and others again which are neither beneficial nor harmful for men but for horses; and others not for animals but only for trees. — Protagoras, 334.

Harmony. He has in his own life a harmony of words and deeds arranged. — Laches, 188.

Harmony is a symphony, and symphony is an agreement; but an agreement of disagreements while they disagree cannot exist; there is no harmony of discord and disagreement. . . . There is an absurdity in saying that harmony is disagreement; harmony is composed of differing notes of higher or lower pitch which disagreed once, but are now reconciled by the art of music. — Symposium, 187.

Harmony of the soul, when perfected, is virtue. — Laws, II, 653.

Harmony, which has motions akin to the revolutions of our souls, is not regarded by him who intelligently uses the Muses as given by them with a view to irrational pleasure, which is the prevailing opinion, but with a view to the inharmonious course of the soul, and as an ally for the purpose of reducing this into harmony and agreement with itself. — Timaeus, 47.

His first object will be not that he may be fair or strong or well, unless he is likely thereby to gain temperance, but he will be always desirous of preserving the harmony of the body for the sake of the concord of the soul. — Republic, IX, 591.

He who intends to be a harmonist must certainly know the things you mention, and yet he may understand nothing of harmony if he has not got beyond the preliminaries of harmony. — Phaedrus, 268.

The restoration of harmony and return to nature is the source of pleasure, if I may be allowed to speak in the fewest and shortest words about matters of the greatest moment. — Philebus, 31.

And when a beautiful soul harmonizes with a beautiful bodily form, and the two are cast in one mold, that will be the fairest of sights to him who has an eye to see it. — Republic, III, 402.

The life of man in every part has need of harmony and rhythm. — Protagoras, 326.

Harp Player. The harp player is certainly a better partner than the just man in playing the harp. — Republic, I, 333.

Harvest. The participation of fruits shall be ordered on this wise. The goddess of harvest has two gracious gifts: one the joy of Dionysus which is not treasured up; the other, which nature intends to be stored. — Laws, VIII, 844.

Haste. To be hasty in coming to a conclusion about important matters, would be very childish and simple. — Laws, I, 635.

The more haste the less speed. — Republic, VII, 528; Statesman, 264.

Hatred. As they hate ruthlessly and horribly, so are they hated. — Laws, III, 697.

What sort of difference creates hatred and anger? Suppose for example that you and I differ about a number; do differences of this sort make us hate one another? Do we not settle at once the issue by calculation? . . . But there are moral differences about which we grow wrathful. — Euthyphro, 7.

Head. The head could neither be left a bare frame of bones, on account of the extremes of heat and cold in the different seasons, nor be allowed to be wholly covered, and so become dull and senseless by an overgrowth of flesh. — Timaeus, 75.

The head is the masterly chief which by nature holds all the ruling senses. — Laws, XII, 943.

The gods, imitating the spherical shape of the universe, inclosed the two divine courses in the spherical body, that, namely, which we now term the head, being the most spiritual part of us and the lord of all that is in us. — Timaeus, 44.

The marrow which, like a field, was to receive the intelligent seed, he made round every way, and called that portion of the marrow "brain," intending that, when an animal was perfected, the vessel containing this substance should be the head. — Timaeus, 73.

Headache. He has been complaining lately of having a headache when he rises in the morning. — Charmides, 155.

There is a constant suspicion that headache and giddiness are to be ascribed to philosophy, and hence all practicing of virtue in the higher sense is absolutely stopped; for a man is always fancying that he is being ill by it. — Republic, III, 407.

The headache will be an unexpected benefit to my young relation, if the pain in his head compels him to improve his mind. — Charmides, 157.

Health. Would he be the happier man in his bodily condition, who is healed, or who never was out of health? — Gorgias, 478.

There are many persons who appear to be in good health, and whom only a physician will discern at first sight not to be in good health. — Gorgias, 464.

Health is a good. — Lysis, 219.

The creation of health is the institution of a natural order and government of one by another in the parts of the body. — Republic, IV, 444.

In health the pleasure exceeds the pain. — Laws, V, 734.

Nothing is pleasanter than health.

But then they never knew this to be the greatest of pleasures until they were ill. — Republic, IX, 583.

I should say that health, regarded as health, is the same, whether of man or woman. — Meno, 72.

Hearing. We may assume sound to be a blow which passes through the ears, and is transmitted by means of the air, the brain, and the blood, to the soul, and that hearing is the motion of this blow, which begins in the head and ends in the region of the liver. — Timaeus, 67.

The pleasant beauty comes through the senses of hearing and sight. — Greater Hippias, 298.

Heart. The gods placed the lung about the heart as a soft spring, that, when anger was rife in it, the heart, beating against the yielding body, might be refreshed and alleviated, and might thus become more ready to accompany passion in the service of reason. — Timaeus, 70.

Hearth. The soil and the hearth of the house of all men is sacred to all gods. — Laws, XII, 955.

Heat. Heat is not the same as fire, nor is cold the same as snow. — Phaedo, 103.

The original figure of fire has a dividing power which cuts our bodies into small pieces, and thus naturally produces that affection to which we give the name of heat. — Timaeus, 62.

Heaven. Opinion once prevailed among men, that the sun and stars are without souls. But if these bodies were things without soul, and had no mind, they could never move according to such exact calculations. And even at that time some ventured to hazard the conjecture that mind is the orderer of all things that there are in heaven. — Laws, XII, 967.

What they saw before their eyes in heaven, all appeared to be full only of stones, and earth, and many other lifeless bodies. Such studies gave rise to much atheism and perplexity, and the poets took occasion to be abusive — comparing the philosophers to she-dogs, uttering vain howlings, and saying other nonsense of the same sort. But now the case is reversed. — Laws, XII, 967.

The argument from the order of motion of the heavens leads men to believe in the gods. If a man looks upon the heaven not lightly and foolishly, he is not so godless, as not to experience a godly effect opposite to that which the many imagine. For these many think that those who handle these matters by the help of astronomy, may become godless; because they see, as far as they can see, things happening by necessity, and not by an intelligent will acomplishing good. — Laws, XII, 966.

Heavy. Heavy and light may be termed either from different points of view. — Republic, V, 479.

Heir. He who makes testamentary dispositions, being a father and having children, shall first of all inscribe as his heir any one of his sons whom he may think fit. If the testator has no sons, but only daughters, let him choose the husband of any one of his daughters, and leave and inscribe him as his son and heir. — Laws, XI, 923.

Help. Let brother help brother. — Republic, II, 362.

We must endeavor to be increasingly helpful to one another. — Letter XIII, 360.

Heracles. Heracles himself is said not to be a match for two. — Phaedo, 89.

Heraclitus. Heraclitus is of the opinion that all things flow and nothing stands; the pushing principle is the cause and ruling power of all things. — Cratylus, 401.

Heraclitus is supposed to say that all things are in motion and nothing at rest; he compares them to the stream of a river, and says that you cannot go into the same water twice. — Cratylus, 403.

Herd. Here is a new division of herds, into land herds and water herds. — Statesman, 264.

Hermes. Zeus feared that the human race would, by internal strife, be exterminated and so he sent Hermes to them, bearing reverence and justice to be the ordering principles of states and the bonds of friendship and conciliation. — Protagoras, 322.

Hero. I doubt whether any muscular hero would be as fearless and confident in offering his body, as you are in offering your mind. — Lesser Hippias, 364.

The hero who has distinguished himself shall receive honor in the army from his youthful comrades; every one of them in succession shall crown him. — Republic, V, 468.

Hesiod. Hesiod says, "Hardly can a man become good, for the gods have placed toil in front of virtue; but when he has reached the goal, then the retainment of virtue, however difficult the acquisition, is easy." — Protagoras, 340.

Hiccough. Let me recommend you to hold your breath, and if this fails, then to gargle with a little water; and if the hiccough still continues, tickle your nose with something and sneeze; and if you sneeze once or twice, even the most violent hiccough is sure to go. — Symposium, 185.

Either he has eaten too much, or from some other cause he has the hiccough. — Symposium, 185.

Hoar Frost. Water which is congealed in a less degree and is only half solid, when upon the earth, and condensed from dew, is called hoar frost. — Timaeus, 59.

Holding One to His Word. I certainly shall not hold you to your word if you now make a different statement. — Protagoras, 349.

Holiness. Holiness or piety is the art of attending to the gods. — Euthyphro, 13.

I cannot simply agree that holiness is justice and that justice is holiness, for there appears to me to be a difference between them. — Protagoras, 331.

Nothing can be holy if holiness is not holy. — Protagoras, 330.

The holy has been acknowledged by us to be loved because it is holy, not to be holy because it is loved. — Euthyphro, 10.

Homer. Homer is the best and most divine of all poets. — Ion, 530.

Homer knows all things human, virtue as well as vice. — Republic, X, 598.

You are possessed by Homer; when anyone reads the verses of another poet you go to sleep, and you know not what to say. But when anyone recites a strain of Homer you wake up in a moment, and your soul dances within you, and you have plenty to say. — Ion, 536.

What is the reason why I lose attention and start dozing and have absolutely no ideas, when anyone speaks of any other poet; but when Homer is mentioned, I wake up at once and am all attention and have plenty to say? — Ion, 532.

I say that Homer intended Achilles to be the bravest of those who went to Troy, and Nestor the wisest, and Odysses the wiliest. — Lesser Hippias, 364.

You praise Homer not by science but by poetical inspiration. — Ion, 536.

I have heard that the Iliad of Homer is a finer poem than the Odyssey in the same degree that Achilles was a better man than Odysseus. — Lesser Hippias, 363.

Homicide. I do indeed believe that to be an involuntary homicide is a less crime than to be a deceiver about goodness or justice. — Republic, V, 451.

Avarice is the chiefest cause and source of voluntary homicide, and hence the worst trials arise. A second cause is the habit of ambition: this creates jealousies, which are troublesome companions, above all to the jealous man himself. And a third cause is cowardly and unjust fear: this has been the occasion of many murders. When a man is doing or has done something which he desires that no one should know it, he will take the life of those who are likely to inform of such things, if he have no other means of getting rid of them. — Laws, IX, 870.

If a beast of burden or other animal cause homicide, except in the case of anything of that kind happening in the public contests, the kinsmen of the deceased shall prosecute the slayer for murder, and the wardens of the country shall try the cause, and let the beast when condemned be slain by them, and cast beyond the borders. — Laws, IX, 873.

They say that homicidal crimes will be punished in the world below, and that when the perpetrators return to this world they will suffer what they did by a natural retribution, and end their lives in like manner by the hand of another. — Laws, IX, 870.

If anyone in an athletic contest, and at the public games, involuntarily kills a friend, when he has been expiated by purification according to the law, he shall be innocent. — Laws, IX, 865.

Homosexuality. When the homosexuals reach manhood, they are lovers of youth, and are not naturally inclined to marry or beget children, which they do, if at all, only in obedience to the law, but they are satisfied if they may be allowed to live unwedded; and such a nature is prone to love and ready to return love, and always embracing that which is sexually akin to him. — Symposium, 192.

When a homosexual finds his other half, whether he be a lover of youth or a lover of another sort, the pair are lost in an amazement of love and friendship and intimacy, and one will not be out of the other's sight, as I may say, even for a moment; yet they could not explain what they desire of one another. For the intense yearning which each of them has towards the other does not appear to be the desire of intercourse, but of something else which the soul desires and cannot tell, and of which she has only a dark and doubtful presentiment. — Symposium, 192.

Suppose Hephaistos to come to a homosexual pair who are lying side by side and say to them, "What do you people want of one another?" they would be unable to explain. And suppose further, that when he saw their perplexity he said: "Do you desire to be wholly one; always day and night to be in one another's company? I am then ready to melt you into one" — there is not a homosexual man when he heard this proposal who would deny that this meeting and melting on one another's arms, this becoming one instead of two, was the very expression of his ancient need. — Symposium, 192.

Those men who are inspired by this love turn to the male, and delight in him who is the more valiant and intelligent nature. — Symposium, 181.

The homosexual abuse of love has led some to deny the lawfulness of love when they see the impropriety and evil of attachments of this sort. — Symposium, 182.

The homosexual women don't care for men, but have female attachments; the female companions are of the same sort. And the homosexual men follow a male; while they are young, they hang about him and embrace him, and they are themselves the best of boys and youths because they have the most manly nature. Some indeed assert that they are shameless, but this is not true; for they do not act thus from want of shame, but because they are valiant and manly, and have a manly countenance, and they embrace that which is like them. — Symposium, 192.

When they grow up, the homosexuals are our statesmen. — Symposium, 192.

In Ionia and other places, and generally in countries which are subject to the barbarians, homosexual loves of youths share the evil repute of philosophy and gymnastics, because they are inimical to tyranny. . . . In Elis and Boeotia, they are very straightforward; the universal sentiment is simply in favor of homosexual connections, and no one, whether young or old, has anything to say to their discredit. — Symposium, 182.

When the lover and beloved come together, having each of them a law, and the lover on his part is ready to confer any favor that he rightly can on his gracious loving one, and the other is ready to yield any compliance that he rightly can to him who is to make him wise and good; the one capable of communicating wisdom and virtue, the other seeking after knowledge, and making his object education and wisdom; when the two laws of love are fulfilled and meet in one — then, and then only, may the beloved yield with honor to the lover. All other loves are the offspring of the common or vulgar goddess. — Symposium, 184, 185

The homosexual practice is repugnant to the moral principle. Suppose we grant that this love is accounted by law to be honorable, or at least not disgraceful, how about virtue? Will such passion implant in the soul of him who is seduced the habit of courage, or in the soul of the seducer the principle of temperance? Who will ever believe this? or rather, who will not blame the effeminacy of him who yields to these pleasures and is unable to hold out against them? Will not all men censure as womanly him who acts like a woman? And what human being will establish by law such a practice? — Laws, VIII, 836.

As to homosexuals, there is a difficulty in determining what they are really seeking; moreover, they are drawn in opposite directions by their feelings — the one inviting them to enjoy the charms of their objects, the other forbidding them such enjoyment. — Laws, VII, 837.

All who are in the flower of their

youth do in a manner raise a pang or emotion in a lover's breast, and seem to be worthy of his affectionate regards. Is not this a way you have with the fair: one, because he has a snub nose, has the epithet "naive" used in his praise; another's beak, as you say, has a royal look; while he who is neither snub nor hooked has a grace of regularity: the dark visage is manly, and the white are angels; and as to the sweet, "honey pale," as they are called, what is the very name but the invention of a lover who uses these pet names, and is not averse to paleness on the cheek of youth? there is nothing you will not say, in order to preserve for your use every flower that has the bloom of youth. — Republic, V, 474, 475.

In the matter of homosexuality, as I may say it between ourselves, I must confess that the laws of Crete and Sparta are quite against us. For if anyone should declare that nature deprecates homosexual or unnatural lusts, adducing the animals as a proof that such unions were monstrous, he might prove his point, but he would be wholly at variance with the custom of those states. — Laws, VIII, 836.

I have a way to make men use natural love and abstain from unnatural, sowing the seeds of human increase in stony places, in which they will take no root. — Laws, VIII, 839.

Whether such practices are honorable or whether they are dishonorable is not a simple question; they are honorable to him who follows them honorably, dishonorable to him who follows them dishonorably. There is dishonor in yielding to the evil, or in an evil manner; but there is honor in yielding to the good, or in an honorable manner. — Symposium, 183.

As wolf to lamb, so lover to his lad. — Phaedrus, 241.

One can recognize the pure enthusiasts. For they love not boys, but intelligent beings whose reason is beginning to be developed, much about the time at which their beards begin to grow. And in choosing them as their companions, they mean to be faithful to them, and not to abuse their inexperience, and play the fool with them, or run away from one to another of them. — Symposium, 181.

The love which arises between the two sexes, is often horrible and coarse, lacking spiritual communion; but the homosexual love is gentle, and has a spiritual communion, which lasts through life. — Laws, VIII, 837.

Loving mere boys should be forbidden by law, because their future is uncertain; they may turn out good or bad, either in body or soul, and the affection which is devoted to them may be thrown away; in this the good are a law in themselves, and the coarser sort of lovers ought to be restrained by force. — Symposium, 181.

Honesty. They say that men ought to profess honesty whether they are honest or not, and that a man is out of his mind who does not make such a profession. Their notion is, that a man must have some degree of honesty; and that if he has none at all he ought not to be in the world. — Protagoras, 323.

They say that honesty is generally less profitable than dishonesty. — Republic, II, 364.

Honey. There is the diffuse class of things, which produce sweetness extending as far as the passages of the mouth; they are included under the general name of honey. — Timaeus, 60.

Honor. I am speaking of the sense of honor and dishonor, without which neither states nor individuals ever do any good or great work. — Symposium, 178.

Honor is a divine good. — Laws, V, 727.

Honor is not to be given to the fair, or the strong, or the swift, or the tall, or the healthy body (although this would be the opinion of the many), any more than to their opposites; but the mean states of all these habits are by far the safest and most moderate; for the one extreme makes the soul braggart and insolent, and the other illiberal and mean; and the possession of money, and property, and distinction, beats to the same tune. — Laws, V, 728.

Not being ambitious they do not care about honor. — Republic, I, 347,

They should entice the rulers with inducements of great honors. — Letter VII, 337.

Even to fail in an honorable object is honorable. — Phaedrus, 274.

Man should honor the living who are aged . . . and his own parents. — Laws, XI, 927, 932.

When a man thinks that life at any price is a good, he does not honor his soul, but dishonors her. — Laws, V, 727.

He who thinks he can honor the soul by word or gift, or any sort of compliance, not making her in any way better, seems to honor her, but honors her not at all. For example, every man, in his very boyhood, fancies that he is able to know everything, and thinks that he honors his soul by praising her, and he is very ready to let her do whatever she may like. But I mean to say that in acting thus he only injures his soul, and does not honor her. — Laws, V, 727.

Hope. Mankind are filled with hopes in every stage of existence. — Philebus, 39.

Man still may hope, that when calamities supervene upon the blessings which God gives him, he will lighten them and change existing evils for the better; and as to the goods, he will not doubt that they will be ever present with him, and that he will be fortunate. — Laws, V, 732.

He who is conscious of no sin has in age a sweet hope which, as Pindar charmingly says, is a kind nurse to him. — Republic, I, 331.

Horse. The well-conditioned horse is erected and well-formed; he has a lofty neck and an aquiline nose, and his color is white, and he has dark eyes and is a lover of honor and modesty and temperance, and the follower of true glory; he needs not the touch of the whip, but is guided by word and admonition only. Whereas the other is a large misshapen animal, put together anyhow; he has a short strong neck; he is flat-faced and of dark color, gray-eyed and bloodshot, the mate of insolence and pride, shag-eared, deaf, hardly yielding to blow or spur. — Phaedrus, 253.

Horses are said to require attention, and not every person is able to attend to them, but only a person skilled in horsemanship. — Euthyphro, 13.

With a horse of better temper, vicious actions would be performed voluntarily, and with a horse of bad temper involuntarily. — Lesser Hippias, 375.

Did ever any man believe in horsemanship, and not in horses? — Apology, 27.

A horse is not useful to everybody, but only to those who know how to use a horse. — Eryxias, 403.

Horse Race. In the center of the two islands was a race course of a stadium in width, and in length allowed to extend all round the island, for horses to race in. — Critias, 117.

We give prizes for single horses — for colts who have not cast their teeth, and for those who are intermediate between the full-grown and the colts, and also for the full-grown horses themselves; and thus the horse races will accord with the nature of the country. — Laws, VIII, 834.

Hospitality. The stranger who comes from abroad should be received in a hospitable spirit. — Laws, XII, 952.

If a stranger is passing along the road, and desires to eat the autumnal fruit, let him, if he will, take of the fresh grape for himself and a single companion without price, as a tribute of national hospitality. — Laws, VIII, 845.

Hound. You are as keen as a Spartan hound in pursuing the track. — Parmenides, 128.

Household. A large household may be compared to a small state. — Statesman, 259.

The house in which order and regularity prevail is good. — Gorgias, 504.

House of Ill Fame. There is disgrace in sitting for hire in a house for ill fame. — Charmides, 163.

Human. Did ever man believe in the existence of human activities, and not of human beings? — Apology, 27.

Am I indeed a wonder more complicated and swollen with passion than the serpent Typho, or a human creature of a gentler and simpler sort, to whom nature has given a moral and intelligent destiny? — Phaedrus, 230.

Of human things we have not as yet spoken, and we must; for to men we are speaking and not to gods. — Laws, V, 732.

Let us grant, that humanity is not to be despised, but is worthy of some consideration. — Laws, VII, 804.

Human Nature. Cronos knew that no human nature invested with supreme power is able to order human affairs and not overflow with insolence and wrong. Which reflection led him to appoint not men but demi-gods, who are of a higher and more divine race, to be the rulers of our cities; he did as we do with flocks of sheep and other same animals. For we do not appoint oxen to be the masters of oxen, or goats of goats; but we ourselves are a superior race, and rule over them. Cities of which some mortal man and not God is the ruler, have no escape from evils and toils. — Laws, IV, 713.

The human gifts which are deemed by us to be essential rarely grow together; they are mostly found in shreds and patches. Quick intelligence, memory, sagacity, cleverness, and similar human qualities, do not often grow together, and persons who possess them and are at the same time high-spirited and magnanimous are not constituted by nature as to live orderly and in a peaceful and settled manner; they are driven any way by their impulses, and all solid principle goes out of them. On the other hand, those steadfast natures which can better be depended upon, which in a battle are impregnable to fear and immovable, are equally immovable when there is anything to be learned; they are always in a torpid state, and are apt to yawn and go to sleep over any intellectual toil. — Republic, VI, 503.

If I had been like other men, I should not have neglected all my own concerns, or patiently seen the neglect of them during all these years, and have been doing yours, coming to you individually, like a father or elder brother, exhorting you to regard virtue; this, I say, would not be like human nature. — Apology, 31.

Human Race. Every man should understand that the human race either had no beginning at all, and will never have an end, but always will be and has been; or had a beginning an immense time ago. — Laws, VI, 781.

Humors. The sharp and briny phlegm and other bitter and bilious humors wander over the body, and . . . create infinite varieties of trouble and melancholy. — Timaeus, 87.

Hunger. If evil were to perish, should we hunger any more, or thirst any more, or have any similar affection? Or may we suppose that hunger will remain while men and animals remain, but not so as to be hurtful? — Lysis, 220.

Hunger may injure us, and may also benefit us. — Lysis, 221.

Must not they be utterly unfortunate whose souls are compelled to pass through life always hungering? — Laws, VIII, 832.

Hunger is a sort of disturbance. — Philebus, 31.

Hunting. Only the best kind of hunting is allowed at all — that of quadrupeds, which is carried on with horses and dogs and men's own persons, and they get the victory over the animals by running them down and striking them and hurling at them, those who have a care of godlike manhood hunting them with their own hands. — Laws, VII, 824.

There remains for our athletes only hunting and catching of land animals, of which the one sort is called hunting by night, in which the hunters sleep in turn and are lazy; this is not to be commended any more than that which has intervals of rest, in which the wild strength of beasts is subdued by nets and snares, and not by the victory of a laborious spirit. — Laws, VII, 824.

Huntsman. I was satisfied like a huntsman whose prey is within his grasp. — Lysis, 218.

Hydra. Even Heracles could not fight against the Hydra, who was a she-Sophist, and had the wit to shoot up many new heads when one of them was cut off. — Euthydemus, 297.

Hymn. Hymns to the gods and praises of famous men are the only poetry which ought to be admitted in our state. For if you go beyond this and allow the honeyed muse to enter, not law and reason, but pleasure and pain will be the rulers in our state. — Republic, X, 607.

Hypocrite. Hypocrites praise one thing, but are pleased at another. — Laws, II, 655.

Hypothesis. I think that you should consider not only the consequences which flow from a given hypothesis; but also the consequences which flow from denying the hypothesis. — Parmenides, 135.

"I wish to assume it as possible before I tell you whether this triangle is capable of being included in this circle": this is a geometrical hypothesis. — Meno, 87.

I

Ibycus. When Ibycus in his old age, against his will, fell in love, he compared himself to an old race horse, who was about to run in a chariot race, shaking with fear at the course he knew so well. — Parmenides, 137.

Ice. Water compressed on the earth is called ice. — Timaeus, 59.

Idea. There are normative ideas, which are distinct from physical things. — Parmenides, 133.

Would you make normative ideas of the just and the good? — Yes. — And would you make a normative idea of fire and water? — I am often undecided, as to whether I ought to include them or not. — Parmenides, 130.

Normative ideas have no relation to physical notions, nor physical notions to them; the relations of either are in their respective spheres. — Parmenides, 134.

Moral ideas are known but not seen. — Republic, VI, 507.

I was afraid that my soul might be blinded if I looked at moral ideas with my eyes or tried by the help of the other senses to comprehend them. — Phaedo, 100.

There certainly are self-existent ideas unperceived by sense, and apprehended only by the mind. — Timaeus, 51.

Reason soars beyond hypotheses to the first principles; and by successive steps she descends from ideas, through ideas, and in ideas she ends. — Republic, VI, 551.

We knew before we were born and at the instant of birth the normative ideas of goodness, justice, and holiness. — Phaedo, 75.

The ideas of the good, and the like, which we imagine to be normative ideas, are unknown to us. — Parmenides, 134.

Ideal. I want to know whether ideals are ever fully realized in language. — Republic, V, 437.

Identity. Even in the same individual there is succession and not absolute unity: a person is called the same; but yet in the short interval which elapses between youth and age, and in which every animal is said to have life and identity, he is undergoing a perpetual process of loss and reparation — hair, flesh, bones, blood, and the whole body are always changing. And this is true not only of the body, but also of the soul, whose habits, tempers, opinions, desires, pleasures, pains, fears, never remain the same in any one of us, but are always coming and going. — Symposium, 207.

Ignorance. Is not ignorance the having a false opinion and being deceived about important matters? — Protagoras, 358.

Ignorance is the greatest of diseases. — Timaeus, 88.

Men are induced to fancy that their own ignorance is wisdom. — Laws, V, 732.

What is ignorance but the aberration of a mind which is bent on truth, and in which the process of understanding is perverted? — Sophist, 228.

Ignorance is a cause of crimes. There is simple ignorance, which is the source of lighter offenses, and double ignorance, which is accompanied by conceit of wisdom; and he who is under the influence of the latter, fancies that he knows about matters of which he knows nothing. — Laws, IX, 863.

The inferiority of a man to himself is ignorance, as the superiority of a man to himself is wisdom. — Protagoras, 358.

Ignorance is involuntary. — Sophist, 230.

Is he not better off in knowing his ignorance? — Meno, 84.

Entire ignorance is not so terrible or extreme an evil, and is far from being the greatest of all; too much cleverness and too much learning, accompanied with ill bringing up, are far more fatal. — Laws, VII, 819.

Nearly all of them seem to be ignorant of the nature and power of the soul. — Laws, X, 892.

The ignorant may fancy himself richer than he is. And still more commonly he may fancy that he is taller or handsomer than he is, or that he has some other advantage of person which he has not really. And yet surely by far the greatest number of people err about the goods of the mind; they imagine that they are a great deal better than they are. — Philebus, 48.

Ignorance may cause punishment by death or exile. — Protagoras, 325.

Herein is the evil of ignorance, that he who is neither good nor wise is nevertheless satisfied: he feels no want, and has therefore no desire. — Symposium, 204.

Ignorance in the powerful is hateful and horrible, because hurtful to others. — Philebus, 49.

Powerless ignorance may be reckoned, and in truth is, ridiculous. — Philebus, 49.

Illegitimate Child. In case a female slave have intercourse with a male slave, freeman or freedman, the offspring shall always belong to the master of the slave; if a free woman have intercourse with a male slave, the offspring shall belong to the master, or of his mistress by a slave — and this be proven — the offspring and the master of the mistress shall be sent away to another country. — Laws, XI, 930.

Illiberality. There should be in the soul no secret corner of illiberality; nothing can be more antagonistic than meanness to a soul which is ever longing after the whole of things both divine and human. — Republic, VI, 486.

Illness. In all well-ordered states every individual has an occupation to which he must attend, and therefore has no leisure to spend in continually being ill. And this we ludicrously enough realize in the case of the craftsmen, but fail to see in the case of the richer people. — Republic, III, 406.

Ill Repute. The ill repute into which these attachments have fallen is to be ascribed to the evil condition of those who make them to be ill reputed. — Symposium, 182.

Illustration. I will not, like a bad

speaker, take the whole of the subject, but will break a piece off as an illustration of my meaning. — Republic, II, 392.

Image. There are two kinds of image-making — the art of making likeness and the art of making appearance. — Sophist, 236.

By images I mean, in the first place, shadows, and in the second place, reflections in water and in solid, smooth and polished bodies. — Republic, VI, 510.

That which being other is also alike the original may fairly be called a likeness or image. — Sophist, 236.

Ideas are patterns fixed in nature, and other things are made in their image, and resemblances of them; and what is meant by the participation of other things in the ideas, is really assimilation to them. — Parmenides, 132.

We have several times acknowledged that names rightly given are likenesses and images of the things which they name. — Cratylus, 439.

Imbecile. If you can find fault with my words, you may be free to call me an imbecile. — Greater Hippias, 291.

Imbecility. Some sons will be of opinion that they should be allowed to indict their fathers on the charge of imbecility when they are degraded by disease or old age. These things only happen as a matter of fact, where the natures of men are very bad. — Laws, XI, 928.

Imitation. Imitation is a kind of production — of images, however, and not of real things. — Sophist, 265.

If they imitate at all, they should imitate the characters which are suitable to their profession — the temperate, righteous, free, courageous, and the like; but they should not depict or be able to imitate any kind of illiberality or other baseness, lest from imitation they should become what they imitate. — Republic, III, 395.

We will not allow those for whom we profess a care and desire that they should be good men, to imitate a woman, whether young or old, quarreling with her husband or striving and vaunting against the gods in conceit of her happiness, or when she is in affliction, or sorrow, or weeping; and certainly not one who is in sickness, love, or labor. — Republic, III, 395.

The passionate and fitful temper furnishes easily a great variety of materials for imitation; the wise and calm temperament, being always nearly equable, is not easy to imitate or to appreciate when imitated. — Republic, X, 604.

When we want to indicate our meaning, either with the voice, or tongue, or mouth, is not indication of anything by means of them identical with their imitation of that thing? —Cratylus, 423.

Did you never observe how imitations in early youth, at last sink into the constitution and become a second nature of body, voice, and mind? — Republic, III, 395.

In the imitative arts, which make likeness, if they succeed in this, and are accompanied by pleasure, may not their works be said to have a charm? — Laws, II, 667.

Thus far then we are pretty well agreed that the imitator has no knowledge worth mentioning of what he imitates. — Republic, X, 602.

In the impersonation the creator

of an imitation is himself the instrument. — Sophist, 267.

Immortality. None of us is born immortal, nor would being so make us happy, as most people think. — Letter VII, 334.

A man shall marry, considering that after a sort the human race naturally partakes of immortality of which all men have the greatest desire implanted in them; for the desire of every man that he may become famous, and not lie in the grave without a name, is only the love of continuity. Now, mankind are coeval with all time, and are even following, and will ever follow, the course of time; in this way they are immortal, leaving children behind them, with whom they are one in the unity of generation. And for a man voluntarily to deprive himself of this gift of immortality, as he deliberately does who will not have a wife or children, is impiety. — Laws, IV, 721.

What is implied in the word "recollection" but the departure of knowledge, which is ever being forgotten and is renewed and preserved by recollection, appearing to be the same although in reality new, according to the law of succession by which all mortal things are preserved, not by absolute sameness of existence, but by substitution, the old worn-out mortality leaving another new and similar one behind? And in this way the mortal body, or mortal anything, partakes of immortality. Marvel not then at the love which all men have of their offspring; for that universal love and interest is for the sake of immortality. — Symposium, 208.

The sum of your objection to immortality is as follows: You want to have proven that the soul is imperishable and immortal, and you think that the philosopher who is confident in death has but a vain and foolish confidence, if he thinks that he will fare better than one who has led another sort of life, in the world below, unless he can prove this. — Phaedo, 95.

If the soul is immortal, great care should be taken of her, not only in respect of the portion of time which is called life, but of eternity. And the danger of neglecting her from this point of view does indeed appear to be awful. If death had only been the end of all, the wicked would have had a good bargain in dying, for they would have been happily quit not only of their body, but of their own evils together with their souls. — Phaedo, 107.

He who is confident in death has but a foolish confidence, unless he is able to prove that the soul is altogether immortal and imperishable. But if he is not able to prove this, he who is about to die will always have reason to fear that when the body is disunited, the soul also may utterly perish. — Phaedo, 88.

The soul of man is immortal and imperishable. — Republic, X, 608.

Conception and generation are a principle of immortality in the mortal creature. — Symposium, 206.

Impartiality. Those who are present at such discussions ought to be impartial hearers of both the speakers; remembering, however, that impartiality is not the same as equality; for both sides should be impartially heard, and yet an equal importance should not be given to both of them; but to the wiser a higher importance should be assigned, and to the less wise a lower. — Protagoras, 337.

Impatience. Nothing is gained by impatience. — Republic, X, 604.

Impeachment. Surely you cannot be engaged in an action before the king. — Not in an action; impeachment is the word which the Athenians use. — Euthyphro, 2.

Imperfect. If a man is imperfect — and this is the ordinary state of most people's minds with regard to intelligence and morality — not even Lynceus could make him see. — Letter VII, 343.

Impetuous. The impetuous is ready to go at that which others are afraid to approach. — Protagoras, 349.

Impiety. If a man be guilty of impiety in word or deed, he shall be tried for impiety at the instance of anyone who is willing to vindicate the laws; and if convicted, the court shall estimate the punishment of each act of impiety; and let all such criminals be imprisoned. — Laws, X, 907.

The impious men waste their service upon the gods, which, when offered by the pious men, is always accepted of them. — Laws, IV, 717.

All impious persons shall depart from their ways and go over to the pious. — Laws, X, 907.

Perhaps you have seen impious men growing old and leaving their children's children in high offices, and that shakes your faith; you have known or heard or been yourself an eyewitness of many monstrous impieties, and have beheld men by these criminal means from small beginnings reaching the pinnacle of greatness, and considering all these things you do not like to accuse the gods; but from some want of reasoning power, and also from an unwillingness to find fault with them, you are led to believe that they exist indeed, but have no thought or just care of human beings. — Laws, X, 900.

They say that the gods exist, not by nature, but only by the laws of state, which are different in different places, according to the legal convention of those who make them; and that the principles of justice have no existence at all in nature, but that mankind are always disputing about them and altering them; and that the alterations which are made by law have no basis in nature, but are of authority for the moment and at the time at which they are made. And the young men fall into impieties, under the idea that the gods are not such as the law bids them to imagine them. — Laws, X, 889, 890.

Implicate. They intended to implicate as many as possible in their crimes. — Apology, 32.

Importance. I know many things, but not anything of much importance. — Euthydemus, 293.

No human thing is of serious importance. — Republic, X, 604.

I wouldn't like to treat minor matters as if they were of major importance. — Letter VII, 330.

Impression. Those who wish to impress figures on soft substances do not allow any previous impression to remain, but make the surface as even and smooth as possible. — Timaeus, 51.

Improvement, Moral. Do you imagine that Cinesias, son of Meles, is concerned with the moral improvement of his hearers, or merely with their pleasure? — Gorgias, 501.

Impudence. Impudence is the insolent refusal to regard the opinion of the better by reason of an overdaring sort of freedom. — Laws, III, 701.

The absence of fear begets impudence. — Laws, III, 701.

Incest. We are all aware that most men, in spite of their lawless natures, are very strictly and precisely restrained from incestual cohabitation with a fair sister or brother, and this not at all against their will, but entirely with their will. — Laws, VIII, 838.

There is no absolute prohibition of incestual cohabitation between brothers and sisters; if the lot favors them, and they have the sanction of the Delphic oracle, the law will still allow them. — Republic, V, 461.

When the poet introduces on the stage a Thyestes or an Oedipus, or a Macareus having had incestual intercourse with his sister, he, when he is found out, is ready to kill himself as the penalty of his sin. — Laws, VIII, 838.

They will never know their real brothers and sisters. Those who were born at the same time with them they will term brothers and sisters, and they are not to intermarry. — Republic, V, 461.

Inclination. The inclinations of youths are fleeting, and often reverse themselves. — Letter VII, 328.

Incontinency. He called the soul a vessel, meaning a vessel of faith or belief, and the unsatiated he called the uninitiated or leaky, and the place in the soul of the uninitiated in which the desires are seated, being the intemperate and incontinent part, he compared to a vessel full of holes, because they can never be satisfied. . . . The uninitiated or leaky persons are the most miserable. For they carry water to a vessel which is full of holes in a similarly holey sieve. — Gorgias, 493.

Incurable. As they are incurable, the time has passed at which they can receive any benefit themselves. — Gorgias, 525.

If the legislator sees an evildoer who is incurable, for him he will make a law and fix a penalty. — Laws, IX, 862.

Indestructible. Soul and body, although not eternal, are indestructible. — Laws, X, 904.

Indicting. You should begin indicting me by indicting him who is my teacher. — Euthyphro, 5.

Indictment. You have put this into the indictment because you had nothing real of which to accuse me. — Apology, 27.

Indifferent, Morally. Things are either good or evil, or morally indifferent. — Gorgias, 467.

Indissoluble. The creator of the universe spoke as follows: My creations are indissoluble. — Timaeus, 41.

Individual. Every individual is his own superior or his own inferior. — Laws, I, 627.

Why single out individuals? Any Athenian gentleman will do him far more good than the sophists. — Meno, 93.

The legislator regards individuals and their possessions, not as belonging to themselves, but as belonging to their whole families; he still more regards the families and their possessions as belonging to the state. — Laws, XI, 923.

Having to take care of the common weal, the legislator cannot order with equal precision the various circumstances of individuals. — Laws, XI, 925.

Indolence. Disgraceful indolence is only a renewal of trouble. — Laws, VI, 779.

Revered friend, the abundance of your wisdom makes you indolent. — Euthyphro, 12.

Infant. Do not nurses, when they want to know what an infant desires, judge by these signs? — when anything is brought to the infant and he is silent, then he is supposed to be pleased, but, when he weeps and cries out, then he is not pleased. — Laws, 792.

Infants are full of spirit almost as soon as they are born, although some of them never seem to attain to the use of reason, and a good many only late in life. — Republic, IV, 441.

Nurses should be careful that the limbs of infants are not distorted by leaning on them when they are too young. — Laws, VII, 789.

Infantry. Crete is not, like Thessaly, a large plain; and for this reason — they have cavalry there, and we have infantry here — the inequality of the ground in our country is more adapted to locomotion on foot; but then, if one has infantrymen, one must have light arms — no one can run carrying a heavy weight, and the lightness of bows and arrows is convenient for foot soldiers. — Laws, I, 625.

Inferior. The inferior or the worse ought not to preside over the better. — Protagoras, 338.

Which is in the truer sense inferior, the man who is overcome by pleasure or by pain? — I should say the man who is overcome by pleasure; for all men deem him to be inferior in a more disgraceful sense, than the other who is overcome by pain. — Laws, I, 633.

Infinite. God revealed a finite element of existence, and also an infinite. — Philebus, 23.

Inflammation. Inflammations of the body come from burnings and inflamings, and all of them originate in bile. — Timaeus, 85.

Informer. The informer is worth many men, because he makes known the misdeeds of others to the rulers. — Laws, V, 730.

Let the authorities take care that no one wrongs the informer in revenge for his giving information. — Laws, XI, 932.

The informer shall have the honor of doing rightly. — Laws, XI, 914.

The informer shall receive, in certain cases, half the value. — Laws, V, 745.

Ingratitude. Did not the very persons whom Cimon was serving ostracize him, in order that they might not hear his voice for ten years? And they did just the same to Themistocles, adding the penalty of exile; and they voted that Miltiades, the hero of Marathon, should be thrown into the pit of death, and he was only saved by the chief Prytanis. — Gorgias, 516.

Inherent. This was inherent in the primal nature. . . . — Statesman, 273.

Inheritance. I shall be satisfied if I leave my sons a little more than I inherited. — Republic, I, 330.

Let the possessor of a lot leave the one of his children who is the best beloved, and one only, to be the heir of his dwellings. — Laws, V, 740.

Injury. Injurer and injured cannot be friends. — Lysis, 214.

Does anyone like to be injured? — Apology, 25.

There is no greater injury which a man can inflict on another than to banish from him divine philosophy. — Phaedrus, 239.

There is reason in supposing that

the finest natures, when under alien conditions, receive more injury than the inferior, because the contrast is greater. — Republic, VII, 491.

I would have you know, that if you kill such a righteous man as I am, you will morally injure yourselves more than you will morally injure me. — Apology, 30.

Injuries are of two kinds — one, voluntary, and the other, involuntary; and the involuntary damages are quite as many and great as the voluntary. — Laws, IX, 861.

I would not have anyone suppose that *all* damages are injuries; for I deny that he who harms another involuntarily does him an injury. I should rather say that an involuntary hurt, whether great or small, is not an injury at all; and, on the other hand, when a benefit is wrongly conferred, the author of the benefit may often be said to injure. — Laws, IX, 862.

Injustice. Injustice, and intemperance, and in general the depravity of the soul, is the greatest evil that there is. — Gorgias, 477.

To do injustice is more to be avoided than to suffer injustice. — Gorgias, 527.

Consider further, most foolish Socrates . . . injustice on a large scale in which the advantage of the unjust is more apparent; and my meaning will be most clearly seen if we turn to that highest form of injustice in which the criminal is the happiest of men, and the sufferers or those who refuse to do injustice are the most miserable — that is to say tyranny, which by fraud and force takes away the property of others, not little by little but wholesale, comprehending in one, things sacred as well as profane, private and public; for which acts of wrong, if he were detected perpetrating any one of them singly, he would be punished and incur great disgrace — they who do such wrong in particular cases are called robbers of temples, and man-stealers and burglars and swindlers and thieves. But when a man besides taking away the money of the citizens has made slaves of them, then, instead of these names of reproach, he is termed happy and blessed, not only by the citizens but by all who hear of his having achieved the consummation of justice. — Republic, I, 343, 344.

Injustice and justice are like disease and health; being in the soul what disease and health are in the body. — Republic, IV, 444.

Let others censure injustice. — Republic, II, 367.

Well, then, Thrasymachus, suppose you begin at the beginning. You say that perfect injustice is more gainful than perfect justice? And do not the unjust appear to you to be wise and good? But still I cannot hear without amazement that you class injustice with wisdom and virtue, and justice with the opposite. — Republic, I, 348.

Men censure injustice, fearing that they may be the victims of it and not because they shrink from committing it. Injustice, when on a sufficient scale, has more strength and freedom and mastery than justice; justice is the interest of the stronger, whereas injustice is a man's own profit and interest. — Republic, I, 344.

He only blames injustice who, owing to cowardice or age or some weakness, has not the power of being unjust. And this is proved by the fact that when he obtains the power, he immediately becomes unjust as far as he can be. — Republic, II, 366.

What shall a man profit, if his injustice be undetected and unpunished? He who is undetected only gets worse, whereas he who is detected and punished has the brutal part of his nature silenced and humanized; the gentler element in him is liberated, and his whole soul is perfected and ennobled by the acquirement of justice and temperance and wisdom. — Republic, IX, 591.

I should never have yielded to injustice from any fear of death. — Apology, 32.

Doing injustice is the greatest of all evils. — Gorgias, 469.

Innocent. No good man will accuse the innocent. — Gorgias, 521.

I was an innocent sufferer. — Letter VII, 346.

Innovation. If sports are disturbed and innovations are made in them, and the young never speak of their having the same likings, either in the bearing of their bodies or in their dress, but he who devises something new and out of the way in figures and colors is held in special honor, we may truly say that this is the greatest injury which can happen in a state. — Laws, VII, 797.

In Egypt, no painter or other artist is allowed to make innovations, leaving the traditional forms and inventing new ones. — Laws, II, 656.

Inquiry. Ought we to inquire into the truth of this, or simply to accept the mere statement on our own authority and that of others? — Euthyphro, 9.

We shall be better and braver and less helpless if we think that we ought to inquire, than we should have been if we indulged in the idle fancy that there is no knowing and no use in searching after what we know not; that is the theme upon which I am ready to fight, in word and deed, to the utmost of my power. — Meno, 86.

Insanity. If a man be insane he shall not be at large in the city, but his relations shall keep him at home in any way which they can. — Laws, XI, 934.

If a mentally deranged man, being master of his property, is the ruin of the house, and his son doubts and hesitates about indicting his father for insanity, let the law in that case provide that he shall first of all go to the eldest guardians of the law and tell them of his father's misfortune, and they shall duly look into the matter, and take counsel as to whether he shall indict him or not. — Laws, XI, 929.

If a mentally ill father is put under tutelage by the court, he shall henceforth be incapable of ordering the least particular of his life; he shall dwell in the house as a child for the remainder of his life. — Laws, XI, 929.

Insatiable. The soul which he compares to a sieve is the soul of the insatiable man, which is full of holes, and therefore incontent; this owing to a bad memory and want of faith. — Gorgias, 493.

Inspiration. He who, not being inspired and having no touch of madness in his soul, comes to the door and thinks that he will get into the temple by the help of art rules — he and his poetry are not admitted; the sane man is inferior when he enters into rivalry with the madman. — Phaedrus, 245.

He who sees the beauty of the earth is transported with the recollection of the true beauty; he would like to fly away, but he cannot; he is like a bird fluttering and looking upward and careless of the world below; and he is therefore esteemed mad. But this is of all inspirations the noblest and best, and comes of the best. — Phaedrus, 249.

There is a great difference between dishonesty and inspiration, and inspiration is the far nobler alternative. — Ion, 542.

The inventions of the poets are inspired only when they make that to which the muse impels them. — Ion, 534.

The soul of the lyric poet does the same, as they themselves tell us; for they tell us that they gather their strains from honeyed fountains out of the gardens and dells of the Muses; thither like the bees, they wing their way. And this is true. For the poet is a light and winged and holy thing, and there is no invention in him until he has been inspired and is out of his senses, and the mind is no longer in him: when he has not attained to this state, he is powerless and is unable to utter his oracles. . . . As the Corybantian revelers when they dance are not in their right mind, so the lyric poets are not in their right mind when they are composing their beautiful strains: but when falling under the power of music and meter they are inspired and possessed; like Bacchic girls who draw milk and honey from the rivers, when they are under the influence of Dionysus, but not when they are in their right mind. — Ion, 534.

Every poet has a muse from whom he is suspended, and by whom he is said to be possessed, which is nearly the same thing; for he is taken possession of. — Ion, 536.

The inspiration of the poets is divine, and often in their strains, by the aid of the Muses and the Graces, they attain truth. — Laws, III, 682.

No man, when in his senses, attains prophetic inspiration; but when he receives the inspired word either his intelligence is enthralled by sleep, or he is demented by some distemper or possession. — Timaeus, 71.

Tell me, Ion: When you produce the greatest effect upon the spectators in the recitation of some striking passage, such as the apparition of Odysseus leaping forth on the floor, recognized by the suitors and casting his arrows at his feet, or the description of Achilles rushing at Hector, or the sorrows of Andromache, Hecuba, or Priam, are you in your right mind? Are you not carried out of yourself, and does not your soul in an ecstasy seem to be among the persons and places of which she is speaking, whether they are in Ithaca or in Troy or whatever may be the scene of the poem? — Ion, 535.

Instruction. The admonitory sort of instruction gives much trouble and does little good. — Sophist, 230.

Integrity. The civil and social virtues of integrity and temperance are acquired by habit and practice rather than by philosophy and reasoning. — Phaedo, 82.

Intellect. Only the intellect is engaged in the contemplation of moral existence. — Philebus, 59.

An impassioned intellect when too eager in the pursuit of knowledge, causes waste. — Timaeus, 88.

Intelligence. For mankind it should be proof that the stars and their whole procession have intelligence, that they move with unbroken uniformity, because their motion carries out a plan; they do not change their paths confusedly, moving now thus, and again thus, and jumping from one orbit to another. However, the majority of us maintain the opposite thesis; because the stars move with uniformity, we imagine them to be unintelligent. . . . The creature which moves in disorderly fashion, including man himself, must be taken to be unintelligent, while the fiery creature moving uniformly through the sky certifies its intelligence. — Epinomis, 982. *Vide* Heaven.

The soul, besides other things, contains intelligence, and the head, besides other things, contains sight and hearing; and the intelligence mingling with these noblest of the senses, and becoming one with them, may be truly called the salvation of all things. — Laws, XII, 961.

Intemperance, Sexual. The truth is that the sexual intemperance for the most part grows into a disease of the soul by reason of the moist and fluid state of one element, and this arises out of the loose consistency of the bones. — Timaeus, 86.

Intention. I maintain that the mere giving or taking away of anything is not to be described either as just or unjust; but the legislator has to consider whether one does it out of a good or bad principle or intention. — Laws, IX, 862.

Many things are not immediately adjacent but have a borderland between them. This is also valid for some deeds of passion, which lie in a mean between the intentional and the unintentional. — Laws, IX, 878.

Intercourse. Excessive intercourse not having the flavor of unfulfilled desire which is created by time intervals, imperceptibly dilutes love from a feeling of oversatiation. — Laws, VI, 776.

Our citizens ought not to fall below the nature of birds and beasts in general, who remain until the age for procreation virgin and unmarried: when arriving at the proper time of life they are coupled, and graciously pair together, and live the rest of their lives in holiness and innocence, abiding firmly in their original compact: surely they ought to be better than the animals. But if they are corrupted by the other Greeks and the barbarians, and they see with their eyes and hear with their ears of the so-called free love everywhere prevailing among them, and they themselves are not able to get the better of the temptation, the guardians of the law shall turn law-givers, and devise a law against them. — Laws, VIII, 840.

Men and women will dwell together, associate at gymnastic exercises, and be brought up together. And so they will be drawn by a necessity of their natures to have intercourse with one another. Necessity is, here, not too strong a word I think. — Republic, V, 458.

Whether such matters are to be regarded jestingly or seriously, I think that the pleasure is to be deemed natural which arises out of the intercourse of men and women; but that the bold attempt is originally due to unbridled lust. — Laws, I, 636.

Our braver and better youth might have greater facilities of intercourse with women given them; their bravery is a good pretext. — Republic, V, 460.

Interest. Let me assure you that I have your interest in view as well as my own. — Gorgias, 455.

Interpretation. Any violent interpretations should be avoided. — Cratylus, 410.

Men could have provided a better and truer interpretation. — Epinomis, 982.

Interpretation has been the most difficult part of my art. — Ion, 530.

Interpreter. It is customary to appoint diviners or interpreters as discerners of the oracles of the gods. Some persons call them prophets; they do not know that they are only repeaters of dark sayings and visions, and are not to be called prophets at all, but only interpreters of prophecy. — Timaeus, 72.

Interrogation. You, as you always do, have recourse to your favorite method of interrogation. — Gorgias, 461.

Intoxication. At the very mention of the word intoxication, one side is ready with their praises and the other with their censures, and this is absurd. — Laws, I, 638.

Let us discourse about the nature of intoxication at large, which is a very important matter, and requires all the wisdom of the legislator to determine. I am not talking of the mere practice of drinking or not drinking wine in general, but about downright intoxication. — Laws, I, 637.

We shall begin by enacting that boys shall not taste wine at all until they are eighteen years of age; we will tell them that fire must not be poured upon fire, whether in the body or in the soul, until they begin to go to labor; afterwards they may taste wine in moderation up to the age of thirty, but while a man is young he should abstain altogether from intoxication and excess of wine; at length he may invite the gods to the festivity of the elder men, making use of the wine to be the cure of the sourness of old age; that in age we may renew our youth, and forget our sorrows; and also in order that the soul, like iron melted in the fire, may become softer and more impressible. — Laws, II, 666.

Intuition. The noble souls know this fact by intuition, while the vulgar souls deny it. — Letter II, 311.

After long acquaintance and study of a subject, intuition, like a blaze kindled by a flying spark, suddenly springs up in the soul and at once becomes self-sufficient. — Letter VII, 341.

Invalids. Unrestrained invalids have a charming way of going on, and the charming thing is that they deem him their worst enemy who tells them the truth, which is simply that, unless they give up eating and drinking and lusting and sleeping, neither drug nor cautery nor spell nor amulet nor anything will be of any avail. — Republic, IV, 426.

Invalids who have no self-restraint will not leave off their habits of intemperance. They are always doctoring and increasing and complicating their disorders, fancying they will be cured by some nostrum which somebody advises them to try — never getting better, but rather growing worse. — Republic, IV, 425.

Invention. Can we suppose that God is ignorant of antiquity, and therefore takes recourse to invention? — Republic, II, 382.

Inventor. He who has the gift of invention is not always the best judge of the utility or inutility of his own inventions to the users of them. — Phaedrus, 274.

Investigation. Thorough investigation of all things is the only way in which the mind can attain truth. — Parmenides, 136.

The investigation of virtue and vice must be founded on a general research into what is true and false of existence. — Letter VII, 344.

Invisible. Allowing that the qualities of virtue, justice, and the like all exist, do men affirm any of them to be visible and tangible, or are they all invisible? — All of them surely are invisible. — Sophist, 247.

Involuntary. Favor me by stating a little more clearly the various complications of the involuntary and voluntary which arise in criminal cases. — Laws, IX, 863.

Iron. Iron is superfluous for the potter and the weaver. — Laws, III, 679.

Irrational. Irrational quantities may be either irrational or rational if taken together. — Greater Hippias, 303.

As irrational as the lines so called in geometry. . . . — Republic, VII, 534.

Irreligious. The irreligious son of a religious father should be called irreligious. — Cratylus, 394.

Irrigation. They shall provide dams against rains doing harm instead of good to the land, when they come down from the mountains into the hollows; and shall keep them back by irrigation works and trenches, in order that they may receive and drink up the rain from heaven, and making fountains and streams for the fields and places which are underneath, may furnish even to the dry places plenty of good water. — Laws, VI, 761.

Island of the Blessed. He who has lived all his life in justice and holiness shall go, when he dies, to the Island of the Blessed. — Gorgias, 523.

J

Jealousy. He who is jealous and will not, if he can help, allow others to partake in a friendly way of any good, is deserving of blame. — Laws, V, 731.

The lover jealously debars his beloved from society; he will not have you intimate with the wealthy, lest they should exceed him in wealth, or with men of education, lest they should be his superiors in knowledge; and he is equally afraid of the power of any other good. — Phaedrus, 232.

Jealousy begets envy. — Menexenus, 242.

Jest. There are jests which you would be ashamed to make yourself, and yet on the comic stage, or again in private, when you hear them, you are greatly amused by them, instead of being disgusted at their unseemliness; there is a disposition in human nature which is inclined to raise a laugh, and this was once restrained by you because you were afraid of being thought a buffoon, but is now let loose again and encouraged by the theatre, and you are often unconsciously betrayed into playing the comic poet in your own person. — Republic, X, 606.

A jest may sometimes pleasantly interrupt the earnest. — Philebus, 30.

The jesting is akin to the earnest. — Letter VI, 323.

Joke. The evil is that he makes a joke of a serious matter. — Apology, 24.

Judges. I know how much more formidable to a man of sense a few good judges are than many fools. — Symposium, 194.

The judge should not be young; he should have learned to know evil, not from his own soul, but from late and long observation of the nature of evil of others: knowledge, and not his own experience, should be his guide. — Republic, III, 409.

The judge governs mind by mind, and he cannot therefore be allowed to have been reared among vicious minds, and to have associated with them, in order that, having gone through the whole calendar of crime, he may infer the crimes of others like their diseases from the knowledge of himself; but the honorable mind which is to form a healthy judgment ought rather to have had no experience or contamination of evil habits when young. — Republic, III, 409.

Good judges are those who are acquainted with all sorts of moral men. — Republic, III, 408.

The judges are required to be men of character — they must possess both wisdom and courage; for the true judge ought not to learn from the theatre, nor ought he to be panic-stricken at the clamor of the many and his own incapacity; nor again, knowing the law, ought he through cowardice and unmanliness carelessly to deliver a wrong judgment, with the very same lips which have just appealed to the gods before he judged. He is sitting, not as a disciple of the theatre, but, in proper place, as their instructor, and he ought to be the enemy of all pandering to the pleasure of the spectators. — Laws, II, 659.

The same officials who judge of the gymnastic contests of men, shall judge of horses; but in music there shall be one set of judges of solo singing, and another who shall judge of choruses. — Laws, VII, 764.

When the pilgrim arrives in the world below, he is delivered from the professors of justice, and finds the true judges who are said to give judgment there. — Apology, 41.

As we know that you are good judges, and will say exactly what you think, we have taken you into our counsels. — Laches, 178.

Judgment. Let us not be hasty in forming a judgment. — Laws, I, 658.

It is difficult to determine accurately the things which are worthy or unworthy of a freeman, but let those who have obtained the prize of virtue give judgment about them in accordance with their feelings of right and wrong. — Laws, XI, 919.

The instrument of judgment is not possessed by the avaricious man, but only by the philosopher. — Republic, IX, 582.

I am extremely desirous to be persuaded by you, but not against my own better judgement. — Crito, 48.

Understanding is not the same as judgment. — Republic, V, 477.

Since judgment and understanding are distinct faculties, the sphere of understanding and of judgment are not the same. . . . We are quite conscious of the distinction between understanding and judgment. — Republic, V, 478.

Judgment and understanding have to do with different kinds of matter (namely, with valuing and knowing the things). — Republic, V, 477.

Do we admit the existence of judgment? — Undoubtedly. — As being the same with knowledge, or another faculty? — Another faculty. — Republic, V, 477.

If true opinion in law courts and knowledge were the same, the perfect judge could not have judged rightly without knowledge; and therefore I must infer that they are not the same. — Theaetetus, 201.

There seems to be something wrong in petitioning a judge, and thus procuring an acquittal instead of informing and convincing him. For his duty is, not to make a present of justice, but to give judgment; and he has sworn that he will judge according to the laws, and not according to his own good pleasure; and neither he nor we should get into the habit of perjuring ourselves — there can be no piety in that. — Apology, 35.

Many lack real virtue, but are not far wrong in their judgment of the vice or virtue of others. Even bad men have a divine instinct which guesses rightly, and very many who are utterly depraved form correct notions and judgments about the difference of good and bad. — Laws, XII, 950.

Judgment is not inferior to knowledge, or less useful in action; nor is the man who has judgment inferior to him who has knowledge. — Meno, 98.

Men shall be entirely stripped before they are judged, for they shall be judged when they are dead; and the judge too shall be naked, that is to say, dead; he with his naked soul shall pierce into the other naked soul as soon as each man dies; and they shall die suddenly and be deprived of all their kindred, and leave their brave attire upon the earth — performed in this manner, the judgment will be just. . . . Judgment was given on the very day on which the men were to die. But since judges and judged were alive, the judgments were not well given. — Gorgias, 523.

Since knowing is the subject matter of understanding, something else must be the subject matter of judgment. — Republic, V, 478.

Judgment is a conclusion of reasoning. — Sophist, 264.

Is judgment also a faculty? — Certainly. — Republic, V, 477.

When we have practiced virtue in common, we shall be better able to judge then. — Gorgias, 527.

With gentleness they were to judge their subjects, of whom they were by nature friends; but when they came in the way of their enemies they were to be fierce with them. — Timaeus, 18.

We should be sorry to judge hastily of you. — Apology, 20.

Our souls are being judged. — Letter VII, 335.

Only a man in his senses can act or judge about himself and his own affairs. — Timaeus, 72.

Jurisprudence. We may observe that any study of jurisprudence turns almost entirely on pleasure and pain. — Laws, I, 636.

Juror. Let the juror decide justly and the pleader argue truly. — Apology, 18.

Just. Can there be any matters more important than the just, the honorable, the good, and the expedient? — First Alcibiades, 118.

Does the just man try to gain any advantage over another just? — Far otherwise; if he did he would not be the simple amusing creature which he is. — Republic, I, 349.

Just men may be expected to pass [after their death] into some gentle social nature which is like their own, such as that of bees or ants. — Phaedo, 82.

He who appears to be the worst of those who have been brought up in laws and humanities, would appear to be a just man if he were to be compared with savages. — Protagoras, 327.

Consider further, most foolish Socrates, that the just is always a loser in comparison with the unjust. First of all, in private contracts: wherever the unjust is the partner of the just you will find that, when the partnership is dissolved, the unjust man has always more and the just less. Secondly, in their dealings with the state: when there is an income tax, the just man will pay more and the unjust less on the same amount of income; and when there is anything to be received the one gains nothing and the other much. Observe also what happens when they take an office; there is the just man neglecting his affairs and perhaps suffering other losses, and getting nothing out of the public, because he is just; moreover he is hated by his friends and acquaintances for refusing to serve them in unlawful ways. — Republic, I, 343.

The just soul and the just man will

live well, and the unjust man will live ill. — Republic, I, 353.

Let us place the just man in his nobleness and simplicity, wishing, as Aeschylus says, to be and not to seem good. There must be no seeming, for if he seem to be just he will be honored and rewarded, and then we shall not know whether he is just for the sake of justice or for the sake of honors and rewards; therefore, let him be clothed in justice only, and have no other covering. Let him be the best of men, and let him be thought the worst; then he will have been put to the proof; and we shall see whether he will be affected by the fear of infamy and its consequences. And let him continue thus to the hour of death; being just and seeming to be unjust. — Republic, II, 361.

You must allow me to repeat of the just the blessings which you were attributing to the fortunate unjust. I shall say of them, what you were saying of the others, that as they grow older, they become rulers in their own city if they care to be; they marry whom they like and give in marriage to whom they will; all that you said of the others I now say of these. And, on the other hand, of the unjust I say that the greater number, even though they escape in their youth, are found out at last and look foolish at the end of their course, and when they come to be old and miserable are flouted alike by stranger and citizen. — Republic, X, 613.

Are not just men gentle, as Homer says? — Gorgias, 516.

The just man, if we regard the idea of justice only, will be like the just state. — Ibid., IV, 435.

There can be no greater difference than between just and unjust. — First Alcibiades, 109.

The view which identifies the just with the pleasant has an excellent moral and religious tendency. For no one will be persuaded to do that which gives him more pain than pleasure. — Laws, II, 663.

But whether the just have a better and happier life than the unjust is a further question which we also propose to consider. I think that they have; but still I should like to examine further, for no light matter is at stake, nothing less than the rule of human life. — Republic, I, 352.

The son of Ariston has decided that the best and justest man is also the happiest and that the worst and most unjust man is also the most miserable. — Republic, IX, 580.

Then this must be our notion of the just man, that even when he is in poverty or sickness, or any other seeming misfortune, all things will in the end work together for good to him in life and death. . . . Look at things as they really are, and you will see that the clever unjust are in the case of runners, who run well from the starting place to the goal but not back again from the goal: they go off at a great pace, but in the end only look foolish, slinking away with their ears dragging on their shoulders, and without a crown; but the true runner comes to the finish and receives the prize and is crowned. And this is the way with the just; he who endures to the end of every action and occasion of his entire life has a good report and carries off the prize which men have to bestow. — Republic, X, 613.

What are plaintiff and defendant doing in a law court — are they not contending about the just and the unjust? — Phaedrus, 261.

Many a man is brave and not just, or just and not wise. — Protagoras, 329.

Are we to require that the just man should never fail to do justice, or may we be satisfied with an approximation, and the attainment of a higher degree of justice in him than is to be found in other men? — Republic, V, 472.

Just and Good. Partisans of the perpetual flux were confidently maintaining that the ordinances which the state commanded and thought just, were just to the state which imposed them, while they were in force; but as to the good, no one had ever yet had the hardihood to contend that the ordinances were really good because they lasted. — Theaetetus, 117.

Justice. But where, amid all this, is justice? Son of Ariston, tell me where. — Republic, IV, 427.

I am far from agreeing that justice is the interest of the stronger. — Republic, I, 347.

The legislator should look, not to the interests of tyrants, or to the power of the people, but to justice always; which is the distribution of legal equality among natural unequals. — Laws, VI, 757.

He who is not on a voyage has no need of a pilot? — No. — Then in time of peace justice will be of no use? — I hardly think so. — Then you think that justice may be of use in peace as well as war? — Yes. — Republic, I, 332, 333.

Justice is useful when money is useless? — That is the inference. — Republic, I, 333.

If we were seeking for a piece of gold, you would not imagine that we were "knuckling under to one another," and so losing our chance of finding it. Why, then, when we are seeking for justice, a thing more precious than much fine gold, do you say that we are weakly yielding to one another and not doing our utmost to get at the truth? Nay, my good friend, we are most willing and anxious to do so, but the fact is that we cannot. And if so, you people who know all these things should pity us and not be angry with us. — Republic, I, 336.

I proclaim justice is nothing else than the interest of the stronger. The different forms of government make laws democratical, aristocratical, tyrannical, with a view of their several interests; and these laws, which are made by them for their own interests, are the justice which they deliver to their subjects, and him who transgresses them they punish as a breaker of the law. In all states there is the same principle of justice, which is the interest of the government; and as the government must be supposed to have power, the only reasonable conclusion is, that everywhere there is one principle of justice, which is the interest of the stronger. — Republic, I, 338.

I will not have you say that justice is advantage or profit or gain or interest, for this sort of nonsense will not do for me; I must have clearness and accuracy. — Ibid., I, 336.

They wanted to arrive at the truth, first, about the nature of justice and injustice, and secondly, about their relative advantages. — Republic, II, 368.

On what principle shall we any longer choose justice rather than the worst injustice? when, if we only unite the latter with a deceitful resemblance to justice, we shall fare well both with gods and men, in life and after death, as most men tell us. Knowing all this, Socrates, how can a man who has any superiority of mind, be willing to honor justice; or indeed refrain from laughing when he hears justice praised? And even if there should be someone who is satisfied that justice is best, still he is not angry with the unjust, but is very ready to forgive them, because he also knows that most men are not just of their own free will. — Republic, II, 366.

The many are of another mind; they think that justice is to be reckoned among goods which are to be pursued for the sake of rewards and of reputation, but in themselves are disagreeable and rather to be avoided. — Republic, II, 358.

Justice is the punisher of those who fall short of the divine law. — Laws, IV, 716.

He meant to say that justice would give each man what is appropriate to him, and this he termed his debt or "due." — Republic, I, 332.

Men are only agreed to a certain extent about justice, and then they begin to disagree. — Cratylus, 412.

Justice frees the evildoer from injustice. — Gorgias, 478.

The universal voice of mankind is saying that justice and virtue are honorable, but grievous and toilsome; and that the pleasures of vice and injustice are easy of attainment. — Republic, II, 364.

There is a great difference between justice and expediency. Many persons have done great wrong and profited by their injustice; others have done rightly and suffered. — First Alcibiades, 113.

Justice is the health of the state. — Protagoras, 346.

Think not of life and children first, and of justice afterwards, but of justice first, that you may be justified before the princes of justice. — Crito, 54.

Would you call justice vice? — No, I would rather say sublime simplicity. — And would you call injustice malignity? — No, I would rather say discretion. — Republic, I, 348.

Justice is of the nature of a spiritual thing. — Protagoras, 330.

When I repeat this notion [that justice is the sun], I am answered by the satirical remark, "What! is there no justice in the world when the sun is down?" And when I earnestly beg my questioner to tell me his own honest opinion, he says, "Fire in the abstract"; but this is not very intelligible. Another says, "No, not fire in the abstract, but the abstraction of heat in the fire." — Cratylus, 413.

No man is of such adamant temper that he would stand fast in justice — that is what they think. No man would dare to be honest when he could with impunity take what he liked, or lie with anyone at his pleasure; for wherever anyone thinks that he can with impunity be unjust, there he is unjust. — Republic, II, 360.

I find myself in far greater perplexity about the nature of justice than I was before I began to learn. — Cratylus, 413.

How are you ever likely to know the nature of justice and injustice, about which you are so perplexed, if you have neither learned them of others nor discovered them yourself? — First Alcibiades, 112.

Is it not by justice that men are just? — Greater Hippias, 287.

Is there or is there not a justice? — Assuredly there is. — Phaedo, 65.

One of them says that justice is the sun. Another man professes to laugh at this, and says that justice is mind. — Cratylus, 413.

What about this thing which you just now called justice, is it just or unjust? — Protagoras, 330.

Justice is the art which gives good to friends and evil to enemies. — Republic, I, 332.

He who really reverences justice, and hates injustice, is discovered in his dealings with inferiors to whom he can easily be unjust. — Laws, VI, 777.

That which is healthy causes health, and that which is unhealthy causes disease. And just actions cause justice, and unjust actions cause injustice. — Republic, IV, 444.

They say that to do injustice is, by nature, good; to suffer injustice, evil; but that the evil is greater than the good. And when men have had experience of both, not being able to avoid the one and obtain the other, they think they had better agree with one another to have neither and thence arise laws and covenants among them. This, as they affirm, is the origin and nature of justice, arising out of a mean or compromise between the best of all, which is to do and not to suffer injustice, and the worst of all, which is to suffer without the power of retaliation; and justice, being in a mean between the two, is tolerated not as a good, but as the lesser evil, and honored by reason of the inability of men to do injustice. For no man who is worthy to be called a man would submit to such an agreement if he were able to resist. — Republic, II, 359.

That justice is only an involuntary practice because of the inability to do injustice will best appear if we imagine something of this kind: suppose we give both the just and the unjust entire liberty to do what they will; then we shall detect the just man in the very act; the just and unjust will be found going the same way — following their interest, which all natures conceive to be their good, and are only diverted into the path of justice by the force of law. — Republic, II, 359.

He who has no share in the administration of justice, is apt to imagine that he has no share in the state at all. — Laws, VI, 768.

Now as you have admitted that justice is one of that highest class of goods which are desired for their rewards, but in a far greater degree for their own sakes — I would ask you in your praise of justice to regard one point only: I mean the inherent good which justice works in its possessor. Let others praise justice, magnifying its rewards and honors; that is the manner of arguing which, coming from them, I am ready to tolerate, but from you who have spent your whole life in the consideration of this question, I expect something better: to show justice to be a good itself. — Republic, II, 367.

We have not [in order to praise justice] introduced the rewards of justice . . . but justice has been shown to be best for its own sake. — Republic, X, 612.

No one has ever blamed injustice or praised justice except with a view to the glories, honors, and benefits which flow from them. No one has ever adequately described either in verse or prose the inherent essence of either of them, or shown that of all the things of a man's soul which he has within him, justice for its own sake is the greatest good, and injustice the greatest evil. Had this been the universal strain, had you sought to persuade us of this from our youth upwards, we should not have been on the watch to keep one another from doing wrong, but everyone would have been his own watchman, because afraid, if he did wrong, of harboring in himself the greatest of evils. — Republic, II, 366, 367.

I cannot imagine any theme about which a man of sense would oftener wish to converse than about justice. — Republic, II, 358.

They have filled the city full of harbors and docks and walls and revenues, and have left no room for justice and temperance. — Gorgias, 519.

You must not wonder that those who attain to beatific vision are unwilling to descend to human affairs; for their souls are ever hastening into the upper world where they desire to dwell; which desire of theirs is very natural. And is there anything surprising in one who passes from divine contemplations to the evil state of man, misbehaving himself in a ridiculous manner; if, while his eyes are blinking and before he has become accustomed to the surrounding darkness, he is compelled to fight in courts of law, or in other places, about the images or the shadows of images or justice, and is endeavouring to meet the conceptions of those who have never yet seen genuine justice? — Republic, VII, 517.

The best way of life is to practice justice. — Gorgias, 527.

I believe that Xerxes or some other rich and mighty man who had a great opinion of his own power, first said that justice is doing good to your friends and harm to your enemies. — Republic, I, 336.

If, on trial, this conception of justice be verified in the individual as well as in the state, then there will be no longer any room for doubt. —Republic, IV, 434.

Justice is positively something. — Greater Hippias, 287.

Is not justice a power? — Lesser Hippias, 375.

Justice, Fugitive of. Does not the fugitive of justice overrun the laws and the whole state? — Crito, 50.

Justice, Natural. Tell me what you mean by natural justice: do you mean that the stronger should take the property of the weaker by force, or that the better should rule the worse? — Gorgias, 488.

Justice, Perverter of. If anyone thinks that he will pervert the power of justice in the minds of the judges, and unreasonably litigate or advocate, let anyone who likes indict him for malpractices of law and dishonest advocacy, and let him be judged in the court of select judges. — Laws, XI, 938.

Justice Fighter. Don't be offended at my telling you the truth — that no man who goes to war with you or any other multitude, honestly fighting against the commission of injustice in the state, will save his life. — Apology, 32.

Justified. The chooser is answerable — God is justified. — Republic, X, 617.

I don't think that you are justified in betraying your own life when you might be saved. — Crito, 45.

[144]

K

King. This, too, is evident, that the king cannot do much with his hands, or with his whole body, towards the maintenance of his empire, compared with what he does by the intelligence and strength of his mind. — Statesman, 259.

Kings we have always had, once hereditary and now elected. — Menexenus, 238.

You allegedly intended to relieve the Syracusans by replacing the tyranny by a kingship. — Letter III, 315.

Knowing. Let us suppose that there is such a person, who knows the past and present as well as the future; you will allow that he is the most knowing of all living men? — Charmides, 174.

Knowledge. Knowledge is the food of the soul; and we must take care, that the Sophist does not deceive us when he praises what he sells, like the dealers who sell the food for the body; for they praise indiscriminately all their goods, without knowing what are really beneficial or hurtful: neither do their customers know, with the exception of any trainer or physician who may happen to buy of them. — Protagoras, 313.

The true lover of knowledge is always striving after being — that is his nature. — Republic, VI, 490.

Knowledge has two parts: the one technical, and the other educational. — Philebus, 55.

The knowledge which we want is one that uses as well as makes. — Euthydemus, 289.

O my friends, hard is it for you who are creatures of a day, to know what is yours — hard, too, to know yourselves. — Laws, XI, 923.

The search for knowledge is wholly directed towards the truth, not caring about gain or fame. — Republic, IX, 581.

Both of us were agreeing that there was nothing mightier than knowledge. — Protagoras, 357.

Those who have knowledge are more confident than those who have no knowledge. — Protagoras, 350.

Only that knowledge which is of the spiritual or invisible, and uses the mind, can make the soul look upwards; and whether a man gapes with his eyes at the heavens or blinks on the ground, seeking to learn something about the physical or visible, I would deny that he can thus comprehend the moral ideas of the spirit; his soul is looking, not upwards, but downwards, even though he study with back-thrown head. — Republic, VII, 529.

Speak out then, and do not hide your knowledge. — Euthyphro, 15.

Knowledge is that which gives a

man not only good fortune but success. — Euthydemus, 281.

Mere reasoning is now most clearly proved to be different from sensual perception. . . . The spiritual scientist does not seek for knowledge in sensual perception at all, but in that other process, in which the mind is alone. — Theaetetus, 187.

If it be knowledge, but not of a valuable sort — what is the use of learning it? — Laches, 183.

Before we begin a posteriori to see and hear, we must have an a priori knowledge. — Phaedo, 75.

The knowledge of things is not to be derived from names. No; they must be studied and investigated in themselves. — Cratylus, 439.

A man who does not know the affairs of others, can never be a statesman, nor an economist. — First Alcibiades, 133.

All knowledge appears to be a good. — Laches, 182.

Knowledge with explanation is the most perfect form of knowledge. — Theaetetus, 206.

Physical knowledge does not only consist in impressions of sense, but also in reasoning about them. — Theaetetus, 186.

All men who have a grain of intelligence will admit that the a priori knowledge which has to do with being and reality, and sameness and unchangeability, is by far the truest of all. — Philebus, 58.

While in company with the body, the soul cannot have pure knowledge. — Phaedo, 66.

What sort of knowledge is there which would draw the soul from matter to spirit? — A study which leads to unexperimental reflection. — Republic, VII, 521, 523.

Let us proceed to inquire whether true knowledge consists in knowing the name only of a thing and not its definition. — Laws, XII, 964.

Why are you so slow of heart to believe that knowledge is virtue? — I fear that I have some reason in doubting whether virtue is knowledge. — Meno, 89.

I reckon that we make the nearest approach to knowledge when we have the least possible concern or interest in the body, and are not saturated with the bodily nature, but remain pure until the hour when God himself is pleased to release us. — Phaedo, 67.

Had we the knowledge at our birth, or did we acquire it afterwards? — Phaedo, 76. (Ed. Note: We have, however, both a priori and a posteriori knowledge.)

In inquiries of this sort [natural sciences] the soul is compelled to use hypotheses, not proceeding to a first principle because unable to ascend above hypotheses. . . . And when I speak of the other branch of cognition, you will understand me to speak of that knowledge which the soul herself attains by the power of reasoning, using the hypotheses not as first principles, but only as hypotheses — that is to say, as steps and points of departure into a philosophical region which is above hypotheses. — Republic, VI, 511.

Is not the knowledge of God one of the noblest sorts of knowledge? — Laws, XII, 966.

When the mind judges the sensible world, then arise beliefs. But when the mind is concerned with cognition, then knowledge is perfected. — Timaeus, 37.

Knowledgeable. If you are knowledgeable, my son, all men will be friendly and attached to you, for you will be useful; but if not, neither father, nor mother, nor relative, nor anyone else, will be your friends. — Lysis, 210.

"Know Thyself." The opposite of "Know thyself" would be, "Know not thyself." — Philebus, 48.

L

Labor. The intention was, that, in the case of the citizens generally, we should put each laborer to that use for which nature designed him, and then every man would do an expert job, and specialized and not versatile. — Republic, IV, 423.

Human labor is not twofold or manifold, for each man plays one part only. In our state, we shall find a shoemaker to be a shoemaker and not a pilot also, and a farmer to be a farmer and not a dicast also, and a soldier a soldier and not a trader also, and the same of all other citizens. — Republic, III, 397.

We are in search of a lover of labor in any line — or he will never be able to undergo the double toil and trouble of body and mind. — Republic, VII, 535.

You will remember the original principle of labor of which we spoke at the foundation of the state, that every man, as we often insisted, should practice one thing only, that being the thing to which his nature was most perfectly adapted. — Republic, IV, 433.

Ladle. Which of the two ladles is appropriate to the soup and the pot? Evidently that of figwood. For it gives the soup a tastier smell, and does not break the pot. But a golden ladle does in either case the opposite. — Greater Hippias, 290.

Lamentation. The presiding judges shall not permit unseemly supplications or womanish lamentations. — Laws, XII, 949.

We shall be right in getting rid of the lamentations of famous men, and making them over to women. — Republic, III, 387.

Does not the morose and ill-natured man appear to you to be full of lamentations and sorrows more than a good man ought to be? — Laws, VII, 792.

If there be nothing after death, still, during the short time that remains for me, I shall save my friends from lamentations. — Phaedo, 91.

Land. As the land is the parent, let the citizens tend her more carefully than children do their mother. For she is a goddess and their queen, and they are her mortal subjects. — Laws, V, 740.

The land and the houses will then have to be appropriated by us as fairly as possible. — Laws, V, 737.

In making the distribution of land, let the individual possessors feel that their particular lots also belong to the whole city. — Laws, V, 740.

Language. As in painting the painter, who wants to depict anything, sometimes uses purple only, or any other color, and sometimes mixes up several colors, as his method is when he has to paint flesh color or anything of that kind, so we shall apply letters to the expression of objects, either single letters when required, or several letters; and then we shall form syllables, and from syllables make nouns and verbs; and thus, at last, from the combinations of nouns and verbs, arrive at language, large and fair and whole. — Cratylus, 424, 425.

How will he ever succeed in making all mankind willing to use the same language about these [sexual] matters? — Laws, VIII, 838.

Names have been so twisted in all manners of ways, that I should not be surprised if the old language were to appear to us now to be quite like a barbarous tongue. — Cratylus, 421.

I [Socrates] shall use the simple words and arguments which occur to me at the moment; for I am certain that this is right, and that at my age I ought not to address you in the ornamental language of a juvenile orator. — Apology, 17.

These four [concepts, descriptions, names, bodies] explain the special quality of any subject as well as they explain its essence because of the inadequacy of language. No intelligent man will, therefore, put into language those things which his understanding has grasped, especially not into the unalterable form of written symbols. — Letter VII, 343.

The fine fashionable language of modern times has twisted and disguised and entirely altered the original meaning of old words. — Cratylus, 418.

Larceny. Larceny is a mean, and robbery a shameless thing. — Laws, XII, 941.

Laughter. In laughing at us, you will be laughing at yourselves. — Protagoras, 357.

A fit of laughter which has been indulged to excess almost always occasions an equally violent reaction. — Republic, III, 388.

There is no man who is in the habit of laughing at another who does not miss virtue and earnestness altogether. — Laws, XI, 935.

Law. The legislator ought to ordain laws with a view to wisdom. — Laws, III, 688.

All of you who are here present I reckon to be kinsmen and friends and fellow citizens, by nature and not by law; for by nature like is akin to like, whereas law is the tyrant of mankind, and often compels us to do many things which are against nature. — Protagoras, 337.

If the law is not the perfect order, why are we compelled to make laws at all? The reason of this has to be investigated. — Statesman, 294.

The law is made with the purpose to benefit the subjects; but sometimes it does definite damage if it is ill made. — Greater Hippias, 284.

The object of laws is to make those who use them happy. — Laws, I, 631.

The law is practically like an obstinate and ignorant tyrant, who will not allow anything to be done contrary to his appointment, or any question to be asked — not even in sudden changes of circumstances, when something happens to be better than what he commanded for someone. — Statesman, 294.

The soul of the child may not be accustomed to feel pleasure and pain in a manner contrary to the law and to those who obey the law. — Laws, II, 659.

The laws have to persuade as well as to threaten. — Laws, IV, 721.

Laws are passed under the idea that they will be useful in after time;

which, in other words, is the future. — Theaetetus, 178.

No one should presume to be wiser than the laws. — Statesman, 299.

Laws are not right which are passed for the good of particular classes and not for the good of the whole state. States which have such laws are not polities but parties, and their notion of justice is simply unmeaning. — Laws, IV, 715.

When a man is driven into believing that nothing is good any more than foul, or just any more than base, do you think that he will still honor and obey the laws? — Republic, VII, 538.

Citizens cannot properly observe the laws by habit only, and without an intelligent understanding of them. — Laws, XII, 951.

Normative laws are creations of mind in accordance with right reason — as you appear to me to maintain, and I am disposed to agree with you. — Laws, X, 890.

Laws are given to the young man, in order to guide him in his conduct whether as ruler or ruled. — Protagoras, 326.

Men should not be subject to human masters but to laws. — Letter, VII, 334.

Law is the sovereign of all. — Gorgias, 484.

Do you know that there are often said to be as many forms of laws as there are of governments? And men say that the law ought not to regard either peace or war or virtue, in general, but only the interests and power and preservation of the existing form of government; this is thought by them to be the best way of expressing the natural definition of justice. — Laws, IV, 714.

The intention of our laws is, that the citizens should be as happy as possible, and as friendly as possible to one another. — Laws, V, 743.

I am speaking of things which in a state and government give not only health and salvation to the body, but also law, or rather preservation of the law in the soul. — Laws, XII, 960.

Under the ancient laws, my friends, the people was not as now the master, but rather the willing servant of the laws. — Laws, III, 700.

There is nothing to prevent us from considering in every point of view the subject of law. — Laws, VI, 781.

The god of intelligent men is law, the god of silly men is pleasure. — Letter, VIII, 355.

The goddess saw the universal wantonness and wickedness of all things, having no limit of pleasure or satiety, and she devised the limit of law and order. You say that the goddess spoiled the soul; but I affirm that she saved her. — Philebus, 26.

To go against the laws, which are based upon long experience, and the wisdom of the counselors who have persuaded the multitude to pass them, would be a far greater and more ruinous error than any adherence to written law. — Ibid., 300.

His nation has been happily preserved for many generations. For laws, and not arbitrary men, were made supreme rulers. — Letters, VIII, 354.

As to the man who violates the simplest and noblest of laws which was the enactment of no mean man, who said, "Take not up that which you have not laid down" — what he ought to suffer at the hands of the gods, God only knows. — Laws, XI, 913.

We should always cooperate with the lead of the best, which is the law. — Laws, I, 645.

Do you expect me to say, that if a rabble of slaves and nondescripts, who are of no use except perhaps for their physical strength, gets together, their announcements are laws? — Gorgias, 489.

Laws and institutions have no beauty in them except in so far as they are pleasant or useful or both. — Gorgias, 474.

The state again compels the children to learn the laws, and live after the pattern which they furnish, and not after their own fancies. — Protagoras, 326.

The differences of men and actions, and the endless irregular movements of human things, do not admit of any universal and simple law. No legislative art can lay down any rule which will last forever. — Statesman, 294.

Is god or man supposed to be the author of your laws? — They may be said to be the work of god. — Laws, I, 624.

The laws would probably say: "Tell us, Socrates, what complaint do you have to make against us which would justify you in attempting to destroy us and the state? In the first place did we not bring you into existence? Your father married your mother by our aid and begat you. Say whether you have any objection to urge against those of us who regulate marriage? Or against those of us who regulate the system of nurture and education of children in which you yourself were trained? Were not the laws, who have charge of this, right in commanding your father to train you in music and gymnastic? Can you deny that you are our child and servant, as your fathers were before you? And if this is true you are not on equal terms with us; nor can you think that you have a right to do to us what we are doing to you." — Crito, 50.

Laws are partly framed for the sake of good men, in order to instruct them, and partly for the sake of those who refuse to be instructed, whose spirit cannot be subdued, or softened, or hindered from going to all evil. — Laws, IX, 880.

The laws would probably say: "Would you, Socrates, have any right to strike your father, when you have been struck by him? And because we think right to destroy you, do you think that you have any right to destroy us in return? And will you, O professor of true virtue, say that you are justified in this?" Do the laws speak rightly, or do they not? — Crito, 51.

If the greater part of mankind behave modestly, the enactments of law may be left to slumber; but, if they are disorderly, the enactments having been passed, let them be carried into execution. — Laws, VI, 785.

Mankind must have laws, and conform to them, or their life would be as bad as that of the most savage beast. And the reason of this is, that no man's nature is able to know what is best for the *social* state of man; or knowing, always able to do what is best. . . . If in the order of nature or by divine destiny a man were able to apprehend the truth about these things, he would have no need of laws to rule over him. But there is no such human mind anywhere, or at least not much; and therefore we must choose the second best, which is law and order. — Laws, IX, 875.

One must make the citizens observe the laws by bringing to bear two motives: fear and reverence. — Letter, VII, 337.

Many things have grown lax among you, which might have been far better, if they had been only regulated by law. — Laws, VI, 781.

The judge shall possess books about judicial matters that he may study them. For of all kinds of studies that of good law has the greatest power of improving the student; otherwise there would be no meaning in the divine and admirable law possessing a name akin to mind. — Laws, XII, 957.

Of all the writings which there are in cities, are not those which relate to laws found to be by far the noblest and the best? — Laws, IX, 858, 859.

Who would like a state that has no laws? — Crito, 53.

Reflection about good and evil when embodied in a decree by a state, is called Law. — Laws, I, 644.

No one accepts readily laws at their first enactment. — Laws, VI, 752.

When the supreme power in man coincides with the greatest wisdom and temperance, then the best laws are by nature framed, and the best constitution; but in no other way will they ever come into being. In one point of view, there may be a difficulty for a city to have good laws, but there is another point of view in which nothing can be easier or sooner effected, granting our supposition. — Laws, IV, 712.

Law, Unwritten. All matters which we are now describing are commonly called by the general name of unwritten laws, and what are termed the laws of our ancestors are all of similar nature. — Laws, VII, 793.

Law of Nature. It is a law of nature that great wisdom and great power attract one another. — Letter, II, 310.

On what principle of justice did Xerxes invade Greece? He acted according to the law of nature: not according to that artificial law, which we frame and fashion, taking the best and strongest among ourselves, and taming them like young lions, saying to them, that with equality they must be content, and that this is the honorable and the just. But if there were a man of sufficient force, he would shake off and break through; he would trample under foot all our formulas and spells and charms, and all our unnatural laws: the slave would rise in rebellion and be the master over us, and the light of natural justice would shine forth. — Gorgias, 484.

Lawful. Surely nothing that is decorously and lawfully done can justly be censured. — Symposium, 182.

Lawgiver. The duty of the lawgiver is to give the citizens punishments and rewards as well as blame and praise. Laws, I, 631.

Lawlessness. When modes of music change, the fundamental laws of the state always change with them. Our guardians, then, must lay the foundations of their fortress in music. The lawlessness too easily steals in, in the form of amusement; and at first sight it appears harmless. There is no harm; were it not that little by little this spirit of lawlessness, finding a home, imperceptibly penetrates into manners and customs; whence, issuing with greater force, it invades contracts between man and man, and from contracts goes on to laws and constitutions, in utter recklessness, ending at last by an overthrow of all rights, private as well as public. — Republic, IV, 424.

Lawlessness — the soil in which all evil is rooted, flourishing and then producing fruits bitter for those who sowed them. — Letter, VII, 336.

Laws, Aim of. The aim of all the laws would be the reverse of war. — Laws, I, 628.

Lawsuit. Men who are always at law with one another, and among whom there are many wrongs done, can never be friends to one another, but only those among whom crimes and lawsuits are few and slight. — Laws, V, 743.

Lawyer. When the philosopher draws the lawyer into upper air and gets him out of his pleas and rejoinders into the contemplation of justice and injustice in their own nature; or from the commonplaces about the happiness of kings to the consideration of government, and of human happiness and misery in general — when that narrow, keen, little legal mind is called to account about all this, he gives the philosopher his revenge; for dizzied by the height at which he is hanging, he is laughed at by every man who has not been brought up as a slave. Such are the two characters: the one of the philosopher, who is trained in liberty and leisure, and may be excused for appearing foolish when he has to perform some menial task; the other of the man who is able to do every kind of service smartly and neatly, but knows not how to wear his cloak like a gentleman. — Theaetetus, 175. *Vide* Profession.

Leader. When men are at war the leader ought to be a brave man. — Laws, I, 640.

There will be discovered to be some natures who ought to study philosophy and to be leaders in the state; and others who are not born to be philosophers, and are meant to be followers rather than leaders. — Republic, V, 474.

In war and in peace one should look to and follow his leader, and in the least things be under his guidance; for example, one should stand or move, or exercise, or wash, or take his meals, or get up in the night to keep guard and deliver massages when he is bidden; and in the hour of danger one should not pursue and not retreat except by order of one's superior. — Laws, XII, 942.

Learning. Is not this to begin with the delicate wine jar in learning the potter's art — which is a foolish thing? — Gorgias, 514.

Don't be a fool and learn by experience. — Symposium, 222.

I am not ashamed to learn, and I ask and inquire, and am very grateful to those who answer me, and never fail to give them my grateful thanks; I never deny my teacher, or pretend that the lesson is a discovery of my own; but I praise his wisdom, and proclaim what I have learned from him. — Lesser Hippias, 372.

He breaks the large vessel in learning to make pots. — Laches, 187.

I should say that learning has a certain accompanying charm which is the pleasure. — Laws, II, 667.

The pleasures of learning are unmixed with pain, and are not the pleasures of the many but of the few. — Philebus, 52.

The philosopher has pleasure in learning; for no one will love that which gives him pain, and in which after much toil he makes little progress. — Republic, VI, 486.

Learned men have a natural authority. — Epinomis, 989.

Legend. Do you believe that there is any truth in ancient legends? — Laws, III, 676.

Legislation. Legislation is entirely a work of human art, based on assumptions which are of spiritual, and not of physical, nature. — Laws, X, 889.

They believe that the state should be as great and as rich as possible, and should possess gold and silver, and have the greatest empire by sea and land; this they imagine to be the true object of legislation, at the same time adding, inconsistently [though fortunately] that the true legislator desires to have the city the best and happiest possible. — Laws, V, 742.

There are things about which it is terrible and unpleasant to legislate, but impossible not to legislate. — Laws, IX, 872.

Legislation was never yet rightly worked out. That was not a bad simile in which I likened the men for whom laws are made to slaves who are doctored by slaves. — Laws, IX, 857.

There can be no doubt that legislation is in a manner the business of a king, and yet the best thing of all is not that the law should rule, but that a man should rule, supposing him to have wisdom and royal power. — Statesman, 294.

There is a sense of disgrace in legislating for crime in a state which will be perfectly adapted to the practice of virtue. — Laws, IX, 853.

Many persons say that legislators ought to impose such laws as the mass of the people will be ready to receive; but this is just as if one were to command gymnastic masters or physicians to treat or cure their pupils or patients in an agreeable manner. — Laws, III, 684.

We are only men who are legislating for the sons of men. — Laws, IX, 853.

Our legislation seems to fall into a difficulty by reason of the vices of mankind. — Laws, VIII, 840.

Legislator. The legislator ought to do a complete, and not half a job; he ought not to let the female sex live softly and waste money and have a luxurious life, while he prescribes a rigorous life for the male sex. — Laws, VII, 806.

The ancient legislators were too good-natured, and made laws without sufficient observation or consideration of human things. — Laws, XI, 922.

Should not the legislator infuse the spirit of persuasion into his words, in order to mitigate the severity of them as far as he can? — Laws, X, 890.

The legislator is of all skilled artisans in the world the rarest. — Cratylus, 389.

A legislator who discourses about laws, gives the citizens education rather than laws. — Laws, IX, 857.

Do not be angry with the legislators. For they are spectacularly trying their hand at reformation, fancying that by legislation they will make an end of the dishonesties and rascalities of men, not knowing that they are in reality only cutting off the head of a hydra. — Republic, IV, 426.

The legislator must give, not two rules about the same thing, but only one. — Laws, IV, 719.

Legislators never appear to have considered that whereas they have two instruments which they might use in legislation, persuasion and force, insofar as a rude and uneducated multitude are capable of being affected by them, they use one only; for they do not combine persuasion with their power, but employ force pure and simple. — Laws, IV, 722.

The legislator should again and again ask himself the simple questions, What is my intention? Do I attain my aim, or do I miss the mark? In this way, and this way only, he may acquit himself and free others from the work of legislation. — Laws, V, 744.

The legislator should always observe the moral principle. — Laws, VIII, 836.

Is our legislator to have no preamble to his laws, but to say curtly — Do this, avoid that, and then threatening with the penalty, to go on to another law; offering never a word of advice or exhortation to those whom he is legislating, after the manner of some doctors? We may entreat the legislator as children might the doctor, to cure our disorders with the gentlest remedies. — Laws, 719, 720.

The legislator ought to be a better judge than all the poets put together. — Laws, XII, 941.

When legislators profess that they are gentle and not stern, we think that they should first of all use persuasion to us. — Laws, X, 885.

Leisure. The difference between slaves and freemen is to be seen in the leisure, which a freeman can always command; he has his talk out in peace, and wanders at will from one subject to another, and from a second to a third, if his fancy prefers a new one, caring not whether his words are many or few; his only aim is to attain the truth. But the lawyer is always in a hurry; there is the water of the clepsydra driving him on, and not allowing him to expatiate at will; and there is his adversary standing over him, enforcing his rights; the affidavit, which in their phraseology is termed the brief, is recited; and from this he must not deviate. — Theaetetus, 172.

Length. The Lacedaemonians would generally prefer the shorter form; although, for my own part, I should certainly decide in favor of the longer; and I would have every law made after the same pattern, if I had to choose. — Laws, IV, 721, 722.

Leontius. The story is that Leontius was coming up from the Piraeus, and observed some dead bodies lying on the ground by the executioner. He felt a desire to see them, and also a disgust and abhorrence of them; for a time he turned away and averted his eyes, and then, suddenly overcome by the impulse, forced them open, and ran up, saying, to his eyes, Take your fill, ye wretches, of the fair sight. — Republic, IV, 439, 440.

Letters of the Alphabet. Some god or divine man, who, as the Egyptians say, was Theuth . . . gave to each and all of them [vowels, semivowels, and mutes] the name of "letters." — Philebus, 18.

Liar. There have been plenty of liars in all ages. — Cratylus, 429.

Liberality. The noble liberality of your nature makes you give many and diverse things, when I am asking for one simple thing. — Theaetetus, 146.

Liberty. Please to remark (for it is hard to believe) that, after a sort, the same evil result happened to us which happened to the Persians; as they led their people into utter servitude, so we, on the other hand, led ours into licentious liberty. — Laws, III, 699.

I would admonish those who want to establish free institutions and to shake off the yoke of servitude, not to become, by desiring excessive liberty, victims of the plague which visited their ancestors who went to extremes in their opposition to authority, not acknowledging reasonable limits of freedom. — Letter, VIII, 354.

Dion believed in liberty for the Syracusans, guided by an order of the best laws. — Letter, VII, 324.

He is dragged into a perfectly lawless life, which by his seducers is termed perfect liberty. — Republic, IX, 572.

We remarked that the Persians grew worse and worse. And we affirm the reason of this deterioration to have been, that they too much restricted the liberty of the people, and introduced too much of despotism, and so destroyed friendship and community of feeling. — Laws, III, 697.

Licentiousness. In a city of the blessed, licentiousness is an unholy thing which the rulers will forbid. — Republic, V, 458.

Lie. How may we devise one of those opportune lies — just one noble lie? — Republic, III, 414.

The lawgiver, who is worth his salt, if he ever ventures to tell a lie to the young for their good, could not invent a more useful lie than the identification of the just with the pleasant; for this fiction entices them to act rightly. — Laws, II, 663.

The fault of telling a lie, especially a bad one, is most serious. — Republic, II, 377.

The true lie is hated not only by the gods, but also by men. Whereas the white lie is in certain cases useful and not hateful; in dealing with enemies — that would be an instance; or again, when those whom we call our friends in a fit of madness or illusion are going to do some harm, then it is useful and is a sort of medicine or preventive. — Republic, II, 382.

No motive can be imagined why God should lie. — Republic, II, 382.

The lying poet has no place in God. — Republic, II, 382.

Life. "Who knows if life be not death and death life?" (Euripides). I have heard a wise man say that at this very moment we live, we are dead, and that the body is a tomb. — Gorgias, 492, 493.

He who is truly a man ought not to care about living a certain time: he knows that none can escape the day of destiny, and therefore he is not fond of life at any price; he leaves all that with God, and considers in what way he can best spend his appointed term. — Gorgias, 512.

Not some but all men would surely prefer a life combined of pleasure and wisdom to a life of either of them. — Philebus, 22.

When we see soul in anything — must we not admit that this is life? — Laws, X, 895.

Your words may remind us that life is a strange affair. — Gorgias, 493.

The mere preservation and continuance of life is not the most honorable thing for men, as the vulgar think, but the continuance of the best life, while we live. — Laws, IV, 707.

Light. Noble is the bond which links together sight and visibility, and great beyond other bonds by no small difference of nature; for light is their bond, and light is no ignoble thing. — Republic, VI, 507.

Likeness. One division is the art of likeness-making; generally a likeness is made by producing a copy which is executed according to the proportions of the original, similar in length and breadth and depth, and also having colors answering to the several parts. — Sophist, 235.

The portrait which has not the shadow of a likeness to the truth, is certainly very blamable. — Republic, II, 377. *Vide* Abstract Art.

Limping. The philosophical aspirant must not limp in his industry. I mean, that he should not be half industrious and half idle: as, for example, when a man is a lover of gymnastic and hunting, but is not fond of learning or of inquiry. And a man may limp in the reverse way. — Republic, VII, 535.

Lisping. When I see a little child, who is not of an age to speak plainly, lisping at his play, that pleases me; there is an appearance of grace and freedom in his utterance, which is natural to his childish years. — Gorgias, 485.

Litigant. There is a stage of the evil in which a man is not only a life-long litigant, passing his days always in the courts either as plaintiff or defendant, but is led by his bad taste to pride himself on this; he is ready to fancy that he is a master in cunning, not knowing that it is far higher and nobler so to order his life as to be able to do without a nodding judge. — Republic, III, 405.

The litigant shall teach and learn what is just quietly, avoiding words of ill omen, or if he utter them, he shall be supposed to speak beside the point, and the judges shall again bring him back to the question at issue. — Laws, XII, 949.

Little Thing. Remember that in any case that little thing turns out to be a source of innumerable woes. — Letter, VIII, 353.

Living. Everything living is born of the dead. — Phaedo, 77. *Vide* Metempsychosis.

You will live, but how? — as a flatterer of all men, and the servant of all men. — Crito, 54.

What is the right way of living? Are we to live always for the sake of fun? If so, in what kind of fun? We ought to pass our lives sacrificing, and singing, and dancing; and then a man will be able to gain heaven's grace, and to defend himself against his enemies. — Laws, VII, 803.

The living, whether things or persons, are generated from the dead. — Phaedo, 71.

Logic. There must be a science which is wholly a science of itself. — Charmides, 167.

We are assuming a general science which having no particular subject matter, is a science of itself. — Charmides, 168.

Logic will not be able to distinguish the physician who knows from one who does not know but pretends or thinks that he knows, or any other professor of anything at all. — Charmides, 171.

I am a great lover of these logical processes of division and generalization; they help me to speak and think. — Phaedrus, 266.

I am afraid that I am very clumsy at these logical processes of division and enumeration. — Philebus, 23.

We should praise or blame the brevity or length of discussions, not by comparing them with one another, but according to a standard of logical suitability. — Statesman, 286.

Logician. I can only suppose that you are a very wise man, who comes to us in the character of a great logician, and who knows when to answer and when not to answer. — Euthydemus, 287.

Loneliness. The loneliness of the primitive men creates in them a feeling of affection and friendship towards one another. — Laws, III, 678.

Longing. In companionship there must be some degree of unfulfilled longing, in order to cement and bind together diversities of character. — Laws, VI, 776.

Loquacity. I should say that the habit which leads a man to neglect his own affairs for the pleasure of conversation, of which the style is far from being equally agreeable to the majority of the hearers, may be fairly termed loquacity. — Sophist, 225.

Lot, the. We are sometimes obliged to use the equality of the lot in order to avoid the discontent of the people. And we invoke god and fortune in our prayers, and beg that they themselves would direct the lot with a view to supreme justice. — Laws, VI, 757.

Love. The person in want is the friend of the person who has abundance, though they are of different sex; and when such friendship becomes intense, we term it love. — Laws, VIII, 837.

Would you say that there is a love which is not the love of beauty, but of itself and of other loves? — Charmides, 167.

Will any others love us, in so far as we are useless to them? — Lysis, 210.

Like the stork, my love will be cherished in turn by the winged love which I have hatched. — First Alcibiades, 135.

Love is always poor, though anything but tender and fair, as the many imagine him; for he is hard-featured and squalid, and has no shoes, nor a house to dwell in; in the bare earth exposed he lies under the open sky, in the streets, or at the doors of houses, taking his rest; and like his mother he is always in distress. — Symposium, 203.

The one is a lover of the body, and hungers after beauty, like some fruit of autumn, and would feign satisfy himself without any regard to the character of the beloved; the other holds the desire of the body to be a secondary matter, and looking rather than loving with his soul, and desiring the soul of the other in a becoming manner, regards the satisfaction of the bodily love as wantonness; he reverences and respects temperance and courage and magnanimity and wisdom, and wishes to live chastely with the chaste object of his affection. — Laws, VIII, 837.

At the touch of love everyone becomes a poet, even though he had no music in him before; this also is a proof that Love is a good poet and accomplished in all the musical arts; for no one can give to another that which he has not himself, or teach that of which he has no knowledge. —Symposium, 196.

As to courage, even the God of War is no match for Love; he is the captive and Love is the lord, for love, the love of Aphrodite, masters him; and the master is stronger than the servant. — Symposium, 196.

Love is a madness. — Phaedrus, 265.

Let us adduce a proof of the tenderness of Love; for he walks not upon the earth, nor yet upon the skulls of men, which are hard enough, but in the hearts and souls of men: in them he walks and dwells and has his home. Not in every soul without exception, for where there is hardness he departs, where there is softness there he dwells; and clinging always with his feet and in all manner of ways in the softest of all soft places, how can he be other than the softest of all things? — Symposium, 195.

Love is the youngest as well as the tenderest of all things, and also he is of flexible form; for without flexure he could not unfold all things, or wind his way into and out of every soul of man without being discovered, if he were hard. And a proof of his flexibility and symmetry of form is his grace, which is universally admitted to be in an especial manner the attribute of Love; ungrace and love are always at war with one another. The fairness of his complexion is revealed by his habitation among the flowers; for he dwells not amid unflowering or fading beauties, whether of body or soul or aught else, but in the place of flowers and scents, there he dwells and abides. — Symposium, 196.

Open loves are held to be more honorable than secret ones. — Symposium, 182.

The love of the noblest and highest, even if their persons are less beautiful than others, is especially honorable. — Symposium, 182.

Love ought to be for the advantage of both parties and for the injury of neither. — Phaedrus, 234.

Aristophanes had a mind to praise Love in another way. Mankind, he said, judging by their neglect of him, have never at all understood the power of Love. — Symposium, 189.

I maintain that Love is the youngest of the gods, and youthful ever. The ancient things of which Hesiod and Parmenides speak, if they were done at all, where done of necessity and not of love; had love been in those days, there would have been no chaining or mutilation of the gods, or other violence, but peace and sweetness, as there is now in heaven, since the rule of Love began. — Symposium, 195.

Love's greatest glory is that he can neither do to nor suffer wrong from any god or any man; for he suffers not by force if he suffers, for force comes not near him, neither does he act by force. For all serve him of their own free will, and where there is love as well as obedience, there is justice. — Symposium, 196.

Pausanias observed that the proposal of Phaedrus was too indiscriminate, and that Love ought not to be praised in this unqualified manner. If there were only one Love, then what he said would be well enough; but since there are two Loves, he should have begun by determining which of them was to be the theme of our praises. We all know that Love is inseparable from Aphrodite, and if there were only one Aphrodite there would be only one Love; but as there are two goddesses there must be two Loves. — Symposium, 180.

The arts of medicine and archery and divination were discovered by Apollo, under the guidance of love and desire; so that he is a disciple of Love. Also the melody of the Muses, the metallurgy of Hephaestus, the weaving of Athene, the empire of Zeus over gods and men, are all due to Love, who was the inventor of them. Love set in order the empire of the gods. — Symposium, 197.

Love has long since been called a tyrant. — Republic, IX, 573.

How can we take precautions against the loves of boys and girls, and of men and women, from which innumerable evils have come upon individuals and cities? How shall we devise a remedy which will be a way of escape out of so great a danger? Truly, there is a great difficulty about that. — Laws, VIII, 836.

The Love who is the son of earthly Aphrodite is essentially earthly, and has no discrimination, being such as the meaner sort of men feel, and is apt to be of women as well as of youths, and is of the body rather than of the soul — the most foolish beings are the objects of this love which desires only to gain an end, but never thinks of accomplishing the end nobly, and therefore does good and evil quite indiscriminately. — Symposium, 181.

Diotima said to me, "What is the reason of love? See you not how all animals, birds as well as beasts, in their desire of procreation, are in agony of union, to which is added the care of offspring, on behalf of whom the weakest are ready to battle against the strongest even to the uttermost, and to die for them, and will let themselves be tormented with hunger or suffer anything in order to maintain their offspring. Man may be supposed to do this from reason. But why should animals have these passionate feelings? . . . Marvel not at this, if you believe that love is of the immortal. Here again the mortal nature is seeking as far as is possible to be everlasting and immortal: and this is only to be attained by generation, because the new is always left in the place of the old."—Symposium, 207.

Must not a man love that which he desires and likes? — Lysis, 221.

You have not the power to resist the words and ideas of your beloved. — Gorgias, 481.

So ancient is the desire of one another which is implanted in us, reuniting our original nature [which was male and female in one], making one of two, and healing the state of man. Each of us when separated is but the indenture of a man, having one side only like a flat fish, and he is always looking for his other half. — Symposium, 191.

Now that he is under the tyranny of love, he becomes always and in waking reality what he was then very rarely and in a dream only. — Republic, IX, 574.

Lover. "Lover of wisdom" and "lover of knowledge" are titles which are rightly applicable to the searching soul. — Republic, IX, 581.

There are cases in which a lover loves, and is not loved, or is perhaps hated; and a man may be the enemy of one who is not his enemy, and is even his friend. — Lysis, 213.

No lover likes to speak with one who has no feeling of love in him. — First Alcibiades, 104.

He who loves your soul is the true lover. — First Alcibiades, 131.

Lovers lavish gifts on those whom they hunt. — Sophist, 222.

The non-lover has all the advantages in which the lover is charged with being deficient. — Phaedrus, 241.

The wise lover does not praise his beloved until he has won him, because he is afraid of accidents. — Lysis, 206.

Lovers sometimes imagine that they are hated by the beloved. — Lysis, 212.

To a lover who is not in his right senses that is agreeable which is not opposed to him; and that which is equal or superior is hateful to him. The lover will, therefore, not brook any superiority or equality on the part of his beloved; he is always employed in reducing him to inferiority. — Phaedrus, 238, 239.

The lover will contrive that the beloved shall be wholly ignorant, and in everything dependent on him; the beloved is to be the delight of his lover's heart, and a curse to himself. — Phaedrus, 239.

The lover may pray, and entreat, and supplicate, and swear, and be a servant of servants, and lie on a mat at the door; in any other case friends and enemies would be equally ready to prevent him, but now there is no friend who will be ashamed of him and admonish him, and no enemy will charge him with meanness or flattery; the actions of a lover have a grace which ennobles them; and custom has decided that they are highly commendable and that there is no loss of character in them; and, what is yet more strange, he only may swear and forswear himself, and the gods will forgive his transgression, for there is no such things as a lover's oath. Such is the entire liberty which gods and men allow the lover. — Symposium, 183.

Great is the encouragement which all the world gives to the lover; neither is he supposed to be doing anything dishonorable; but if he succeeds he is praised, and if he fail he is blamed. And in the pursuit of his love the custom of mankind allows him to do many strange things, which morality would bitterly censure if they were done from any motive of interest, or wish for office or power. — Symposium, 182, 183.

The coarser sort of lovers ought to be restrained by force. — Symposium, 182.

Evil is the vulgar lover who loves the body rather than the soul, and who is unstable because he is a lover of the fleeting; and therefore when the bloom of youth which he was desiring is faded, he takes wings and flies away, in spite of all his promises and vows; whereas the love of the noble mind, which is in union with the everlasting, is life-long. — Symposium, 183.

Lovers repent of the kindness which they have shown, when their love is over. — Phaedrus, 264.

Everyone selects the object of his affections according to his character, and this he makes his god, and fashions and adorns as a sort of image which he is to fall down and worship. The followers of Zeus desire that their beloved should have a soul like him; and, therefore, they seek some philosophical and imperial nature, and when they have found him and loved him, they do all they can to create such a nature in him. — Phaedrus, 252.

Loyalty. Loyalty is the greatest virtue in the hour of danger. — Laws, I, 630.

He who is loyal in a civil broil is worth his weight in gold and silver. — Laws, I, 630.

Lunacy. The lunacy of a man is often not observable, except to those who live with him. — Laws, XI, 929.

Lung. When the lung, which is to the body the steward of the air, is obstructed by rheums and has the passage stopped up, having no egress in one part, while in another part too much air enters in, then the parts which are unrefreshed by the air corrode, while in other parts the excess of wind forcing its way through the veins distorts them and consumes the body at the center, and is there shut in and holds fast the midriff; thus numberless painful diseases are produced, accompanied by copious sweats. — Timaeus, 84.

Lust. The greatest and sharpest want and desire breaks out last, and is the fire of sexual lust, which kindles in men every species of wantonness and madness. — Laws, VI, 783.

Luxury. Some say that luxury and intemperance and license, if they are duly supported, are happiness and virtue; all the rest is mere bauble, custom contrary to nature, fond inventions of men nothing worth. — Gorgias, 492. *Vide* Happy; Many.

Luxury makes the disposition of youth morose and irascible and vehemently excited by trifles. — Laws, VII, 791.

Especially the young men are habituated to lead a life of luxury and idleness both of body and mind; they do nothing, and are incapable of resisting either pleasure or pain. — Republic, VIII, 556.

Luxury and softness are blamed, because they relax and weaken man, making him a coward.—Republic, IX, 590.

If you were founding a city of pigs, how would you feed the beasts? — But what would you have? — Why, you should give them the conveniences of life. People who are comfortable are accustomed to lie on sofas, and dine off tables, and they should have dainties and desserts in the modern fashion. — Now I understand: the question which you would have me consider is, not only how a state, but how a luxurious state is to be created. And possibly there is no harm in this, for in such a state we shall be more likely to see how justice and injustice grow up. — Republic, II, 372.

In my opinion the healthy constitution of the state is the one which I have described. But if you wish also to see a luxurious state at fever heat, I have no objection. For I suspect that many will not be satisfied with the simpler way of life. They will be for adding sofas, and tables, and other furniture; also dainties, and perfumes, and incense, and courtesans, and cakes, all these not of one sort only, but in every variety; we must go beyond the necessaries of which I was at first speaking, such as houses, and clothes, and shoes: the arts of the painter and the embroiderer will have to be set in motion, and gold and ivory and all sorts of materials must be produced. — Republic, II, 372, 373.

Scythians and Thracians, both men and women, drink unmixed wine, which they also pour on their garments, and this they think a happy and glorious institution. The Persians, again, are much given to other luxuries, but they have more moderation in them than the Thracians and Scythians. — Laws, I, 637.

No man under the sun, even brought up in self-indulgence, can mature to a wise and temperate age, if facing a life which accustomed to Italian and Syracusan banquets consists in filling oneself up twice a day, never sleeping alone at night, and indulging in luxurious habits. — Letter VII, 326.

Lycurgus. The good order of Lacedaemon is due to Lycurgus. — Republic, X, 599.

I think that we degrade, not Lycurgus, but ourselves, if we imagine that he laid down laws mainly with a view to war. — Laws, I, 630.

Lyric Poet. They introduce the young discipline to the poems of other excellent poets, who are the lyric poets. — Protagoras, 326.

M

Madness. There are two kinds of madness; one produced by human infirmity, the other by a divine release from the ordinary ways of men. — Phaedrus, 265.

There is a kind of madness, which is a possession of the Muses; this enters into a delicate and virgin soul, and there inspiring frenzy, awakens lyric and other poetry. — Phaedrus, 245.

If the ancient inventors of names had thought madness a disgrace or dishonor, they would never have called prophecy, which is the noblest of arts, by the very same name as madness, thus inseparably connecting them; but they must have thought that there was an inspired madness which was no disgrace. — Phaedrus, 244.

That might have been truly said if madness were simply an evil; but there is also a madness which is a special gift of heaven, and the source of the chiefest blessings among men. For prophecy is a madness, and the prophetess at Delphi and the priestess of Dodona, when out of their senses have conferred great benefits on Greece, but when in their senses few or none. — Phaedrus, 244.

Some sorts of madness originate in evil and passionate nervousness, and are increased by education; out of a slight quarrel this class of madmen will often raise a storm of abuse against others, and nothing of that kind ought to be allowed to exist in a well-ordered state. — Laws, XI, 934.

The divine madness is subdivided into four kinds, prophetic, initiatory, poetic, erotic, having four gods presiding over them; the first is the inspiration of Apollo, the second that of Dionysus, the third that of the Muses, the fourth that of Aphrodite or Eros. — Phaedrus, 265.

No mad or senseless person can be a friend of God. — Republic, II, 382.

Excessive pains and pleasures are justly to be regarded as the greatest illnesses of the soul, for a man who is in great pain, in his irrational eagerness to attain the one and to avoid the other, is not truly able to see or to hear anything; but he is mad, and is at the same time quite incapable of any participation in reason. — Timaeus, 86.

A man who is deranged and not right in his mind, will fancy that he is able to rule, not only over men, but also over the gods. — Republic, IX, 573.

Magician. Gods are not magicians who transform themselves. — Republic, II, 383.

Magnet. The magnet not only attracts iron rings, but also imparts to them a similar power of attracting other rings; and sometimes you may see a number of pieces of iron and rings suspended from one another so as to form quite a long chain: and all of them derive their power of suspension from the original magnet. Now this is like the Muse, who first gives to men inspiration herself: and from these inspired persons a chain of other persons is suspended, who take the inspiration from them. — Ion, 533.

Magnitude. Do not the same magnitudes appear larger to your sight when near, and smaller when at distance? — Protagoras, 356.

Suppose we differ about magnitude, do we not quickly put an end to that difference by measuring? — Euthyphro, 7.

Maintaining. Maintain the traits you already maintain. — Letter X, 358.

Majority Opinion. What, are you for going by the opinion of the majority? — Yes; what other way is there? — If you were deliberating about the gymnastic training of your son, would you follow the advice of the majority of us, or the opinion of a skillful master? His one vote would be worth more than the vote of all us four. — Certainly. — Laches, 184.

Making. He distinguished making from doing and working: making anything might sometimes become a disgrace, but work is never any disgrace. — Charmides, 163.

Malice. Is not malice an unrighteous pleasure, and also a pain? — Philebus, 49.

Man. All things which have life are animals, but there is a special kind of animal which we call "man". — Eryxias, 401.

Man, having a share of the spiritual attributes, is the only of the animals who has any gods, because he alone is of their kindred; and he raises altars and images of them. He is not long in inventing language and names; and he also constructed houses and clothes and shoes and beds, and drew sustenance from the earth. — Protagoras, 322.

Nothing is more uncommon than a very large or very small man. — Phaedo, 90.

Every man is pleased when he is spoken to in his own language and spirit. — Gorgias, 513 .

Man is a changeable, though no mean, animal. — Letter XIII, 360.

The case of non-human animals is not so important; they are only worth mentioning for the sake of illustration, but what relates to man is of the highest importance. — Laws, V, 735.

There can be no doubt that man is a troublesome animal, and therefore is not, and is not likely to become, very manageable. — Laws, VI, 777.

And one of these portions of the universe is thine own, stubborn man, which, however little, has the whole in view. — Laws, X, 903.

Every man thinks himself wiser than other men in some things, and their inferior in others. — Theaetetus, 170.

I am a man, and like other men, a creature of flesh and blood, and not of wood and stone. — Apology, 34.

The manner in which the best men are treated in their own state is so grievous that no single thing on earth is comparable to it. — Republic, VI, 488.

Will you do me the favor of saying whether man is an animal? — Certainly he is. — Gorgias, 516.

Man is one of the three things — soul, body, or the union of the two. — First Alcibiades, 130.

Man is superior to all other animals in understanding, and alone has justice and religion. — Menexenus, 237.

We may assume that there are three classes of men — lovers of wisdom, lovers of ambition, lovers of gain. — Republic, IX, 581.

Making this world, the Deity framed one visible animal comprehending within all other animals of a kindred nature. — Timaeus, 30, 31.

Man of Understanding. The man of understanding will look at the city which is within him, and take heed that no disorder occur in it, such as might arise either from superfluity or from want. In the city which is his own he certainly will be a statesman, though in the land of his birth perhaps not. He will be a ruler in the city which exists in idea only; for I do not believe that there is such an one anywhere on earth. But whether such an one exists, or ever will exist in fact, is no matter; for he will live after the manner of that ideal city, having nothing to do with any other. — Republic, IX, 592.

Management. There appears to be one management of men and another of beasts. — Statesman, 262.

Will he continue to administer his house himself, or will he commit its management to you, if he believes that you have a better idea of it? — Lysis, 209.

Mankind. I hope that you depart in peace and kindness towards us, as you are going the way of all mankind. — Laws, XI, 923.

Manners. There would be small wisdom in legislating about manners in general; we may assume that the direction in which education starts a man will determine his future life. — Republic, IV, 425.

Manure. Manure is a good thing when laid about the roots, but utterly destructive if thrown upon the shoots and young branches. — Protagoras, 334.

Many, the. Why should we trouble ourselves about the opinion of the many, who just say anything that happens to occur to them? — Protagoras, 353.

But why, my dear Crito, should we care about the opinion of the many? Good men are the only persons who are worth to be considered. — Crito, 44.

The opinion of the many must be regarded, because they can do the very greatest evil to anyone who has lost their good opinion. — I only wish, that they could; for then they could also do the greatest good, and that would be well. But the truth is, that they can do neither good nor evil: they cannot make a man wise or make him foolish. — Crito, 44.

The many can kill us. — Crito, 48.

The many enslave the nobler natures, and being unable to satisfy their pleasures, they praise temperance and justice because they are cowards. — Gorgias, 492.

There is a difficulty in speaking to the many, from a fear of their misconceiving and misunderstanding what is said. — Laws, II, 672.

Marathon. He who has presented to him that conflict, would know what manner of men they were who received the onset of the barbarians at Marathon, and by their victory first taught other men that the power of the Persians was not invincible. And I assert that those men are the fathers not only of ourselves, but of our liberties and of the liberties of all who are on the continent, for that was the battle to which the Greeks looked back when they ventured to fight for their own safety in the conflicts which followed. — Menexenus, 240.

The men of Marathon only showed the Greeks that it was possible to ward off the barbarians by land. — Menexenus, 241.

Mare. Is not a beautiful mare a beauty? — Greater Hippias, 288.

Market Place. In the market place men win distinction. — Gorgias, 485.

Marriage. They would advise you neither to avoid a poor marriage, nor specially to desire a rich one. . . . And he who is conscious of being too headstrong, ought to decide to become the relation of orderly parents; and he who is of the opposite temper ought to seek the opposite alliance. . . . Every man shall follow, not after the marriage which is most pleasing to himself, but after that which is most beneficial to the state. — Laws, VI, 773.

Many persons form marriages of an improper kind, with a view to the procreation of children. — Statesman, 310.

He who marries is to consider, that one of the two houses in the lot is the nest and nursery of his chicks, and there he is to marry and make the home of himself and his children, going away from his father and mother. — Laws, VI, 776.

There are cases in which the blood relations of the diseased man refuse to obey, and are ready to do anything rather than marry the kinswoman, when there is some bodily or mental sickness or defect in the party whom they are bidden to marry. — Laws, XI, 925.

Marrow. The worst of all is when the marrow is diseased, either from excess or defect. — Timaeus, 84.

Material, Parable of. The warp and the woof cannot be made of the same materials, but the warp is necessarily superior as being stronger, and having a certain character of firmness, whereas the woof is softer and has a proper degree of elasticity. — Laws, V, 735.

Materialist. Either the materialist shall teach us that we are wrong in saying that the spirit exists; or, if he be not able to say anything better, then he must yield to us and live for the remainder of his life in the belief that there are moral ideas. — Laws, X, 899.

The real aborigines, children of the dragon's teeth, are deterred by no shame at all, but obstinately assert that nothing has any existence which they are not able to hold in their hands. — Ibid., 246.

By the uninitiated I mean the materialists who believe in nothing but what they can hold fast in their hands, and who will not allow that invisible moral ideas have any existence. They are very stubborn and repulsive mortals, yes, outer barbarians. — Theaetetus, 155, 156.

Maternity. For the women of the guardians, maternity will be an easy job. — Well, it ought to be. — Republic, V, 460.

Mathematician. You surely would not regard the skilled mathematician as a dialectician? — Assuredly not; I have hardly ever known a mathematician who was capable of philosophizing. — Republic, VII, 531.

Mathematics. Mathematics stirs up him who is by nature dull, and makes him quick to learn, retentive, shrewd, and, aided by art divine, he makes progress quite beyond his natural powers. — Laws, V, 747.

Matter. Philosophy shows the soul that [matter] is visible and tangible, but that what she sees in her own intangible nature is intellectual and invisible. — Phaedo, 83.

Maturity. No creature is born having that degree or kind of intelligence which he is destined to have in maturity; and in the intermediate period, in which he has not yet acquired his own proper sense, he rages and roars without rhyme or reason; and when he has once got on his legs he jumps about without rhyme or reason. — Laws, II, 672.

Mean, the. Let man know how to choose the mean and avoid the extremes on either side, as far as possible, not only in this life but in all that which is to come. For this is the way of happiness. — Republic, X, 619.

The true life should neither seek for forbidden pleasures, nor, on the other hand, entirely avoid pains, but should embrace the middle state, which is gracious and propitious. — Laws, VII, 792.

Meanness. I hardly like to talk of the little meannesses, for they are beneath mention. — Republic, V, 465.

Meaning. Whether the syllables of a name are the same or not the same, that makes no difference, provided the meaning is retained. — Cratylus, 393.

The etymologist is not put out by the addition or transposition or subtraction of a letter or two, or indeed of all the letters, for this need not interfere with the meaning. — Cratylus, 394.

Even a very slight permutation of the letters of a word will sometimes give an entirely opposite meaning. — Cratylus, 418.

We see the figure and color of certain alphabetical letters, and we hear the elevation or depression of the sound of them when spoken: but we do not comprehend by sight and hearing their meaning. — Theaetetus, 164.

Can we imagine spiritual being to be devoid of meaning, and to remain in awful unmeaningness an everlasting fixture? — That would be a terrible admission. — Sophist, 249.

I shouldn't wonder if he who said this had no notion of his own meaning. — Charmides, 162.

Don't elaborate on my words, but understand their meaning. — Theaetetus, 166.

Shall we say that spiritual being has meaning without having physical life? How can that be? — Sophist, 249.

I have no objection to your giving names any signification that you please, if you will only tell me the intended meaning. — Charmides, 163.

Means. Some things are for the sake of something else. — Philebus, 53.

Do men appear to you to will always that which they do, or do they not often will only a further objective, for the sake of which they do that which they do; for example, when patients take medicine at the bidding of a physician, do they will the drinking of the unpleasant medicine, or the health for the sake of which they drink? — Gorgias, 467.

Measure. Measure and symmetry are everywhere reckoned as beauty and virtue. — Philebus, 64.

Want of measure and proportion in any mixture must always of necessity be fatal. — Philebus, 64.

Suppose the salvation of human life to depend on the choice of odd and even, and on the knowledge of when men ought to choose the greater or less — what would be the saving principle of our lives? Surely knowledge — knowledge of measuring, when the question is one of excess and defect, and arithmetic, when the question is of odd and even. — Protagoras, 356, 357.

Measurement. The points that I mean are length and shortness, excess and defect, with all of which the art of measurement is conversant. — Statesman, 283.

Mechanical. Why is "mechanical" a term of reproach? Because it implies a weakness of the selective principle. — Republic, IX, 590.

Medicine. Before the time of Herodicus, the guild of Asclepius did not practice our present system of medicine, which may be said to educate diseases. But Herodicus, being a trainer, and himself of a sickly constitution, by a happy combination of training and doctoring, found out a way of torturing, first and principally himself, and secondly the rest of the world — by the invention of lingering death; for he had an incurable disease which he perpetually tended; he was in constant torment whenever he departed in anything from his usual regimen, and so dying hard, by the help of science he struggled on to old age. — Republic, III, 406.

When patients do not require medicines, but have only to be put under a regimen, the inferior sort of practitioner is deemed to be good enough; but when medicine has to be given, then the physician should be more of a man. — Republic, V, 459.

We ought always to manage diseases by regimen, as far as a man can spare the time, and not provoke a disagreeable enemy by medicines. — Timaeus, 89.

Medicine may be regarded generally as the knowledge of the loves and desires of the body, and how to fill or empty them. — Symposium, 186.

Medicine is a sort of ministration or service, tending to the attainment of some object. — Euthyphro, 13.

When a carpenter, for instance, is ill he asks the physician for a rough and ready remedy; an emetic or a purge or cautery or the knife, — these are his remedies. And if anyone tells him that he must go through a course of dietetics, and swathe and swaddle his head, he replies at once that he has no time to be ill, and that he sees no good in a life which is spent in nursing his disease to the neglect of his ordinary calling; and therefore bidding farewell to this sort of physician, he resumes his customary diet, and either gets well and lives and continues his business, or, if his constitution fails, he dies and has done with it. — Republic, III, 406.

I shall not be a rash practitioner of medicine. — Charmides, 158.

To require the help of medicine, not when a wound has to be cured, or on occasion of an epidemic, but just because, by their lives of indolence and luxury, men fill themselves like pools with waters and winds, compelling the ingenious sons of Asclepius to give diseases the names of flatulence and flux — is not this a disgrace? — Yes, and those are certainly strange and new-fangled names of diseases. — Republic, III, 405.

Meletus. Meletus has a quarrel with me [Socrates] on behalf of the poets. — Apology, 23.

Melissus. Melissus and the others

say that "all is one and at rest." — Theaetetus, 183.

Melody. Sounds which are smooth and clear, and form a single pure melody, are beautiful as sounds, and not as expressions of feelings; for they cause a natural pleasure. — Philebus, 51.

Let us follow the scent like hounds, and go in pursuit of beauty of figure, and melody, and song, and dance; if these escape us, there will be no use in talking about true education, whether Greek or barbarian. — Laws, II, 654.

Memory. The lessons which we have learned as children make a wonderful impression on our memories, for I am not sure that I could remember all that I heard yesterday, but I should be much surprised if I forgot any of these things which I have heard very long ago. — Timaeus, 26.

I have a wretched memory, and when anyone makes a long speech to me I never rememeber what he is talking about. — Protagoras, 334.

Memory may be rightly described as the preservation of perception. — Philebus, 34.

You would have some difficulty to recall it. — Why? I can remember fifty names after hearing them once. — I am sorry, I almost forgot your photographic memory. — Greater Hippias, 285.

Mental Health. Let us, in the first place, be careful of admitting into our souls the notion that there is no truth or health or validity in any arguments at all; but let us rather say that we ourselves are still spiritual invalids, and that we must improve ourselves like men and do our best to gain mental health. — Phaedo, 90. *Vide* Research.

Mercenary. Many a mercenary soldier will take his stand and be ready to die at his post, and yet they are generally and almost without exception insolent, unjust, violent men, and the most senseless of human beings. — Laws, I, 630.

Merchant. The honorable merchants when they might make a great deal of money are sober in their wishes, and prefer a moderate to a large gain. But the mass of mankind are the very opposite: their desires are unbounded. — Laws, XI, 918.

May not he who takes wares of the soul about and sells them be quite as truly called a merchant as he who sells meats and drinks? — Sophist, 224.

Then there is the situation of the city — to find a place where nothing need be imported is practically impossible. But if the trader goes empty-handed, having nothing which they require who would supply his need, he will come back empty-handed. And therefore what they produce at home must be not only enough for themselves, but such both in quantity and quality as to accommodate those from whom their wants are supplied. Importers and exporters, who are called merchants, [will be needed]. Then they will need a market-place, and a money-token for purposes of exchange. — Republic, II, 370, 371.

Metempsychosis. The ancient doctrine of metempsychosis affirms that the souls go from hence into the other world, and return hither, and are born from the death. — Phaedo, 70.

Men who have chosen the portion of injustice, and tyranny, and violence, will [after their death] pass into wolves, or hawks and kites; whither else can we suppose them to go? — Phaedo, 82. *Vide* Just.

Midday. We ought always to talk and not to sleep at midday. — Phaedrus, 259.

Middle Course. All men ought to avoid the life of unmingled pain or pleasure, and pursue always a middle course. — Laws, VII, 793.

Midwife. The midwives know better than others who is pregnant and who is not. Did you ever remark that they are also most cunning matchmakers, and have an entire knowledge of what unions are likely to produce a brave brood? — Theaetetus, 149.

The midwives who are respectable women avoid the practice of matchmaking, because they are afraid of being called procuresses; and yet the true midwife is also the true and only matchmaker. — Theaetetus, 150.

No woman, as you are probably aware, who is still able to conceive and bear, is a midwife, but only those who are past bearing. . . . Artemis could not allow the barren to be midwives, because one cannot know the mystery of birth, without one's own experience; and therefore she assigned this office to those who by reason of age are past bearing. — Theaetetus, 149.

Such are the midwives, whose work is a very important one, but not so important as mine; for women do not bring into the world at one time real children, and at another time idols which are with difficulty distinguished from them; if they did, then the discernment of the true and false birth would be the crowning achievement of the art of midwifery. — Theaetetus, 150.

Midwifery. My art of midwifery is in most respects like that of midwives; but the difference lies in this, that I attend men and not women, and I practice on their souls when they are in labor, and not on their bodies; and the triumph of my art is in examining whether the thought which the mind of the young man is bringing to the birth is a false idol or a noble and true creation. And like the midwives, I am barren, and the reproach which is often made against me, that I ask questions of others and have not the wit to answer them myself, is very just; the reason is, that the god compels me to be a midwife, but forbids me to bring forth. And therefore I am not myself wise. Theaetetus, 150.

The office of a midwife I [Socrates], like my mother, have received from God; she delivered women, and I deliver men; but they must be young and noble and fair. — Theaetetus, 210.

Might. The young men are told that the highest right is might. — Laws, X, 890.

Military. Your military way of life is modeled after the camp, and is not like that of dwellers in cities; and you have your young men herding and feeding together like young colts. No one takes his own individual colt and drags him away from his fellows against his will, raging and foaming, and gives him a groom for him alone, and trains and rubs him down privately, and gives him the qualities in education which will make him not only a good soldier but also a governor of a state and of cities. — Laws, II, 666.

Let us define piracy, man-stealing, tyranny, the whole military art — one and all as a hunting by force. — Sophist, 222.

Mimicry. When anyone makes himself appear like another in his figure or in his voice, imitation is the name for this part of the fantastic art. Let this, then, be named the art of mimicry. — Sophist, 267.

Mind. Has mind a greater share of beauty than pleasure, that is, is mind or pleasure the fairer of the two? — Philebus, 65.

Mind, the ruling power, persuaded necessity to bring the greater part of created things to perfection, and thus in the beginning, when the influence of reason got the better of necessity, the universe was created. — Timaeus, 48.

Mind is not inferior to nature. — Laws, X, 890.

He who has not contemplated the mind, is not able to give a reason of such things as have reason. — Laws, XII, 968.

In going to war for mind I ought to have weapons of another make from those which I used before for pleasure. — Philebus, 23.

Are not mind and wisdom names which are to be appreciated most? — Philebus, 59.

The mind becomes informed, improved, and preserved by learning and reasoning; but an idle mind speedily forgets whatever it has learned. — Theaetetus, 153.

The mind more often faints from the severity of study than from the severity of gymnastics: the toil is more entirely the mind's own, and is not shared with the body. — Republic, VII, 535.

Of what nature is the movement of mind? That is a hard question. — Laws, X, 897.

Do you not believe with Anaxagoras, that mind or soul is the ordering and containing principle of all things? — Cratylus, 400.

After practicing minute comparisons of definitions and names and sense perceptions, after examining them in benevolent dispute by the application of question and answer, at last understanding of each blazes up suddenly, and the mind, exerting all its faculties, is flooded with light. — The mind. — Letter VII, 344.

Minding. Never mind if someone despises you as a fool, and insults you, if he has a mind; let him strike you, by Zeus, and do you be of good cheer and do not mind the insulting blow, for you will never come to any harm in the practice of virtue, if you are a really good and true man. — Gorgias, 527.

Misanthropy. Misanthropy arises from too great confidence in men; you trust a person and think him altogether true and good and faithful, and then in a little while he turns out to be false and knavish; and then another and another, and when this repeats itself several times to a man, especially within the circle of his own most trusted friends, as he deems them, and he has often been irritated by them, he at last hates all men, and believes in his disappointment that no one has any good in him at all. — Phaedo, 89.

Miscarriage. By the use of potions and incantations the midwives are able to arouse the pangs and to soothe them at will; they can make those bear who have a difficulty in bearing, and if they choose they can cause a miscarriage. — Theaetetus, 149.

Misconduct. Realize your misconduct towards us, so that you may treat other people better. — Letter I, 310.

Misdeed. A thousand misdeeds arise out of harsh and uncivil natures. — Laws, I, 649.

Miser. The miser will be an ignoble competitor in a state for any prize of victory, or other object of honorable ambition; he is too much afraid of awakening his expensive appetites and inviting them to help and join in the struggle; in true oligarchical fashion he fights with a small part only of his resources, and the result commonly is that he loses the prize and saves his money. — Republic, VIII, 555.

Miserable. Of two miserables one cannot be the happier. — Gorgias, 473.

When a man has health and wealth and lasting power, but also the injustice and insolence of his own nature — I can scarcely make you believe that such a one is miserable rather than happy. — Laws, II, 661.

Misfortune. Perturbations of the soul arise out of misfortune. — Laws, I, 632.

Misologist. The danger of becoming misologists is one of the great misfortunes than can happen to us. For as there are misanthropists or haters of men, there are also misologists or haters of moral ideas, and both spring from the same cause, which is ignorance of the world. — Phaedo, 89.

Mistake. There is a class of ignorant persons who do not make mistakes in life, because they trust others. — First Alcibiades, 117.

What a way you have! When you make a mistake which has been already detected, you want to have a new and different demonstration of the mistake. — First Alcibiades, 113.

If he did fewer things he would make fewer mistakes. — Euthydemus, 281.

Do you imagine that he who is mistaken about the sick is a physician in that he is mistaken and at the time that he is mistaken? True, we say that the arithmetician or grammarian or physician has made a mistake, but this is only a way of speaking; for the fact is that neither the grammarian nor any other person of skill ever makes a mistake insofar as he is what his name implies: they all of them err only when their skill fails them. — Republic, I, 340.

Mixed Life. Reason intimates to us that we should seek the good, not in the unmixed life, but in the mixed. There is far greater hope of finding that which we are seeking in the life which is well mixed than in that which is not. — Philebus, 61.

Model. A model or example of this process has first to be framed. — Statesman, 279.

Moderation. Moderation is the appointment of nature, and deters men from all frenzy and madness of love, and from all adulteries, and makes them good friends to their own wives. — Laws, VIII, 839.

Modesty. Modesty is not good for a needy man. — Charmides, 161.

Their modesty is so great that they are driven to contradict themselves. — Gorgias, 487.

Modesty is becoming in youth. — Charmides, 158.

The soul which is over-full of modesty and has no element of courage in many successive generations, is apt to grow very indolent, and at last to become utterly paralyzed and useless. — Statesman, 310.

The legislator terms the fear of a bad reputation modesty, and the confidence which is the reverse of this he terms impudence. — Laws, I, 647.

Moment. The moment seems to apply change from one to the other; and it does not change from a continuing state of rest, nor from a continuing state of motion, but there is a singular nature, which we call the moment, placed between rest and motion, and which is not in any time, and into this and out of this that which is in motion changes into rest, and that which is at rest into motion. — Parmenides, 156.

Monarch. Because men are offended at the one monarch, and can never be made to believe that anyone can be worthy of such authority, or can unite the will and the power in the spirit of virtue and knowledge to do justly and holily to all; they fancy that a monarch would wrong and harm and slay whom he pleases of us; for if there could be such a monarch as we describe, they would acknowledge that we ought to be too glad to have him, and that he alone would be the happy ruler of a true and perfect state. — Statesman, 301.

Monarchy. If one man of great merit exercises the rule, the state is a monarchy; if more than one, an aristocracy. — Republic, IV, 445.

Monarchy, when bound by good prescriptions or laws, is the best, and when lawless is the most bitter and oppressive to the subjects. — Statesman, 302.

Money. I give my pupils their money's worth, and even more, as they themselves admit. — Protagoras, 328.

Take care of your money. — Protagoras, 357.

Money and honor have no attraction for them. — Republic, I, 347.

Silver is useful only because it enables us to supply our bodily needs. — Eryxias, 402.

I see your indifference about money, which is a characteristic rather of those who have inherited their fortunes than of those who have acquired them; the makers of fortunes have a second love of money as a creation of their own, resembling the affection of authors for their own poems, or of parents for their children, besides that natural love of it for the sake of use and profit which is common to them and all men. And hence they are very bad company, for they can talk about nothing but the praises of wealth. — Republic, 1, 330.

Monster. I certainly should not like to leave the tale wandering all over the world without a head; a headless monster is such a hideous thing. — Laws, VI, 752.

Month. The month is created when the moon completes her orbit. — Timaeus, 39.

Moon. The moon goes its way, now waxing, now waning, as she lights up one day after another, until she has accomplished fifteen days and nights; and they constitute a period, such that the dullest creature whom God has accorded the faculty to learn, may learn it. — Epinomis, 978.

Moral Ideas. Anyone who maintains the existence of moral ideas, will admit that they cannot exist in us. . . . Moral essence has nothing to do with us, nor we with it; moral essences have to do with themselves alone, and we with ourselves. . . . Great is the difficulty of affirming self-existing moral ideas. — Parmenides, 133.

If a materialistic opponent argues that these self-existent ideas, as we term the moral ideas, cannot be known, no one can prove to him that he is wrong, unless he who is disputing their existence be a man of great genius and cultivation, and is willing to follow a long and laborious demonstration — he will remain unconvinced, and still insist that they cannot be known. — Parmenides, 133.

The moral ideas cannot be set forth except through the medium of examples. — Statesman, 277.

These are only a few of the difficulties which are involved in the hypothesis of the spiritual existence of moral ideas. He who hears of them will often doubt or deny their existence, and will maintain that even if they do exist, they must be unknown to man, and he will think that there is reason in what he says, and will be amazingly hard of being convinced. A man must be a man of intellectual ability before he can understand the particular class of spiritual essence. — Parmenides, 135.

Moral Philosophy. What is to become of moral philosophy? What resource is there, if the moral ideas are unknown? — Parmenides, 135.

Unless the moral philosopher is able to abstract and define by mere thinking the idea of good, and unless he can run the gauntlet of all objections, not by appeals to observation, but to spiritual reflection, never faltering at any step of the argument — unless he can do all this, you would say that he knows neither the idea of good nor any particular good; he apprehends only a shadow, if anything at all. — Republic, VII, 534.

Anyone who has no natural aptitude for justice and moral ideals will, though very intelligent in the research of physical subjects, not attain to an understanding of moral concepts. — Letter VII, 344.

This was the moral method which I adopted: I first assumed some moral idea which I judged to be the best, and then I affirmed as good any action which seemed to agree with it; and actions which disagreed with it I regarded as bad. — Phaedo, 100.

Moralists. Shall we be guilty of an impropriety in calling the moralists lovers of judgment rather than lovers of knowledge, and will they be very angry with us for thus describing them? On the other hand, those who love the truth are lovers of knowledge rather than lovers of judgment. — Republic, V, 480.

Morality. People will think and speak better about morality if we conduct ourselves more righteously. — Letter II, 311.

Mother of Men. This our land did prove that she was going to be the mother of men, for in those days she alone and first of all brought forth wheat and barley for man whom she regarded as her true offspring. — Menexenus, 237, 238.

Motherhood. A woman proves her motherhood by giving milk to her young ones. — Menexenus, 237.

They will bring the mothers to the fold when they are full of milk, taking the greatest care that no mother recognizes her own child; and other wet nurses may be engaged if more are required. Care will also be taken that the process of suckling shall not be protracted too long; and the mothers will have no getting up at night or other trouble, but will hand over all this sort of thing to the nurses and attendants. — Republic, V, 460.

Motion. Someone says to me: "O Stranger, are all things in rest and nothing in motion, or is the exact opposite of this true, or are some things in motion and others at rest?" To this I shall reply that some are in motion and others at rest. — Laws, X, 893.

That which is not in motion must be at rest, and again, that which is not at rest must be in motion. Yet spaceless spirit is placed outside of both these classes. Is this possible? — Sophist, 250.

Spiritual being is neither in motion nor at rest. — Sophist, 250.

To conceive that anything can be moved without a mover is hard or indeed impossible, and equally impossible to conceive that there can be a mover without something that will be moved: motion cannot exist where either of these things is wanting. — Timaeus, 57.

The proverb which prohibits moving what is better left alone is applicable to many things. — Laws, XI, 913.

Too many of our modern philosophers are, in their search after the nature of things, always going round and round and get dizzy, and then they imagine that the world is going round and round and moving in all directions. And this appearance, which is only within them and an opinion of their own, they suppose to have a real existence in the external world; they think that there is nothing stable or permanent, but only flux and motion. — Cratylus, 411.

Now that we teach that the soul imparts motion to the body, we do not distrust her ability to set any weight whatsoever in motion. As we maintain that soul is the universal cause, it is obvious that she is universally the condition of all movement. — Epinomis, 988.

Have we not heard from the ancients, who concealed their wisdom from the many in poetical figures, that Oceanus and Tethys, the origin of all things, are streams, and that nothing is at rest? And now the moderns, in their superior wisdom, have declared the same openly, that the cobbler too may hear and learn of them, and no longer foolishly imagine that some things are at rest and others in motion — having learned that all is in motion, he will duly honor his teachers. — Theaetetus, 180.

Much. Never too much. — Charmides, 165.

The ancient saying, "Never too much" is really well said. — Menexenus, 247.

Multitude. The multitude is seldom willing to meet unless they get a little honey. — Republic, VIII, 565.

Murder. There are murders of kinsmen, either perpetrated by the hands of kinsmen, or by their contrivance, and out of malice prepense, which mostly happen in ill-regulated states, but also in a country where a man would not expect to find them. — Laws, IX, 872.

They say that he did not kill him, and even if he did, the killed man was but a murderer, and I ought not to take any notice. That shows, how little they know of justice. — Euthyphro, 4.

Muscle. The muscles are elastic, and they cover the bones, which have also a covering or environment of flesh and skin which contains them. — Phaedo, 98.

Muses. The name of the Muses would seem to be derived from their making philosophical inquiries. — Cratylus, 406.

Music. Music is the counterpart of gymnastic, and trains the guardians by the influence of habit, by harmony making them harmonious, by rhythm rhythmical, but not giving them science; and the words, whether fabulous or possibly true, have kindred elements of rhythm and harmony in them. — Republic, VII, 522.

In music there first arose the universal conceit of omniscience and general lawlessness; licentious freedom came following afterwards, and men fancying that they knew what they did not know, had no longer any fear. — Laws, III, 701.

The excellence of music is to be measured by pleasure. But the pleasure must not be that of chance persons; the fairest music is that which delights the best and best educated. — Laws, II, 658.

Music is full of guesswork; as is seen in the harmonizing of sounds of an instrument, not by rule, but by conjecture; and this is especially the case in flute music, which tries to discover the pitch of notes by lucky shots for them, and therefore has very little of scientific calculation. — Philebus, 56.

If a man makes a mistake in music, he may do himself the greatest injury by welcoming evil dispositions. — Laws, II, 669.

When a man allows music to play and pour over his soul through his ears, which are the funnel, those sweet and soft and melancholy airs, and his whole life is passed in warbling and the delights of song; in the first stage of the process the passion or spirit which is in him is tempered like iron, and made useful, instead of brittle and useless. But in the next stage he begins to melt and consume, until the passion of his soul is melted out of him. — Republic, III, 411.

Musical effects evidently depend upon the numeration of tones and motions. — Epinomis, 978.

Musician. When I note the harmony and correspondence of a man and his words — such a one I deem to be the true musician. — Laches, 188.

Myself. If I know the things of my soul, I shall know myself. — First Alcibiades, 132.

Mystery. I envy you for having been initiated in the great mysteries before you were initiated into the little. — Gorgias, 497.

Mystic. Many are the thyrsus-bearers, but few are the mystics. — Phaedo, 69.

Myth. I quite acknowledge that the scientific explanation of the myths are attractive. — Phaedrus, 229.

What would you like? Shall I, as an elder, speak to you as younger men in an apologue or myth, or shall I argue the question? — I think that the myth will be more interesting. — Protagoras, 320.

Because we do not know the truth about ancient times, we make, in the fables of mythology, falsehood look like truth; and there is practical use in this. — Republic, II, 382.

N

Nail. Those who formed us well knew that women and other animals would some day be framed out of men, and they further knew that many animals would require the use of nails for many purposes; wherefore also they stamped in men at their first creation the forms of nails. They fashioned skin, hair, and nails at the extremities of the limbs. — Timaeus, 76.

Nakedness. Not long ago the Greeks were of the opinion, which is still generally held by the barbarians, that the sight of a naked man was ridiculous and improper; and when first the Cretans and then the Lacedaemonians introduced the custom, the wits of that day might equally have ridiculed the innovation. But when experience showed that to let all things uncovered was far better than to cover them up, then the man appeared to be a fool who directs the shafts of his ridicule at any other sight but that of folly and vice, or seriously inclines to weigh the beautiful by any other standard but that of good. — Republic, V, 452.

Name. I would not have him speak of the name, but of the thing which is intended by the name. — Theaetetus, 177.

How can the name of any color be rightly applied to anything, since the very whiteness is a flux or change which is passing into another color, and will not remain white? — Theaetetus, 182.

If you are not too particular about names, you will be all the richer in wisdom as you grow older. — Statesman, 261.

There is no use in disputing about a name. — Meno, 87.

Even in foreign names, if you analyze them, a meaning is still discernible. — Cratylus, 401.

We often put in and pull out letters in words, and give names as we please and change the accents. — Cratylus, 399.

The first imposers of names must surely have been considerable persons; they were philosophers. — Cratylus, 401.

To say that names which we do not understand are of foreign origin — this is very likely the true answer, and some of them may be foreign words. — Cratylus, 421.

Narrator. The worse the narrator is the more unscrupulous he will be; nothing will be beneath him: moreover he will be ready to imitate anything not as a joke, but in right good earnest, and before a large audience. He will attempt to represent the roll of thunder, the rattle of wind and hail, or the various sounds of pulleys, of pipes, of flutes, and all sorts of instruments; also he will bark like a dog, bleat like a sheep, and crow like a cock; and there will be very little narration. — Republic, III, 397.

National Characteristics. And so of the individual; we shall be right in arguing that he has the same qualities in his own soul which are found in the nation; and he may be correctly described in the same terms, because he is affected in the same manner. ... Individuals of a state have certain national characteristics and habits. There would be something ridiculous in thinking that the quality of spirit or passion, which is characteristic of the Thracians, Scythians, and in general of the northern nations, when found in states, does not originate in the individuals who compose them. And the love of knowledge is a special characteristic of our part of the world. — Republic, IV, 435.

Natural Science. When I was young, I had a prodigious desire to know that department of philosophy which is called natural science; this appeared to me to have lofty aims, as being the science which has to do with causes of things, and which teaches why a thing is, and is created and destroyed. — Phaedo, 96.

Nature. One conceives fire and water and earth and air to be the first elements of all things, and calls them nature. — Laws, X, 891.

Those who use the term "nature" mean to say that nature is the first creative power; but if the soul turns out to be the primeval element and not fire or air, then in the truest sense and beyond other things the soul may be said to have a natural or creative power: and this would be true if you proved that the soul is older than the body. — Laws, X, 892.

This is the tree. Yes, indeed, and a delightful and shady resting place, full of summer sounds and scents. There is the lofty and spreading plane tree, and the agnus castus high and clustering, in the fullest blossom and the greatest fragrance; and the stream which flows beneath the plane tree is deliciously cold to the feet. Moreover, there is a sweet breeze, and the grasshoppers chirrup; and the greatest charm of all is the grass like a pillow gently sloping to the head. — Phaedrus, 230.

Navigator. The navigator seeks the knowledge of the kindness or fury of the winds. — Epinomis, 976.

Necessity. All this seems to flow necessarily out of our previous admissions. — Phaedo, 72.

Necessity, not geometrical, but another sort of necessity which lovers know, and which is far more convincing and constraining to the mass of mankind. — Republic, V, 458.

What necessities are divine and not human? — I conceive them to be those of which he who has no knowledge at all cannot be a god, or hero to mankind. — Laws, VII, 818.

He who made the proverb "that not even God himself can fight against necessity," meant divine necessity; for as to the human necessities, nothing can be more ridiculous than such an application of the words to God. — Laws, VII, 818.

Neck. Fearing to pollute the divine soul any more than necessary, the creators gave to the mortal nature of man a separate habitation in another part of the body, placing the neck between them to be the isthmus and boundary line, which they constructed between the head and the breast, to keep them distinctly apart. — Timaeus, 69.

Need. The good man is enough for

himself and his own happiness, and therefore is least in need of other men. — Republic, III, 387.

If a man could live without food or drink, and yet suffer neither hunger nor thirst, would he want either money or anything else in order to supply his needs? — Eryxias, 401.

Needy. The most needy will be the most grateful; for they are the persons who will be most relieved. — Phaedrus, 233.

Negative. The words inexpedient, unprofitable, unadvantageous, ungainful are negative. — Cratylus, 417.

Negligent. Occupied with public affairs, they are too apt to be negligent and careless of their own children and their private concerns. — Laches, 180.

Neighbors. Many small injuries done by neighbors to one another through their multiplication, may cause a weight of enmity, and make neighborhood a very disagreeable and bitter thing. Wherefore a man ought to be very careful of committing any offense against his neighbor, and especially of encroaching on his neighbor's land. — Laws, VIII, 843.

Nemesis. Nemesis, the messenger of Justice, is appointed to watch over all matters. — Laws, IV, 717.

Nestor. Nestor is said to have excelled all men in the power of speech, and yet more in his temperance. — Laws, IV, 711.

Neutral. There is no reason why the wise man should not live in a neutral state — neither rejoicing nor sorrowing. — Philebus, 33.

Nile. The Nile is our never-failing savior. — Timaeus, 22.

Niobe. The poet writes of the sufferings of Niobe. — Republic, II, 380.

Noble. Suppose that a man thinks he has done wrong to another, the nobler he is the less able is he to feel indignant at any suffering, which the injured person may inflict upon him — this he deems to be just, and his anger refuses to be excited by it. But when he thinks that he is the sufferer of the wrong, then he boils and chafes, and is on the side of what he believes to be justice. His noble spirit will not be quelled until he either slays or is slain; or until he hears the voice of the shepherd, that is, reason, bidding his dog bark no more. — Republic, VI, 440.

Nothing can be nobler than to do anything for anybody for the sake of virtue. — Symposium, 185.

I want you to see that the noble and the good may possibly be something different from saving and being saved. — Gorgias, 512.

Is anything noble which is evil and hurtful? — Laches, 192.

Come, now, and let us gently reason with the unjust, who is not intentionally in error. "Gentleman," we will say to him, "what do you think of things esteemed noble and ignoble? Is not the noble that which subjects the beast to the man, or rather to the god in man; and the ignoble that which subjects the man to the beast?" He can hardly avoid saying Yes — can he now? — Republic, IX, 589.

Non-Existent. The non-existent one, since it in no way partakes of being, neither perishes nor comes into being. It experiences no change at all; for if it were liable to change, it would come into being and perish. — Parmenides, 163.

Noon. You must wait until it gets cooler; don't you see that the hour is noon, and the scorching sun is standing over our heads? Let us rather stay and talk over what has been said, and then return in the cool. — Phaedrus, 242.

Nose. When the air channel through the mouth is not open, the streams of the mouth are replenished through the nose. — Timaeus, 78.

Not-Being. Not-being in the abstract is inconceivable, unutterable, unspeakable, indescribable. — Sophist, 238.

Nourishment. The provision of food and of all other things which mingle their particles with the particles of the human body, and minister to the body, may be called by the general term of nourishment — unless you have a better name to offer. — Statesman, 288, 289.

Novelty. The love of novelty arises out of pleasure in the new, and weariness of the old. — Laws, I, 657.

Novice. To delight in always bringing forward oppositions in argument, is no true refutation, but only proves that he who uses such immature arguments is a novice who has got but a little way in the investigation of truth. — Sophist, 259.

Number. He who never looks for number in anything, will not himself be looked for in the number of famous men. — Philebus, 17.

It is a great fortune to men, if they accept Uranus' gift of number. — Epinomis, 977.

If number were banished from us, we could never become wise. For man could not attain full virtue, if his soul were without rational discourse; a human creature that could not recognize two and three, odd and even, but was entirely unacquainted with number, could not give a rational account of things wherefore it had sensations only. — Epinomis, 977.

Disorderly, unregulated, unrhythmical, and dissonant motion, and all else that participates in evil, is void of number. — Epinomis, 978.

Nursling. A variety of pleasures would utterly ruin the nursling, coming at the beginning of his education. — Laws, VII, 792.

If during the first three years of life every possible care is taken that the nursling should have as little of sorrow and fear, and in general of pain as is possible, might we not expect at this age to make his soul more gentle and cheerful? — Laws, VII, 792.

O

Oath. As the opinions of men about the gods are changed, the laws should also be changed: a rational legislation ought to do away with the oaths of the parties on either side; they should instead write down the charges, but not add an oath.

A judge who is about to deliver his sentence shall take an oath. — Laws, XII, 948.

No one shall call the gods to witness, when he says or does anything false or deceitful or dishonest, unless he would be the most hateful of mankind to them. And he is most hateful to them who takes a false oath, and never thinks of the gods; and in the second place, he who tells a falsehood in the presence of his superiors. — Laws, XI, 917.

Obedience. He is by far the best, who rather than the Olympic or any other victory of peace or war, desires to win the palm of obedience to the laws of his country, and who, of all mankind, is the person reputed to have obeyed them best during his whole life. — Laws, V, 729.

Object. All this anxiety has regard not to the means which are provided for the sake of an object, but to the object for the sake of which they are provided. — Lysis, 220.

Odd Number. The odd is a particular number; number is wider in extent than the odd. — Euthyphro, 12.

The name of the general is not confined to it; the particular, though not being the general, may also lay claim to it. For example, the number three may be called by its specific name, and also be called odd, which is not the same as three; and this may be said not only of three but also of five, and every alternate number — each of them without being oddness is odd. — Phaedo, 103, 104.

Offering. Brass and iron are instruments of war — let a man, therefore, offer what he likes which is made of wood only, and in like manner of stone to the public temples, but of woven work let him not offer more than one woman can execute in a month. — Laws, XII, 956.

Office. The offices should be held equally by women and men. — Republic, V, 460.

When there has been a contest for office, and the victorious monopolize the government, and refuse any share of office to the defeated party, they live watching one another, in perpetual fear that someone will come into office who has a recollection of former wrongs, and will rise up against them. — Laws, IV, 715.

The good men take office, not because they want it but because they cannot help it; nor under the idea that they are going to have any benefit or enjoyment themselves, but as a necessary duty, and because they are not able to commit the task of ruling to anyone who is better than themselves, or indeed as good. — Republic, I, 347.

The probability is that if a city were composed entirely of good men, then to avoid office (which thus can be managed well by anyone) would be as much an object of ambition as to obtain office is at present. — Republic, I, 347.

To seek office oneself instead of awaiting the call of compulsion has been thought disgraceful. — Republic, I, 347.

Official. Officials are servants of the rulers, not themselves rulers. — Statesman, 290.

Offspring, Intellectual. Men whose bodies only are pregnant, betake themselves to women and beget children — this is the character of their love; their offspring, as they hope, will preserve their memory and give them the blessedness and immortality which they desire in the future. But pregnant souls — for there are men who are more creative in their souls than in their bodies — conceive that which is proper for the soul to conceive and retain. And what are these conceptions? — wisdom and virtue in general. . . . And he who in youth has the seed of temperance and justice implanted in him and is himself inspired, when he comes to maturity desires to beget and generate. And when he finds a fair and noble and well-nurtured soul . . . in company they tend that which he brings forth, and they are married by a far nearer tie and have a closer friendship than those who beget mortal children, for the children who are their common offspring are fairer and more immortal. Who, when he thinks of Homer and Hesiod and other great poets, would not rather have their children than ordinary human ones? Who would not emulate them in the creation of children such as theirs, which have preserved their memory and given them everlasting glory? There is Solon, too, who is the revered father of Athenian laws; and many others there are, who have done many noble works, and have been the parents of virtue of every kind; and many temples have been raised in honor of their children, which were never raised in honor of the mortal children of anyone. — Symposium, 208, 209.

Oil. Physicians always forbid their patients the use of oil in their food, except in very small quantities, just sufficient to take away the disagreeable sensation of smelling meats and sauces. — Protagoras, 334.

Old Age. He will not think that old age of itself brings wisdom. — Laches, 188.

Those who have reached old age, fall out of acquaintance with the young. — Laches, 180.

Old age is no burden to you, not because you are of a happy disposition, but because you are rich. — Republic, I, 329.

I am afraid that you will laugh at me if I continue the games of youth in old age. — Menexenus, 236.

Men of old age flock together; we are birds of a feather, as the old proverb says; and at our reunions the lament of my acquaintance commonly is — I cannot eat, I cannot drink; the pleasures of youth and love are fled away: there was a good time once, but now that is gone, and life is no longer life. Some complain of the slights which are put upon them by relations, and they will tell you sadly of how many evils their old age is the cause. But to me, these complainers seem to blame that which is not really in fault. For if old age were the cause, I too being old would have felt as they do. But this is not my experience. How well I remember the aged poet Sophocles, when in answer to the question, How does love suit with age, Sophocles — are you still the man you were? Peace, he replied; most gladly have I escaped the thing of which you speak; I feel as if I had escaped from a mad and furious master. — Republic, I, 329.

When the root of the triangles is relaxed by having undergone many conflicts with many things in the course of time, they are no longer able to cut or assimilate the food which enters into them, but are easily subverted by the new bodies which come in from without. In this way the whole animal is overcome and decays, and this state of things is called old age. — Timaeus, 81.

Neither can a good poor man lightly bear old age, nor can a bad rich man, grown old, ever be at peace with himself. — Republic, I, 330.

Certainly old age has a great sense of calm and freedom; when the passions relax their hold, then, as Sophocles says, we are freed from the grasp not of one mad master only, but of many. — Republic, I, 329.

As he is older he may be expected to be wiser than we are. — Theaetetus, 171.

I am old and my memory is bad. — Laches, 189.

Clearly you and I will be compelled to reply that the old men are right; their way of thinking is far better than any other which now prevails in the world. — Laws, II, 658.

I believe that we old men would have the greatest pleasure in hearing a rhapsodist recite the Iliad and Odyssey, or one of the Hesiodic poems. — Laws, II, 658.

Oligarchy. When the rich disregard the laws, such a government is called oligarchy. — Statesman, 301.

Oligarchies have both the extremes of great wealth and utter poverty. — Republic, VIII, 552.

In oligarchical states, from the general spread of carelessness and extravagance, men of no ignoble quality have often been reduced to beggary. And still they remain in the city; there they are, ready to sting and fully armed, and some of them owe money, some have forfeited their citizenship; a third class are in both predicaments; and they hate and conspire against the acquirers of their property, and against everybody else, and are eager for revolution. — Republic, VIII, 555.

Olive. She made the olive spring up as a boon to their descendants, and to be the help of their toils. — Menexenus, 238.

Olive Oil. Olive oil is very bad for all plants, and generally most injurious to the hair of every animal with the exception of man, but beneficial to human hair and to the human body generally. — Protagoras, 334.

Omen. I shall speak only words of good omen. — Letter, VI, 323.

One. If one exists, number must exist. — Parmenides, 144.

The one is different from the others. — Parmenides, 146.

The original one must be seen not only as one and many and infinite, but also in some definite number. — Philebus, 16.

Oneness. There is no impropriety in our inquiring of the dualists [about the meaning of being]. And what about the assertors of the oneness of the all — must we not endeavor to ascertain from them what they mean by "being"? . . . Shall we say that being is one and a whole only as having the attribute of unity? Or shall we say that being is not a whole at all? That is a hard alternative to offer. For being having in a certain sense the attribute of one, is yet proved not to be the same as one, and the all is therefore more than one. — Sophist, 244, 245.

Opinion. They have differences of opinion about good and evil, just and unjust, honorable and dishonorable: there would have been no quarrels among them, if there had been no such differences. The same things, as it appears, are hated by the gods and loved by the gods, are both hateful and dear to them. Upon this view the same things will be pious and also impious. — Euthyphro, 7, 8.

Human opinions are not stable. — Letter, VI, 323.

Some opinions are to be regarded, and others are not to be regarded. — Crito, 46.

There is nothing that I admire more than your magnanimous disregard of any opinion. — Euthydemus, 303.

Opinion is darker than knowledge, but lighter than ignorance; it is an intermediate between them. — Republic, V, 478.

Opposing. I cannot oppose you when I agree with you. — Theaetetus, 162.

There is a difficulty in opposing many millions of mouths. — Laws, VII, 810.

Opposites. We admitted before that opposites are simply generated from opposites; but now this seems to be utterly denied. — But you do not observe that there is a difference in the two cases. For then we were speaking of contrary opposites, while now of contradictory opposites. — Phaedo, 103.

The greatest friendship is of opposites. — Lysis, 216.

All opposites are, even though not expressed in words, generated out of one another, and there is a passing or process from one to the other of them. — Phaedo, 71.

Every opposite has one opposite only and no more. — Protagoras, 332.

The number two is certainly not opposed to the number three. — Phaedo, 104.

I have described the dances which are appropriate to noble bodies and generous souls. But it is necessary also to consider and know uncomely persons and thoughts, and those which are intended to produce laughter in comedy. For serious things cannot be understood without laughable things, nor opposites at all without opposites, if a man is really to have intelligence of either. And for this reason he should learn them both, in order that he may not in ignorance do or say anything which is ridiculous and out of place. — Laws, VII, 816.

Are not all things which have opposites generated out of their opposites? I mean such things as good and evil, just and unjust — and there are inumerable other opposites which are generated out of opposites. — Phaedo, 70.

The weaker is generated from the stronger, and the swifter from the slower. And the worse is from the better, and the more just is from the more unjust. And we are convinced that all opposites are generated out of one another. — Phaedo, 71.

These two forms or ideas, the one of greatness, and the other of smallness, have existence. — Parmenides, 149.

The nature of the light and the heavy will be best understood when examined in connection with our notions of above and below; for it is quite wrong to suppose that the universe is parted in two regions, separate from and opposite to each other, the one a lower one to which all things tend which have any bulk, and an upper one to which things only ascend against their will. — Timaeus, 62.

Optimism. The best soul takes care of the world and guides it along the good path. — Laws, X, 897. *Vide* World.

Oratory. Discussion is one thing, and making an oration is quite another. — Protagoras, 336.

Orators and lawyers persuade men by their art and do not teach them. — Theaetetus, 201.

He who would be a skillful rhetorician has no need of truths — for in courts of law men literally care nothing about truth, but only about plausibility: and this is based on probability, to which he who would be an astute orator should therefore give his whole attention. And they say also that there are causes in which the actual facts ought to be withheld, and only the probabilities should be told. — Phaedrus, 272.

The perfection of oratory is, like the perfection of all things, partly accomplished by natural talent, assisted by art. — Phaedrus, 269.

Order. No other animal attained to any perception of order, but man only. Now the order of motion is called rhythm, and the order of the voice, in which high and low are duly mingled, is called harmony; and both together are termed choric song. — Laws, II, 664, 665.

Orphan. Do you know where you will have to look if you want to discover his rogueries? Let him be the guardian of an orphan, or have some other great opportunity of acting dishonestly. — Republic, VIII, 554.

Men should have a fear of the gods above, who regard the loneliness of orphans. — Laws, XI, 927.

We ought to take measures that the misfortune of orphanhood may be as little sad as possible. — Laws, XI, 926.

Orpheus. Orpheus attracted the listeners by his voice. — Protagoras, 315.

Overcome. When you speak of being overcome, what do you mean, but that you choose the greater evil in exchange for the lesser good? — Protagoras, 355.

P

Pain. This is the advantage of enduring your pain — that you get well. — Gorgias, 478.

Pain deters from good. — Timaeus, 69.

Painter. The creations of the painter look alive, and yet if you ask them a question they preserve a solemn silence. — Phaedrus, 275.

Painters are wise in what relates to the making of likenesses, and similarity of other things. — Protagoras, 312.

Would a painter be any worse because, after having delineated with consummate art an ideal of a perfectly beautiful man, he was unable to show that any such man could ever have existed? Well, and were we not creating an ideal of a perfect state? — Republic, V, 472.

We do not examine and analyze a painting of inanimate things of nature; all that is required from the artist is a sort of indistinct and deceptive mode of shadowing them forth. But when an artist endeavors to paint the human form we are quick at finding out defects, and our familiar knowledge makes us severe judges of anyone who does not render every point of similarity. — Critias, 107. *Vide* Abstract Art.

Pairing. We shall have to invent some ingenious kind of lots which the less worthy may draw on each occasion of their pairing, and then they will accuse their own ill-luck and not the rulers. — Republic, V, 460.

The chief officials were to contrive secretly, by the use of certain lots, so to arrange the nuptial meeting, that the bad of either sex and the good of either sex should pair with their like, and there was to be no quarreling on this account, for they were to imagine that the union was a mere chance, and was to be attributed to the lot. — Timaeus, 18.

Pan. There is reason in Pan being the double-natured son of Hermes. — Cratylus, 408.

Pangs of Labor. These are the pangs of labor, my dear Theaetetus; you have something within you which you are bringing to the birth. — Theaetetus, 148.

Panharmonic Style. A proper way of feeding and living may be likened to the composition of melody and song in the panharmonic style, and in all the rhythms. — Republic, III, 404.

Parable. You ask a question, to which a reply can only be given in a parable. — And that is a way of speaking to which you are not at all accustomed. — Republic, VI, 487.

Pardon. The citizens ask the lawgiver to pardon them if they are sometimes unable to fulfill the duties which he in his ignorance imposes upon them. — Laws, XI, 926.

Parents. Neither god, nor a man who has understanding will ever advise anyone to neglect his parents. — Laws, XI, 930.

A man and his wife shall leave to his and her father or mother their own dwelling places, and themselves go to a colony and dwell there, and visit and be visited by their parents. — Laws, VI, 776.

If your father and mother love you, no one can doubt that they are very ready to promote your happiness. — Lysis, 207.

You are not to wonder at good fathers having bad sons, or at good sons having bad fathers. — Protagoras, 328.

Parenthood. No man should bring children into the world who is unwilling to persevere to the end in their nurture and education. — Crito, 45.

Parmenides. Parmenides is venerable and awful, as in Homeric language he may be called. — Theaetetus, 183.

Parmenides was [at the time of the great Panathenaea] about sixty-five years old, very white with age, but well favored. — Parmenides, 127.

Parricide. If a man could be slain more than once, most justly would he who in a fit of passion has slain father or mother, undergo many deaths. — Laws, IX, 869.

Partaking. I would like to know whether there are certain ideas of which all other things partake; similars, for example, become similar, because they partake of similarity; and great things become great, because they partake of greatness; and just and beautiful things become just and beautiful, because they partake of justice and beauty? — Parmenides, 130.

Participation. Participation is an active or passive energy, which arises out of a certain power of elements meeting with one another. — Sophist, 248.

Particulars. The rhetorician must have a keen eye for the observation of particulars. — Phaedrus, 263.

Partisan. At this moment [in the prospect of my death] I am sensible that I have not the objective temper of a philosopher; like the vulgar, I am only a partisan. For the partisan, when he is engaged in a dispute, cares nothing about the rights of the question, but is anxious only to convince his hearers of his own assertions. And the difference between him and me at the present moment is only this — that whereas he seeks to persuade his hearers that what he says is true, I am rather seeking to convince myself. — Phaedo, 91.

Partnership. By contracts you mean partnerships? — Exactly. — Republic,

Passion. Passion is hard to be striven against and contended with, and by irrational force overturns many things. — Laws, IX, 863.

Is not the passionate element wholly set on ruling and conquering and getting fame? — Republic, IX, 581.

The young man is drawn opposite ways: while his father is watering and nourishing the rational principle in his soul, the others are encouraging the passionate and appetitive; and he being not originally of a bad nature, but having kept bad company, is at last brought by their joint influence to a compromise, and gives up the kingdom which is within him to the intermediate principle of ambition and passion, and becomes arrogant and covetous. — Republic, VII, 550. I, 333.

Patience. To be patient under suffering is best; we should not give way to impatience. — Republic, X, 604.

Patient. Where there is an agent,

must there not also be a patient? — Gorgias, 476.

Patriarchal Rule. Among primitive societies the eldest ruled, because government originated with them in the authority of a father and mother, whom, like a flock of birds, they followed, forming one troop under the patriarchal rule and sovereignty of their parents, which of all sovereignties is the most just. — Laws, III, 680.

Every family would be under patriarchal rule, and, owing to their separation from one another, would have peculiar customs about the gods and themselves. — Laws, III, 681.

Patroclus. The notion that Patroclus was the beloved one is a foolish error into which Aeschylus has fallen. ... Patroclus was the lover of Achilles rather than his love. — Symposium, 179.

Pauper. Nearly everybody is a pauper who is not a ruler. — Republic, VIII, 552.

Whenever you see paupers in a state, somewhere in that neighborhood there are hidden away thieves, and cutpurses and robbers of temples, and all sorts of malefactors. — Republic, VIII, 552.

Payment. Money I have none, and therefore I pay in praise, which is all I have. — Republic, I, 338.

You must pay them well in money and not merely in thanks. — Cratylus, 391.

If you always pay immediately you will be accommodated readily. — Letter, XIII, 363.

Peace. Peace, and the song of peace — let us have them by all means. — Laws, VII, 801.

Peace with one another, and good will, are the best. — Laws, I, 628.

Every man of us should live the life of peace as long and as well as he can. — Laws, VII, 803.

The victors of a civil war can never have peace until they cease to sentence men to exile and death and to take revenge on the opposition party. They should rather exercise self-control and make equitable laws which do not discriminate against the defeated party. — Letter, VII, 336, 337.

No one can be a sound legislator who orders peace for the sake of war, and not war for the sake of peace. — Laws, I, 628.

Peacemaker. Let us be your peacemakers. — Protagoras, 337.

Pedestrian. We should have begun by dividing pedestrians into biped and quadruped. — Statesman, 266.

Penalty. I can but suffer the penalty of ignorance; and the penalty is to learn from the wise. — Republic, I, 337.

Penalty more than enough will fall upon our heads. — Laws, VII, 790.

It is almost impossible to the legislator not to leave the courts some discretion on the question of the amount of penalty. — Laws, IX, 875.

He who has slain a father shall himself be slain at some time or other by his children; for where a family is polluted with blood there is no other penalty, nor can the pollution be washed out until the homicidal soul has given life for life, like for like. — Laws, IX, 872.

They do not know the inherent penalty of injustice — not stripes and death, as they suppose, which evildoers often escape, but a penalty which cannot be escaped: to be injust. — Theaetetus, 176.

He who obeys the law will never know its penalties, but he who despises the law shall be liable to a double penalty, the first coming from the gods, and the second from the law. — Laws, VIII, 843.

I do not understand how a penalty can be a payment. — Republic, I, 347. *Vide.* Punishment.

The man who fills his moneybags, and starves his soul . . . is blind, not realizing that consequences follow his wicked acts of violence. — Letter, VII, 335.

Penelope's Web. A philosopher's soul will not ask philosophy to emancipate her in order that when set free she may deliver herself up again to the thralldom of pleasures and pains, doing a work only to be undone again; she will weave instead of unweaving her Penelope's web. — Phaedo, 84.

People. Most of the people have no understanding, and only repeat what their rulers are pleased to tell them. — Protagoras, 317.

Perception. The union or communion of soul and body in one feeling and motion, may be truly called perception. — Philebus, 34.

Perception, Sensual. Sensual perception has no part in spiritual science or merely reasoning knowledge. — Theaetetus, 186.

Perfection. Life which is wholly concerned with the virtue of body and soul; and to this end all freemen ought full of toil and trouble as the pursuit after Pythian and Olympic victories, which debars a man from every employment of life. For there ought to be no by-work which interferes with this duty. Night and day are not long enough for the perfection of body and soul; and to this end all freemen ought to arrange the time of their employments during the whole course of the twenty-four hours, from morning to evening and from evening to the morning of the next sunrise. — Laws, VII, 807.

Performance. His performances in prose are bad enough, but nothing at all in comparison with his verse. — Lysis, 204.

Perfume. In making perfumes they first contrive that the liquid substance which is to receive the scent shall be as odorless as possible. — Timaeus, 50.

As to frankincense and similar perfumes, used in the service of the gods, which come from foreign countries, or to materials which are not produced domestically and are not necessary — no one should import them. — Laws, VIII, 847.

Pericles. There is Pericles, again, magnificent in his wisdom. — Meno, 94.

Pericles was the first to establish payment for service among the Athenians — and made them thus idle and cowardly, and encouraged them in the love of talk and of money. — Gorgias, 515.

At first, Pericles was glorious and his character unimpeached by any verdict of the Athenians — this was during the time when they were not so good — yet afterwards, when they had been made good and gentle by him, at the very end of his life they convicted him of theft, and almost put him to death, clearly under the notion that he was a malefactor. — Gorgias, 516.

Pericles is said to have enriched his wisdom, not by the light of nature, but through his association with wise men. — First Alcibiades, 118.

In addition to his natural gifts, Pericles acquired comprehensive power from his happening to know Anaxagoras. He was imbued with the higher philosophy, and attained the knowledge of mind and matter, which was the favorite theme of Anaxagoras, and hence he drew what was applicable to his art. — Phaedrus, 270.

Perjury. Everyone who is guilty of adultery in the agora tells a falsehood, and deceives, and when he invokes the gods, he is perjured. — Laws, XI, 917.

Either of the parties in a legal case may bring an accusation of perjury, touching the evidence in whole or in part, previous to the final decision of the case. — Laws, XI, 937.

It is a dreadful thing to know that almost half the people who are in the habit of meeting one another are perjured. — Laws, XII, 948.

Period. The whole orbit of the moon constitutes a unity, called a period. — Epinomis, 978.

Perplexity. Being in perplexity I am always changing my opinion. — Lesser Hippias, 376.

As we are all in the same perplexity, why should one of us be preferred to another? — Laches, 200.

He made an unintelligible attempt to hide his perplexity. — Charmides, 169.

Persians. The Persians are shepherds — sons of a rugged land, which was a stern mother, and well fitted to produce a sturdy race, able to live in the open air and watch, and to fight also, if fighting was required. — Laws, III, 695.

First I will tell you how the Persians, rulers of Asia, were enslaving Europe. — Menexenus, 239.

Person. Do we not consider a human being as a moral person? — Laws, I, 644.

Persuasion. Persuasion is the crown of rhetoric. — Gorgias, 453.

The rhetorician about justice and injustice gains the ears of the multitude, not by instruction, but by persuasion. — Gorgias, 459.

Can you be persuaded better than out of your own mouth? — First Alcibiades, 114.

Can you persuade us, if we refuse to listen to you? — Republic, I, 327.

Persuasion is truly the greatest good because it gives men freedom for themselves and rule over others. Priceless is the word which can convince the judges in the courts, or the senators in the council, or the citizens in the assembly. If you have the power of persuasion, you will have the physician your slave, and the trainer your slave, and the money-maker to whom you talk, will be found to gather treasures, not for himself, but for you who are able to speak and persuade multitudes. — Gorgias, 452.

Mere knowledge of the truth will not give you the art of persuasion. — Phaedrus, 260.

Before you are hard upon us and threaten us, you should argue with us and persuade us — you should first attempt to teach and convince us. — Laws, X, 885.

Let us summon as far as possible all the power of persuasion which we possess, and unreservedly consider the whole matter. — Laws, X, 887.

The art of the lawyer, of the popular orator, and the art of conversation may be called the art of persuasion. — Sophist, 222.

The legislator can take the story of armed men springing up out of sown teeth as a proof that he can persuade the minds of the young of anything; he has only to use all his efforts to make the whole community utter one and the same word in their songs and tales and discourses all their life long. — Laws, II, 663, 664.

The rhetorician in the courts of law only creates belief about just and unjust — he is only persuading and not instructing. — Gorgias, 455.

Pessimist. You are just the same pessimist — always speaking evil of yourself and of others. — Symposium, 173.

I think that you are, pessimistically, too ready to speak evil of men; and, if you will take my advice, I would recommend you to be more careful. Perhaps there is no city in which it not easier to do men harm than to do them good. — Meno, 94.

Pestilence. The wantonness and overbearingness of the intemperate love affecting the seasons is the source of pestilence, and brings many difrent sorts of diseases on animals and plants. — Symposium, 188.

Petitio Principii. To bid us add those things which we already have, in order that we may learn what we already know, is a rare sort of darkness: a petitio principii. — Theaetetus, 209.

Pettifogger. The pettifogger is a servant, and is disputing about a fellow servant before his master, who is seated, and has the cause in his hands; the trial is never about some indifferent matter, but always concerns himself; and often he has to run for his life. The consequence has been, that he has become keen and shrewd; he has learned how to flatter his master in word and indulge him in deed; but his soul is small and unrighteous. His slavish condition has deprived him of growth and uprightness and independence; dangers and fears, which were too much for his truth and honesty, came upon him in early years, when the tenderness of youth was unequal to them, and he has been driven into crooked ways; from the first he has practiced deception and retaliation, and has become stunted and warped. And so he has passed out of youth into manhood, having no soundness in him; and is now, as he thinks, a master of wisdom. Such is the pettifogger. — Theaetetus, 173.

Philosopher. When I see one of your young men studying philosophy, I consider him ingenious and becoming a man of a liberal education, and him who neglects philosophy I regard as an inferior man, who will never aspire to anything great and noble. But if I see him continuing to study philosophy in later life, and not leaving off, I think that he ought to be whipped; for such a one, even though he has natural gifts, becomes effeminate. Shunning the city, he creeps into a corner for the rest of his life, and talks in a whisper with three or four admiring youths, but never speaks out like a freeman in a satisfactory manner. — Gorgias, 485.

He is most like to have been a philosopher who has done his own work, and not troubled himself with the doings of other men in his lifetime. — Gorgias, 526.

Suppose that someone were to take you, or anyone of your philosophical sort, off to prison, declaring that you have done wrong when you had done no wrong, you must allow that you would not know what to do: there you would stand giddy and gaping, and not having a word to say; and when you went up before the court, even if the accuser were a poor creature and not good for much, you would die if he were disposed to claim for you the penalty of death. — Gorgias, 486.

Philosophers are probably right. — Laws, X, 888.

Those who passed their days in the pursuit of philosophy are ridiculously at fault when they have to appear and plead in a court of law. — Theaetetus, 172.

Philosophers appear in various shapes; they walk to and fro in cities, as Homer says, looking from above upon human life; and some think nothing of them, and others can never think enough; and sometimes they appear as statesman, and sometimes as Sophists; and then, again, they seem to be no better than madmen. — Sophist, 216.

The wicked will say that the life which philosophers desire is truly death, and that they have found them out to be deserving of the death which they desire. — Phaedo, 64.

He who has lived as true philosopher has reason to be of good cheer when he is about to die. — Phaedo, 64.

The philosopher, and he only, will know himself, and be able to examine what he knows or does not know, and see what others know, and think that they know and do really know; and what they do not know, and fancy that they know, when they do not. No other person will be able to do this. — Charmides, 167.

We philosophers belong to a brotherhood which is free, and are not the servants of the argument; but the argument is our servant, and must wait our leisure. Where is the judge or spectator who has a right to censure or control us, as he might the poets? — Theaetetus, 173.

This was what we foresaw, not without fear and hesitation, that neither cities nor states nor individuals will ever attain perfection until the small class of philosophers are by some chance compelled to take care of the state; or until kings are divinely inspired with a true love of true philosophy. That either or both of these alternatives are impossible, I see no reason to affirm; if they were so, we might indeed be justly ridiculed as dreamers and visionaries. — Republic, VI, 499.

The lords of philosophy have never known their way to the Agora, or the council, or any other political assembly; the eagerness of political societies in the attainment of offices — clubs, and banquets, and revels, and singing girls, do not enter even into their dreams. Whether any event has turned out well or ill in the city, what disgrace may have descended to anyone from his ancestors are matters of which the philosopher no more knows than he can tell, how many pints are contained in the ocean. Neither is he conscious of this ignorance. For he does not hold aloof in order that he may gain a reputation; but the truth is, that the outer form of him only is in the city; his mind, disdaining the littleness and nothingness of human things, is "flying all abroad," as Pindar says, measuring the things which are under and on the earth and above the heaven, interrogating the whole nature of each and all, but not condescending to anything which is within reach. — Theaetetus, 173.

The philosopher looks like an awkward creature, and conveys the impression that he is stupid. When he is reviled, he has nothing personal to say in answer to the civilities of his adversaries, for he knows no scandals of anyone, and they do not interest him; and therefore is laughed at for his sheepishness; and when others are being praised and glorified, he cannot help laughing very sincerely in the simplicity of his heart; and this again makes him look like a fool. When he hears a tyrant or king eulogized, he fancies that he is listening to the praises of some keeper of cattle — a swineherd, or shepherd, or cowherd, who is being praised for the quantity of milk which he squeezes from them; and he remarks that the milked human creature is less tractable than cows. Then, again, he observes that the great man is of necessity as ill-mannered and uneducated as any shepherd — for he has no leisure, and is surrounded by a wall, which is his mountain pen. — Ibid., 174.

The philosopher always reasons about being. — Sophist, 254.

The very qualities which make a man a philosopher may, if he be ill-educated, serve to divert him from philosophy, no less than riches and their accompaniments and the other so-called goods of life. This is the class out of whom come those who are the authors of the greatest evil to states and individuals; and also of the greatest good when the tide carries them in the direction of good; but a small man never was the doer of any great thing either to individuals or states. — Republic, VI, 495.

May we not say of the philosopher that he is a lover, not of a part of wisdom only, but of the whole? And he who dislikes learning, especially in youth, when he has no power of judging what is good and what is not, such a one we maintain not to be a philosopher or a lover of knowledge, just as he who refuses his food is not hungry, and may be said to have a bad appetite. Whereas he who has a taste for every sort of knowledge and who is curious to learn and is never satisfied, may be justly termed a philosopher. Am I not right? Glaucon said: If curiosity makes a philosopher, you will find many a strange being will have a title to the name. Certainly not, I replied; true philosophers are lovers of the vision of truth. — Republic, V, 475.

Everyone will admit that a nature having in perfection all the qualities which we required in a philosopher, is a rare plant which is seldom seen among men. — Republic, 491.

The philosopher is a lover of learning. — Phaedo, 82.

The philosopher is the only one who has wisdom as well as experience. — Republic, IX, 582.

At the end of the first thousand years the good souls and also the evil souls both come to cast lots and choose their second life, and they may take any that they like. And then the soul of a man may pass into the life of a beast, or from the beast again into the man. But the soul of him who has never seen the truth will not pass into the human form, for man ought to have intelligence. And therefore the mind of the philosopher alone has wings. But, as he forgets earthly interests and is rapt in the divine, the vulgar deem him crazy, and rebuke him; they do not see that he is inspired. — Phaedrus, 249.

Take this parable to the gentleman who is surprised at finding that philosophers are not honored in their cities; explain it to him and try to convince him that it would be far more surprising if they were honored. Say to him, that, in deeming the best spirits of philosophy to be useless to the rest of the world, he is right; but also tell him to attribute their uselessness to the fault of those who will not use them, and not to themselves. — Republic, VI, 489.

O my friend, do not attack the multitude: they will change their minds, if, not in an aggressive spirit, but gently and with a view of soothing them and removing their dislike of learning, you show them your philosophers as they really are, and then mankind will see that he of whom you are speaking is not such as they supposed — if they view him in this new light, they will surely change their notion of him, and answer in another strain. Who can be at enmity with one who loves them, who that is himself gentle and free from envy will be jealous of one in whom there is no jealousy? Nay, let me answer for you, that in a few this harsh temper may be found but not in the majority of mankind.— Republic, VI, 500.

I will illustrate my description of the philosophers by the jest which the clever, witty Thracian handmaid made about Thales, when he fell into a well as he was looking up at the stars. She said, that he was so eager to know what was going on in heaven, that he could not see what was before his feet. This is a jest which is equally applicable to all philosophers. For the philosopher is wholly unacquainted with his next-door neighbor; he is ignorant, not only of what he is doing, but whether he is or is not a human creature; he is searching into the essence of man, and is unwearied in discovering what belongs to such a nature to do or suffer different from any other. — Theaetetus, 174.

He whose desires are drawn towards knowledge in every form will be absorbed in the pleasures of the soul, and will not feel bodily pleasure only — I mean if he be a true philosopher and not a sham one. Such a one is sure to be temperate and by no means covetous; for the motives which make another person desirous of having and spending money, have no place in his character. — Republic, VI, 485.

Are not those philosophers who are verily deprived of the knowledge of the true being . . . blind? — Republic, VI, 484.

At present the students of philosophy are quite young; beginning when they are hardly past childhood, they devote only the time saved from moneymaking and housekeeping to such pursuits; and even those of them who are reputed to have most of the philosophic spirit, when they come within sight of the great difficulty of the subject, I mean dialectic, take themselves off. In later life they may, perhaps, go and hear a lecture, and about this they make much ado, for philosophy is not considered by them to be their proper business: at last, when they grow old, in most cases they are extinguished more truly than Heracleitus' sun, inasmuch as they never light up again. — Republic, VI, 498.

A disciple of philosophy may be compared to a man who has fallen among wild beasts — unable to join in the wickedness of his fellows, neither would he be able alone to resist all their fierce natures, and therefore he would be of no use to the state or to his friends, and would have to throw away his life before he had done any good to himself or others. And he reflects upon all this, and holds his peace, and minds his own business. He is like one who retires under the shelter of a wall in the storm of dust and sleet which the driving wind hurries along; and when he sees the rest of mankind full of wickedness, he is content if only he can live his own life and be pure from evil, and depart in peace, with bright hopes. — Republic, VI, 496.

The true disciple of philosophy is likely to be misunderstood by other men; they do not perceive that he is ever pursuing death and dying. — Phaedo, 64.

You will soon observe whether a man is just and gentle, or rude and unsociable; these are the signs which distinguish even in youth the philosophical nature from the unphilosophical. . . . Then, besides other qualities, we must try to find a naturally well-proportioned and gracious mind, which will move easily towards the cognition of the true being of everything. . . . And must not that be a blameless study which he only can pursue who has the gift of a good memory, and is quick to learn — noble, gracious, the friend of truth? — Republic, VI, 486, 487.

The philosopher has greatly the advantage; for he has of necessity always known the taste of the other pleasures: but the lover of gain has not necessarily tasted the sweetness of learning and knowing truth. The lover of wisdom has a great advantage over the lover of gain, for he has a double experience. — Republic, IX, 582.

Philosopher-Politician. If contemplative philosophy and political action are both good, but tend to different ends, and the philosopher-politicians participate in both, and are in a mean between them, then they are talking nonsense, for they are worse than either. . . . These philosopher-politicians who aim at both fall short of both in the attainment of their respective ends. — Euthydemus, 306.

Philosophical Temper. The philosophical temper will make them gentle to their friends and fierce to their enemies. — Timaeus, 18.

Philosophy. If you do not appreciate philosophy, let it alone. — Letter, II, 312.

I would like to see philosophy appreciated even by plain people. — Letter, II, 312.

Is not spiritual philosophy the practice of death? — Phaedo, 80.

Philosophy [general science] is not like the other sciences [special]. — Charmides, 165.

Philosophy is the only science which is the science of itself and of the other sciences as well. — Charmides, 166.

Philosophy is the acquisition of knowledge. — Euthydemus, 288.

Philosophy if pursued in moderation and at the proper age, is an elegant accomplishment, but too much philosophy is the ruin of human life. — Gorgias, 484.

What is the value of philosophy which converts a man of sense into a fool, who is helpless, powerless, when the danger is greatest, to save either himself or others — being a man who may be boxed on the ears with impunity? — Gorgias, 486.

The study of philosophy should not be pushed too much into detail. — Gorgias, 487.

The impulse that carries you towards philosophy is noble and divine — never doubt that — though philosophy often seems to be useless, and is called by the vulgar idle talking. — Parmenides, 135.

Philosophy, regarded only as a knowledge of knowledge or science of sciences will not teach a man the knowledge of health or of building. — Charmides, 170.

We have little time for philosophy. — Phaedo, 66.

Philosophy, the noblest pursuit of all, is not likely to be much esteemed by those of the opposite faction; not that the greatest and most lasting injury is done to her by her opponents, but by her own pretenders, the same of whom you suppose the accuser to say, that the greater number of them are arrant rogues, and the best are useless; in which opinion I agree.... Truth is the leader of the philosopher, whom he follows always and in all things; failing in this, he is an impostor. — Republic, VI, 489, 490.

The worthy disciples of philosophy will be but a small remnant.... Those who belong to this small class have tasted how sweet and blessed a possession philosophy is, and have also seen enough of the madness of the multitude. — Republic, VI, 496.

I do not wonder that the many refuse to believe; for they have never seen that of which we are now speaking realized; they have seen only a conventional imitation of philosophy, consisting of words artificially brought together, not like those of ours having a natural unity. But a human being who in word and work is perfectly molded into the proportion and likeness of virtue — such a man ruling in the city they have never yet seen. — Republic, VI, 489.

Philosophy, Socrates, if pursued in moderation and in your youth, is an elegant accomplishment, but too much philosophy is the ruin of any human life. Even if a man is gifted, still, if he carries philosophy into later age, he is necessarily ignorant of all those things which a gentleman ought to know, especially of the human pleasures and desires. And people of this sort, when they betake themselves to politics or business, are as ridiculous as I imagine the politicians to be, when they make their appearance in the arena of philosophy. — Gorgias, 485.

Philosophy is the noblest and greatest of arts. — Phaedo, 60, 61.

And so philosophy is left desolate, with her marriage rite incomplete: for her own have forsaken her, and other unworthy persons, seeing that she has no kinsmen to be her protectors, rush in and dishonor her; and fasten upon her the reproaches which her reprovers utter, who affirm of her pretenders that some are of no account and the many accountable for many evils. The puny creatures who, seeing this land open to them — a land well stocked with fair names and showy titles — like prisoners running out of prison into a sanctuary, take a leap out of their trades into philosophy. For, although philosophy be in a low estate, still there remains a dignity about her which is not to be found in the arts. — Republic, VI, 495.

If the perfect philosopher is or has been or hereafter shall be compelled to take charge of the state, we are ready to admit, that this our constitution has been, and is — yea, and will be whenever the Muse of Philosophy is queen. There is no impossibility in all this; that there is a difficulty, we acknowledge ourselves. — Republic, VI, 499.

The time will come when philosophy will have a firmer grasp of you, and then you will not refuse to understand even the meanest things. — Parmenides, 130.

There is one peculiarity in their case: when they begin to reason about their dislike of philosophy, if they have the courage to hear the argument out, and do not run away, they grow at last strangely discontented with themselves; their rhetoric fades away, and they become speechless as children. — Theaetetus, 177.

If you want to stop me, silence philosophy, which is my love. — Gorgias, 482.

Philosophy, Natural. I don't mean to say anything disparaging of anyone who is a student of natural philosophy. I should be very sorry if Meletus could lay that to my charge. But the simple truth is, that I have nothing to do with these studies. — Apology, 19.

Phlegm. The white phlegm, being capable of relief by expiration, is less severe, and only discolors the body, generating white, leprosies and similar diseases. — Timaeus, 85.

Physical Culture. Physical culture has two branches, dancing and wrestling. — Laws, VII, 795.

Physician. The good physician is he who is able to separate fair love from foul, or to convert one into the other. — Symposium, 186.

In the case of physicians, if their patient die against their will, they shall be held guiltless by the law. — Laws, IX, 865.

The physician may often be too happy if he can restore health, without any very great infliction of pain. — Laws, III, 684.

Do you imagine that the physician knows whether health or disease is the more terrible to a man? Had not many a man better never get up from a sick bed? — Laches, 195.

If a rude physician chanced to observe a gentle physician talking to the patient in an almost philosophical language, beginning at the beginning of the disease, and discoursing about the whole nature of the body — he would say to his colleague: Foolish fellow, you are educating the sick man, rather than healing him; and he does not want to be a doctor, but to get well. — Laws, IX, 857.

Who is best able to do good to his friends and evil to his enemies in time of sickness? — The physician. — Republic, I, 332.

In time of health there is no need of a physician. — Republic, I, 332.

Is the physician a healer of the sick or a maker of money? And remember that I am now speaking of the true physician. No physician, insofar as he is a physician, considers his own good in what he prescribes, but the good of his patient; for the true physician is also a ruler having the human body as a subject, and is not a mere moneymaker. — Republic, I, 342.

Are not those physicians the best who have treated the greatest amount of healthy and sick people? — Republic, III, 408.

Physicians do not treat the body by the body. If they did, we would not allow them ever to be sickly; but they cure the body with the mind. — Republic, III, 408.

The cure of many diseases is unknown to the physicians of Greece, because they are ignorant of the whole [body and soul], which ought to be studied also; for the part can never be well unless the whole is well. — Charmides, 156.

Skillful physicians are those who,

besides knowing their art, have from their youth upwards had the greatest experience of disease of others; they also had better not be in robust health, and should have had all kinds of diseases in their own persons. — Republic, III, 408.

In prescribing food and drink would a physician wish to outdo another physician? — He would not; but he would want to overreach the non-physician. — Republic, I, 350.

The practitioner is a madman or a pedant who fancies that he is a physician, because he has read something in a book, or has stumbled on a few drugs, although he has no real understanding of the art of medicine. — Phaedrus, 268.

Picture. Our discussion may be compared to a picture of some living being which had been fairly drawn in outline, but had not yet attained the life of clearness which is given by the blending of colors. — Statesman, 277.

Piety. Piety is an art which men have of doing business with one another. — Euthyphro, 14.

Piety is doing as I am doing; that is to say, prosecuting anyone who is guilty of murder, sacrilege, or any other similar crime — whether he be your father or mother, or some other person, that makes no difference — and not prosecuting them is impiety. — Euthyphro, 5.

Piety is that which is dear to the gods and impiety is that which is not dear to them. — Euthyphro, 6.

Is not that which is pious necessarily just? — Euthyphro, 11.

Piety or holiness is an abiding by a particular law, namely divine law; there is also an abiding by another particular law, namely human law. — Euthyphro, 12.

Piety is one of the greatest virtues, and often eludes even the most noble persons. — Epinomis, 989.

Does piety or holiness, which has been defined as the art of attending to the gods, benefit or improve them? Would you say that when you do a holy act you make any of the gods better? — Euthyphro, 13.

That thing or person which is dear to the gods is pious. — Euthyphro, 7.

Justice is the more extended notion of which piety is only a part. — Euthyphro, 12.

Pilgrimage. As I am going to another place [world below], I ought to be thinking and talking of the nature of the pilgrimage which I am about to take. — Phaedo, 61.

Pilot. The circumstance that the pilot, like a passenger, sails in the ship is not to be reckoned as essential; this is accidental only, and has nothing to do with the name of pilot, which is significant of his skill and of his authority. — Republic, I, 341.

The pilot-philosopher is aware that there is no certainty as to which of his fellow passengers he has benefited, and which of them he has injured in not allowing them to be drowned. He considers that if a man who is afflicted by great and incurable bodily diseases is only to be pitied for having escaped danger, much more must this be true of one who has great and incurable diseases, not in his body, but in his soul. — Gorgias, 512.

When there is a storm, there must surely be a great advantage in having a pilot. — Laws, IV, 709.

Piracy. Let not any desire of catching men and of piracy by sea enter into your souls and make you cruel and lawless hunters. — Laws, VII, 823.

Pity. You should not envy wretches who are miserable and not to be envied, but only pity them. — Gorgias, 469.

The feeling of pity which had been nursed, and has acquired strength at the sight of the misfortunes of other men, will come out in our own misfortunes, and cannot easily be controlled. — Republic, X, 606.

He sometimes pities me for my lack of education and experience. — Greater Hippias, 293.

The unjust and the unfortunate are always to be pitied in any case. — Laws, V, 731.

Places. There is a difference in places, and some beget better men and others worse; and we must legislate accordingly. Some places are subject to strange and fatal influences by reason of diverse winds and violent heats, some by reason of waters; or, again, from the character of that subsistence which the earth supplies them, which not only affects the bodies of men for good or evil, but produces similar results in their souls. And in all such qualities those spots excel in which there is a divine inspiration, and in which the gods have their appointed lots, and are propitious to the dwellers in them. — Laws, V, 750.

Plan. A good plan shared by two minds and approved as the best by many, can be materialized. — Letter, VIII, 357.

Plato. I [Plato] have not written any book concerning the subject to which I devote myself, nor shall I ever compose one in future. For there is no possibility of putting it in words. Letter, VII, 341.

It is impossible for what is written not to be revealed. For this reason, I have never written anything; there is not, and will not be, any written work of Plato's own. What are now called his dialogues are the work of a Socrates, revised and modernized. — Letter, II, 314.

Plato pretends to know what is advantageous for a democracy, but he never addresses the assembly. — Letter, V, 322.

Play. People are apt to fancy that when the plays of children are altered they are merely plays, not seeing that the most serious and detrimental consequences arise out of the change. — Laws, VII, 798.

In states generally no one has observed that the plays of childhood have a great deal to do with permanence or want of permanence in legislation. For when plays are ordered with a view to children having the same plays, the more solemn institutions of the state are allowed to remain undisturbed. — Laws, VII, 797.

Songs appear to have been invented, which are really charms, and are designed to implant harmony. And, because the mind of the child is incapable of enduring serious training, they are called plays and songs, and are performed in a play. — Laws, II, 659.

Pleasant. Is the pleasant to be pursued for the sake of the good, or the good for the sake of the pleasant? — Gorgias, 506.

If you ask me in turn which of their lives is pleasantest, each of them will be found praising his own and depreciating that of others.... But what ought to be the criterion for the most pleasant life? Is any better than experience and wisdom and reason? — Republic, IX, 581, 582.

Pleasure. Pleasure is the greatest incitement of evil. — Timaeus, 69.

I know that Pleasure is diverse. To hear her same name you would imagine that she is one, and yet surely she takes the most various and even unlike forms. For do we not say that the intemperate has pleasure, and that the temperate has pleasure in his very temperance, and that the fool is pleased when he is full of foolish fancies and hopes, and that the wise man has pleasure in his wisdom; and may not he be justly deemed a fool who says that these pairs of pleasures are respectively alike? — Philebus, 12.

Do you think that someone who asserts all pleasure to be good, will tolerate the notion that some pleasures are good and some bad? — Philebus, 13.

As Orpheus says, some have attained maturity in their pleasures. — Laws, II, 669.

Pleasure is the veriest impostor in the world. — Philebus, 65.

The pleasures are children, who have not yet attained any degree of reason. — Philebus, 65.

Do you put into the balance the pleasures, near and distant, and weigh them, and then say which outweighs the other? — Protagoras, 356.

You say that all pleasant things are good; now no one can argue that pleasure is not pleasure, but he may argue that pleasures are oftener bad than good, and still you call them all good, and at the same time are compelled, if you are pressed, to acknowledge that they are unlike. — Philebus, 13.

Let there be no wisdom in the life of pleasure, nor any pleasure in the life of wisdom, for if either of them is the chief good, it cannot be supposed to want anything, but if either is shown to want anything, then it cannot really be the chief good. — Philebus, 20.

A small pleasure, if unalloyed with pain, is always pleasanter and truer and fairer than a great or often-repeated one of another kind. — Philebus, 53.

Pleasure will rank fifth but not first; no, not even if all the oxen and horses and animals in the world in their pursuit of enjoyment this assert; and the many trusting in them, as diviners trust in birds, determine that pleasures make up the good of life, and deem the lusts of animals to be better witnesses than the inspirations of divine philosophy. — Philebus, 67.

The rest of the world are of the opinion that a life which has no bodily pleasures and no part in them is not worth having, and that he who thinks nothing of bodily pleasures is almost as though he were dead. — Phaedo, 65.

If anyone says to him that some pleasures are the satisfactions of good and noble desires, and other of evil desires, and that he ought to use and honor some and chastise and master the others — whenever this is repeated to him he shakes his head and says that they are all alike, and that one is as good as another. — Republic, VIII, 561.

The bad commonly delight in false pleasures, and the good in true pleasures. — Philebus, 40.

Immediate pleasure differs widely from future pleasure. — Protagoras, 356.

Do you think that the philosopher ought to care about the pleasures — if they are to be called pleasures —

of eating and drinking, and the pleasures of love? — By no means. — Phaedo, 64.

In all of us, even in good men, there is such a latent wild-beast nature, which peers out in sleep. — Republic, IX, 572.

Everyone appears to have unlawful pleasures and appetites, but in some persons they are controlled by the laws and by reason, and the better desires prevail over them; in the case of others they are stronger, and there are more of them. I mean those which are awake when the reasoning and human and ruling power is asleep; then the wild beast within us, gorged with meat and drink, starts up and having shaken off sleep, goes forth to satisfy his desires; and there is no conceivable folly or crime — not excepting incest or any other unnatural union, or parricide, or the eating of forbidden food — which at such time, when he has parted company with all shame and sense, a man may not be ready to commit. — Republic, IX, 571.

Are you satisfied at having a life of pleasure — without any pain? — Protagoras, 355.

What good can the just man have which is separated from pleasure? — Laws, II, 663.

When men are overcome by eating and drinking and other sensual desires which are pleasant, and they, knowing them to be evil, nevertheless indulge in them, is not that what you would call being overcome by pleasure? — Protagoras, 353.

Pleasure and Pain. Pleasures are avoidances of pain. — Philebus, 44.

Pleasure and pain are two fountains which nature lets flow, and he who draws from them where and when, and as much as he ought to, is happy; and this holds of men and animals — of individuals as well as states; and he who indulges in them ignorantly and in excess, is the reverse of happy. — Laws, I, 636.

With those who declare that all pleasures are a cessation of pain, I do not agree, but use them as witnesses of the existence of some pleasures which are imaginary and in no way real. — Philebus, 51.

One should not rush headlong into pleasures, for one will not be free from pains. — Laws, VII, 792.

Pleasures and pains and desires are a part of human nature, and on them every mortal being must of necessity hang and depend with the most eager interest. — Laws, V, 732.

I think that by pleasure he must mean the negative of pain. — Philebus, 43.

The true discipline of pleasure and pain which, when rightly ordered, is a principle of education, has been often relaxed and corrupted in human life. — Laws, II, 653.

Pleasure and pain engender folly and forgetfulness and dullness and lawlessness. — Letter, III, 315.

How singular is the thing called pleasure, and how curiously related to pain, which might be thought to be the opposite of it; for they never come to a man at the same instant, and yet he who pursues either of them is generally compelled to take the other. They are two, and yet they grow together out of one head or stem; if Aesop had noticed them, he would have made a fable about God trying to reconcile their strife. — Phaedo, 60.

Dullness, folly, forgetfulness and wantonness often result from pleasure and pain. — Letter, III, 315.

Do you remember how at the sight of tragedies the spectators smile through their tears. And are you aware that even at a comedy the soul experiences a mixed feeling of pain and pleasure? — Philebus, 48.

In the temperate life the pleasures exceed the pains, and in the intemperate life the pains exceed the pleasures in greatness and number and intensity. — Laws, V, 734.

Pleasure, Sexual. Our citizens should not allow sexual pleasures to strengthen with indulgence but should by toil divert the aliment and exuberance of them into other parts of the body; and this sublimation will happen if no immodesty be allowed in the practice of love. Then they will be ashamed of excessive intercourse, and they will find pleasure, if seldom enjoyed, to be a less imperious mistress. — Laws, VIII, 841.

Is not a man more likely to abstain from pleasures of love, when his physique is in good condition — in training, in fact — than when it is in poor form? — Laws, VIII, 839.

Pledge. Give a pledge, and evil is nigh at hand. — Charmides, 165.

Pluto. They shall give to Pluto his own in the twelfth month, which is sacred to him, according to the law. To such a deity warlike men should entertain no aversion, but they should honor him as being always the best friend of man. For the connection of soul and body is no way better than the dissolution of them, as I am ready to maintain quite seriously. — Laws, VIII, 828.

Poet. Did we not imply that the poets are not always capable of knowing what is good or evil? — Laws, VII, 801.

Every one of these poets has said many things well and many things the reverse of well. — Laws, VII, 811.

A poet might quarrel with an actor who spoiled his poems in repeating them. — Charmides, 162.

Poets are to us in a manner the fathers and authors of wisdom. — Lysis, 214.

Like a fountain, the poet allows the stream of thought to flow freely and his art being imitative, he is often compelled to represent men under opposite circumstances, and thus to say two different things; neither can he tell whether there is any truth in either of them, or in one more than in the other. — Laws, IV, 719.

The poets are only the interpreters of the gods by whom they are severally possessed. Was not this the lesson which the God intended to teach when by the mouth of the worst of poets he sang the best of songs? — Ion, 534.

The poets were men of genius, but they had no knowledge of what is just and lawful in music; raging like Bacchanals and possessed with inordinate delights — mingling lamentations with hymns, and paeans with dithyrambs; imitating the sounds of the flute on the lyre, and making one general confusion of forms. And by composing such licentious poems, and adding to them words as licentious, they have inspired the multitude with lawlessness and defiance. — Laws, III, 700.

Some poet will make dithyrambs, another hymns of praise, another choral strains, another epic or iambic verses — he who is good at one is not good at any other kind of verse. — Ion, 534.

He who cannot rise above his own compilations and compositions, which he has been long patching and piecing, adding some and taking away some, may be justly called poet or speech-writer or law-writer. — Phaedrus, 278.

Poetry. We must beg Homer and the other poets not to be angry if we strike out these and similar passages in their works, not because they are unpoetical, or unattractive to the popular ear, but because the greater the charm of them as poetry, the less are they meet for the ears of boys and men who are to be sons of freedom. — Republic, III, 387.

Skill in poetry is the principal part of education. — Protagoras, 339.

Poetry is really imaginative rather than descriptive. — Phaedo, 61.

Poetry feeds and waters the passions instead of withering and starving them; she lets them rule instead of ruling them as they ought to be ruled, with a view to the happiness and virtue of mankind. — Republic, X, 606.

Poetry and mythology are, in some cases, wholly imitative. — Republic, III, 394.

Let this then be the explanation which we give of our reasons for dismissing poetry, and let us make an apology to her, that she may not charge us with any harshness or want of politeness. We will tell her, "that there is an ancient quarrel between philosophy and poetry." Not withstanding this, let us assure our sweet friend that if she will only prove her title to existence in a well-ordered state we shall be delighted to receive her, knowing that we ourselves also are very susceptible of her charms. — Republic, X, 607.

Point of Vantage. One needs a point of vantage to judge what is good for states and individuals. — Letter, VII, 326.

Poison. By talking, heat is increased, and this interferes with the action of the poison; those who excite themselves are sometimes obliged to drink the poison two or three times. — Phaedo, 63.

There are two kinds of poisons used among men. There is one kind of poison which injures bodies by the use of bodies according to nature; and there is another kind which injures by sorceries, and incantations, and magic bonds, as they are termed, and induces one class of men to injure others as far as they can, and persuades others that they are liable to be injured by the powers of the magician. And when men are disturbed at the sight of waxen images at the doors, there is little hope in trying to persuade them that they should despise all such things. But we must have a law concerning poisoning, and we must entreat, and exhort, and advise men not to have recourse to such practices, by which they scare the multitude out of their wits, as if they were children. — Laws, XI, 933.

Policy. The right policy is to do the most damage to your enemies and the most benefit to your friends. — Letter, VIII, 352.

Political. The best and wisest of our citizens are unable to impart their political wisdom to others. — Protagoras, 319.

Political Action. This, then, is the perfection of the web of political action. There is a direct intertexture of brave and temperate natures, when statesmanship has drawn the two sorts of lives into communion by unanimity and kindness. — Statesman, 311.

Political Science. Political science is concerned with tame animals, and is also confined to gregarious animals. — Statesman, 264.

Politician. That politician who curries favor with the citizens and indulges them and fawns upon them and has a presentiment of their wishes, and is skillful in gratifying them, he is esteemed as a great statesman. — Republic, IV, 426.

There are some politicians whom the applause of the multitude has deluded into the belief that they are really statesmen, and they are not much to be admired. — What do you mean? You should have more feeling for them. When a man cannot measure, and a great many others who cannot measure declare that he is four cubits high can he help believing them? — He cannot. — Republic, IV, 426.

They know that no politician is honest, nor is there any champion of justice at whose side they may fight and be saved. — Republic, VI, 496.

Why don't you know that when a politician writes he begins with the names of his approvers? He begins thus: "Be it enacted by the senate, the people, or both, as a certain person who was the author proposed"; and then he rehearses all his titles, and proceeds to display his own wisdom to his admirers with a great flourish in what is often a tedious composition. And if the law is passed, then, like the poet, he leaves the theatre in high delight; but if the law is rejected, and he is not thought good enough to write, then he and his party are mourning. This shows how far they are from despising, or rather how highly they value the practice of writing. — Phaedrus, 258.

There is nothing of which great politicians are so fond as of writing speeches, which they bequeath to posterity. And when they write them, out of gratitude to their admirers, they append their names at the top. — Phaedrus, 257.

We shall see who are the false politicians who win popularity and pretend to be politicians and are not, and separate them from the wise king. — Statesman, 292.

Politics. There seems to be a difficulty in so ordering acts and words in politics, that there should be no dispute about them. — Laws, I, 636.

I wonder why most of the great men of the past — Pittacus, Bias, Thales of Miletus, Anaxagoras — did not take an active part in politics. — Greater Hippias, 281.

There is sometimes a difficulty in apprehending that the true art of politics is concerned, not with private but with public good; for public good binds together states, but private only distracts them — nor do men always see that the gain is greater both to the individual and the state, when the state and not the individual is first considered. — Laws, IX, 875.

Your countrymen are right in admitting the tinker and the cobbler to advise about politics. — Protagoras, 324.

We put aside the so-called good results of politics. — Euthydemus, 292.

If I had engaged in politics, I should have perished long ago, and done no good either to you or to myself. — Apology, 31.

There may be trouble and danger in any political undertaking. But we are now discoursing, and not acting. — Laws, V, 736.

To what doctrine do we give the

power of determining whether we are to use persuasion or force in relation to any particular thing or person, or whether the use of them is to be allowed at all? — That, if I am not mistaken, will be politics. — Statesman, 304.

That common doctrine which is over them all, and guards the laws, and all things that are in the state, and truly weaves them all into one, if we would describe under a name characteristic of this common nature, most truly we may call politics. — Statesman, 305.

Every man ought to share in political virtue, and states could not exist if this were otherwise. — Protagoras, 323.

When the foundation of politics is in the letter only and in custom, and knowledge is divorced from action, can we wonder at the miseries that are there, and always will be, in states? Any other art, built on such a foundation, would be undermined — there can be no doubt of that. Ought we not rather to wonder at the natural strength of the political bond? For states have endured all this, time out of mind, and yet some of them still remain and are not overthrown, though many of them, like ships foundering at sea, are perishing, and have perished, and will hereafter perish, through the incapacity of their pilots and crews, who have the worst sort of ignorance of the highest truths — I mean to say, that they are wholly unacquainted with politics, of which, above all other doctrines, they believe themselves to have acquired the most perfect knowledge. — Statesman, 301, 302.

Pollution. If anyone intentionally pollutes the water of another, either by poisonous substances, or by digging, let the injured party bring the cause before the wardens of the city. — Laws, VIII, 845.

I am amused at your making a distinction between one who is a relative and one who is not a relative; for surely the pollution is the same in either case, if you knowingly associate with the murderer when you ought to clear yourself by proceeding against him. The real question is whether the murdered man has been justly slain. If justly, then your duty is to let the matter alone; but if unjustly, then even if the murderer is under the same roof with you and eats at the same table, proceed against him. — Euthyphro, 4.

Polus. I praise you, Polus, for being a rhetorician rather than a reasoner. — Gorgias, 471.

And there is Polus, who has schools of diplasiology, and gnomology, and eikonology. — Phaedrus, 267.

Ponder. To ponder is the same as to consider. — Cratylus, 411.

Popularity. Popularity is a road to success. — Letter IV, 321.

Population Control. The number of weddings is a matter which must be left to the discretion of the rulers, whose aim will be to control the population; and they will have to consider the effects of wars and diseases, in order to prevent the state becoming either too large or too small. — Republic, V, 460.

Poseidon. Poseidon fell in love with Cleito and had intercourse with her. — Critias, 113.

Possessed. Spiritually possessed they say many grand things. — Meno, 99.

Possession. I should distinguish "having" from "possessing": for example, a man may buy and keep under his control a garment which he does not wear; and then we should say, not that he has, but that he possesses the garment. — Theaetetus, 197.

Possibility. I will ask you, if you have no objection, to assist me, first of all, in considering the advantages of this [ideal plan], and then I will return to the question of possibility. — Republic, V, 458.

They do not see that some of these things are possible, and some of them are impossible; and the builder of a state will intend only what is possible, and will not indulge in vain wishes or attempts to accomplish that which is impossible. — Laws, V, 742.

Pot. Brazen pots, when they are struck, continue to sound unless someone puts his hand upon them. — Protagoras, 329.

Poverty. In a worldly estate, do you see any greater misfortune than poverty? — Gorgias, 477.

The community which has no poverty will always have the noblest principles. — Laws, III, 679.

I am in utter poverty by reason of my service to the god. — Apology, 23.

I have a witness of the truth of what I say; my poverty is a sufficient witness. — Apology, 31.

They will take care that their families do not live beyond their means; having an eye to poverty. — Republic, II, 372.

Power. Every man has power who does that which he wishes at the time when he wishes: I am not speaking in any special case of his being prevented by disease or something of that sort. — Lesser Hippias, 366.

The very bad men come from the class of those who have power. And yet in that very class there may arise good men. — Gorgias, 526.

There ought to be no great and unmixed powers; and this is under the idea that a state ought to be free and wise and harmonious. — Laws, III, 693.

Power is a good thing, and yet power which is exercised without understanding is an evil. — Gorgias, 467.

In that sort of way anyone may have great power: he may burn any house that he pleases, and the docks and triremes of the Athenians, and all their other vessels — but this is in some sense not great power. — Gorgias, 469.

I don't admit that the powerful is strong, only that the strong is powerful. For there is a difference between power and strength; the former is given by knowledge as well as by madness and rage, but strength comes from nature and a healthy state of the body. — Protagoras, 350, 351.

They say that tyranny or democracy, or any other conquering power, makes the continuance of the power which is possessed by them the first or principal object of their laws. — Laws, IV, 714.

If anyone gives too great a power to anything, too much food to the body, too large a sail to a vessel, too much authority to the mind, and disregards the mean, everything is overthrown, and, in the wantonness of excess, runs in the one case to disorder, and in the other to injustice, which is the child of excess. There is no soul of man, young and irresponsible, who will be able to sustain the temptation of arbitrary power — no one who will not, under such circumstances, become filled with folly, that worst of diseases, and then be hated by his dearest friends: when this happens his kingdom is undermined, and all his power vanishes from him. — Laws, III, 691.

Practice. I advised him to practice my proposed ideals for the state. — Letter, VII, 327.

They acquire their medical skill by obeying and observing their masters; by practice, and not by theoretical study. — Laws, IV, 720.

Mankind have been agreed of old, that if great subjects are to be adequately treated, they must practice on slighter and easier matters before they aspire to the greatest of all. — Sophist, 218.

Praise. Praise and blame educate a man, and make him more tractable and amenable to the laws which are to be enacted. — Laws, V, 730.

You will see how ready I am to praise you when you talk sense. — Gorgias, 510.

To honor with hymns and panegyrics those who are still alive is perilous; a man having run out his whole life, should make a fair ending, and then we will praise him and let all that we have to say apply equally to man and women who have been distinguished in virtue. — Laws, VII, 802.

I would rather praise the god Love first, and then speak of his gifts; this is always the right way of praising everything. — Symposium, 195.

Prayer. The prayer of a fool is full of danger, being likely to end in the opposite of what he desires. — Laws, III, 688.

All men who have any degree of right feeling pray at the beginning of every enterprise great or small. — Timaeus, 27.

The prayers of a father or a mother who is specially dishonored by his or her children, are heard by the gods; but if a man is honored by his children, and in the gladness of his heart earnestly entreats the gods in his prayers to do them good, he is equally heard, and ministered to his request. If not, the gods would be very unjust, and that we affirm to be contrary to their nature. — Laws, XI, 931.

Prayer of Socrates. Beloved Pan, and all ye other gods who haunt this place, give me beauty in the inward soul; and may the outward and inward man be at one. May I reckon the wise to be the wealthy, and may I have such a quantity of gold as none but the temperate can carry. — Phaedrus, 279.

Preamble. It is a matter of great importance, that our reasons in proof of the existence of gods [normative laws] and their higher concern for justice than man, should carry some sort of persuasion with them. This would be the best and noblest preamble of all our laws. — Laws, X, 887.

I imagine that all this language of conciliation, which the legislator utters in the preface of the law, is intended to create good-will in the person whom he addresses, in order that, by reason of this good-will, he might more intelligently receive the law. And therefore, in my way of speaking, this is more rightly described as the preamble than as the matter of the law. And I must further proceed to observe that the legislator should not make laws without preambles. — Laws, IV, 723.

Precision. Nothing delighted me more than the precision of their movements. — Protagoras, 315.

The free use of words and phrases, rather than minute precision, is generally characteristic of a liberal education, and the opposite is pedantic; but sometimes this precision is necessary. — Theaetetus, 184.

Predecessors. I habitually praise our predecessors of former times before and above contemporaries, for while I watch over myself against the envy of the living, I fear the wrath of the dead. — Greater Hippias, 282.

Predestination. The combination of a living being has a predestined term of life. — Timaeus, 89.

Pregnancy. If I were not afraid of appearing to be ridiculous, I would say that a pregnant woman should of all women be most carefully tended during that year, and kept from violent or excessive pleasures and pains; let her preserve gentleness and benevolence and kindness at that time of her life. — Laws, VII, 792.

Shall we make a law that the pregnant woman shall walk about and fashion the still unborn infant as a thing of wax which is still flexible? — Laws, VII, 789. *Vide.* offspring.

Prejudice. Don't make the observers of your interests prejudiced against you. — Letter, XIII, 362.

Pretense. You give your disciples only the pretense of wisdom. — Phaedrus, 275.

I will not pretend to be more than I am. — Lesser Hippias, 372.

Price. When a man undertakes a work, the law gives him the same advice which was given to the seller, that he should not attempt to raise the price, but simply ask the value; this the law enjoins also on the contractor; for the craftsman assuredly knows the value of his work. — Laws, 921.

Pride. Your pride has been too much for the pride of your admirers. — First Alcibiades, 103.

Man is blamed for pride and sullenness when the lion and serpent element in him grows and increases out of proportion. — Republic, IX, 590.

Primitive. We may accept his witness to the fact that there was a time when primitive societies existed. — Laws, III, 680.

Principle. A principle which has any soundness should stand firm not only now and then, but always and forever. — Meno, 89.

A principle is above hypotheses. Republic, VI, 510.

Principle, Moral. Is there not such a moral principle? — Crito, 48.

Do we suppose the spiritual or moral principle, which has to do with justice and injustice, to be inferior to the body? — Crito, 48.

The intellectual principle is dark and inapprehensible to the bodily eye, and can be seen only by the spiritual eye. — Phaedo, 81.

Let us note that in everyone of us there are two guiding and ruling principles which lead us whither they will; one is an innate desire of pleasure, the other an acquired opinion which is in search of the best; and these two are sometimes in harmony and then again at war, and sometimes the one, sometimes the other conquers. — Phaedrus, 237.

Principles, First. Every man should expend his chief thought and attention on the consideration of his first principles: Are they or are they not rightly laid down? and when he has sifted them all the rest will follow rightly. — Cratylus, 436.

Prison. There shall be three prisons in the state: the first of them is to be the common prison, for the safekeeping of the generality of offenders; another is to be called the "house of correction"; another, to be situated in some wild and desolate region of the country, shall be called by some name expressive of retribution. — Laws, X, 908.

Private. Without the regulation of private life in cities, stability in the laying down of laws is hardly to be expected. — Laws, VII, 790.

In private life there are many little things which are so small and of such frequent occurrence, that there would be an impropriety in making them penal by law; and if made penal, they are the destruction of the written law, because mankind gets the habit of frequently transgressing in small matters. The result is that you cannot legislate about them, and still less can you say nothing. — Laws, VII, 788.

Where there is no common but only private feeling, that disorganizes a state. — Republic, V, 462.

Probability. All is probability with you, and yet surely you had better reflect whether you are disposed to admit of probability and figures of speech in matters of such importance. Any geometrician who argued from probabilities and likelihoods in geometry, would not be worth an ace. — Theaetetus, 162, 163.

Procreation. There is a certain age at which human nature is desirous of procreation; and this procreation must be in beauty and not in deformity. — Symposium, 206.

The human seed having life, and becoming endowed with respiration, produces, in that part in which it respires, a lively desire of emission, and thus creates in us the love of procreation. Wherefore also in men the organ of generation becoming rebellious and masterful, like an animal disobedient to reason, seeks, by the raging of the appetites, to gain absolute sway; and the same is the case with the wombs and the other organs of women. — Timaeus, 91.

Divorced persons who have no children, or but a few at the time of their separation, should choose their new partners with a view to the procreation of children. — Laws, XI, 930.

The animal within men is desirous of procreating children, and when remaining without fruit long beyond its proper time, gets discontented and angry and wandering in every direction through the body, closes up the passages of the breath, by obstructing respiration, drives them into the utmost difficulty, causing all varieties of nervous and somatic disease, until the desire of the man and the woman cause the emission of seed into the womb, as into a field, in which they sow animals. — Timaeus, 91.

They shall beget and rear children, handing on the torch of life from one generation to another. — Laws, VI, 776.

Procuress. Procuress is a name given to those women who join man and women in an unlawful and unscientific way. — Theaetetus, 150.

Prodigy. Those who follow out of the course of nature are prodigies. —Cratylus, 394.

Production. He who brings into existence something that did not exist before is said to be a producer, and that which is brought into existence is said to be produced. — Sophist, 219.

Conditions which are not required for the existence of a thing are not useful for the production of it. — Eryxias, 402.

Things which are made by nature

are the work of divine art, and things which are made by man out of these are works of human art. And so there are two kinds of making or production, the one human and the other divine. — Sophist, 265.

Profession. In every profession the inferior sort are numerous and good for nothing, and the good are few and beyond all price. — Euthydemus, 307.

Professor. Are we to maintain that all the professors of minor arts are philosophers? — Republic, V, 475.

When I contemplate any of those who pretend to educate others, I am amazed. They all seem to me to be such outrageous beings, if I am to confess the truth: so that I do not know how I can advise the youth to study philosophy. — Euthydemus, 307.

Profit. Would things profit us, if we only had them and did not use them? — Euthydemus, 280.

Profligacy. The utterly bad man is in general profligate, and therefore poor. — Laws, V, 743.

Progress. Progress is brought about when the craftsmen of the past cannot stand comparison with those of today. — Greater Hippias, 281.

You have really made progress toward combining private pursuit with public interest. — Greater Hippias, 282.

Prolonging. Do you think that all our cares are to be directed to prolonging life to the uttermost? — Gorgias, 511.

Prometheus, Tale of. Prometheus found that the other animals were suitably furnished, but that man alone was naked and shoeless, and had neither bed nor arms of defense. Not knowing how he could devise his salvation, he stole the mechanical arts of Hephaestus and Athene, and fire with them, and gave them to man. Thus man had the wisdom necessary to support of life, but political wisdom he had not; for that was in the keeping of Zeus. But Prometheus is said to have been afterwards prosecuted for theft. — Protagoras, 321.

Promise. Lovers' promises are made to be foresworn. — Philebus, 65.

I must beg you to be absolved from the promise which (as Euripides would say) was a promise of the lips and not of the mind. — Symposium, 199.

The promise is so vast, that a feeling of incredulity creeps in. — Euthydemus, 274.

Proof. If the proof, although not quite precise, is fair, that is fair enough. — First Alcibiades, 130.

Pardon me; I do not want this "if you wish" or "if you will" sort of argument to be proven, but I want you and me to be proven; and I mean by this that the argument will be best proven if there be no "if." — Protagoras, 331.

I will give you a notable proof of the truth of what I am saying. — Euthyphro, 5.

That [proof] would be a difficult task, although I could make the matter very clear indeed to you. — I understand; you mean to say that I am not so quick of apprehension as the judges: for to them you will be sure to prove fast that that act is unjust. — Euthyphro, 9.

Prophecy. There is no great prophecy in knowing, and no great difficulty in telling, after the evil has happened. — Laws, III, 691.

I [Socrates] am about to die, and that is the hour in which men are gifted with prophetic power. And I prophesy to you who are my murderers, that immediately after my death punishment far heavier than you have inflicted on me will surely await you. — Apology, 39.

Prophet. The prophet knows the future. — Charmides, 174.

Proportion. With a view to health and disease, and virtue and vice, there is no proportion or disproportion more important than that of the soul to the body. — Timaeus, 87.

Proposition. What was before a conjecture is now a proposition. — Philebus, 38.

A true proposition says that which is. — Cratylus, 385.

The combination of concepts is the essence of a proposition. — Theaetetus, 202.

Propositions may be true or false. — Cratylus, 385.

Proprietor. Hearing of enormous landed proprietors of ten thousand acres and more, our philosopher deems this to be a trifle, because he has been accustomed to think of the whole earth. — Theaetetus, 174.

Propriety. A man should seek to behave with propriety, whether his genius be set at good fortune, or whether at the crisis of his fate, when he seems to be mounting high and steep places, the gods oppose him in some of his enterprises. — Laws, V, 732.

Prose. The poets have already declared in verse the Greek glory to all mankind and therefore any commemoration in prose which we might attempt would hold a second place. — Menexenus, 239.

Prosecuting. I suppose that someone is prosecuting you, for I cannot believe that you are the prosecutor of anybody else. — Euthyphro, 2.

Prospect. Distant prospects are apt to make the world spin round us, especially in childhood. — Laws, II, 662.

Prosperity. Prosperity brings deliverances from misfortune. — Laws, I, 632.

Prosperity makes men jealous. — Menexenus, 242.

Prostitution. I would command men to abstain from any female field in which that which is sown is not likely to grow. — Laws, VIII, 839.

Prostrate. Only he who is standing upright and not he who is prostrate can be laid prostrate. — Protagoras, 344.

Protagoras. Protagoras of Abdera, and Prodicus of Ceos, and a host of others, have only to whisper to their contemporaries: "You will never be able to manage either your own house or you own state until you appoint us to be your ministers of education" — and this ingenious device of theirs has such an effect in making men love them that their companions all but carry them about on their shoulders. — Republic, X, 600.

Protagoras would be a better judge of the arguments which are likely to convince us in a court of law than any layman. — Theaetetus, 178.

You have quiet made up your mind that you will be a pupil of Protagoras, although you do not know him. — Protagoras, 313.

Proteus. You have literally as many forms as Proteus; and now you go all manner of ways, twisting and turning, and, like Proteus, become all manner of people at once. — Ion, 541.

Providence. Execute your plans more effectively through the kindness of providence. — Letter, VII, 337.

You may ascribe the deliverance of

Sicily to a special providence, that is, to god. — Letter, VIII, 353.

Proxeni. From their earliest youth, all boys, when they are told that they are the proxeni of a particular state, feel kindly towards the state of which they are the proxeni, as to a second country. — Laws, I, 642.

Psychosomatic. All good and evil, whether in the body or in human nature, originates in the soul, and overflows from thence, as from the head into the eyes. And therefore if the head and the body are to be well, you must begin by curing the soul; that is the first thing. And the psychosomatic cure has to be effected by the use of certain charms, and these charms are fair words. — Charmides, 156, 157.

Let no one persuade you to cure the head, until he has first given you his soul to be cured by the charm. For this is the great error of our day in the treatment of the human body, that physicians separate the soul from the body. — Charmides, 157.

Public Opinion. The legislator who wants to master any of the passions which keep men in bondage may easily know how to subdue them. He only has to get the sanction of public opinion thoughout the state. That will be the surest foundation of the law which he can make. — Laws, VIII, 838.

The public are the new Sophists. . . . All those mercenary individuals, whom the multitude call Sophists, do but teach the collective opinion of the many, which are the opinions of their assemblies. — Republic, VI, 492, 493.

Public opinion is a marvelous force, if no breath of opposition ever assails it. — Laws, VIII, 838.

There neither is, has been, nor ever can be an education of virtuous character independent of public opinion. — Republic, VI, 492.

Public Property. No house of all the 5040 belongs to the individual inhabitant or to the whole family, in the same sense as it is the public property of the state. — Laws, IX, 877.

Pugnacious. He is very pugnacious, and that is the reason why I want you to argue with him. — Lysis, 211.

Punishment. If he suffers punishment he will probably be corrected and improved; for no penalty which is inflicted according to law is designed for evil, but always makes him who suffers either better or not so bad. And if a citizen be guilty of any great and unmentionable wrong, let the judge deem him to be incurable, remembering what an education he has had from youth unward, and yet has not abstained from the greatest of crimes. The penalty of death is to him the least of evils; and others will be benefited by his example. — Laws, IX, 854.

Let no one be outlawed for any offense whatever, nor be banished beyond the frontier, but let him receive punishment — death, or bonds, or blows, or uncomfortable positions, standing or posted at a temple on the borders of the land, or let him pay money penalties. In cases of death, let the judges be the guardians of the law, and a court selected according to merit from last year's magistrates. — Laws, IX, 855.

Let there be a general rule, that the disgrace and punishment of the father is not to be visited on the children, except in the case of some one whose father, grandfather, and great-grandfather have successively undergone the penalty of death. — Laws, IX, 856.

We should make punishments stern here in this life. — Laws, IX, 881.

Punishment is useful, because giving deliverance from great evils. — Gorgias, 478.

Not to suffer punishment, is to perpetuate one's injustice. — Gorgias, 479.

To suffer punishment is another name for being justly corrected. — Gorgias, 476.

To suffer punishment is the way to be released from one's injustice. — Gorgias, 479.

Not to be punished is a greater evil than to be punished. — Gorgias, 474. *Vide* Evildoer.

He who escapes punishment is worse than he who suffers it. — Gorgias, 479.

He who is punished suffers what he deserves. — Gorgias, 477.

One undoubtedly punishes for the sake of prevention. — Protagoras, 324.

When a state has good courts, and the judges are well trained and scrupulously tested, the determination of the penalties or punishments which shall be inflicted on the guilty may fairly and with advantage be left to them. — Laws, IX, 876.

He who is punished and suffers retribution, suffers justly. — Gorgias, 476.

All men agree as to the propriety of punishing a murderer. — Euthyphro, 8.

They do not argue that the evildoer should not be punished. — Euthyphro, 8.

No one punishes the evildoer under the notion, or for the reason, that he has done wrong — only the unreasonable fury of a vengeful beast acts in that way. — Protagoras, 324.

Surely neither god nor man will ever venture to say that the doer of evil is not to be punished. — Euthyphro, 8.

The wicked are miserable because they are required to be punished, and yet are benefited by receiving punishment. — Republic, II, 380.

He who is wanting in justice, whether he be a child only or a grown-up man or woman, must be taught and punished, until by punishment he becomes better. — Protagoras, 325.

The proper object of punishment is twofold; he who is rightly punished ought either to become better and profit by it, or he ought to be made an example to his fellows, that they may see what he suffers, and fear and become better. — Gorgias, 525.

Men commit all sorts of crimes, and there is nothing that they will not do or say for vindication's sake, in order to escape punishment. — Euthyphro, 8.

Rhetoric is of use for the evildoer, if, instead of concealing and excusing his iniquity, he voluntarily brings it to light and accuses himself so that he may be healed through punishment. — Gorgias, 480.

Still grander are the rewards of heaven which Musaeus and his son (Eumolpus) vouchsafe to the just; they take them down into the world below, where they have the saints lying on couches at a feast, everlastingly drunk, crowned with garlands; their idea seems to be that an immortality of drunkenness is the highest meed of virtue. This is the style in which they praise justice. But about the wicked there is another strain; they bury them in a slough in Hades, and make them carry water in a sieve;

also while they are yet living they bring them to infamy, and inflict upon them punishments. — Republic, II, 363.

He who desires to inflict rational punishment does not retaliate for the past wrong, for that which is done cannot be undone, but he has a regard to the future, and is desirous that the man who is punished, and he who sees him punished, may be deterred from doing wrong again. — Protagoras, 324.

Not that man is punished because he did wrong, for that which is done can never be undone, but in order that in future times, he, and those who see him corrected, may utterly hate injustice, or at any rate abate much of their evil-doing. Having an eye to all these things, the law, like a good archer, should aim at the right measure of punishment, and in all cases at the deserved punishment. — Laws, XI, 934.

Punishment disciplines us, makes us more just, and cures us of evil. — Gorgias, 478.

Punishment is a deliverance from the greatest of evils, namely wickedness. — Gorgias, 478.

Puppet. May we not regard every living being as a puppet of the gods, which may be their plaything only, or may be created with a purpose? — Laws, I, 644.

Pure. We should try to understand what is the nature of the pure. — Philebus, 52.

No impure thing is allowed to approach the pure. — Phaedo, 67.

Purgative. Diseases which are not dangerous should not be irritated by purgatives. — Timaeus, 89.

Purge. He who without a despotism sets up a new government and laws, even he attempt the mildest of purgations, may think himself happy if he can complete his work. — Laws, V, 735.

A rare purge — not the sort of purgation which the physicians make of the body; for they take away the worse and leave the better part, but the tyrant does the reverse. If he is to rule, I suppose that he cannot help himself. What a blessed alternative: to be compelled to dwell only with the many bad, and to be by them hated, or not to live at all! — Republic, VIII, 567.

Purification. To the discerning art belongs purification, to the purifying art mental purification. — Sophist, 231.

Purification is the separation of the soul from the body: the habit of the soul gathering and collecting herself into herself, out of all the courses of the body; the dwelling in her own place alone, as far as she can; the release of the soul from the chains of the body. — Phaedo, 67.

The best of all purifications and quadrupeds and polypeds were cre- the next best is a rolling motion, as in sailing or in any other mode of conveyance which is not fatiguing; the third sort of motion may be in use in a case of extreme necessity, but in any other will be adopted by no man of sense: I mean the purgative treatment of physicians. — Timaeus, 89.

Purpose. Can a bad thing be used to carry out a good purpose? I should say not. — Eryxias, 404.

Puzzle. We shall surely loose the puzzle if we find the answer. — Philebus, 34.

Q

Quadruped. This is the reason why quadrupeds and polypeds were created: God gave the more senseless of the beings the more support that they might be more attracted to the earth. And the most foolish of them, who trailed their bodies entirely upon the ground and have no longer any need for feet, he made without feet to crawl upon the earth. — Timaeus, 92.

Quality. I suspect that quality may appear a strange term to you, and that you do not understand the word when thus generalized. Then I will take a particular case: the producing power or agent becomes neither heat nor whiteness, but hot and white. Neither the agent nor patient have any absolute existence, but as they come together and generate sensations and objects of sense, the one becomes of a certain quality, and the other is percipient. — Theaetetus, 182.

There are two qualities which should be cultivated in the soul: first, supreme courage; secondly, supreme fear. — Laws, I, 649.

Question. They shall attain the greatest skill in asking and answering questions. — Republic, VII, 534.

No intelligent person will object to the method of questions — quite the reverse. — Theaetetus, 167.

I like to answer a question which is fairly put. — Protagoras, 317.

In that world they do not put a man to death for asking questions; certainly not. — Apology, 41.

Quickness. That which accomplishes much in a little time — that I call quickness in running, speaking, and every other sort of action.— Laches, 192.

Quietness. Quietness is the essence of temperance. — Charmides, 159.

R

Race, Girls'. Let the girls who are not grown up race naked in the stadium and the double course, and the horse course and the long course, and let them run on the race ground itself; those who are thirteen years and upwards shall descend into the arena in suitable dresses. — Laws, VIII, 833.

Rain. They ought to take care that the rains from heaven flow off easily [instead of remaining in the streets]. — Laws, VI, 779.

Random, At. Do not anwser at random what is not your real opinion. — Gorgias, 500.

Rape. Anyone who does violence to a free woman or a youth, shall be slain with impunity by the raped person, or by his or her father or brothers or sons. If a man find his wife suffering violence, he may kill the violator, and be guiltless in the eye of the law. — Laws, IX, 874.

Let us refuse to believe the tale of Theseus son of Poseidon, or of Peirithous son of Zeus, going forth to perpetrate a horrid rape. — Republic, III, 391.

Rarity. Only what is rare is valuable; and water, which as Pindar says, is the best of all things, is the cheapest. — Euthydemus, 304.

Reaction, Emotional. I must confess — at a tale of pity my eyes are filled with tears, and when I speak of horrors, my hair stands on end and my heart throbs. — Ion, 535.

Reading. I seized the books and read them as fast as I could in my eagerness to know the better and the worse. — Phaedo, 98.

Reading and writing are the same as doing. — Charmides, 161.

Reason. Cities as well as individuals should live according to reason. — Laws, I, 645.

At first all things were without reason. — Timaeus, 53.

Reason with whom decision ought to rest. — Republic, IX, 582.

You talk about the reason of man being degraded to the level of the brutes, which is a telling argument with the multitude, but not one word of proof or demonstration do you offer. — Theaetetus, 162.

Is not that farthest from reason which is at the greatest distance from law and order. — Republic, IX, 587.

This will never cease, and is not now beginning, but is, as I believe, an everlasting quality of timeless reason, as such, which never grows old in us. — Philebus, 15.

Reason rules the universe. — Philebus, 30.

Reason moves in the sphere of the self-moved or spiritual in voiceless silence. — Timaeus, 37.

If a man refuses to acknowledge normative ideas or species of spiritual existences, he will be at his wit's end; in this way he will utterly destroy the power of reasoning. — Parmenides, 135.

Reasoning is the peculiar instrument of the philosopher. — Republic, IX, 582.

Reason (Ground). And this they declare to me to be justice and the reason, for a reason is that because of which a consequence is created, and someone comes and whispers in my ear that justice is so called because partaking of the nature of the reason. — Cratylus, 413.

I presuppose the existence of goodness; if you grant my assumption, I hope to be able to show you the essence of the reason. — Phaedo, 100.

We must admit that the soul is the reason of good and evil, base and honorable, just and unjust, and of all other opposites, if we suppose her to be the universal condition. — Laws, X, 896.

Rebelliousness. I was thinking of the rebelliousness of mankind when I said that the permanent establishment of these things is very difficult. — Laws, VIII, 839.

Recapitulation. All of them agree in asserting that a speech should end in a recapitulation, though they do not all agree in the use of this word. — Phaedrus, 267.

Recollection. When the soul has lost the memory of some perception or knowledge, and recalls this of herself, that recovery is termed recollection. — Philebus, 34.

Recollection, Associative. What is the feeling of lovers when they recognize a lyre, or a garment, or anything else which the beloved has been in the habit of using? Do not they, from knowing the lyre, form in the mind's eye an image of the youth to whom the lyre belongs? And this is associative recollection: and in the same way anyone who sees Simmias may remember Cebes; and there are endless other things of the same nature. — Phaedo, 73.

Reconciliation. In music there is a reconciliation of opposites; and I suppose that this must have been the meaning of Heraclitus, although his words are not accurate; for he says that one is united by disunion, like the harmony of the bow and the lyre. — Symposium, 187.

Recreation. A man may sometimes set aside meditations about eternal things, and for recreation turn to consider the truths of generation; thus he attains a pleasure not to be repented of, and makes for himself during his life a wise and moderate pastime. Let us continue to grant ourselves this indulgence. — Timaeus, 59.

He will plant his seeds in the garden of letters only as an amusement, or he will write his memoirs against the forgetfulness of old age, to be treasured by him and his equals when they, like him, have one foot in the grave; and he will rejoice in beholding their tender growth; and they will be his recreation while others are watering the garden of their souls with drinking parties and the like. A recreation as noble as the other is ignoble, when a man is able to pass time joyfully in the discourse about justice and similar topics. — Phaedrus, 276.

Redemption. Such misdeeds are beyond redemption; such stains cannot be cleansed. — Letter, VIII, 352.

Referee. Let us choose an arbitrator, referee or president to watch over the speeches and reduce them to their proper length. — Protagoras, 338.

Refining. The workmen begin the

process of refining by sifting away the earth and stones and the like; they then draw off in the fire, which is the only way of extracting them, the more precious elements of copper, silver, and sometimes adamant, which have an affinity to gold; these are at last refined away by the use of tests, and the gold is left quite pure. — Statesman, 303.

Reform. Another piece of good fortune must not be forgotten — that we have escaped division of land and the abolition of debts; a city which is driven to legislation upon such matters can neither allow the old ways to continue, nor yet venture to alter them drastically. We must hope that a slight reform may be cautiously effected in a length of time. And such a redistribution can be accomplished by those who, having abundance of land and also many debtors, are willing, in a kindly spirit, to share with those who are in want, remitting some and dividing some, holding fast in a path of moderation, and deeming poverty to be the increase of a man's desires and not the diminution of his property. — Laws, V, 736.

When the legislator attempts to inaugurate reforms, everyone meets him with the cry, "that he is not to disturb vested interests" — declaring with imprecations that he is introducing agrarian law and cancellation of debts, until a man is at his wit's end. — Laws, III, 684.

Refutation. Refutation is the greatest and chiefest of purifications, and he who has not been refuted, is in the highest degree impure. . . . As the physician considers that the body will receive no benefit from taking food until the internal obstacles have been removed, so the instructor of the soul is conscious that his patient will receive no benefit from the applications of knowledge until he is refuted, and from refutation learns modesty; he must be cleared out, and learn to think that he knows only what he knows, and no more. — Sophist, 230.

There are two ways of refutation, one which is yours; but mine is of another sort. — Gorgias, 472.

Do you not think that you have been sufficiently refuted, when you say that which no human being will allow? — Gorgias, 473.

You are raising hobgoblins, instead of refuting me. — Gorgias, 473.

Such is their skill in the war of words, that they can refute any proposition whether true or false. — Euthydemus, 272.

Say rather, dear Agathon, that you cannot refute the truth; for Socrates is easily refuted. — Symposium, 201.

I prophesy that the youth whichever he answers, will be refuted. — Euthydemus, 275.

I am one of those who are very willing to be refuted if I say anything which is not true, and very willing to refute anyone else who says what is not true, that is to say, just as ready to be refuted as to refute; for I hold that the gain [of the truth is the greatest benefit]. — Gorgias, 458.

Regimen. Medical regimen is not a pleasant but a beneficial thing. — Gorgias, 478.

Registration. To every man the first year is the beginning of life, and ought to be registered in the temples of their fathers as the beginning of existence both to boy and girl. And in every phratria let there be written down on a whited wall the list of the archons by whom the years are reckoned. And near to them let the living members of the phratria be inscribed, and when they depart life let them be erased. — Laws, VI, 785.

Now the day was that day of the Apaturia which is called the registration of youth, at which our parents gave prizes for recitations. — Timaeus, 21.

Regulation. If all these things were done in this way according to written regulations, and not according to art, what would be the result? — Human life, which is bad enough already, would then become utterly unendurable. — Statesman, 299.

Rejoicing. Neither rejoice overmuch nor grieve overmuch. — Menexenus, 248.

We rejoice when we think that we prosper, and again we think that we prosper when we rejoice. — Laws, I, 657.

There is nothing wrong in rejoicing at the misfortunes of enemies. But it is wrongful in feeling joy instead of sorrow at the sight of our friends' misfortunes. — Philebus, 49.

Relative. I am about to speak of an illustrious philosophy, in which all things are said to be relative; you cannot rightly call anything by any name, such as great or small, or heavy or light, for the great will be small and the heavy light. Becoming is by us incorrectly called being; for nothing really is, but all things are becoming. — Theaetetus, 152.

Does not the greater in the order of nature appear to you to be only relative to the less, and the less only relative to the greater? — Statesman, 283.

While to the just all these things are the best of possessions, to the unjust they are the greatest of evils. Sight, and hearing, and perception, and life are, if not servicing justice and virtue, a great evil. — Laws, II, 661.

If a person were to go from the lower to the middle region, would he not imagine that he is going up; and he who is standing in the middle and sees whence he has come, would he not imagine that he is already in the upper region, if he has never seen the true upper world?—Republic, IX, 584.

The same wind is blowing, and yet one of us may be cold and the other not, or one may be slightly and the other very cold. Now is the wind, regarded not in relation to us but absolutely, cold or not; or are we to say, with Protagoras, that the wind is cold to him who is cold, and not to him who is not? — Theaetetus, 152.

Relativist. The relativist maintains that the truth varies with the individual opinion. And the best of the joke is that he acknowledges as true the opinions of those who believe his opinion to be false; for in admitting that the opinions of all men are true, in effect he grants that the opinion of his opponents is true. — Theaetetus, 171.

Relaxation, Judicial. By the relaxation of justice each power in the state is rent asunder from one another; they no longer incline in the same direction, but fill the city with faction, and make many cities out of one, and soon bring all to destruction. — Laws, XII, 945.

Relevance. You are literally always talking of cobblers and fullers and cooks and doctors, as if this would pertain to our argument. — Gorgias, 491.

Religion. The world is always

jealous of novelties in religion. — Euthyphro, 3.

Offenses are the greatest when they are committed against religion. — Laws, X, 884.

Religious. Then there would come forth the most religious of animals; and as human nature was of two kinds, the superior race would hereafter be called man. — Timaeus, 42.

Relive. Any man whose head is not filled with senile illusions is not willing to relive his life, when he retrospects it. — Epinomis, 974.

Remembering. If at your age you cannot remember, what will you do by and by, when you get older? — Gorgias, 466.

Often a man remembers that which he has seen, even if he closes his eyes. Theaetetus, 163.

Having been in an ecstasy I cannot well remember. — Phaedrus, 263.

Repair. The misfortune of which I was the cause I will also repair. — Gorgias, 447.

Repeating. It is good to repeat twice and thrice what is good. — Gorgias, 499.

He repeated himself two or three times, either from want of words or from want of efforts. — Phaedrus, 235.

Repose. True repose comes from labor. — Laws, VI, 779.

Reproof. He who does not fly from reproof will be sure to take more heed of his moral life. — Laches, 188.

Republic. He will seek to establish a republic guided by the best and justest laws without taking resort in the least to executions and banishments. — Letter, VII, 351.

Reputation. To be thought or not to be thought well of by the rest of the world is no light matter. — Laws, XII, 950.

Parents and tutors are always telling their sons and wards that they are to be just; but why? not for the sake of justice, but for the sake of reputation. — Republic, II, 363.

The generality of cities are right in exhorting men to value a good reputation in the world, for there is no truth greater and more important than this — that he who is really good seeks for reputation, not without, but with a possession of goodness. — Laws, XII, 950.

You will most likely be victors in the contest, if you so order your lives as not to misuse the reputation of your ancestors, knowing that to a man who has any self-respect, nothing is more dishonorable than to be honored, not for his own sake, but on account of the reputation of his ancestors. The honor of parents is a fair and noble treasure to their posterity, but to have the use of a treasure of wealth and honor, and to leave none to posterity, because you have neither money nor reputation of your own, is alike base and dishonorable. — Menexenus, 247.

Good men do everything to leave a good reputation for posterity, too. — Letter II, 311.

Some men say that to have a bad reputation though being really just, is disadvantageous, while having a good reputation without being really just, is very profitable. — Republic, II, 365.

He who has a feeling of reverence and shame about the commission of any action, fears and is afraid of an ill reputation. — Euthyphro, 12.

Rescuing. In time of war, men have died in rescuing a companion or kinsman, when others who have neglected the duty of rescuing have escaped in safety.

Research. We ought not to listen to the sophistical argument about the impossibility of research; such pessimism will make us idle, and is sweet music in the ears of lazy men. But the argument about the possibility of inquiry will make us active and enterprising. — Meno, 81. *Vide* Mental Health.

Some natural phenomena do not excite thought because the sense is an adequate judge of them; but where the senses are not reliable, further research is necessary. — Republic, VII, 523.

We ought to research. — Euthyphro, 9.

They say that we ought not to busy ourselves in searching out the causes of things. — Laws, VII, 821.

Respiration. When the respiration is going in and out, and the fire, which follows at the same time, is moving to and from, and entering through the belly, reaches the meat and drink, it dissolves them, and, dividing them into small portions and guiding them through the passages where it goes, draws them as from a fountain into the channels or veins, and makes the stream of the veins flow through the body as through a conduit. — Timaeus, 78, 79.

Responsibility. Those who want to be kings ought to be kings responsible for their actions. The rule of law should be supreme not only over ordinary citizens, but even more over the kings themselves, in case they do not observe the constitution. — Letter, VIII, 355.

Restitution. If the purchaser of a slave who has epilepsy or some other incurable disorder of body or mind, which is not discernible to the ordinary man, be a physician, he shall have no right of restitution; nor shall there be any right of restitution if the seller has told the truth beforehand to the buyer. But if a skilled person sells to another who is not skilled, let the buyer appeal for restitution. — Laws, XI, 916.

Restoration. Eating is a sort of restoration. — Philebus, 31.

Restraining. While the soul is senseless and intemperate and unjust and evil, her desires ought to be restrained, and she ought to be prevented from doing anything that does not tend to her own improvement.—Gorgias, 505.

Retailer. Retailers are weak in bodily strength, and therefore unable to do anything else; for all they have to do is to be in the market, and take money of those who desire to buy goods, and in exchange for goods to give money to those who desire to sell. — Republic, II, 371.

Retaliation. What of doing evil in retaliation for evil, which is the morality of the many — is that just or unjust? — Not just. — Crito, 49.

We ought not to retaliate or render evil for evil to anyone, whatever evil we may have suffered from him. This opinion has never been held, and never will be held, by any considerable number of persons. Tell me, then, whether you agree with and assent to my first principle, that neither injury nor retaliation nor warding off evil by evil is ever right. — Crito, 49.

This [teachableness of virtue] is the notion of all who retaliate upon others. And the Athenians, too, like other men, retaliate on those whom they regard as evildoers. — Protagoras, 324.

Retribution. If you become worse you shall belong to the worse souls, or if better to the better. This is a meaningful retribution, which neither you nor any other unfortunate shall ever claim to have escaped. If you say: "I am small and will creep into the depths of the earth, or I am high and will fly up to heaven," you still are not so small or so high, as to be able to escape judgment, but you shall pay the due penalty. — Laws, X, 905.

Retribution is the suffering which waits upon injustice; and whether a man escape or endure this, he is miserable — in the former case, because he is not cured; in the latter, because he perishes in order that the rest of the world may be saved. — Laws, V, 728.

There is a law of the goddess Retribution. — Phaedrus, 248.

Revelry. Must we not appoint a sober man and a wise man as master of revels? For if the head of drinkers be himself young and drunken, and not wise, only by some special good fortune will he be saved from doing some great evil. — Laws, I, 640.

In the presence of those whom they think wise, some persons are ashamed of dancing and singing in base fashion, or of deliberately lending their countenance to such proceedings; and yet, they have a secret pleasure in them. — Laws, II, 656.

Reverence. We fancy that our children will inherit reverence from us, if we rebuke them when they show a want of reverence. But this quality is not really imparted to them by the present style of admonition, which only tells them that the young ought always to be reverential. A sensible legislator will rather exhort the elders to reverence the younger, and above all take heed that no young man sees or hears him doing or saying anything base; for where old men have no shame, there young men will most certainly be devoid of reverence. The best way of training the young, is to train yourself at the same time; not only to admonish them, but to be seen always doing that of which you would admonish them. — Laws, V, 729.

Divine fear we have called reverence and shame. — Laws, II, 671.

We are wrong in saying that where there is fear there is also reverence; and we should say, where there is reverence there is also fear. But there is not always reverence where there is fear; for fear is wider in extent than reverence, which is only a part of fear. — Euthyphro, 12.

Revile. Are there not many cases in which we observe that, when a man's desires violently prevail over his reason, he reviles himself, and is angry at the violence within him, and that in this struggle his spirit is on the side of his reason? — Republic, IV, 440.

Revival. Revival, if there be such a thing, is the birth of the dead into the world of the living. — Phaedo, 72.

Revolution. Clearly, all revolutions originate in divisions of the actual governing power; a government which is united, however small, cannot be shaken. — Republic, VIII, 545.

In time of revolution men sometimes revenge themselves unduly on their adversaries. — Letter, VII, 325.

Citizens who are of the same race and live in the same cities, may unjustly conspire, and having the superiority in numbers, may overcome and enslave the few just; and when they prevail, the state may be truly called its own inferior. — Laws, I, 627.

Revolutionist. Young as I was, I believed that these revolutionists would introduce a new era of justice. But soon I discovered that the former government was by comparison a golden age. Observing this, I withdrew in disgust of the abusive regime. — Letter VII, 325.

Rhapsode. The rhapsode has always to wear fine clothes, and to look as beautiful as he can is a part of his art. — Ion, 530.

The rhapsode is obliged to give close attention to the spectators, for if he makes them weep, he himself shall laugh when he gets his fee, but if they laugh, he will weep at losing it. — Ion, 535.

The rhapsode will know what a woman ought to say, and what a freeman and what a slave ought to say, and what a ruler and what a subject. — Ion, 540.

No man can be a rhapsode who does not understand the meaning of the poet. For the rhapsode ought to interpret the mind of the poet to his hearers, and he cannot do this well unless he knows what he means. — Ion, 530.

You rhapsodists are the interpreters of the poets. — That is true. — Then you are the interpreters of interpreters. — Ion, 535.

Rhetoric. Rhetoric is an art of which the effect is produced through the medium of discourse. — Gorgias, 450.

One should make right use of his rhetoric gifts as well as of his athletic. — Gorgias, 457.

The rhetorician can speak more persuasively to the multitude than any of them, and on any subject. Such is the power and quality of rhetoric. — Gorgias, 456.

Rhetoric is the art of persuasion in the courts and other assemblies, and concerned with the just and unjust. — Gorgias, 454.

The whole of which rhetoric is a part appears to be a process, not of art, but the habit of a bold and ready wit, which knows how to behave in the world: this I sum up under the word "flattery." — Gorgias, 463.

Rhetorician. Every rhetorician has speeches ready made; nor is there any difficulty in improvising that sort of stuff. — Menexenus, 235.

The rhetorician ought not to abuse his strength any more than a pugilist or pancratiast or other master of fence; because he has powers which are more than a match either for enemy or friends, he ought not therefore to strike, stab, or slay his friends. — Gorgias, 456.

The rhetorician need not know the whole truth; he has only to discover some way of persuading the ignorant that he has more knowledge than those who know. — Gorgias, 459.

The rhetorician can speak against all men and on any subject, and in general he can persuade the multitude of anything better than any other man. — Gorgias, 457.

Did you not say just now that the rhetoricians are like tyrants, and that they kill whom they will, and expropriate or exile anyone they dislike? — Gorgias, 466.

We cannot give the title of wisdom to those who declare to defend us by their rhetoric in the law courts, while they are far astray from proper comprehension of genuine justice. — Epinomis, 976.

Rheums. The nature of rheums is not understood by most professors of medicine. — Timaeus, 88.

Rhythm. Rhythm was given by the

Muses on account of the irregular and graceless ways which prevail among mankind generally, and to help us against them. — Timaeus, 47.

Whereas other animals have no perception of order or disorder in their movements, that is, of rhythm and harmony, as they are called, to us the gods have given the pleasurable sense of harmony and rhythm, and by this they stir us into life, and we follow them and join hands with one another in dances. — Laws, II, 653, 654.

The poet is like a painter who will make a likeness of a cobbler though he understands nothing of cobbling; and this is good enough for those who know no more that he does, and judge only by colors and figures. The poet lays on certain colors of each of the arts in the shape of nouns and verbs, himself understanding their nature only enough to imitate; and other people, who are as ignorant as he is and judge only from words, imagine that if he speaks of cobbling in meter and harmony and rhythm, or of military tactics, or of anything else, he speaks very well — such is the sweet influence which melody and rhythm have naturally. — Republic, X, 601.

Rich. Those who have the means are rich — their children begin education soonest and leave off latest. — Protagoras, 326.

The richest must be in the worst condition because they appear to be most in want of things. — Eryxias, 406.

Riches. There is no one whom I could not persuade to concede that riches are bad for some men. — Eryxias, 395.

I would not have anyone fond of heaping up riches for the sake of his children, in order that he may leave them as rich as possible. The condition of youth which is free from flattery, and at the same time not in need of the necessaries of life, is the best and most harmonious of all, being in accord with our nature. Let parents, then, bequeath to their children riches, not in possessions but in reverence. — Laws, V, 729.

Their untold riches are useless to them on the field of battle. — Laws, III, 697.

And so they grow richer and richer, and the more they think of making a fortune the less they think of virtue; for when riches and virtue are placed together in the scales of the balance, the one always rises as the other falls. — Republic, VIII, 550.

The value of a man is often judged by riches. — Eryxias, 396.

Establish laws which will not direct your thoughts primarily to riches. From the three things — soul, body, and money — soul is the highest value, next body, subject to the soul, and thirdly money, subject to the soul and the body. — Letter VIII, 355.

Riddles. I will state it to you in riddles, so that it will not be understood by everybody. — Letter II, 312.

At feasts, punning riddles are being asked, which have a double sense. — Republic, V, 479.

Ridicule. We draw the distinction of jest and earnest, and allow a man to make use of ridicule in jest and without anger about any thing or person, but not if he be angry and have a set purpose. . . . He who is engaged in the practice or reviling cannot revile without attempting to say what is ludicrous; and this is the use of ridicule, employed in a moment of anger, which we censure. — Laws, XI, 935.

Ridiculous. Those who are weak and unable to defend themselves, when they are laughed at, may be truly called ridiculous. — Philebus, 49.

Riding. The art of riding is most befitting to a freeman. —Laches, 182.

When a person is ignorant of riding, and has horses which are useless to him, if someone teaches him that art, he makes him also richer, for what was before useless has now become useful to him, and in giving him knowledge he has also conferred riches upon him. — Eryxias, 403.

Right. What do you mean by the word "right"? — Meno, 97.

The word "right," like everything else, has to be explained. — Republic, V, 449.

Can we be right in praising that in another which a man would abominate and be ashamed of in his own person? — Republic, X, 605.

A man who is good for anything ought not to calculate the chance of living or dying; he ought only to consider whether in doing anything he is doing right or wrong — acting the part of a good man or of a bad. . . . I say again that the greatest good of man is daily to converse about virtue, and that the life which is unexamined is not worth living. What I say is true, although a thing of which it is hard for me to persuade you. . . . The difficulty is not in avoiding death, but in avoiding unrighteousness; for that runs faster than death. I am old and move slowly, and the slower runner has overtaken me, and my accusers are keen and quick, but the faster runner, who is unrighteousness, has overtaken them. — Apology, 28, 38, 39.

Righteousness. He who does not believe in the gods, and yet has a righteous nature, hates the wicked and dislikes and refuses to commit crimes, and avoids unrighteous men, and loves the righteous. — Laws, X, 908.

The sum and substance of our thoughts may be worded thus: the life which is by the gods deemed to be happy is the righteous. We shall affirm this to be a most certain truth. — Laws, II, 664.

What is righteousness? That is an inquiry which I shall never be weary of pursuing as far as in me lies. — Euthyphro, 15.

The moral is that a man ought to live always as righteously as possible. — Meno, 81.

Risk. All great things are attended with risk. — Republic, VI, 497.

Rite. No man shall have sacred rites in a private house. But when he is disposed to sacrifice, let him place his offerings in the hands of the priests, who have publicly under their care the holy rite. — Laws, X, 909.

River. Suppose that we three have to pass a rapid river, and I being the youngest of the three and experienced in rivers have the duty thrown upon me of making the attempt first by myself; leaving you in safety on the bank, I am to examine whether the river is passable by older men like yourselves. I mean to say that the argument in prospect is likely to be too violent. — Laws, X, 892.

Rivet. Each pleasure and pain has a sort of rivet with which it fastens the soul to the body and nails her down and makes her believe that to be good what is pleasant to the body. — Phaedo, 83.

Road. The road which we are taking may be disagreeable to some but is agreeable to others. — Laws, VII, 810.

They should have care of the ways within the town, and of the different high roads which lead out of the country into the city. — Laws, VI, 763.

Hard or easy, this is the road we must tread. — Epinomis, 992.

Robbers. I will proclaim the law about robbers of temples and similar incurable, or almost incurable criminals. — Laws, IX, 854.

Robbers' Code. Do you think that a band of robbers and thieves, or any other gang of evildoers could act at all if they injured one another? — Republic, I, 351.

Robbing. We allegedly use your plans to rob you of your rule. — Letter III, 315.

Rock. The earth when compressed by the air into an indissoluble union with water becomes rock. — Timaeus, 60.

Rogue. Did you never observe the narrow intelligence flashing from the keen eye of a clever rogue — how eager he is, how clearly his paltry soul sees the way to his end; he is the reverse of blind, but his keen eyesight is forced into the service of evil, and he is mischievous in proportion to his cleverness? — Republic, VII, 519.

Rogues have stings. — Republic, VIII, 552.

Role. The same person will hardly be able to play the serious role in life, and at the same time be an imitator and imitate many other roles as well; for even when two species of imitation are nearly allied, the same persons cannot succeed in both. — Republic, III, 395.

Rough. He is really rough; he makes always difficulties before accepting something. — Greater Hippias, 289.

Roughness. Roughness is hardness mingled with inequality, and smoothness is produced by the joint effect of quality and density. — Timaeus, 63.

Rule. We agreed that those persons are good men who are able to rule themselves, and bad men who are not. — Laws, I, 644.

As to a ruling without laws — this is a hard saying. — Statesman, 293.

All rules fail for the divine. — Republic, VI, 492.

He who refuses to rule is liable to be ruled by one who is worse than himself; there can be no greater punishment. — Republic, I, 347.

The rule of the stronger prevails very widely among all creatures, and is according to nature; and yet, the rule of the wiser is not contrary to nature, but according to reason, being the rule of law over willing subjects, and not a rule of compulsion. — Laws, III, 690.

Wise rule is a doctrine, a doctrine of a particular kind, having at once a judicial and commanding nature. — Statesman, 292.

Ruler. The good ruler is not meant by nature to regard his own interest, but that of his subjects; and he who is aware of this will choose rather to receive a benefit from another than to have the trouble of conferring one. — Republic, I, 347.

This is the reason why no one is willing to rule; because no one likes to take in hand the reformation of evils which are not his concern without remuneration. For, in the execution of his work, and in giving his orders to another, the true artist does not regard his own interest, but always that of his subjects; and therefore in order that rulers may be supported and willing to rule, they must be paid. — Republic, I, 347.

The pilot should not humbly beg the sailors to be commanded by him; neither are "the wise men to go to the doors of the rich." The ruler who is good for anything ought not to beg his subjects to be ruled by him; although the present governors of mankind are of a different stamp; they may be justly compared to the mutinous sailors, and the true helmsmen to those who are called by them good-for-nothings and star-gazers. — Republic, VI, 489.

Our inquiry is concerned with the ruler — and not with his opposite. — Statesman, 260.

You must contrive for your future rulers another and a better life than that of a ruler, and then you may have a well-ordered state; for only in the state which offers this, will they rule who are truly rich, not in silver and gold, but in virtue and wisdom, which are the true blessings of life. Whereas if they go to the administration of public affairs, poor and hungering after their own private advantage, thinking that hence they are to snatch the chief good, order there can never be; for they will be fighting about office, and the civil and domestic broils which thus arise will be the ruin of the rulers themselves and of the whole state. — Republic, VII, 521.

Generally they call them masters, but in democratic states they simply call them rulers. — Republic, V, 463.

There must be rulers and subjects in states. — Laws, III, 689.

The rulers of the state are the only persons who ought to have the privilege of lying, either at home or abroad; they may be allowed to lie for the good of the state. But nobody else is to meddle with anything of the kind. — Republic, III, 389.

Are the rulers of states absolutely infallible, or are they sometimes liable to error? — Republic, I, 339.

It is in the interest of the rulers that there should be no strong bond of friendship or society among their subjects, as our Athenian tyrants learned by experience; for the love of Aristogeiton and the constancy of Harmodius had a strength which undid their power. — Symposium, 182.

The ruler is clearly the shepherd of the polled herd, who have no horns. — Statesman, 265.

Wise rulers cannot err while they regard the one great rule of distributing justice to the citizens with intelligence and art. — Statesmen, 297.

One wise man may often be superior to ten thousand fools, and he ought to rule them, and they ought to be his subjects. — Gorgias, 490.

Ruler and Subject. Often rulers and their subjects may come close together, whether on a pilgrimage or a march, as fellow soldiers or fellow sailors; aye and they may observe the behavior of each other in the very moment of danger — for where danger is, there the poor is not in the least despised by the rich — and very likely the wiry sunburnt poor man may be placed in battle at the side of a wealthy one who has never spoilt his complexion and has plenty of superfluous flesh — when he sees such a one puffing and at his wits' end, how can he avoid drawing the conclusion that men like him are only rich because no one has the courage to despoil them? And when they meet in private will not people be saying to one another, "Our warriors are not good for much"? — Republic, VIII, 556.

The interests of rulers require that their subjects should be poor in spirit. — Symposium, 182.

Rumormonger. These rumormongers are the accusers whom I dread; for their names I do not know and cannot tell. — Apology, 18.

Running. If you want to see Crison and me in the same stadium, you must bid him slacken his speed to mine, for I cannot run quickly, and he can run slowly. — Protagoras, 336.

Running Away. To run away, and to be caught in running away, is the very height of folly. — Protagoras, 317.

Rust. When the parts grow old and are disunited, this comes out in the form of what is called rust. — Timaeus, 59.

S

Sacrifice. Sacrificing is giving to the gods, and prayer is asking of the gods. — Euthyphro, 14.

The practice of men sacrificing one another still exists among many nations. — Laws, VI, 782.

Safety. Safety at sea is the good of navigation. — Republic, I, 346.

Salamis. The sailors of Salamis became the schoolmasters of Greece, teaching the Greeks not to fear the barbarians at sea. — Menexenus, 241.

Salt. I have met with a philosophical work in which the utility of salt has been made the theme of an eloquent discourse. — Symposium, 177.

Cooks shall be allowed to throw in salt by handfuls, whereas the noncook will not be allowed to put in as much as he can take between his fingers. — Lysis, 209.

Salutation. Is it a better form of salutation to bid "joy," or to wish customarily "do well"? This salutation I mostly use when writing to a friend. — Letter III, 315.

Salvation. The salvation of human life has been found to consist in the right choice of pleasures and pains. — Protagoras, 357.

Sameness. Sameness itself and difference are contrary to one another. So sameness will never be in what is different, nor difference in what is the same. — Parmenides, 146.

Sanitation. In all that relates to the sanitation of the city, the wardens should have a care of cleanliness, and no citizen should encroach upon any public property either by buildings or digging. — Laws, VI, 779.

Sanity. Man-made sanity is inferior to heaven-sent madness. — Phaedrus, 244.

Saps. There are numerous kinds of water which have been mingled with one another, and are distilled through plants; and this class is called by the general name of juices or saps. — Timaeus, 59.

Satire. A composer of iambic or satirical lyric verse, shall not be permitted to ridicule any of the citizens, either by word or image, either in anger or without anger. — Laws, XI, 935.

Saving. I am speaking of the saver and not of the spender. — Laws, V, 743.

Scholar. If there are no teachers neither are there scholars. — Meno, 96.

The scholar learns whatever he studies with facility, and has a capacious and reliable memory . . . but no one will call a person wise on account of any of these erudite gifts. — Epinomis, 976.

School. When the day breaks, the time has arrived for youth to go to school. — Laws, VII, 808.

Science. The science of science will also be the science of absence of science. — Charmides, 166.

Each science is distinguished from other sciences, not as science, but by the nature of the subject matter. — Charmides, 171.

Natural science is only hypothetical descending to experiment and facts instead of going up to a principle; but spiritual science passes out of hypotheses, and goes up to a principle proceeding only in ideas by reasoning. — Republic, VI, 510.

At present, the language of the geometricians is in flat contradiction to the merely contemplative science. For they speak of finding the side of a square, and applying and adding as though they had a practical end in view. This is ridiculous; for knowledge only is the real object of the whole science. — Republic, VII, 527.

He and I have a notion that there is not one knowledge or science of the past, another of the present, a third of the future; but that of all three there is one science only: for example, there is one science of medicine which is concerned with the inspection of health equally in all times, present, past, and future. — Laches, 198.

Wisdom eludes us if we turn to the scientific branches. — Epinomis, 974.

Not by any science, and not because they were scientists, did Themistocles and other statesmen govern states. And this is the reason why they, wise men, were unable to make others like themselves — because wisdom is not grounded on science. — Meno, 99.

Scientist. You rhapsodes and actors, and the poets whose verses you sing, are wise men; and I am a scientist, who only speaks the truth. — Ion, 532.

When the scientist turns towards nature, then he goes blinking about, and is first of one opinion and then of another and seems to have no stability. — Republic, VI, 508.

Natural intelligence and a brilliant memory cannot make a scientist love all subject matters. — Letter VII, 344.

Scratching. Take the pleasures of unseemly disorders, for example, the relief of itching and other ailments by scratching, which is the only remedy required. For what in heavens's name is the feeling to be called which is thus produced? Pleasure or pain? — Some mixed experience. — Philebus, 46.

Do you include itching and scratching, provided you have enough of scratching, and continue scratching through life, in your notion of happiness? — Gorgias, 494.

Scribe. Is the scribe to be regarded as doing nothing when he reads or writes? — Charmides, 161.

Scylla and Charybdis. I passed the baleful strait of Scylla and Charybdis. — Letter VII, 345.

Sea. The sea is pleasant as a daily companion, but has also a bitter and brackish quality; filling the streets with merchants and shopkeepers, and begetting in the souls of men uncertain and unfaithful ways. — Laws, IV, 705.

We who dwell along the borders of the sea, are just like ants and frogs round a pond. — Phaedo, 109.

Searching. If a person wishes to make a search in the house of another, he shall enter naked, or having only a short tunic and no upper girdle. — Laws, XII, 954.

Seasons. The observation of the seasons and of months and years is quite essential to farming and navigation, and not less essential to military strategy. — Republic, VII, 527.

Security. When a man becomes surety, let him give the security in a distinct form, acknowledging the whole transaction in a written document. — Laws, XII, 953.

Sedition. Whoever by promoting a man to power enslaves the laws, and subjects the city to factions, using violence and stirring up sedition contrary to law, him we will deem the greatest enemy of the whole state. — Laws, IX, 856.

Seed. He who has the seed about the spinal marrow too fruitful and overflowing, like a tree overladen with fruit, has many throes. — Timaeus, 86.

Animal seeds are unseen by reason of their smallness, and formless. — Timaeus, 91.

Would an intelligent farmer with serious intention plant seeds during the heat of summer in some garden of Adonis, and enjoy watching it bearing fine fruit within eight days? If he did so at all, wouldn't he act just in a holiday spirit, by way of pastime? For serious purposes, he would sow his seeds in fitting soil, and be well content if they arrived at maturity within eight months. — Phaedrus, 276.

Seeing. When you are caught in a well, as they say, and the self-assured adversary closes one of your eyes with his hand, and asks whether you can see his cloak with the eye which he has closed, how will you answer the inevitable man? — I should answer, not with that eye but with the other. — Theaetetus, 165.

Seeming. If anyone does something, under the idea that this is for his interests when really not for his interests, he may be said to do what only seems best to him. — Gorgias, 468.

Self. You must take in consideration the fact, that each of us is born not for himself alone. — Letter IX, 358.

Self, Moral. I would have you to look to yourselves; that is a service which you may always be doing to me and mine as well as to yourselves, even if you don't agree with me now. But if you take no thought of yourselves, and act not according to the precepts which I have given you, all will be of no avail, however ardently you agree with me now. — Phaedo, 115.

Self-Accusation. The guilty should be the first to accuse himself, and should use rhetoric for disclosing his own misdeeds and delivering himself from wickedness, which is the greatest of all evils. — Gorgias, 480.

Rhetoric is of use for the culprit, if he behaves bravely, closing, like a patient, his eyes manfully, and letting the judging physician cut and operate him, in the hope of attaining the good and honorable — regardless of pain: if he have done things worthy of flogging, allowing himself to be beaten, or of imprisonment, to bonds, or of fine, to be fined, or of exile, to be exiled, or of death, to die. — Gorgias, 480.

Self-Composed. We exclaim, How calm! How temperate! in describing the moderate and quiet working of the mind; and again we speak of actions as deliberate and gentle, and of the voice as smooth and deep, and of all rhythmical movement, and of restrained artistry in general as having a proper solemnity. All these qualities we do not term impetuous, but self-composed. — Statesman, 307.

Self-Control. Is not the calm, and temperance, and disdain of the passions which even the many call self-control, a quality belonging only to those who preserve a decent indifference toward their desires, and live in philosophy? — Phaedo, 68.

The whole multitude of men lack temperance in their lives, either from ignorance or from want of self-control or both. — Laws, V, 734.

Instead of having any shame or self-control, he will be always whining and lamenting on slight occasions. — Republic, III, 388.

We admonished him to lead the kind of life which would be most conducive to self-control. — Letter VII, 331.

Self-Deception. There is nothing worse than self-deception — when the deceiver is always at home and always with you — that is, indeed, terrible. — Cratylus, 428.

Self-Defense. They also need the faculty of self-defense against mean and unjust persons. — Letter VI, 322.

If brother kill brother in a civil broil, or under other like circumstances, if the other have begun, and he only defend himself, let him be free from guilt, as he would be if he has slain an enemy. And if a citizen kill a citizen, in self-defense, let him be free in like manner, and so also stranger who kills stranger, or slave who kills slave. — Laws, IX, 869.

Suppose a man to be a skillful boxer — he in the fullness of his strength goes and strikes his father or mother; but that is no reason why the trainer or fencing master should be held in detestation or banished from the city — surely not. For they thought this art for a good purpose, as an art to be used against enemies and evildoers, in self-defense, not in aggression, and others have perverted their instructions, making a bad use of their strength and skill. — Gorgias, 457.

Self-Existent. Let us see in what way the self-existent can be discovered. — First Alcibiades, 129.

Self-Knowledge. If we have no self-knowledge and no wisdom, can we ever know our own good and evil? — First Alcibiades, 133.

At times, I fancy that anybody can know himself; at other times, the task of self-knowledge appears to be very difficult. — First Alcibiades, 129.

They met together and dedicated in the temple of Apollo at Delphi, as the first fruits of their wisdom, the far-famed inscriptions, which are in all men's mouths, "Know thyself," and "Nothing too much." — Protagoras, 343.

Self-Love. "Every man by nature is and ought to be his own friend." But the excessive self-love is in reality the source to each man of all offenses; for the exorbitant lover is blinded about the beloved, so that he judges wrongly of the just, the good, and the honorable, and thinks that he ought always to prefer his own interest to righteousness. — Laws, V, 731.

Self-Moved. What is the definition of that which is named "soul"? Can we conceive of any other than that which has been already given — the motion which is self-moved? — Laws, X, 895, 896.

Self-Praise. To praise myself would be ill manners. — Charmides, 158.

Self-Respect. My motive was a concern for my self-respect — I feared to become a man of words instead of actions. — Letter VII, 328.

Self-Rule. What do you mean by his "ruling over himself"? — Just what is commonly said, that a man should be master of himself: ruler of his own pleasures and pains. — Gorgias, 491.

There is something paradoxical in the expression "master of himself"; for the master is also the servant and the servant the master; and in all these modes of speaking the same person is predicated. But the real meaning of the expression, I believe, is that, when the better principle of the human soul controls the worse, then a man is said to be the master of himself. — Republic, IV, 431.

One man is the master of his pleasures and passions, another the slave of them — and this language describes facts. — Laws, IX 863.

Self-Sufficiency. There is a consolation in a country producing all things self-sufficiently at home; and, yet, owing to the ruggedness of the soil, not providing anything in great abundance. — Laws, IV, 705.

Selling. The art of selling is distinguished as the sale of a man's own production; another is the exchange of the works of others. — Sophist, 223.

Semimaterialist. We have discovered the source of this vain opinion of all those semimaterialists, who manufacture the soul according to their own materialistic notions; they affirm the spirit to be last, and the matter to be first. — Laws, X, 891.

Sensation. The way will be to ask whether sensation is or is not the same as knowledge. — Theaetetus, 163.

I wonder that he did not begin his great work on Truth with a declaration that a pig or a dog-faced baboon, which has sensation, is the only measure of all things. He might have condescended to inform us that he was no wiser than a tadpole and did not even aspire to be a man — would not this have produced an overpowering effect? — Theaetetus, 161.

Sense. Whatever things are learned or done with sense are profitable, but when done without sense they are harmful. — Meno, 88.

Senses. The senses are variously named hearing, seeing, smelling; there is the sense of heat, cold, pleasure, pain, desire, fear, and many more. — Theaetetus, 156.

Is the body, if invited to share in the inquiry, a hinderer or a helper? Have sight and hearing any truth in them? Are they not, as the poets are always telling us, inaccurate witnesses? And what is to be said of the other senses? Must not, then, existence be revealed to the soul in thought only? — Phaedo, 65.

Philosophy pointed out to the soul that the eye is full of deceit, and also observation by means of the ear and the other senses, and persuaded her to retire from them in all but the necessary use of them. — Phaedo, 83.

Sensuality. Those then who know not wisdom and virtue, and are always busy with gluttony and sensuality, go down and up again as far as the mean; and in this region they move at random throughout life, but they never pass into the moral upper world; thither they neither look, nor do they ever find their way, neither are they filled with spiritual being, nor do they taste of pure and abiding pleasure. Like cattle, with their eyes always looking down and their heads stooping to the earth, that is, to the dining table, they fatten and feed and breed, and, in their excessive love of these delights, they kick and but at one another with horns and hoofs which are made from iron; and they kill one another by reason of their insatiable lust. For they fill themselves with that which is not substantial and incontinent. — Republic, IX, 586.

Sentence. A sentence which has no subject is impossible. — Sophist, 263.

Sepulchre. The sepulchres are to be in places which are not cultivated, and there shall be no monuments to them, either large or small, but they shall occupy only that part of the country which is naturally adapted for receiving and concealing the bodies of the dead with as little hurt as possible to the living. No man, living or dead, shall deprive the living of the sustenance which the earth, our mother, is naturally inclined to bear to them. — Laws, XII, 958.

Serious. The matter is serious, and must be seriously considered. — Cratylus, 421.

Perhaps he is serious, and not merely talking for the sake of talking. — Laches, 196.

They think that their serious pursuits should be for the sake of fun. — Laws, VII, 803.

When one sees anywhere the written work of anyone, whether that of a lawgiver in his laws or whatever it may be in some other field, the subject investigated cannot have been his most serious concern — that is, if he is himself a serious man. His most serious interests have dwelled in the most seclusive realm of his activity. If, however, he still has put his most serious matters in writing, "then surely" not the gods, but mortals "have utterly blasted his wits." — Letter VII, 344.

No serious man will ever think of writing about serious matters for the broad public so as to make them a prey to doubt and envy. — Letter VII, 344.

Servant. The language used to a servant ought always to be that of command; and we ought not to jest with them — this is a foolish way which many people have of setting up their slaves, and making the life of servitude more disagreeable both for them and for those who command them. — Laws, VI, 778.

Old servants, who are supposed to be attached to the family, from time to time talk privately in the same [indecent] strain. — Republic, VIII, 549.

Service. Any service which the lover does is not to be accounted flattery or dishonor, and the beloved has also one way of voluntary service which is not dishonorable, and this is virtuous service. — Symposium, 184.

Servility. I [Socrates] thought that I ought not to stoop to servility in the hour of danger. — Apology, 38.

Serving. Every man should remember the universal rule, that he who is not a good servant will not be a good master; a man should pride himself more upon serving well than upon commanding well; first upon serving the laws, which is also serving of the gods; in the second place, upon having served ancient and honorable men in the days of his youth. — Laws, VI, 762.

Servitude. Excessive and savage servitude makes men mean and abject, and haters of their kind, and therefore makes them undesirable associates. — Laws, VII, 791.

The proper measure of servitude is to serve god; the improper to serve men. — Letter VIII, 354.

Sex, Transformation of. Tradition

says that Caeneus, the Thessalian, was changed by a god from a woman into a man; but the reverse transformation of sex is impossible — or no punishment would be more proper than that the man who throws away his shield should be changed into a woman. — Laws, XII, 944.

Sexes, Equality of the. If the male and female sex appear to differ in their fitness for any art or pursuit, we should say that such pursuit or art ought to be assigned to one or the other of them; but if the difference consists only in women bearing and men begetting children, this does not amount to a proof that a woman differs essentially from a man in that respect of which we are speaking; and we shall therefore continue to maintain that the wives of our guardians ought to have the equal pursuits as their husbands. — Republic, V, 454.

The female and male dogs share everything alike; the difference between them is only of weaker and stronger nature. — Republic, V, 451.

In the administration of a state neither a woman as a woman, nor a man as a man has any special function, but the gifts of nature are equally diffused in both sexes; all the pursuits of men are the pursuits of women also. — Republic, V, 455.

Sexes, the. Let me treat of the nature of man; for the original human nature was not like the present, but different. The sexes were originally three in number, not two as they are now; there was man, woman, and the union of the two, having a name corresponding to this double nature; this once had a real existence, but is now lost, and the name only is preserved as a term of reproach. — Symposium, 189.

Shadow. We have been grasping at a shadow. — Lysis, 218.

Shadow arises from intercepting the light by dark patches. — Sophist, 266.

Shame. When he is left alone he will not mind saying or doing many things which he would be ashamed of anyone hearing or seeing. — Republic, X, 604.

The fear of a bad reputation we and all men term shame. — Laws, I, 647.

It is more shameful to do than to suffer wrong. — Gorgias, 475.

Sheep. Sheep lie asleep at noon about the fountain. — Phaedrus, 259.

Shelter. Defenses against heat and cold are shelters. — Statesman, 279.

Shepherd. Hill shepherds would necessarily be unacquainted with the crafts of those who live in cities, and with the various devices which are suggested to them by interest and ambition, and all the wrongs which they contrive against one another. — Laws, III, 677.

They did not use blows or bodily force, as the manner of shepherds is. — Critias, 109.

Shivering. To the convulsion of the body the name of shivering and trembling is given. — Timaeus, 62.

Shoemaker. A shoemaker smooths out leather upon a last. — Symposium, 191.

Shoes. When we take care of our shoes, do we not take care of our feet? — First Alcibiades, 128.

Shrewdness. Is not shrewdness a quickness or cleverness of the soul? — Charmides, 160.

Shuffling. He shuffles up and down in order to conceal the difficulty into which he has got himself. — Laches, 196.

Sicilian. In case anyone lives in Sicilian fashion, do not call upon him to aid you, and do not believe that he can serve you loyally. — Letter VII, 336.

Sickness. What use is there in giving to the body of a sick man a quantity of the best food or drink or any other pleasant thing, which may be really as bad for him as if you gave him nothing, or even worse if rightly estimated? — Gorgias, 505.

Shall we not be right in saying, that if a person would wish to see the greatest pleasures he ought to go and look, not at health, but at sickness? And here you must distinguish: do not imagine that I am asking whether those who are very sick have *more* pleasure than those who are well, but understand that I am speaking of the intensity of pleasure. — Philebus, 45.

Side, Left. Those who make the left side weaker than the right act contrary to nature. . . . He who is perfectly skilled in boxing or wrestling, is not unable to fight from his left side, and does not limp and draggle in confusion when his opponent makes him change his position, and compels him to exert himself on the other side. — Laws, VII, 795.

Sight. Sight is the keenest of our bodily senses. — Phaedrus, 250.

God gave us the sight to the end that we might behold the courses of intelligence in the heaven, and apply them to the courses of our own intelligence which are akin to them, the unperturbed to the perturbed; and that we, learning them and being partakers of the true computations of nature, might imitate the absolutely unerring courses of god and regulate our own vagaries. — Timaeus, 47.

Sight in my opinion is the source of the greatest benefit to us, for had the eyes never seen the stars, and the sun, and the heaven, none of the words which we have spoken about the universe would have ever been uttered. — Timaeus, 47.

Sight is by far the most costly and complex piece of workmanship which the artificer of the senses ever contrived. — Republic, VI, 507.

When the light of day surrounds the stream of vision . . . [it reaches] the soul, producing that perception which we call sight. — Timaeus, 45.

Sight and hearing are the best of our senses. — Phaedo, 65.

Silence. In painting, or statuary, or many other arts, the work may proceed in silence. — Gorgias, 450.

Silent. Observe, Meletus, that you are silent, and have nothing to say. — Apology, 24.

Similarity. He who would deceive others, and not be deceived, must exactly know the real similarities and differences of things. — Phaedrus, 262.

When you are reminded by similarity, you are also aware whether the similarity is perfect or imperfect. — Phaedo, 74.

Simplicity. Good language and grace and rhythm depend on simplicity — I mean the simplicity of a truly and nobly ordered mind, not that other simplicity which is only a euphemism for folly. — Republic, III, 400.

Simplicity in music is the parent of temperance in the soul, and simplicity in gymnastic, of health in the body. — Republic, III, 404.

Sin, Expiation of. They produce a host of books, according to which they perform their ritual, and persuade not only individuals, but whole cities, that expiations and atonements for sin may be easily made by sacrifices and amusements which fill a vacant hour. — Republic, II, 364.

Singing. His singing was an infliction to the audience. — Gorgias, 502.

Will not any man whose heart is warm within him, be more ready and less ashamed to sing — I do not say before a large audience, but before a moderate number? — Laws, II, 666.

Sinner. The way of improving sinners is by pain and suffering; for there is no other way in which they can be delivered from their evils. — Gorgias, 525.

There the sinners are, hanging up as examples, in the prison house of Hades, a warning spectacle to all unrighteous men who come thither. — Gorgias, 525.

Size. The same size viewed from near and far appears different. — Republic, X, 602.

Skin. The fleshy nature was not wholly dried up, but a large sort of peel was parted off and remained over, which is now called skin. — Timaeus, 76.

Slanderer. These slanderers attempt to set you against me out of envy. — Apology, 18.

Slave. The right treatment of slaves is to behave properly to them — to do them, if possible, even more justice than to those who are free. — Laws, VI, 777.

We ought neither to punish slaves in hot blood or so as to anger them, nor yet to leave them unpunished lest they become self-willed. A like rule is to be observed in the case of the free-born. — Laws, VII, 794.

Ought the slave to govern his master, and would he who governed be any longer a slave? — Meno, 73.

Do you think that anyone is happy in the condition of a slave? — Lysis, 207.

Suffering of injustice is not fit for a man but only for a slave, who indeed had better die than live; for when he is wronged and trampled upon, he is unable to help himself, or any other about whom he cares. — Gorgias, 483.

Slaves ought to be punished as they deserve, and not admonished as if they were freemen, which will make them only conceited. — Laws, VI, 777.

Many a man has found his slaves better in every way than brethren or sons, and many times they have saved the lives and property of their masters and their whole house — such tales are well known. But may we not also say that in general the soul of the slave is corrupt, and that no man ought to trust them as a class? — Laws, VI, 776.

Slavery. They are to fear slavery more than death. — Republic, III, 387.

Their present maladministration of their government is due to the prevalence of slavery and despotism among them. — Laws, III, 698.

Sleep. Much sleep is not required by nature, either for our souls or bodies. For no one who is asleep is good for anything, any more than if he were dead; but he of us who has the most regard for life and reason keeps awake as long as he can, reserving only so much time for sleep as is expedient for health; and much sleep is not required, if the habit of not sleeping be once formed. Public officers who keep awake at night are terrible to the bad, and are honored and reverenced by the just and temperate, and are useful to themselves and to the whole state. — Laws, VII, 808. *Vide* Pleasure.

When the night approaches, and the surrounding atmosphere is now deprived of fire: the eyes no longer see, and we feel disposed to go to sleep. — Timaeus, 45.

That any citizen should continue during the whole night in sleep, and not be seen by all his servants, always the first to awake and the first to rise — this should be deemed unworthy of a freeman. — Laws, VII, 808.

Sluggishness. Too great slowness or gentleness is termed sluggishness or cowardice. — Statesman, 307.

Small. There is greater difficulty in seeing and hearing the small than the great. — Laws, X, 902.

There is always less difficulty in fixing the mind on small matters than on great. — Statesman, 236.

Sneezing. I wonder whether the principle of order in the human frame requires these sort of noises and ticklings, for I no sooner applied the sneezing than I was cured from the hiccough. — Symposium, 189.

Snow. Water which is congealed in a less degree and is only half solid, when above the earth is called snow. — Timaeus, 59.

Sober. The calm and sober guardians are the captains over their unsober fellow workers; and without their help there is greater difficulty in fighting against drink than in fighting against enemies, when the commander of the army is not himself unperturbed. — Laws, II, 671.

Society. I will legislate with a view to the society, considering what is best both for the state and for the family, holding as I ought to the affairs of an individual as of minor importance. — Laws, XI, 923.

Socrates. At any rate, the world has decided that Socrates is in some way superior to other men. — Apology, 34.

Anyone who has the least sense will acknowledge the wonderful clearness of Socrates' reasoning. — Phaedo, 102.

I did not know that Socrates is a master in the art of love. — Symposium, 193.

I never could have thought that I should have met with a man like him [Socrates] in wisdom and endurance. — Symposium, 219.

What shall be done to a man who has never had the wit to be idle during his whole life; but has been careless of what the many care about — wealth, and family interests, and military offices, and speaking in the assembly, and poets, and parties? Reflecting that I was really too honest a man to follow in this way and live, I did not go where I could do no good to you or to myself; but where I could do the greatest good privately to everyone of you. — Apology, 36.

I am the only politician of my time. Now, seeing that I look to what is best and not to what is most pleasant, being unwilling to practice those graces which you recommend, I shall have nothing to say in the justice of court. I shall be tried just as a physician would be tried in a court of little boys at the indictment of a cook. — Gorgias, 521.

Anyone who has an intellectual affinity to Socrates is liable to be drawn into a discussion with him; and whatever subject may be started by him, he will be continually carried round and round by him; Socrates will not let him go until he has completely and thoroughly sifted him. — Laches, 187.

I always wonder at you, Socrates. For when you are in the country, you really are like a stranger who is being led about by a guide. Do you ever cross the border? I rather think that you never venture even outside the gates. — Phaedrus, 230.

The halt, the blind, the maimed were not more stationary in Athens than Socrates. — Crito, 53.

I might have proved to Meletus that I was about to lead a better life. — Euthyphro, 16.

Men of Athens, I honor and love you; but I shall obey God rather than you, and while I have life and strength I shall never cease from the practice and teaching of philosophy, exhorting anyone whom I meet after my manner: O my friend, why do you care so much about laying up the greatest amount of money and honor and reputation, and so little about wisdom and truth and the greatest improvement of the soul, which you never regard or heed at all? — Apology, 29.

I have a benevolent habit of pouring out myself to everybody, and would even pay for a listener. — Euthyphro, 3.

I see not only that you are in love, but that you are already far gone in your love. Simple and foolish as I am, the gods have given me the power of understanding these sorts of affections, too. — Lysis, 203.

The hour of departure has arrived, and we go our ways — I to die, and you to live. Which is better God only knows. — Apology, 42.

Such was the end, Echecrates, of our friend Socrates, whom I may truly call the wisest, and justest, and best of all the men whom I have ever known. — Phaedo, 118.

Socratic Method. And I begin, in spite of all that has been said, to interrogate quite gently: "But if all this be true, I still want to know, what is justice." Thereupon they think that I ask tiresome questions, and am leaping over the barriers, and have been already sufficiently answered, and they try to satisfy me with one derivation after another, and at length they quarrel. — Cratylus, 413.

Solids. After plane geometry, we took solids in revolution, instead of taking solids at rest. . . . The ludicrous state of solid geometry made me pass over this branch and go on to astronomy, or motion of solids. — Republic, VII, 528.

Solon. Solon was the wisest of the seven sages. — Timaeus, 20.

One of our tribe said that in his judgment Solon was not only the wisest of men, but also the noblest of poets. If Solon had only made poetry the business of his life, and had not been compelled to attend to other matters, in my opinion he would have been as famous as Homer or Hesiod, or any poet. — Timaeus, 21.

Solvent. Pleasure — mightier agent far in washing the soul than any soda or lye; and sorrow, fear, and desire mightier solvents than any others. — Republic, IV, 430.

Soldier. In their life the soldiers rejoiced their friends with their virtue, and their death they gave in exchange for the salvation of the living. — Menexenus, 237.

Son. Dear is the son to the father — the younger to the elder. — Laws, III, 687.

Truly, then, a tyrannical son is a

blessing to his father and mother. — Republic, IX, 574.

From the time of Xerxes to this there has never been a really great king among the Persians, although they are called great. And I would argue that this is not to be attributed to fortune; the reason is rather the evil life which is generally led by the sons of very rich and royal persons; for never will boy or man, young or old, excel in virtue, who has been thus educated. — Laws, III, 695, 696.

Why do the sons of good fathers often turn out ill? Let me explain that — which is far from being wonderful. — Protagoras, 326.

Soothsayer. The soothsayers are courageous. For who but one of them can know to whom to die or to live is better? — Laches, 195.

Begging priests and soothsayers go to rich men's doors and persuade them that they have a power committed to them of making an atonement for their sins or those of their fathers by sacrifices or charms, with rejoicings and games; and they promise to harm an enemy at a small charge; with magic arts and incantations binding the will of Heaven to their work. — Republic, II, 364.

Sophist. The Sophist disputes, and teaches to dispute. — Sophist, 232.

The Sophist has been shown to have conjectural or apparent knowledge only, and not the truth. — Sophist, 233.

[The Sophist] makes the worse appear the better cause. — Apology, 18.

The Sophist accomplishes by words the change which the physician works by the aid of drugs. — Theaetetus, 167.

Is not a Sophist one who deals wholesale or retail in the food of the soul? — Protagoras, 313.

Sophists are the only professors of moral improvement. — Laches, 186.

The Sophist presides over the art of making eloquent speakers. — Protagoras, 312.

The members of all the other states, with the exception of that which has knowledge, may be set aside as being not statesmen but partisans, — upholders of the most monstrous idols, and themselves idols; and, being the greatest imitators and magicians, are also the worst Sophists. The term Sophist appears to have been most correctly transferred to the politicians, as they are called. — Statesman, 303.

Do the Sophists not profess to make men able to dispute about law and about politics in general? — Why, they would have no disciples worth speaking of, if they did not make these claims. — Sophist, 232.

Do you really think, as people often say, that our youth are corrupted by Sophists in any degree worth speaking of? Are not the public men who say these things themselves the greatest of all Sophists? Will the influence of a Sophist stem the tide of public praise or blame, or not rather be carried away in the stream of public opinion? No opinion of any single Sophist can be expected to overcome in such an unequal contest. — Republic, VI, 492.

Sophisticated. He is not sophisticated, but a plain person who cares for nothing but the truth. — Greater Hippias, 288.

Sophistry. Sophistry is a hunt after the souls of rich young men of good repute. — Sophist, 223.

Sorb apple. A sorb apple may be

halved for pickling, or an egg divided with a hair. — Symposium, 190.

Sorrow. When any sorrow happens to ourselves, then we pride ourselves on the quality of quietness and endurance; this is the manly part, and our rapture at somebody else's sorrow is deemed to be the part of a woman. — Republic, X, 605.

When some pitiful hero is drawling out his sorrows in a long oration, the best of us delight in giving way to sympathy, and are in raptures at the excellence of the poet who stirs our feelings most. — Republic, X, 605.

We entreat our fathers and mothers to be assured that they will not please us by sorrowing and lamenting over us. But if the dead have any knowledge of the living, they will displease us most by making themselves miserable and by taking their misfortunes to heart, and they will please us best if they bear their loss lightly and temperately. And if they will direct their minds to the care and nurture of our wives and children — in a way that is more agreeable to us. — Menexenus, 248.

There is in us a natural feeling which is just hungering after sorrow and weeping, and desiring to be indulged, and this emotion, which is kept under control in our own calamities, is the same which is satisfied and delighted by the poets: the better nature in each of us, not having been sufficiently trained by reason or habit, is taken unawares because the sorrow is another's; and the spectator fancies that there can be no disgrace to himself in praising and pitying anyone who comes telling him what a good man he is, and making unseasonable lamentations. — Republic, X, 606.

Soul. The soul is more lasting than the body; but no one knows whether the soul, after having worn out many bodies, might not perish herself and leave her last body behind her. — Phaedo, 91. *Vide* Coat.

Neither good nor evil occur to that which has no soul; only a soul experiences them. — Letter VII, 334, 335.

The soul is like the eye: when resting upon its shining object, the soul perceives and understands, and is radiant with intelligence. — Republic, VI, 508.

I am right in bidding everyone to honor his own soul, which everyone seems to honor, but no one honors as he ought. — Laws, V, 727.

Of all the things which a man has, next to the gods, his soul is the most divine. — Laws, V, 726.

Nothing is more honorable than the soul, and he who thinks otherwise of her has no idea how grossly he undervalues his wonderful possession. — Laws, V, 727.

And they, imitating the Creator, received from him the immortal principle of the soul; and around this they fashioned a mortal body, and made the whole body to be a vehicle of the soul, and constructed within a soul of another nature which was mortal. — Timaeus, 69.

What makes each one of us to be what we are is only the soul. — Laws, XII, 959.

Is the soul visible or invisible? — Invisible. — Phaedo, 79.

Only the soul of a philosopher, guileless and true, or the soul of a lover, who is not without philosophy, may acquire wings in the third recurring period of a thousand years. — Phaedrus, 249.

What is that which holds and carries and gives life and motion to the entire nature of the body? What is that but the soul? — Cratylus, 400.

Is not one part of us body, and the rest of us soul? — Phaedo, 79.

A diseased soul is a far more miserable companion than a diseased body. — Gorgias, 479.

When using the sense of sight and hearing or some other sense, the soul wanders and is confused; the world spins round her, and she is like a drunkard. — Phaedo, 79.

Surely there is nothing belonging to us which has more valuable existence than the soul. — First Alcibiades, 130.

Is not the soul which has an order of her own better than that which has no order of her own? — Gorgias, 506.

An intelligent man confides in the kinship of the soul rather than in that of the blood. — Letter VII, 334.

My notion is that the soul is like a book. Memory and perception meet, and they and their attendant feelings seem to me almost to write down words in the soul, and when the inscribing feeling writes truly, then true opinion and true propositions grow in our souls — but when the scribe within us writes falsely the result is false. — Philebus, 39.

Every soul may be said to wear out many bodies, especially in the course of a long life. — Phaedo, 87. *Vide* Coat.

We believe that the soul is the universal condition. — Epinomis, 988.

If the soul is ever to know herself, must she not look at the soul? — First Alcibiades, 133.

May not our body be said to have a soul? — Clearly. — Philebus, 30.

So much we will take as settled, that soul is older than body. — Epinomis, 980.

My notion is, that the soul has no separate organ, but that she conceives the *universals* of all things by herself. . . . The soul views some things by herself and others through the bodily organs. — Theaetetus, 185.

Has not the soul functions which nothing else can fulfill? Are not these functions peculiar to the soul, and can they rightly be assigned to any other agency? — To no other. — Republic, I, 353.

To see the soul as she really is, not as we now behold her, marred by communion with the body and other miseries, you must contemplate her with the eye of reason, in her original purity; and then her beauty will be revealed, and justice and injustice will be manifested more clearly. — Republic, X, 611.

Habits of mind, reasonings, judgments, purposes, and memories are prior to length, breadth, depth, and strength of bodies, if the soul is prior to the body. — Laws, X, 896.

There appear to be as many forms of the soul as there are forms of the state. — Republic, IV, 445.

Wisdom and reason cannot exist without soul. — Philebus, 30.

The right way is to place the goods of the soul first and highest in the scale; and in the second place, the goods of the body; and in the third place, those of money and property. — Laws, III, 697.

The philosopher is entirely concerned with the soul and not with the body. He would like, as far as he can, to be quit of the body and turn to the soul. — Phaedo, 64.

I am not talking or arguing with the face of Alcibiades, but with the real Alcibiades; and that is with his soul. — First Alcibiades, 130.

Soul, Selling One's. Who can imagine that a man who sold his son or daughter into slavery for money would be the gainer, however large might be the sum which he received? And will anyone say that he is not a miserable caitiff who remorselessly sells his soul to the most godless and detestable? — Republic, IX, 589, 590.

Sound. Equal sounds are greater when near, and lesser when at a distance. — Protagoras, 356.

The sound which moves swiftly is acute, and the sound which moves slowly is grave, and that which is uniform is equable and smooth, and the reverse is harsh. A great body of sound is loud, and the opposite is low. Respecting the harmony of sounds I must hereafter speak. — Timaeus, 67.

Sow. Courage is not a thing which every sow would have. — Laches, 196.

Space. Space is eternal, admits not of destruction, provides a home for all created things, and is perceived without the help of sense, but by pure understanding. — Timaeus, 52.

Span of Life. The whole race and every individual has an appointed span of life, apart from violent casualties; for the triangles are originally framed with power to live for a certain time, beyond which no man can prolong his life. — Timaeus, 89.

Sparta. There is a very ancient philosophy which is more cultivated in Crete and Sparta than in any other part of Greece, and there are more philosophers in those countries than anywhere else in the world. — Protagoras, 342.

Many have noted that the true Spartan type of character has the love of philosophy even stronger than the love of gymnastics; they are conscious that only a perfectly educated man is capable of uttering proverbial expressions. Such were Thales of Miletus, and Pittacus of Mytilene, and Bias of Prienne, and our own Solon, and Cleobolus the Lindian, and Myson the Chenian. All these were lovers and emulators and disciples of Spartan culture. — Protagoras, 342, 343.

The laws of Sparta, in as far they relate to pleasure, appear to me to be the best in the world; for that which leads mankind in general into the wildest pleasure and license, the law has clean driven out; and neither in the country nor in towns which are under the rule of Sparta, will you find revelries and the many incitements of pleasure which accompany them, and stir them up to the utmost. — Laws, I, 637.

Spartan. The Spartan is renowned for brevity. — Laws, I, 641.

The Spartan rule is, "Fight or depart." — Theaetetus, 169.

An Athenian can point out the license which exists among Spartan women. — Laws, I, 637.

If a man converses with the most ordinary Spartan, he will find him seldom good for much in general conversation, but at any point in the discourse he will be darting out some notable saying, terse and full of meaning, with unerring aim; and the person with whom he is talking seems to be like a child in his hands. — Protagoras, 342.

Speaker. They will be sure to listen if they find that you are a good speaker. — Euthyphro, 9.

A speaker whose actions do not correspond to his words is an annoyance to me, and the better he speaks the more I hate him, and then I seem to be a hater of discourse. — Laches, 188.

Speaking. I can only speak as I think. — Laws, VII, 806.

Do not be afraid to speak. — Sophist, 238.

There never is nor ever will be a real art of speaking which is unconnected with the truth. — Phaedrus, 260.

Spectator. The competitor in a race is bidden by the spectators to run when he is already running. — Phaedo, 61.

Speech. I cannot manage these long speeches: I only wish that I could. — Protagoras, 335.

The comparison of a drunken man's speech with those of sober men is hardly fair. — Symposium, 214.

The river of speech which goes out of a man and ministers to the intelligence is the fairest and noblest of all streams. — Timaeus, 75.

You are aware that speech signifies all things, and is always turning them round and round, and has two forms, true and false. — Cratylus, 408.

Suppose that we strip all poetry of song and rhythm and meter, there will still remain speech. — Gorgias, 502.

I am afraid that my mistress may be angry with me if I publish her speech. — Menexenus, 236.

What is both precious and beautiful is the talent to create a nice and eloquent speech to a law court or a council meeting or any other official assembly whom you are addressing, to convince your audience, and to carry off the greatest of all prizes, your own salvation and that of your friends. — Greater Hippias, 304.

There are some writers of speeches who do not know how to use the speeches which they compose; and also some persons who are of themselves unable to write speeches, but are able to use speeches which others compose for them. And this proves that the art of writing speeches is not the same as the art of holding them. — Euthydemus, 289.

The writers of speeches always appear to me to be extraordinary men. For their art is a part of the great art of enchantment; it acts upon dicasts and crowds, charming and consoling them. — Euthydemus, 289, 290.

I am speaking like a book, but I believe that what I am saying is true. — Phaedo, 102.

Speech, Freedom of. Shall we allow a stranger to run down Sparta in this fashion? — Yes; for we have granted him freedom of speech. — Laws, VII, 806.

Spending. Spending money rightly in right time is a good habit. — Letter XIII, 362.

Spendthrift. I meant to refer to the class of idle spendthrifts, of whom the more courageous are the leaders and the more timid the followers, the same whom we were comparing to drones, some stingless, and others having stings. These two classes are the plagues of every city in which they are generated, being what phlegm and gall are to the body. And the good physician and law-giver of the state ought, like the wise beemaster, to keep them at a distance and prevent, if possible, their ever coming in; and if they have anyhow found a way in, then he should have them and their cells cut out as speedily as possible. — Republic, VIII, 564.

Spirit. Passion or spirit appeared at first sight to be a sort of desire, but

[245]

now we should say the contrary; for in the conflict of the soul spirit is arranged on the side of the rational principle. — Republic, IV, 440.

Is he likely to be brave who has no spirit, whether horse or dog or any other animal? Have you never observed how irresistible and unconquerable spirit is, the presence of which makes the soul of any creature fearless and invincible? — Republic, II, 375.

The spirit began a rational life enduring throughout all time. The body of heaven is visible, but the spirit invisible, and partakes of reason and intelligence. — Timaeus, 36.

Love is the great spirit, and like all that is spiritual he is intermediate between the divine and the mortal. — Symposium, 202.

The spirit imposes its law as a sovereign who is subject to none. — Epinomis, 982.

As the state is composed of three classes, traders, auxiliaries, counselors, so there is in the individual soul besides desire and reason, a third element which is passion or spirit. — Republic, IV, 441.

Spiritual. Would they say that the invisible or spiritual is corporeal? — They would not venture to deny the existence to justice, wisdom, and the like, or to maintain that these normative phenomena are corporeal. — Sophist, 247.

The spiritual philosopher rises out of the region of nature and lays hold of spiritual being. — Republic, VII, 525.

The spiritual scientist must pass from the region of amoral facts to the region of moral ideas. — Republic, VII, 525.

When I was worn out with my investigations about physical phenomena . . . I thought that I had better have recourse to value ideas, and seek also in these spiritual phenomena the truth about things. — Phaedo, 100.

Sport. He who changes the sports is secretly changing the manners of the young, and making the old to be dishonored among them and the new to be honored. — Laws, VII, 797.

Sports should not be altogether without dangers, but contain, to a certain degree, perils in order to discriminate the man of courage from the man of fear. This will rather prepare the whole city for the true conflict of life. — Laws, VIII, 831.

Sportsman. Should not the good sportsman follow the track, and not be lazy? — Laches, 194.

Spring. I do not understand the meaning of the name Tethys. — Well, that is almost self-explanatory, being only the name of a spring, a little disguised; for that which is strained and filtered may be likened to a spring, and the name Tethys is made up of these two words. — Cratylus, 402.

Standard. Tell me what this is, and then I shall have a standard to which I may look. — Euthyphro, 6.

When you speak of beautiful things, as, for example, bodies, colors, figures, sounds, institutions, do you not call them beautiful in reference to some standard? Bodies, for example, are beautiful in proportion as they are useful, or as the sight of them gives pleasure to the spectators? — Gorgias, 474.

Standards of Conduct. Thus educated, the youths will rediscover for themselves those apparently trifling standards of conduct which their predecessors have altogether neglected. I mean such things as these: when the young are to be silent before their elders; how they are to show respect to them by standing and making them sit; what honor is due to parents; what garments or shoes are to be worn; the mode of dressing the hair; deportment and manners in general. — Republic, IV, 425.

Stars. Stars are the measure of time. — Timaeus, 42.

The stars are the most beautiful of all sights to the eye, and as they move through the figures of the most beautiful and most glorious of dances they complete their task to all living creatures. They are not really the tiny spots they seem to be; the body of any star is enormous. We may rightly assume that the sun as a whole is larger than the earth as a whole, and every one of the moving stars is of astonishing magnitude. — Epinomis, 982, 983.

Vain would be the attempt of telling about all the figures of the stars moving as in a dance, and their meetings with one another, and the return of their orbits on themselves, and their approximations. — Timaeus, 40.

State. The states are as bad as the men. — Republic, IV, 426.

An oracle says that when a man of brass or iron guards the state, it will then be destroyed. — Republic, III, 415.

Our state will be a reality, and not a dream only, and will be administered in a spirit unlike that of other states, in which men fight with one another about shadows only and are distracted in the struggle for power, which in their eyes is a great good. Whereas the truth is that the state in which the rulers are most reluctant to govern is always the best and most quietly governed, and the state in which they are most eager, the worst. — Republic, VII, 520.

Any restless state may indeed be spoken of in the plural number, being many states in one — a game of cities at which men play. Any ordinary city, however small, is in fact two cities, one the city of the poor, the other of the rich, at war with one another; and in either division there are many smaller ones, and you would make a great mistake if you treated them as a single state; but if you deal with them as many, and give the money or means or persons of the one to the others, you will always have a great many friends, and not many enemies. — Republic, IV, 422, 423.

As the state is not like a beehive, and has no natural head who is the recognized superior in body and mind, mankind are obliged to meet and make laws, and endeavor to approach as nearly as they can to the good form of government. — Statesman, 301.

No man ought to have pre-eminent importance in a state because he surpasses others in wealth, any more than because he is swift or handsome or strong, unless he have some virtue in him. — Laws, III, 696.

A divisive state is not one, but two states, the one of the poor men, the other of the rich men, who are living on the same spot and ever conspiring against one another. — Republic, VIII, 551.

The state, if once started well, goes on with accumulating force like a wheel. — Republic, IV, 424.

A state in which the better citizens win a victory over the inferior classes, may be truly said to be better than itself. — Laws, I, 627.

We cannot suppose that states are made of "oak and rock," and not out of the human natures which are in them, and which in a figure turn the scale and intelligently draw other things after them. — Republic, VIII, 544.

If we could wait until the second generation which has been indoctrinated with the new laws from its childhood, and has been nurtured in them, takes part in the public elections — then there would be little danger of a state thus founded not being permanent. — Laws, VI, 752.

Until philosophers are kings, or the kings of this world have the spirit and power of philosophy, and political greatness and wisdom meet in one, and those commoner natures who pursue either to the exclusion of the other are compelled to stand aside, cities will never have rest from their evils — no, nor the human race, as I believe — and then only will this our state have a possibility of life and behold the light of day. Such was the thought which I would fain have uttered if it had not seemed too extravagant; for to be convinced that in no other state can there be happiness is indeed a hard thing. — Republic, V, 473.

If our settlement of the country is to be perfect, we ought to have some institution, which will tell what is the aim of the state, and will inform us how we are to attain this, and what law or what man will advise us to that end. Any state which has no such institution is likely to be void of mind and sense, and in all her actions will proceed by mere chance. — Laws, XII, 962.

Even as they are [without property], our guardians will probably be the happiest of men; but our object in the construction of the state is the greatest happiness of the whole, and not of any one class; and in a state which is ordered with a view to the good of the whole, we think that we are most likely to find justice, as in the ill-ordered state injustice: and, having found them, we shall then be able to decide which of the two is the happier. — Republic, IV, 420.

A state arises out of the needs of mankind; no one is self-sufficing, but all of us have many wants. Can any other origin of a state be imagined? — Republic, II, 369.

Statement. Statements are true or false. — Sophist, 264.

Any statement must have a certain quality. The true statement says how things are; the false statement does not say how things are. — Sophist, 263.

Statesman. A great statesman is just the man to have a great mind. — Laches, 197.

The most powerful and dignified men among our statesmen are ashamed of writing speeches and leaving them in a written form because they are afraid of posterity, and do not like to be called Sophists. — Phaedrus, 257.

No one has ever shown himself a good statesman in his own state. — Gorgias, 517.

No one can be a great statesman who looks only, or first of all, to external warfare. — Laws, I, 628.

The statesmen seem to be much more like their subjects in character. — Statesman, 275.

The great statesman will do many things by his art without regard to the laws, when he is of opinion that something other than that which he has written down and enjoined to be observed during his absence would be better. — Statesman, 300. *Vide* Compulsion.

If not by science, the only alternative which remains is that statesmen guide by wisdom, which is in politics what divination is in religion. — Meno, 99.

Great statesmen above all may be said to be divine and illuminated, being inspired and possessed by divine wisdom. — Meno, 99.

The intention of a reasonable statesman is not what the many declare to be the object of a good legislator. — Laws, **V, 742.**

All the results of politics, and they are many, as for example, wealth, freedom, tranquility, are neither good nor evil per se; but statesmanship makes us wise, and imparts wisdom to us, if that is the art which is likely to do us good, and make us happy. — Euthydemus, 291.

Statesmanship. The knowledge of the natures and habits of men's souls will be of the greatest use in the art which has the management of them; and that art is statesmanship. — Laws, I, 650.

Had in his government wisdom and reign been united in the same person, such statesmanship would have shone forth gloriously among Greeks and non-Greeks. — Letter VII, 335.

Considering how great and terrible the whole art of war is, can we imagine any superior art but statesmanship? — Statesman, 305.

Rulers may be truly called those who possess statesmanship, whether they rule or not. — Statesman, 292.

Statue. How energetically you polish them up, as if they were two statues. — Republic, II, 361.

Stimulant. When a man goes of his own accord to a physician, and takes a stimulant, he is quite aware that soon, and for many days afterwards, he will be in a bodily state which he would die rather than accept as the permanent condition of his life. — Laws, I, 646.

Stolen Goods. If anyone knowingly receives stolen goods, he shall undergo the same punishment as the thief. — Laws, XII, 955.

Stone. Though shouting, I cannot induce you to hear me. Sitting beside me, you might be a stone as well, a real millstone without ears and brain. — Greater Hippias, 292.

Stool. He would act like a person who pulls away a stool from someone when he is about to sit down, and then laughs and claps his hands at the sight of his friend sprawling on the ground. — Euthydemus, 278.

Story. This made us discourse too long, and, nevertheless, the story never came to an end. — Statesman, 277.

Whether these stories about the strange behavior of gods have a good or bad influence I should not like to be severe upon them, because they are ancient; but I must say, that looking at them with reference to the duties of children to their parents, I cannot praise them, or think that they are useful, or at all true. — Laws, X, 886.

Friends should not keep their stories to themselves, but have them in common. — Critias, 112.

Strange. Everyone looks strange when you do not know him. — Statesman, 291.

Stranger. We must allow the strangers to use language in their own way, and not quarrel with them about words, but be thankful for what they give us. — Euthydemus, 285.

A stranger finding his way into great cities ought to be very cautious. — Protagoras, 316.

Our citizens should show their respect to Zeus, the god of hospitality, not driving away strangers at meal and sacrifices and by savage proclamations, as is the manner which prevails among the children of the Nile. — Laws, XII, 953.

Is he not rather a god, who comes to us in the disguise of a stranger? — Sophist, 216.

Strategy. How can generalship and military strategy be regarded as other than a science? — Statesman, 304.

Stream. When a stream is flowing out, there should be water flowing in too; and remembrance of the right rules is the flowing in of failing wisdom. — Laws, V, 732.

Strength. Strength, as strength, whether of man or woman, is the same. — Meno, 72.

Striking. If a man strikes, there must be something which is stricken. — Gorgias, 476.

Stubbornness. At three, four, five, and six years the childish nature will require sports; now is also the time to get rid of stubbornness in him, by inflicting punishment. — Laws, VII, 793.

Student. Even if a teacher could be found, as matters now stand, the students who are very conceited would not mind him. — Republic, VII, 528.

The students of the art are filled with lawlessness. — Republic, VII, 537.

Study. What are the studies which will lead a man to wisdom?. — Epinomis, 973.

If a man grasps several questions aright, the benefit accruing to him is great. To the man who pursues his studies in the proper way, all geometric constructions, all systems of numbers, all duly ordered harmonious progressions should reveal themselves; and they will reveal themselves, if, as I say, a man arranges his studies scientifically, with his mind's eye fixed on their single end. As such a man reflects, he will receive the disclosure of a single bond of intelligible interconnection between all these issues. — Epinomis, 991, 992.

I am amused at your fear that the world may criticize you for insisting upon unpractical studies. — Republic, VII, 527.

In all our sessions for study we are to relate the peculiar fact to its species; there are questions to be asked and wrong theories to be refuted. As for tests that pretend to be such but are not, there is no effort so useless as that spent on them. — Epinomis, 991.

Study of God. No Greek should fear that the study of God is a forbidden activity. . . . The proverb about not knowing one's own identity would be true, if the deity felt wrath against the able investigator, and not rather a pure joy at seeing him developing in goodness by its aid. — Epinomis, 988.

Style. I have composed a beautiful discourse, a work distinguished by a subtle style. — Greater Hippias, 286.

Subject Matter. Each science has a subject matter which is different from it. — Charmides, 166.

Subjection. Not speaking the same language, they will more easily be held in subjection. — Laws, VI, 777.

Subjection is disastrous both to

masters and subjects, to their children and all their posterity. — Letter VII, 334.

Substance. What we term the substance of each color is neither the active nor the passive element, but something which passes between them. — Theaetetus, 154.

Subversion. Every man who is worth anything will bring the conspirator to trial for making a violent and subversive attempt to change the government. — Laws, IX, 856.

Success. Often you have assumed that only a trifle stood between you and full success. — Letter VIII, 353.

Sufficient. He who is sufficient wants nothing — that is implied in the word sufficient. — Lysis, 215.

Suggestion. They may accept a suggestion of ours, having nothing of their own to offer. — Sophist, 247.

Suicide. A man should wait, and not commit suicide until God summons him.... Man is a prisoner who has no right to open the door of his prison and run away. — Phaedo, 62.

Why is suicide held not to be right? Why, when a man is better dead, is he not permitted to be his own benefactor, but must wait for the hand of another? — Phaedo, 61, 62.

What shall he suffer who slays him who of all men is said to be nearest and dearest to him? I mean the suicide, who deprives himself by violence of his appointed share of life, not because under the compulsion of some painful misfortune, nor because he has had to suffer from irremediable and intolerable shame, but who from indolence or cowardice imposes upon himself an unjust penalty. Those who meet their death in this way shall be buried alone; they shall be buried ingloriously, in such places as are nameless, and no column or name shall mark the place of their interment. — Laws, IX, 873.

Sun. While the sun and the heavens go round, all things human and divine are and are preserved, but if the sun were to be arrested in his course, then all things would be destroyed. — Theaetetus, 153.

The sun is the brightest of the heavenly bodies which revolves about the earth. — Theaetetus, 208.

The sun and the moon and the other stars move in the same kind of path — not in many paths, but in one only which is circular, and the aberrations are only apparent. — Laws, VII, 822.

God lighted a fire, which we now call the sun. — Timaeus, 39.

The sun is the author of generation and nourishment and growth, though he himself is not generation. — Republic, VI, 509.

The creature composed of fire moves with utter uniformity, holding its course uniformly through the sky. — Epinomis, 982.

The infallible regularity and uniformity of the sun's path proves convincingly his intelligent life. — Epinomis, 982. *Vide* Intelligence.

Superintend. A carpenter shall not be the foreman of a smith, under the pretext that in superintending many servants who are working for him, he is likely to superintend them better, because more revenue will accrue to him from them than from his own art. — Laws, VIII, 846.

Superior. Do you mean by superior the stronger or the better? Are the superior and better and stronger the same or different? — Gorgias, 488.

The drive of the strong individual

to have more than the many, is conventionally said to be shameful and unjust, and is called injustice, whereas nature herself intimates that it is just for the better to have more than the worse, than the more powerful than the weaker; and in many ways she shows that justice consists in the superior ruling over and having more than the inferior. — Gorgias, 483.

Suppliant. Of offenses committed, whether against strangers or fellow countrymen, that against suppliants is the greatest. For the god who witnessed to the agreement made with the suppliant, becomes in a special manner the guardian of the sufferer; and he will certainly not suffer unavenged. — Laws, V, 730.

Supplication. Perhaps there may be someone who is offended at me, when he calls to mind how he himself on a similar, or even less serious occasion, had recourse to prayers and supplications with many tears, and how he produced his children in court, which was a moving spectacle, together with a posse of his relations and friends; whereas I, who am probably in danger of my life, will do none of these things. — Apology, 34.

Supply and Demand. The wage earner and the tavern keeper, and many other occupations — all alike have the same object; they seek to satisfy our demand and equalize our possession by supply. — Laws, XI, 918.

Surmise. The sphere of surmise is to the sphere of certainty as the copy to the original. — Republic, VI, 510.

Surpass. They ought to surpass men rather than children. — Letter IV, 320.

Swan. Swans, when they perceive that they must die, having sung all their life long, do then sing more than ever, rejoicing in the thought that they are about to go away to the god whose ministers they are. But men, because they are themselves afraid of death, slanderously affirm of the swans that they sing a lament at the last. Because the swans are sacred to Apollo and have the gift of prophecy and anticipate the good things of another world, therefore they sing and rejoice on that day more than they ever did before. . . . I too, believing myself to be the consecrated servant of Apollo, and the fellow servant of the swans and thinking that I have received from my master gifts of prophecy which are not inferior to theirs, would not go out of life less merrily than the swans. — Phaedo, 85.

Sweet. When the composition of the particles which dissolve in the moisture of the mouth, is congenial to the tongue, and smooths and oils over the roughness, and relaxes the parts which are unnaturally contracted, and contracts the parts which are relaxed, and disposes them all according to their nature; that sort of remedy of violent affections is pleasant and agreeable to every man, and has the name sweet. — Timaeus, 66.

Sweetmeats. All professional athletes know that a man who is to be in good condition should abstain from sweetmeats. — Republic, III, 404.

Swiftness. That which is done with swiftness is done swiftly, and that which is done with slowness, slowly? — Protagoras, 332.

In all that concerns body or soul, swiftness and activity are clearly better than slowness and quietness. — Charmides, 160.

Swimming. Whether a man has

fallen into a swimming pool or into a great ocean, he has to swim all the same. — Republic, V, 453.

Swimming surely saves a man from death, for there are occasions on which he must know how to swim. — Gorgias, 511.

Syllable. If anyone could express the essence of each thing in letters and syllables, would he not express the nature of each thing? — Cratylus, 423.

Synonym. Now is the time to rehabilitate Simonides, by the application of your charming philosophy of synonyms, which distinguishes "will" and "wish," and many similar words which you mentioned in your admirable speech. — Protagoras, 340.

T

Tale. We shall have to reject all the terrible and appalling names which describe the world below — Cocytus and Styx, ghosts under the earth, and sapless shades, and any other words of the same type, the very mention of which causes a shudder to pass through the inmost soul of him who hears them. I do not say that these tales may not have a use of some kind; but there is a danger that the nerves of our guardians may become affected by them. — Republic, III, 387.

Listen to a tale which a child would love to hear, and you are not too old to be amused as a child. — Statesman, 268.

Talking. I prefer to talk with another when he responds pleasantly, and is light in hand; if not, I would rather have my own say. — Sophist, 217.

Talking is natural, whether friendship or mere pleasure is the motive. — Phaedrus, 232.

Tame. Are tame animals ever hunted? — Yes, if you include man under tame animals. But if you like you may say that there are no tame animals, or that, if there are man is not among them; or you may say that man is a tame animal and is not hunted; you shall decide which of these alternatives you prefer. — Sophist, 222.

Tarentine. Among our Tarentine colonists I have seen the whole city drunk at a Dionysiac festival. — Laws, I, 637.

Tartarus. He who has lived unjustly and impiously shall go to the house of vengeance and punishment, which is called Tartarus. — Gorgias, 523. *Vide* Island of the Blessed.

Taste. What is taste? That is what the argument has to show — the point being what is according to nature, and what is not according to nature. — Laws, V, 733.

Tax, Citizenship. They make a tax law which fixes a certain sum of money as the qualification of citizenship (or franchise); the money fixed is more or less as the oligarchy (or democracy) is more or less exclusive; and they forbid anyone whose property is below the amount fixed to share in the government (or election): these regulations they effect by force, if intimidation has not already done the work. — Republic, VIII, 551.

Taxes. Their fondness for money makes them unwilling to pay taxes. — Republic, VIII, 551.

Let no one pay any duty either on the importation or exportation of goods. — Laws, VIII, 847.

Teacher. Teachers themselves should be compelled to learn. — Laws, VII, 811.

Students cannot learn unless they have a teacher. But then a teacher is hardly to be found. — Republic, VII, 528.

Do not mind whether the teachers of philosophy are good or bad, but think only of philosophy herself. — Euthydemus, 307.

That the teacher is younger, or not as yet in repute — anything of that sort is of no account with me. — Laches, 189.

Knowledge is the first qualification of any teacher. — First Alcibiades, 111.

Can we call them teachers who do not acknowledge the possibility of their own vocation? — Meno, 95.

There would be no difficulty in finding a teacher of those who are wholly ignorant. — Protagoras, 328.

All men are teachers of virtue, each one according to his ability, and you say that there is no such teacher. You might as well ask, who teaches Greek? For of that too there will not be any teachers found. — Protagoras, 328.

If a man is able to teach, I honor him for being paid. — Apology, 19.

The men who dwell in the city are my teachers, and not the trees, or the country. — Phaedrus, 230.

I maintain that every one of us should seek out the best teacher whom he can find, first for ourselves, and then for the youth, regardless of expense or anything. — Laches, 200.

Teaching. He who transmits them [sciences] may be said to teach them, and he who receives to learn them, and he who has them in possession in the aforesaid aviary may be said to know them. — Theaetetus, 198.

The design which you meditate of teaching what you do not know, and have not taken any pains to learn, is downright insanity. — First Alcibiades, 113.

They say that they are able to teach anyone who will give them money, however old or stupid. — Euthydemus, 304.

Tears. Tears and cries are the inauspicious signs by which infants show what they love and hate. — Laws, VII, 792.

Tediousness. I wanted to get rid of any impression of tediousness which we may have experienced in the discussion about weaving, and the rotation of the universe, and in the discussion concerning the Sophist and being and not-being. — Statesman, 286.

Temperance. He thought temperance was doing things orderly and quietly. — Charmides, 159.

Temperance is the same as modesty. — Charmides, 160.

If this gift of temperance is already yours, you have no need of any charms. — Charmides, 158.

Man should veil his excessive sorrow or joy, and seek to behave with temperance, whether his genius be set at good fortune, or whether at the crisis of his fate, when he seems to be mounting high and steep places, the gods oppose him in some of his enterprises. — Laws, V, 732.

When opinion conquers [forbidden desire], and by the help of reason leads us to the best, the conquering principle is called temperance. — Phaedrus, 237.

Where temperance is, there health is speedily imparted, not only to the head, but to the whole body. — Charmides, 157.

Temperance is a sort of order and control of certain pleasures and desires; this is implied in the saying of "a man being his own master." — Republic, IV, 430.

Temperance is self-knowledge. — Charmides, 165.

Temperance is the acknowledged ruler of the pleasures and desires, and no pleasure ever masters Love; he is their master and they are his servants; and if he conquers them he must be temperate indeed. — Symposium, 196.

When a man's pulse is healthy and temperate, and he goes to sleep cool and rational, after having supped on a feast of reason and meditation, and come to a knowledge of himself, having indulged his appetites neither too much nor too little, but just enough to lay them to sleep, and prevent them and their enjoyments and pains from interfering with his better self: when, again, before going to sleep he has allayed his passionate anger, if he has had a quarrel — when, after pacifying the two irrational elements, he rouses up the third or rational element before he takes his rest, then he attains virtue most nearly, and is least likely to be the sport of fanciful and lawless dreams. — Republic, IX, 572.

Temperate. Do you mean those fools — the temperate? — Gorgias,, 461.

"Know thyself!" and "Be temperate!" are the same. — Charmides, 164.

Tending. We should tend them carefully, not only out of regard to them, but yet more out of respect to ourselves. — Laws, VI, 777.

Terminology. Nothing obstructs the things which are now termed straight from being termed round and the round straight; and those who interchange the names, using them in the reverse way, will find the things or concepts of them no less stable than they are now. — Letter VII, 343.

Terrible. The terrible and the hopeful are the things which do or do not create fear. — Laches, 198.

Territory. The territory must be sufficient to maintain a certain number of inhabitants in a moderate way of life — more than this is not required. — Laws, V, 737.

Test of Knowledge. Must not the creature be fond of learning who determines what is friendly and what is unfriendly by the test of knowledge and ignorance? — Republic, II, 376.

Testing. What is more suitable than a harmless drink of wine, to test the character of a man? What is there cheaper, or more innocent? For do but consider which is the greater risk: Would you rather test a man of harsh and uncivil nature by having him as a companion at the festival of Dionysus, or would you, if you wanted to apply a touchstone to a man who is prone to love, entrust your wife, or your sons, or daughters to him, periling your dearest interests in order to discover his character? I do not believe that anyone will doubt that that test is a fair test, and safer, cheaper, and speedier than any other. — Laws, I, 650.

I consider that if a man is to test another's soul for its good or bad qualities, he ought to have three qualities — knowledge, good will, and frankness. — Gorgias, 487.

Theages. Everything in the life of Theages conspired to divert him from philosophy; but ill health kept him away from politics. — Republic, VI, 496.

Theatre. The theatres from being mute have become vocal, as though they had understanding of good and bad in music and poetry. — Laws, III, 701.

Theft. He who steals a little steals

with the same wish as he who steals much, but with less power. He who takes up anything more than he has deposited is unjust in the highest degree; and therefore the law is not disposed to inflict a less penalty on the one than on the other, because his theft is less, but on the ground that the thief may possibly be in the one case still curable, and the other case is incurable. — Laws, XII, 941.

As to the desire of thieving in town or country, may that never enter into your most passing thoughts. — Laws, VII, 823.

The guilty thief ought not to believe, that he is doing nothing base, but only what the gods themselves do. For this is untrue and improbable. He who steals or robs, acts contrary to the law, and is therefore guilty. — Laws, XII, 941.

Theory. I know too well that theories which rest their proof upon plausibility are impostors, and unless great caution is observed they are apt to be deceptive. — Phaedo, 92.

Thessalians. There was a time when the Thessalians were famous among the other Greeks only for their riches and their riding; but now they are equally famous for their wisdom. — Meno, 70.

Things. People seem to forget that some things have physical and visible qualities, which may be easily shown to an inquirer, without any trouble; while the spiritual and noblest things have no outward quality, which alone is visible to man and adaptable to the eye of the sense. We ought, therefore, to practice ourselves in understanding the moral ideas with the eye of the mind; for immaterial things are shown only in thinking, and in no other way. — Statesman, 285, 286.

There are three aspects to be noted about things: for one, the existence of the things, for another the definition of this existence, for another, its name. — Laws, X, 895.

Here are two kinds of things. One is physical generation, and the other is spiritual essence. — Philebus, 54.

The material things you can touch and see and perceive with the senses, but the intelligible things you can only conceive with the mind — they are invisible and not seen. — Phaedo, 79.

Let us not speak of physical things at all as having stability or erroneously imagine ourselves to indicate any of them by the term "this" or "that," for they are too volatile to be detained in any such expressions. — Timaeus, 49.

Thirst. Thirst is a cause of destruction and a pain. — Philebus, 32.

Thirst is relative to drink. — Republic, IV, 439.

Thirst or any similar desire may sometimes be a good and sometimes an evil to us. — Lysis, 221.

Thought. Thought is the unuttered conversation of the soul with herself. — Sophist, 263.

Thought is best when the mind is gathered into itself and none of these things trouble it — neither sounds nor sights nor pain nor any pleasure — when it has as little as possible to do with the body, and has no bodily sense or feeling, but is aspiring after thinking. And in this the philosopher dishonors the body; his soul runs away from the body and desires to be alone and by itself. — Phaedo, 65.

There is no harm in repeating a sound thought. — Laws, VI, 754.

He who is always occupied with the cravings of desire and ambition, and is eagerly striving after them, must have all his thoughts mortal. But he who has been earnest in the love of knowledge and wisdom, must have thoughts immortal. — Timaeus, 90.

Thought and mind and law are prior to matter which is hard and soft, and heavy and light. — Laws, X, 892.

Must you not say that everything is made up of thoughts, and that all things think? — Parmenides, 132.

Threshing. When grain is shaken and winnowed by fans and other instruments used in the threshing of corn, the close and heavy particles are borne away and settle in one direction, and the loose and light particles in another. — Timaeus, 52.

Thrift. He who receives money unjustly as well as justly, and spends neither justly nor unjustly, will be a rich man if he be also thrifty. — Laws, V, 743.

Time. Time is the true test of most things. — Symposium, 184.

The moving image of eternity we call time. Days and nights are the parts of time, and the past and future are created species of time. — Timaeus, 37.

Until the creation of time, all things had been made in the likeness of the original. — Timaeus, 39.

Now the sight of day and night, and the revolution of the months and years, have given us the invention of number, and a conception of time, and the power of inquiring about the nature of the whole; and from this source we have derived philosophy, than which no greater good ever was or will be given by the gods to mortal man. — Timaeus, 47.

Timocracy. I know of no name for a government of honor other than timocracy, or perhaps timarchy. — Republic, VIII, 545.

In the fear of admitting philosophers to power, because they are no longer to be had simple and earnest, but are made up of mixed strain; and in turning from them to passionate and less complex characters, who are by nature fitted for war rather than peace; and in the value set by them upon military stratagems and contrivances, and in the waging of everlasting wars — timocracy will be for the most part peculiar. — Republic, VIII, 547, 548.

Timocrat. Timocrats invent illegal modes of expenditure; neither they nor their wives care much about the law. — Republic, VIII, 550.

The young timocrat should have more of self-assertion, and be somewhat less sophisticated, and yet friend of culture; and he should be a good listener, but not a speaker. Such a man is apt to be rough with slaves, unlike the educated man, who is too proud for that; and he will also be courteous to freemen, and remarkably obedient to authority; he is a lover of power and a lover of honor; claiming to be a ruler, not because he is eloquent, but because he is a good soldier. — Republic, VIII, 549.

Timocrats will have a fierce secret longing after gold and silver, which they will hoard in dark places, having magazines and treasures of their own for the deposit and concealment of them; also castles which are just nests for their eggs, and in which they will spend large sums on their wives, or on any others whom they please. And they are miserly because they have no means of openly acquiring the money which they prize; they will spend that which is another man's on the gratification of their desires, stealing their pleasures and running away like children from the law, their father: they have been schooled not by gentle influence but by force, for they have neglected her who is the true Muse, the companion of reason and philosophy, and have honored gymnastic more than music. — Republic, VIII, 548.

Timocrat man will despise riches only when he is young; but as he grows older he will be more and more attracted to them, because he has a trait of the avaricious nature in him, and is not single-minded towards virtue, having lost his best guardian. — Republic, VIII, 549.

Tinker. Are you not exactly like a bald little tinker who has just got out of durance and come into a fortune; he washes the dirt off him and has a new coat, and is decked out as a bridegroom going to marry his master's daughter, who is left poor and desolate? — Republic, VI, 495.

Tool. The tools which would teach their own use would be too costly. — Republic, II, 374.

The mere handling of tools will not make a man a skilled workman, or master of defense, nor be of any use to him who knows not the nature of each, and has never bestowed any attention upon them. — Republic, II, 374.

Torch Race. There is to be an equestrian torch race in the evening. — Indeed, that is a novelty. Will the horsemen carry torches and pass them to one another during the race? — Republic, I, 328.

Torpedo. As to my being a torpedo, if the torpedo is torpid as well as the cause of torpidity in others, then indeed I am a torpedo, but not otherwise; for I perplex others, not because I am clear, but because I am utterly perplexed myself. — Meno, 80.

Torpedo Fish. You seem in your appearance and in your power over others to be very like the flat torpedo fish, who torpifies those who come near him with the touch, as you have now torpified me. For my soul and my tongue are really torpid, and I do not know how to answer you. — Meno, 80.

Touchstone. The one sure touchstone of all is the writing of the legislator, which the righteous judge ought to have in his mind as the antidote of all other words. — Laws, XII, 957.

Toy. Man is created to be a toy for God, and this, truly considered, is the best of him. — Laws, VII, 803.

Trade. Retail trade in a city is not by nature intended to do any harm, but quite the contrary; for is not he a benefactor who reduces the inequalities and immeasurabilities of goods to equality and measure? And this is what the power of money accomplishes, and the merchant may be said to be appointed for this purpose. — Laws, XI, 918.

Trade, Foreign. A state which makes money from the cultivation of its soil only, and has no foreign trade, must consider what it will do about the emigration of its own people to other countries, and the reception of strangers from elsewhere. The intercourse of cities with one another is apt to create a confusion of manners; strangers are always suggesting novelties to strangers. — Laws, XII, 949.

Had there been domestic abundance there might have been a great foreign trade, and a great return of gold and silver. — Laws, IV, 705.

Tradition. Such a tradition will be a second legal standard of honorable and dishonorable, having a second notion of right. — Laws, VIII, 841.

Tragedy. Tragedy has her face turned towards pleasure and gratification. — Gorgias, 502.

Socrates was insisting that the genius of comedy was the same as that of tragedy, and that the writer of tragedy ought to be a writer of comedy also. — Symposium, 223.

Training. There are two processes of training all things, including body and soul; in the one, we treat them with a view to pleasure, and in the other with a view to the highest good. — Gorgias, 513.

There is a very great difference between one who has been trained and one who has not been. — Laws, VII, 795.

Are not those who train in gymnasia, at first beginning, reduced to a state of weakness? — Laws, I, 646.

Traitor. The traitor has no friend; as time advances he becomes known, and lays up in store for himself isolation in crabbed age when life is on the wane: so that, whether his children or friends are alive or not, he is equally solitary. — Laws, V, 730.

Traveler. A traveler standing at a strange place at which three roads meet and not knowing his way, will ponder over the right direction, and will not move forward until he is sure that he is going right. Now, we are in the same position, for a strange discussion on the subject of law has arisen, which requires the utmost consideration. — Laws, VII, 799.

Traveling. I used to travel about the world, thinking that I was doing something. — Symposium, 173.

Treasure. Let us speak of treasure: May I never pray the gods to find the hidden treasure, which a man has laid up for himself and his family, he not being one of my ancestors, nor lift, if I should find, such a treasure. — Laws, XI, 913.

Treatment. Eminent physicians say to a patient who comes to them with bad eyes, that they cannot cure his eyes by themselves, but if his eyes are to be cured, his head must be treated; and then again they say that to think of curing the head alone, and not the rest of the body also, is the height of folly. — Charmides, 156.

We can hardly say that any one course of treatment is perfectly adapted to a particular constitution, for that which does good in one way does harm in another. — Laws, I, 636.

Everywhere in such places the youth shall make gymnasia for themselves, and warm baths for the aged, placing by them abundance of dry wood, for the benefit of those laboring under disease — there the weary frame of the rustic, worn with toil, will be kindly received, and experience far better treatment than at the hands of a conceited doctor. — Laws, VI, 761.

Tree. These are the trees and plants and seeds, which by cultivation are now adapted to our use; anciently there were only the wild kinds, which are older than the cultivated. — Timaeus, 77.

Trial. If there were a law at Athens, such as there is in other cities, that a capital trial should not be decided in one day, then I [Socrates] believe that I should have convinced you [of my innocence]; but now the time is too short. — Apology, 37.

Tribute. There is a tribute of deeds and of words. — Menexenus, 236.

Trojan Horse. No one can suppose that we are merely Trojan horses, in whom are perched several unconnected senses, not meeting in some spiritual center, of which they are the instruments, whether you term this center soul or not, with which through these we perceive objects of sense. — Theaetetus, 184.

True. Man should live a true man as long as possible, for then he can be trusted. — Laws, V, 730.

No man should be angry at what is true. — Republic, V, 480.

"True Life." Some philosophers invite the young men to lead a "true life" according to nature, which is to live in real dominion over others, and not in legal subjection to them. — Laws, X, 890.

Truism. He is uttering not a wonder but a truism. — Parmenides, 129.

Trust. For effective service Dionysius could trust neither those unrelated with him, nor his younger brothers. None of them was he able to secure by way of persuasion or kinship, so that he could trust him as a reliable officer in the government; in this failure, he was seven times inferior to Darius. For Darius trusted even those who were not his brothers but only his associates. — Letter VII, 332.

Trustee. The property disappeared in the hands of trustees. — Theaetetus, 144.

Truth. I am not ashamed or afraid to tell the truth. — Letter II, 310.

I have no particular liking for anything but the truth. — Euthyphro, 14.

Grasp the truth as a whole and in the right way, and you will have no difficulty in understanding the preceding remarks. — Republic, VI, 491.

Are there people who say things as they are? — Yes, all persons who speak the truth. — Euthydemus, 284.

If you could only persuade everybody, Socrates, as you do me, of the truth of your words, there would be more peace and fewer evils among men. — Theaetetus, 176.

A man is not to be reverenced above the truth. — Republic, X, 595.

What essence is to generation, truth is to belief. — Timaeus, 29.

Surely we are not now simply contending in order that my opinion or yours may prevail, but I presume that we ought both of us to be fighting for truth. — Philebus, 14.

We are no respecters of persons, but seekers of the truth. — Sophist, 246.

Truth gives to learning rightness and utility. — Laws, II, 667.

Truth, stranger, is a noble thing and a lasting, but a thing of which men are hard to be persuaded. — Laws, II, 663.

There was a tradition in the temple of Zeus at Dodona that oaks first gave prophetic utterances. The men of that day deemed that if they heard the truth even from "oak and rock," that was enough for them; whereas you seem to think not of the truth but of the speaker, and of the country from which the truth comes. — Phaedrus, 275.

I would ask you to be thinking of the truth and not of Socrates: agree with me, if I seem to you to be speaking the truth; or if not, withstand me might and main, that I may not deceive you as well as myself in my enthusiasm. — Phaedo, 91.

I must remain loyal to the truth. — Letter VII, 330.

The discovery of the truth is a common good. — Gorgias, 505.

In philosophy you must train and exercise yourself, now that you are young, or truth will elude your grasp. — Parmenides, 135.

I am afraid that the truth is sometimes discourteous. — Gorgias, 462.

You can never refute the truth. — Gorgias, 473.

Summon the whole house of Pericles, or any other great Athenian family: I only am left alone and cannot agree, for you do not convince me; you only produce many false witnesses against me, in the hope of depriving me of my inheritance, which is the truth. — Gorgias, 472.

The point is not who said the words, but whether they are true or not. — Charmides, 161.

Of two things, one is true. — Charmides, 160.

As the time is equally divided in which we are asleep or awake, in either sphere of existence the soul contends that the thoughts which are present to her at the time are true; and during one half of our lives we affirm the truth of the one, and during the other half, of the other; and are confident of both. — Theaetetus, 158.

Is truth or falsehood to be determined by duration of time? That would be in many ways ridiculous. But can one certainly determine in any other way which of these opinions is true? — Theaetetus, 158.

O men of Athens, I have spoken the truth and the whole truth; I have concealed nothing, I have dissembled nothing. — Apology, 24.

A man is not to be reverenced more than the truth. — Republic, X, 595.

Tutor. Neither sheep nor any other animal can live without a shepherd, nor can children be left without tutors. — Laws, VII, 808.

Two. When two go together, one sees before the other. — Protagoras, 348.

There are two things, let us call them by two names — first, good and evil, and then pleasant and painful. — Protagoras, 355.

Tyrannical Contender. I exhort tyrannical contenders to stop dreaming of the so-called happiness of men who are only greedy and senseless. They should adopt a kingly habit and subject themselves to kingly laws. — Letter VIII, 354.

Tyranny. The leaders of the people deprive the rich of their estates and distribute them among the people . . . and charge them with plotting against the people and being friends of the oligarchy. Then come impeachments and judgments and trials. When a tyrant first appears above ground he is a protector. How then does a protector begin to change into a tyrant? Clearly when he does what the man is said to do in the tale of the Arcadian temple of Lycaean Zeus. The tale is that he who has tasted the entrails of other victims is destined to become a wolf.

And the protector of the people is like him; having a mob entirely at his disposal, he is not restrained from shedding the blood of kinsmen; by the favorite method of false accusation he brings them into court and murders them, making the life of man to disappear, and with unholy tongue and lips tasting the blood of his fellow citizens; some he kills and others he banishes, at the same time hinting at the abolition of debts and partition of lands; and after this, what will be his destiny? Must he not either perish at the hands of his enemies, or from being a man become a wolf — that is, a tyrant?

Then comes the famous request for a bodyguard, which is the device of all those who have got thus far in their tyrannical career — "Let not the people's friend," as they say, "be lost to them." The people readily assent; all their fears are for him — they have none for themselves. And he, the protector of whom we spoke, is to be seen standing up in the chariot of state with the reins in his hand, no longer protector, but tyrant absolute.

At first, in the early days of his power, this creature is full of smiles, and he salutes every one whom he meets — he to be called a tyrant, who is making promises in public and also in private, liberating debtors, and distributing land to the people and his followers, and wanting to be so kind and good to everyone! But when he has disposed of foreign enemies by conquest or treaty, and there is nothing to fear from them, then he is always stirring up some war or other, in order that the people may require a leader.

Has he not also another object, which is that they may be impoverished by payment of taxes, and thus compelled to devote themselves to daily wants and therefore less likely to conspire against him? Clearly. And if any of them are suspected by him of having notions of freedom, and of resistance to his authority he will have a good pretext for destroying them.

Now he begins to grow unpopular. Then some of those who joined in setting him up speak their minds to him and to one another, and the more courageous of them cast in his teeth what is being done. And the tyrant, if he means to rule, must get rid of them; he cannot stop while he has a friend or an enemy who is good for anything. And therefore he must look about him and see who is valiant, who is high-minded, who is wise, who is wealthy; happy man, he is the enemy of them all, and must seek occasion against them whether he will or no, until he has purged the state.

He will rob the citizens of their slaves; he will then set them free and enroll them in his bodyguard. What a blessed creature must this tyrant be; he has put to death the others and has these for his trusted friends. And these are the new citizens whom he has called into existence, who admire him and are his companions, while the good hate and avoid him.

The tyrant will maintain a fair and numerous and various and ever-changing army of his. The people, from whom he has derived his being, will maintain him and his companions; they cannot help themselves. The parent will discover what a monster he has been fostering in his bosom; and, when he wants to drive him out, he will find that he is weak and his son strong. The tyrant will use violence, beat his father if he opposes him, having first disarmed him. He is a parricide, and a cruel guardian of an aged parent; and this is real tyranny, about which there can be no longer a mistake: as the saying is, the people who would escape the smoke which is the slavery of freemen, has fallen into the fire which is the tyranny of slaves. Thus liberty, getting out of all order and reason, passes into the harshest and bitterest form of slavery. — Republic, VIII, 565-569.

Last of all comes the most beautiful

of all, man and state alike, tyranny and the tyrant. — Republic, VIII, 562.

You would not wish to be a tyrant? — Not if you mean by tyranny what I mean. — Gorgias, 469.

How does tyranny arise? — out of democracy of course. — Republic, 562.

Euripides praises tyranny as godlike; and many other things of the same kind are said by him and by the other poets. And therefore, the tragic poets being wise men will forgive us if we do not receive them into our state, because they are the eulogists of tyranny. But they will continue to go to other cities and attract mobs, and hire voices fair and loud and persuasive, and draw the cities over to tyrannies. Moreover, they are paid for this and receive honor from tyrants; but the higher they ascend our constitution hill, the more their reputation fails, and seems unable from shortness of breath to proceed further. — Republic, VIII, 568.

Lycurgus, a good and wise man, realized that Argos and Messene have ruined themselves and their cities, because they transformed kingship into tyranny. — Letter VIII, 354.

Tyrant. The tyrannical man will commit the foulest murder, or eat forbidden food, or be guilty of any other horrid act. Love is his tyrant, and lives lordly in him, and being himself a king emancipated from all control, he leads him on — like man like state — into the performance of reckless deeds in order to maintain himself and his rabble, which evil communications have brought in from without, or which he himself has allowed to break loose within him by reason of a similar character in himself. — Republic, IX, 574, 575.

If the people yield, well and good; but if they resist him, as he began beating his own father and mother, so now, if he has the power, he beats them, and will keep his dear old fatherland or motherland, as the Cretans say, in subjection to his young retainers whom he has introduced to be their rulers and masters. — Republic, IX, 575.

Small and great evils are comparative terms, and all these things, in the misery and evil which they inflict upon a state, do not come within a thousand miles of the tyrant. . . . They choose from among themselves the one who has most of the tyrant in his own soul. He will be the most fit to be a tyrant. — Republic, IX, 575.

The longer a tyrant lives the more of a tyrant he becomes. — Republic, IX, 576.

The tyrant grows worse from having power: he becomes and is of necessity more jealous, more faithless, more unjust, more friendless, more impious, than he was at first. — Republic, IX, 580.

The tyrant must be always getting up a war. — Republic, VIII, 567.

He first takes their property. — Republic, IX, 574.

No one has ever portrayed a tyrant perishing for lack of money. — Letter I, 310.

If anyone is suspected by the tyrant of having notions of freedom, and of resistance to his authority, he will have a good pretext for destroying him by placing him at the mercy of the enemy. — Republic, VIII, 567.

The tyrant is he who begins to

make a party against the rich. — Republic, VIII, 566.

Tyrants are always either the masters or servants and never the friends of anybody; the tyrant never tastes of true freedom or friendship. — Republic, IX, 576.

When tyrants are only private individuals and before they get power, this is their character; they associate entirely with their own flatterers or ready tools; or if they want anything from anybody, they in their turn are equally ready to bow down before them: they profess every sort of affection for them; but when they have gained their point they know them no more. — Republic, IX, 575, 576.

The tyrant will not be the friend of anyone who is greatly his inferior, for the tyrant will despise him, and will never seriously regard him as a friend. — Gorgias, 510.

When the tyrant is rude and uneducated, if there is anyone who is his superior in virtue, he may be expected to fear him, but will never be able to be really friendly with him. — Gorgias, 510.

Most of those fearful examples, as I believe, are taken from the class of tyrants, and kings, and potentates, and public men, for they are the authors of the greatest and most impious crimes, because they have the power. — Gorgias, 525.

Any tyrant should transform tyranny into kingship, if possible. — Letter VIII, 354.

Tyrants kill whom they will, and expropriate or exile anyone whom they dislike. — Gorgias, 466.

A judge whose mind can enter into and see through human nature, must not be like a child who looks only at the outside and is dazzled at the pompous aspect which the tyrant assumes to the beholder. . . . He who is the real tyrant is the real slave, and is obliged to practice the greatest adulation and servility, and to be a flatterer of the vilest of mankind. He has desires which he is utterly unable to satisfy, and has more wants than anyone, and is truly poor, if you know how to inspect the whole soul of him: all his life long he is beset with fear and is full of convulsions and distractions. He is the purveyor and cherisher of every sort of vice, and the consequence is that he is supremely miserable, and that he makes everybody else as miserable as himself. . . . I say that he is by far the most miserable of all men. — Republic, IX, 577, 579, 580, 578.

The case of the tyrant will be still worse, if you suppose him to be everywhere surrounded and watched by enemies. Is this not the sort of prison in which the tyrant will be bound, who is full of all sorts of fears and lusts? His soul is dainty and greedy, and yet, of all men in the city, he may not go on a journey, or see the things which other freemen desire to see, but he lives in his hole like a woman hidden in the house, and is jealous of any other citizen who goes into foreign parts and sees anything of interest. — Republic, IX, 579.

The request of a tyrant contains something of a compulsion. — Letter VII, 329.

U

Unbeliever. You do not understand the nature of the complaint of the unbelievers, and fancy that their minds rush into impiety only from a love of sensual pleasure. — Laws, X, 886.

Those who, besides believing that the world is void of gods, are intemperate, and have at the same time good memories and quick wits, are worse; although both of them are unbelievers, much less injury is done by the one than by the other. The one may talk loosely about the gods and about sacrifices and oaths, and perhaps by laughing at other men he may make them like himself. But the other unbeliever, who is deemed a superior person, is full of stratagem and deceit — men of this sort are prophets and jugglers of all kinds, and out of their ranks sometimes come tyrants and demagogues and generals and hierophants of private mysteries and the ingenuities of so-called Sophists. — Laws, X, 908.

Unchangeable. Only the spiritual things are unchangeable, and body is not included in this class. — Statesman, 269.

Unconsciously. My motive would be just a fear of my unconsciously fancying that I knew something of which I was ignorant. — Charmides, 166.

Unconsciousness. When you are describing the state in which the soul is unaffected by the shocks of the body, say unconsciousness. — Philebus, 34.

Understanding. I ask whether a man can understand all things. — That would be too great a happiness for man. — Sophist, 233.

The mental faculty which is concerned with geometry and the cognate sciences I suppose that you would term understanding and not reason. — Republic, VI, 511.

One thing which every man thinks is, that there are great differences in the understanding of men. — Theaetetus, 171.

Any man however dull can understand them [laws], if he go over them often. — Laws, X, 891.

Let us have a clear understanding, and not be satisfied with half an explanation. — Republic, X, 601.

How can a man understand the name of that of which he does not know the nature? — To be sure he cannot. — Theaetetus, 147.

I purposely use the same images as before, in order that you may the better understand me. — Gorgias, 517.

Understanding is the greatest blessing. — Epinomis, 977.

Do you imagine that he did not understand the meaning of his own words, because you don't understand them? — Charmides, 162.

Shall we say that we understand all that which we see and hear? for example, shall we say that not having learned, we do not understand the language of foreigners when they speak to us? or shall we say that hearing them, we also understand them? or suppose that we see letters which we do not understand, shall we say that we do not see them? or shall we maintain that, seeing them, we must understand them? — Theaetetus, 163.

Certainly understanding is a faculty, and the mightiest of all faculties. — Republic, V, 477.

Undervalue. There is a danger that men may undervalue an art which they have so easy an opportunity of learning. — Euthydemus, 304.

Underworld Code. Could an army, or a band of robbers and thieves, or any other gang of the underworld act at all if they lived without code, injuring one another indiscriminately? — No indeed . . . this would render them incapable of common action. — Republic, 1, 351.

Unfriendliness. Unfriendliness has solitude for company. — Letter III, 321.

Ungracefulness. Voluntary ungracefulness comes from excellence of the bodily frame, and involuntary from the defect of the bodily frame. — Lesser Hippias, 374.

Union. If the original idea had been carried out, and a single union formed, their power would have been invincible in war. — Laws, III, 686.

Unity. Can there be any greater good than the bond of unity? — Republic, V, 462.

Must it not be of the unity, or single nature, which the cognition recognizes as attaching to all? — Parmenides, 132.

There is unity where there is community of pleasures and pains — where all the citizens are glad or grieved on the same occasions of joy and sorrow. — Republic, V, 462.

This unity of feeling we admitted to be the greatest good. — Republic, V, 464.

Zeno is your second self in his writings too; he puts what you say in another way, and half deceives us into believing that he is saying something new. For you, in your writings, declare that the all is one; and he on the other hand says, There is no many. You affirm unity, he denies plurality. And so you both deceive the world into believing that you are asserting different things when really you are saying much the same. This is a strain of art beyond the reach of most of us. — Parmenides, 128.

The wise men of our time are either too quick or too slow in conceiving plurality in unity. — Philebus, 17.

Universe. The universe is called Cosmos or order, not disorder or misrule. — Gorgias, 508.

Let us begin by asking whether the physical universe is guided by irrational causes or intelligent reasons. — Philebus, 28.

The spiritual universe contains in itself all intelligible essences, just as the physical world contains all visible creatures. — Timaeus, 30.

As the universe is a sphere, all the extremities being equidistant from the center are equally extremities, and the center which is equidistant from them is equally to be regarded as the opposite of them all. Such being the nature of the world, when a person says that anything is above and below, may he not justly be charged with using an improper expression? For the center of the world cannot be rightly called either above or below, but is the center and nothing else. — Timaeus, 62.

There is a time when God assists the universe on its way and guides it by imparting rotation to it. — Statesman, 269.

Unjust. The unjust life is not only more evil, but also more unpleasant than the just life. — Laws, II, 663.

To be unjust is more evil than to be poor and sick. — Gorgias, 477.

Gods and men appear to be associated in making the life of the unjust more blessed than the life of the just. — Republic, II, 362.

Man may be unjust, but he is unjust against his will. — Laws, IX, 860.

When Thrasymachus says that the life of the unjust is more advantageous than that of the just, his new statement appears to be of a far more serious character. — Republic, I, 347.

Unlawful. To think that a thing can go at one time in one direction and at another time in another, is unlawful. — Statesman, 299.

Unmarried. If a man will not listen, and remains unsocial among his fellow citizens, and is still unmarried at thirty-five years of age, he shall pay a yearly fine. — Laws, VI, 774.

Use. Knowledge, whether of money-making, or of medicine, or of any other art which knows only how to make a thing, and not to use that which is made, is of no use to us. — Euthydemus, 289.

The wrong use of a thing is far worse than the non-use; for the one is an evil, and the other is neither a good nor an evil. — Euthydemus, 280.

What is the guiding principle which makes health and strength, and beauty and wealth advantageous or the reverse? Are not these things advantageous when they are rightly used, and harmful when they are not rightly used? — Meno, 88.

The excellence of any implement refers to the use of it. The user of anything has the greatest experience, and intimates to the maker the good or bad qualities which develop themselves in use; for example, the flute player will tell the flute maker which of his flutes responds in playing; he will tell him how to make them, and the other will attend to him. — Republic, X, 601.

Usury. No one shall deposit money with another whom he does not trust as a friend, nor shall he lend money upon usury; in this case, the borrower shall not be required to pay either capital or interest. — Laws, V, 742.

V

Vainglorious. The more vainglorious the beauties, the more difficult is the capture of them. — Lysis, 206.

Valiant. There are times and seasons in which we are by nature more than commonly valiant and bold. — Laws, I, 649.

Validity. My object is to test the validity of the argument. — Protagoras, 333.

Valor. Hosts of men and the multitude of riches alike yield to valor. — Menexenus, 240.

Unless a man be pre-eminent in valor, he cannot help being ridiculous. — Laches, 184.

Justice and temperance and wisdom, when united with valor, are better than valor alone; for a man cannot be faithful and good in civil strife without having all virtue. — Laws, I, 630.

Valuation. The valuation is out of the sphere of knowledge. — Theaetetus, 201.

The valuation of anything is, though an exercise of the mind, no definition or knowledge. — Theaetetus, 202. *Vide* Judgment.

Variance, at. I would rather that the whole world should be at odds with me, and oppose me, rather than that I myself should be at variance with myself, and contradict myself. — Gorgias, 482.

Vegetarian. We hear of human beings who do not even venture to taste the flesh of a cow and have no animal sacrifices, but only cakes and fruits soaked in honey; from animals they abstain under the idea that they ought not to eat them, and may not stain the altars of the gods with blood. In those days men are said to have lived a sort of Orphic life, having the use of all vegetarian things, but abstaining from all animal things. — Laws, VI, 782.

Vice. We shall be right in calling vice a discord and disease of the soul. — Sophist, 228.

One may see that virtue is one, but that the forms of vice are innumerable; there being four special ones which are deserving of note. — Republic, IV, 445.

Victory. Education certainly gives victory, although victory sometimes produces forgetfulness of education; for many have grown insolent from victory in war, and this insolence has engendered in them innumerable evils; and many a victory has been and will be suicidal to the victors; but education is never suicidal. — Laws, I, 641.

Let us say nothing, at present, of victories and defeats. Let us only consider that some things are honorable, and some things dishonorable. — Laws, I, 638.

We cannot say that victory or

defeat in battle affords more than a doubtful proof of the goodness or badness of institutions. — Laws, I, 638.

There is a victory and defeat — the first and best of victories, the lowest and worst of defeats — which each man gains or sustains at the hands, not of another, but of himself; this shows that there is a war against ourselves going on in every individual of us. — Laws, I, 626.

Violence. Too great sharpness or quickness or hardness is termed violence or madness. — Statesman, 307.

Shall we say that violence, if exercised by a rich man, is just, and if by a poor man, unjust? — Statesman, 296.

Are you about to use violence, without even going through the forms of justice? — Charmides, 176.

Virtue. Is not the virtue of each thing dependent on order and arrangement? — Gorgias, 506.

Without virtue all possessions and pursuits are dishonorable and evil. — Menexenus, 246.

Virtue is the health and beauty and well-being of the soul, and vice is the disease and weakness and deformity of the soul. — Republic, IV, 444.

Vice cannot know virtue, but a virtuous nature, educated by time, will acquire a knowledge both of virtue and vice: the virtuous, and not the vicious man has wisdom. — Republic, III, 409.

Virtue comes by the gift of God, rather than by nature. — Meno, 99.

Virtue is the power of governing mankind. — Meno, 73.

True virtue: a unanimous and harmonious soul. — Republic, VIII, 554.

Virtue is either wholly or partly wisdom. — Meno, 89.

Virtue is the quality of which all men must be the partakers, and which is the very condition of their learning or doing anything else. — Protagoras, 325.

You are quite right in beginning with virtue. — Laws, I, 631.

How would you explain the virtues? What principle of correctness is there in those charming words — wisdom, understanding, justice, and the rest of them? — Cratylus, 411.

The question is, whether virtue is knowledge or of another species? — Meno, 87.

There was one principle in particular about which we were agreed — that a man's whole energies throughout life should be devoted to the acquisition of the virtue proper to a man, whether this was to be gained by study, or habit, or some other kind of possession, or desire, or opinion, or knowledge. — Laws, VI, 770.

The investigation of virtue must be completed by constant practice throughout a long time. — Letter, VII, 344.

I was not surprised that an intelligent man suddenly became enthused with the virtuous life which he neglected in his youth. — Letter, VII, 339.

There is nothing surprising in states going astray — the reason is that their legislators have improper aims: certain groups should rule in the state, whether they be good or bad; or some citizens should be rich, no matter whether or not at the cost of enslavement; or all citizens should be free, whether they deserve it or not. However, laws generally should look

Watchdog. To keep watchdogs, who, from want of discipline or hunger, or some evil habit or other, would turn upon the sheep and worry them, and behave not like dogs but wolves, would be a foul and monstrous thing. — Republic, III, 416.

The dog is a watcher, and the guardian is also a watcher; and regarding them in this point of view only, is not the noble youth very like a well-bred dog? I mean that both of them ought to be quick to observe, and swift to overtake the enemy; and strong too, if, when they have caught him, they have to fight with him. — Republic, II, 375.

Water. Water admits of a division into two kinds, the one liquid and the other fusile. The liquid kind is composed of the small and unequal particles of water; and moves itself and is moved because of the inequality of the particles whereas the fusile kind being formed of large and equal elements is more stable than the other, and is solid and compact by reason of its equability. — Timaeus, 58.

If there is a deficiency in the supply of water, let the man dig down on his own land as far as the brick clay, and if at this depth he finds no water, let him carry water from his neighbors, as much as is required for his servants' drinking. — Laws, VIII, 844.

Water is the greatest element of nutrition in gardens, but is easily polluted. You cannot poison the soil, or the sun, or the air, which are the other elements of nutrition in plants, or divert them or steal them; but all these things may very likely happen in regard to water, which must therefore be protected by law. — Laws, VIII, 845.

Weakness. When there is weakness in a state there is also likely to be illness, the occasion of which may be very slight, one part introducing their democratical, the other their oligarchical allies, and the state may fall sick, and be at war with itself. — Republic, VIII, 556.

I will proclaim the law, not without an eye to the weakness of human nature. — Laws, IX, 854.

When a body is weak the addition of a slight touch from without may bring on illness. — Republic, VIII, 556.

Wealth. O Socrates, you will never be able to persuade me that gold and silver and similar things are not wealth. But I am very strongly of opinion that things which are useless to us are not wealth. . . . Useless things would no longer be regarded as wealth, whereas that would be wealth which enabled us to obtain what is useful to us. — Eryxias, 402.

The means by which oligarchy was maintained was excess of wealth. And the insatiable desire of wealth was also the ruin of oligarchy. — Republic, VIII, 562.

It remains to investigate what constitutes wealth; for unless you know this, you probably cannot come to an understanding as to whether it is a good or an evil. . . . What is useful to us is wealth, and what is useless to us is not wealth. — Eryxias, 399, 400.

The false admiration of wealth is bruited about among Greeks and non-Greeks. — Laws, IX, 870.

Wealth is well known to be a great comforter. — Republic, I, 329.

If we did not want the things of which we now stand in need, there would be no use in this so-called wealth. We now wish for wealth only in order that we may satisfy the desires and needs of the body in respect to our various wants. And therefore if the possession of wealth is useful in ministering to our bodily wants, and bodily wants were unknown to us, we should not need wealth, and possibly there would be no such thing as wealth. — Eryxias, 401.

Wealth is what is useful to this end [satisfaction of needs].—Eryxias, 401.

Nothing can be nobler and better than that the truth about wealth should be spoken — namely, that riches are for the sake of the body as the body is for the sake of the soul. They are good, and wealth is intended by nature to be for the sake of them, and is therefore inferior to them both. This argument would seem to show that he who would be happy ought not to seek to be rich, or rather he should seek to be rich justly and temperately, and then there would be no murders in states, which require to be purged away by other murders. — Laws, IX, 870.

He who spends on honorable objects, and acquires wealth by just means only, can hardly be remarkably rich, any more than exceedingly poor. The argument then is right in declaring that the immensely rich are not good, and, if they are not good, they are not happy. — Laws, V, 743.

The possession of justice in the soul is preferable to the possession of wealth. — Laws, XI, 913.

The war is against two enemies — wealth and poverty; one of whom corrupts the soul of man with luxury, while the other drives him by pain into utter shamelessness. What remedy can a city of sense find against this diseases? — Laws, XI, 919.

There is a principle of order and harmony in the acquisition of wealth; this also he will observe, and will not allow himself to be dazzled by the opinion of the world, and heap up riches to his own infinite harm. — Republic, IX, 591.

The excessive lust for wealth, and the neglect of all other things for the sake of money-making, was the ruin of oligarchy. — Republic, VIII, 562.

It is better that a person should not be wealthy, if his poverty prevents the fulfillment of his desires, and these desires are evil. — Eryxias, 397.

Weaving. To weave is to separate or disengage the warp from the woof. — Cratylus, 388.

No rational man would seek to analyze the notion of weaving for its own sake. — Statesman, 285.

Web. To me there seem to be a great many holes in their web. — Phaedrus, 268.

Well Done. Better a little which is well done, than a great deal imperfectly. — Theaetetus, 187.

Wet Nurse. There is the difficulty of getting the wet nurses to comply. — Laws, VII, 790.

Whole. That which has parts must be a whole of all the parts. Or would you say that a whole, although formed out of parts, is a single notion different from all the parts? — Theaetetus, 204.

I think that there is no difference between a whole and all. — Theaetetus, 205.

You yourself do not appreciate things as a whole but dissect and separate each general concept, so that you do not conceive the magnificent continuity of reality. — Greater Hippias, 301.

Wicked. The law would not have the wicked fancy that by raising temples and altars they can propitiate the gods with sacrifices and prayers, while they are really multiplying their crimes infinitely. — Laws, X, 910.

Upon this earth there dwell wicked men who would fain persuade their keepers by fawning flattery and prayers and supplications that it is lawful for them to encroach upon mankind with impunity. — Laws, X, 906.

They honor the wicked men when they are rich or have other sources of power, while they despise and neglect those who may be weak and poor, even though acknowledging that these are better than the others. — Republic, II, 364.

Wickedness. Wickedness is not easily concealed. — Republic, II, 365.

Will. Individuals would make regulations at variance with one another, and repugnant to the laws and habits of the living and their own previous habits, if a person were simply allowed to make any will which he pleases, and this were to take effect in whatever state he may be at the end of life; for most of us lose our senses in a manner, and are prostrated in mind when we think that we are soon about to die. — Laws, XI, 922.

Wily. When you say that Odysseus is wily, you clearly mean that he is false? — Exactly. — Lesser Hippias, 365.

Wine. Wine warms the soul as well as the body. — Timaeus, 60.

The drinking of wine intensifies our pleasures and pains, and passions and loves. — Laws, I, 645.

The winegrower is likely to be a better prophet of the sweetness or dryness of the vintage which is not yet gathered, than the musician. — Theaetetus, 178.

Winnowing. A winnowing machine separates off the elements most unlike from one another, and thrusts the similar elements together. — Timaeus, 53.

Wisdom. Not he who has riches, but he who has wisdom, is delivered from his misery. — First Alcibiades, 134.

How can there be the least shadow of wisdom when there is no harmony? And he is a partaker of wisdom who lives according to reason. — Laws, III, 689.

They should not neglect the higher wisdom for the sake of that wisdom which is concerned with the necessities of human life. — Letter, VI, 323.

Every man ought to be loved who says and manfully pursues and works out anything which is at all like wisdom: at the same time we shall do well to see them as they really are. — Euthydemus, 306.

The Spartans pretend to be ignorant, just because they do not wish to have it thought that they rule the world by wisdom, and not by valor of arms; considering that if the reason of their superiority were disclosed, all men would be practicing their wisdom. — Protagoras, 342.

None of these things will be well or beneficially done, if wisdom be wanting. — Charmides, 174.

Wisdom is the essence of virtue. — Epinomis, 977.

Wisdom always makes men fortunate: for by wisdom no man would ever err, and therefore he must act rightly and succeed, or his wisdom would be wisdom no longer. At last we somehow contrived to agree in a general conclusion, that he who had wisdom had no longer need of fortune. — Euthydemus, 280.

All of us have the innate capacity

of acquiring wisdom. — Epinomis, 974.

Surely courage is one thing, and wisdom another. — Laches, 195.

They believe that wisdom may be overmastered by anger, or pleasure, or pain, or love, or perhaps fear — just as if wisdom were a slave, and might be dragged about anyhow. Wisdom is a noble and commanding thing, which cannot be overcome, and will not allow a man to do anything which is contrary to it; wisdom will have strength to help him. — Protagoras, 352.

Wisdom is only utilization of knowledge. — Charmides, 174.

Man is confident that he possesses an innate capacity, though what it is, he cannot tell. Does not the case stand much thus with our desperate search for wisdom, a search so much more difficult than might be anticipated by those of us who can observe themselves and others with profound understanding? — Epinomis, 974.

Surely wisdom is good fortune; even a child may know that. — Euthydemus, 279.

Wisdom is claimed by the mass of mankind, arousing in them a disputing spirit and a lying conceit. — Philebus, 49.

As to wisdom and true conviction, happy is the man who acquires them even in his later years. — Laws, II, 653.

Wisdom is strength. — Protagoras, 350.

Those who are already wise are no longer lovers of wisdom; nor can they be lovers of wisdom who are ignorant to the extent of being evil. There remain those who have the misfortune to be ignorant, but are not yet hardened in their ignorance, or void of understanding, and do not as yet fancy that they know what they do not know: and therefore those who are the lovers of wisdom are as yet neither good nor bad. But the bad do not love wisdom any more than the good; for neither is unlike the friend of unlike, nor like of like. — Lysis, 218.

All other things hang upon the soul, and the things of the soul hang upon wisdom, if they are to be good. — Meno, 89.

I am far from saying that wisdom and the wise man have no existence. — Theaetetus, 166.

All men agree with one another on the necessity of wisdom, but on the choice of the wise way, they disagree. — Epinomis, 979.

Wisdom is the only good, and folly the only evil — all other things are indifferent. — Euthydemus, 281.

How I wish that wisdom could be infused through the medium of touch, out of the full into the empty man, like the water which the wool soaks out of the full vessel into an empty one. — Symposium, 175.

Every one of us, whether individual or state, ought to pray and endeavor that he may have wisdom. — Laws, III, 688.

The supreme difficulty is to know how we are to become good men. To get all other so-called good things is both possible and not too difficult — to get the wealth we need, or do not need, the bodily strength we need or do not need. And as for the soul, that it must be wise, there again we are all agreed; but on the question what wisdom it needs, the multitude are hopelessly in discord. — Epinomis, 979.

According to your report, earlier

thinkers appear to have been ignorant; the fate of Anaxagoras is said to have been just the opposite to yours, for when he inherited a sizable fortune, he neglected it and lost it all — so mindless was his wisdom — and the same kind of story is told of other great philosophers of former generations. Your success, I admit, is fine evidence of the wisdom of the present generation as compared with their predecessors, and it is a popular sentiment today that the wise men must above all be wise for themselves; of such wisdom the criterion is in the end the ability to make a lot of money. — Greater Hippias, 283.

Wise. Every man ought by all means to try and make himself as wise as he can. — Euthydemus, 282.

Some men are wise, even though they can neither read nor swim. — Laws, III, 689.

Which rejoice and sorrow most — the wise or the foolish? — Gorgias, 498.

The wise man will want to be ever with him who is better than himself. — Phaedo, 62.

A wise man is not likely to talk nonsense; let us try to understand him. — Theaetetus, 152.

I know that you are as much wiser than I am, as you are younger. — Euthyphro, 12.

When the wax of the soul is deep and abundant, and smooth and perfectly tempered, then the impressions which pass through the senses and sink into the heart of the soul, as Homer says in a parable, meaning to indicate the likeness of the soul to wax — these being pure and clear, and having a sufficient depth of wax, are also lasting, and minds such as these easily learn and easily retain, and are not liable to confusion, but have true imprints, for they are well spaced, and having clear impressions of things, as we term them, quickly distribute them into their proper places on the block. And such men are called wise. — Theaetetus, 194.

Is not the wiser always the handsomer? — Protagoras, 309.

I am called wise, for my hearers always imagine that I myself possess the wisdom which I find wanting in others. — Apology, 23.

The wise man is late for a fray, but not for a feast. — Gorgias, 447.

As to the epithet "wise" — wise in what? In all things small as well as great? — Laches, 192.

He who has learned the lessons we have described has certainly a reputation of wisdom. Whether such a man really is wise is the question we hope to determine. — Epinomis, 979.

They will call me wise even although I am not wise when they want to reproach me. — Apology, 38.

Wish. A man should not desire or endeavor to have all things according to his wish, while his wish is at variance with his reason. — Laws, III, 687.

The wish which a man has is, that all things may come to pass in accordance with the will of his soul. — Laws, III, 687.

Witchcraft. Witchcraft has no place at our oar. — Laws, I, 649.

Witness, False. If a man be twice convicted of false witness, he shall not be required, and if thrice, he shall not be allowed to bear witness. — Laws, XI, 379.

Every man who is engaged in any suit ought to be very careful of bringing false witness against anyone, either intentionally or unintentionally if he can help, for justice is truly said to be a modest virgin. A witness ought to be very careful not to sin against justice, especially in what relates to the loss of arms: he must distinguish the throwing them away when necessary, and not make that a reproach, or bring an undeserving action against some person on that account. — Laws, XII, 943.

Wolf. The wolf is the fiercest of animals. — Sophist, 231.

Wolves may come down on the fold from without. — Republic, III, 415.

The doers of unjust acts declare that the gods are lenient and divide the spoil with them. That is as if wolves might be supposed to toss a portion of their prey to the dogs, and they, mollified by the gift, suffered them to tear the flocks. This is the opinion of those who maintain that the gods are venal. — Laws, X, 906.

Woman. In most places women will not endure to have the truth spoken without raising an outcry. — Laws, VI, 781.

The grown-up women, no longer employed in spinning wool, are actively engaged in weaving the web of life, which will be no cheap or mean employment, and in the duty of serving and taking care of the household and bringing up children — in these they will observe a sort of mean, not participating in the toils of war. — Laws, VII, 806.

He would be utterly ridiculous, who would attempt to compel women to show how much they eat and drink in public. There is nothing at which the female sex is more likely to take offense. For women are accustomed to creep into dark places, and when dragged out into the light they will exert their utmost powers of resistance. — Laws, VI, 781.

Woman's nature is inferior to that of men in capacity of virtue. — Laws, VI, 781.

A woman is only a lesser man. — Republic, V, 455.

A woman's virtue may be easily described: her virtue is to order her house, and keep what is indoors, and obey her husband. — Meno, 71.

You are quite right in maintaining the general inferiority of the female sex; at the same time many women are in many things superior to many men, though, speaking generally, what you say is true. — Republic, V, 455.

Need I waste time in speaking of the art of weaving, and the management of pancakes and preserves, in which womenkind does really appear to be great, and in which the superiority of the other sex is the most laughable thing in the world? — Republic, V, 455.

If women are to have the same duties as men, they must have the same education. — Republic, V, 451.

We did not forget the women whose natures should be equally developed like those of men, and should share with them in their military pursuits, and in their ordinary way of life. — Timaeus, 18.

Unlike the Amazons, the women would be unable to take part in archery or any other skilled use of missiles. — Laws, VII, 806.

Woman, Old. Children make use of old women, to tell them nice tales. — Greater Hippias, 286.

Word. There will be no difference between words that are and are not set to music. — Republic, III, 398.

Does not the word express more than the fact? — Republic, V, 473.

Every spoken word is in a manner plainer than the unspoken. — Phaedrus, 238.

I was right after all in saying that words have a sense. — Euthydemus, 287.

The rhetorician ought to make a regular division, and acquire a distinct notion of two classes of words: words with fluctuating meaning, and words with steady meaning. He who made such a distinction would have an excellent principle. — Phaedrus, 263.

Word-Catching. Are you not ashamed to be word-catching, and when a man trips in a word, thinking that to be a piece of luck? — Gorgias, 489.

Word Splitter. My good friend, take my advice, and stop that eternal questioning; learn "the arts of business, and acquire the reputation of common sense," leaving to others those philosophical niceties; whether they are better described as follies or absurdities, they will only give you poverty for the inmate of your dwelling. Cease, then, to emulate those paltry splitters of words, and emulate only the man of substance and honor, who is well to do. — Gorgias, 486.

Work. A work is spoiled when not done at the right time. — Republic, II, 370.

They will work, in summer commonly stripped and barefoot, but in winter substantially clothed and shod. — Republic, II, 372.

Work is no disgrace. — Charmides, 163.

Working Class. The people are a third class, consisting of those who work with their own hands; they are not politicians, and have not much to live upon. This, when assembled, is the largest and most powerful class in a democracy. — Republic, VIII, 565.

World. No man of sense will believe that the world is a sick man who has a running nose. — Cratylus, 440.

The world is the fairest of creations and the divine artificer is the best of the causes.... He put intelligence in soul, and soul in body, and framed the universe to be the best and fairest work in the order of nature.... For the Deity intended to make this world like the fairest and most perfect of intelligible beings. — Timaeus, 29, 30.

The world must of necessity be the copy of something. — Timaeus, 29.

We must not say that the world is self-moved always. — Statesman, 269.

World Below. After death, as they say, the genius of each individual, to whom he belonged in life, leads him to a certain place in which the dead are gathered together for judgment, whence they go into the world below. — Phaedo, 107.

Worth. Will life be worth having, if the spirit of man be destroyed? — Crito, 48.

When the bodily constitution is gone, life is no longer endurable, though pampered with all kinds of meats and drinks, and having all wealth and all power; and shall we be told that when the very essence of the vital principle of justice is undermined and corrupted, life is still worth having to a man? — Republic, IV, 445.

Wrestling. As regards wrestling, the tricks which Antaeus and Cercyon devised in their systems out of the vain spirit of competition, do not deserve to have much said about them; but the true stand-up wrestling and art of liberating the neck and hands and sides, working with energy and constancy, with a composed strength, and for the sake of health, these are always useful, and not to be neglected. — Laws, VII, 796.

Writing. I would be very sorry if my treatise were poorly written. — Letter, VII, 341.

Anyone can see that there is no disgrace in the fact of writing. There may however be a disgrace in writing, not well, but badly. — Phaedrus, 258.

He will not seriously incline to "write in water" or that black fluid one calls ink, or in dumb characters which have not a word to say for themselves and cannot express the truth. — Phaedrus, 276.

I have enough religion for my own needs, as you might say of a bad writer — his writing is good enough for him. — Phaedrus, 242.

A love of controversy led me to write the book in the days of my youth; the motive, however, of writing, was not the ambition of an old man, but the pugnacity of a young one. — Parmenides, 128. *Vide* Conscience.

O most ingenious Theuth, the invention of yours will create forgetfulness in the learners' souls, because they will not use their memories; they will trust to the external written characters and not remember of themselves. — Phaedrus, 275.

He would be a simple person, and quite without understanding of the oracles of Thamus and Ammon, who should leave in writing or receive in writing any art under the idea that the written word would be intelligible or certain; or who deemed that writing was at all better than knowledge and recollection of the same matters. — Phaedrus, 275.

If he wrote at all, his motive was a disgraceful ambition either to appear as the author of the doctrine or as a man of culture. — Letter, VII, 344.

I am speaking of an intelligent writing which is graven in the soul of him who is learned, and can defend itself, and knows when to speak and when to be silent. — You mean the word of knowledge which has a living soul, and of which the written word is properly no more than an image? — Phaedrus, 276.

Wrong. I should be very wrong in refusing to aid in the improvement of anybody. — Laches, 200.

Shall we say that the omitting of wrong is unpleasant? — Laws, II, 663.

He who voluntarily does wrong and disgraceful things, if there be such a man, will be the good man? — There I cannot agree with you. — Nor can I agree with myself; and yet that seems to be the necessary deduction. As I was saying before, I wander up and down, and being in perplexity am always changing my opinion. — Lesser Hippias, 376.

It would be a monstrous thing to say that those who do wrong voluntarily are better than those who do wrong involuntarily. — And yet that appears to be the inference. — Lesser Hippias, 375.

You wrong me by stating something contrary to facts. — Letter III, 315.

As I am convinced that I never wronged another, I will assuredly not wrong myself. — Apology, 37.

When the state is wronged all are wronged. — Laws, VI, 768.

Those who would live happily should in the first place do no wrong to another, and ought not themselves to be wronged by others; to attain the first is not difficult, but there is great difficulty in acquiring the power of not being wronged. No man can be perfectly secure against wrong, unless he has become perfectly good; and cities are like individuals in this: For a city if good has a life of peace, but if evil, a life of war. — Laws, VIII, 829.

He will wrongly use that which he wrongly took. — Gorgias, 521.

Wrongdoer. One can afford to forgive as well as pity, the wrongdoer who is curable, and refrain and calm one's anger, not giving way to passion. But upon him who is incapable of reformation and incurably evil, the vials of our wrath should be poured out. — Laws, V, 731.

X

Xanthippe. Socrates' wife Xanthippe sat by him, and held his child in her arms. — Phaedo, 60.

Xerxes. After Darius came Xerxes, who again was brought up in the royal and luxurious fashion. Might we not justly say to him, O Darius, why did you not learn wisdom from the misfortunes of Cyrus, instead of bringing up Xerxes in the same way in which he brought up Cambyses? For Xerxes, being the creation of the same education, met with much the same fate as Cambyses. — Laws, III, 695.

Y

Yawning. A person when another yawns in his presence catches the infection of yawning from him. — Charmides, 169.

Year. The year is created when the sun completes his orbit. — Timaeus, 39.

Young. Young citizens must be habituated to forms and strains of virtue. — Laws, II, 656.

Young men are often enthusiasts of philosophy. — Letter, VII, 338.

Almost all young persons are alike beautiful in my eyes. — Charmides, 154.

The young man should not be told that in committing the worst of crimes he is far from doing anything outrageous. — Republic, II, 378.

At your young age, you are too much disposed to look to the opinions of men. — Parmenides, 130.

Why, my dear boy, you are young, and your ear is quickly caught, and your mind influenced by popular arguments. — Theaetetus, 162.

We should take counsel with our elders; for we are still young — too young to determine such a matter. — Protagoras, 314.

The young of all creatures cannot be quiet in their bodies or in their voices; they are always wanting to move, and cry out; at one time leaping and skipping, and overflowing with sportiveness and delight at something, and then again uttering all sorts of cries. — Laws, II, 653.

The characters of young men are subject to many changes in the course of their lives. — Laws, XI, 929.

Let the younger answer; he will incur less disgrace if he makes a mistake. — Theaetetus, 165.

The younger will be more severe. — Apology, 39.

They are young and there is still hope of them. — Protagoras, 328.

Being younger, I am not so experienced. — Laches, 181.

Youth. Youth and love live and move together. — Symposium, 195.

Youths will not grow up to honor if they are too rebellious and take no pains about themselves. — Laches, 179.

Any youth, when he first tastes intellectual subtleties, is delighted, and fancies that he has found a treasure of wisdom; in the first enthusiasm of his joy he sets every stone, or rather every thought rolling; he puzzles himself first and above all, and then he proceeds to puzzle his neighbors, whether they are older or younger, or of his own age — that makes no difference; neither father nor mother does he spare; no human being who has ears is safe from him, hardly even his dog. — Philebus, 15, 16.

So long as the youth has been and is well brought up, the ship of our state will have a good going. — Laws, VII, 813.

Youth is always able to improve. — Theaetetus, 146.

I beheld young men and girls holding friendly intercourse with one another. And there naturally arose in my mind a sort of apprehension — I could not help thinking how one is to deal with a city in which youths and girls are well nurtured, and have nothing to do, and are not undergoing excessive and servile toils which extinguish wantonness, and whose only cares during their whole life are sacrifices and festivals and dances. How will they abstain from desires which thrust many a man and woman into perdition? The ordinances already made may possibly get the better of most of these desires; moreover, the eye of the rulers is required always to watch over the young, and never to lose sight of them; and these provisions do, as far as human means can affect anything, exercise a regulating influence upon the desires in general. — Laws, VIII, 835, 836.

I never met any youth who was his equal in natural gifts: for he has a quickness of apprehension which is almost unrivaled, and he is remarkably gentle, and also most courageous; there is a union of qualities in him such as I should scarcely have thought that the combination was possible; for those who, like him, have quick and ready and retentive wits, have generally also quick tempers; they are ships without ballast; and the steadier sort, when they have to face study, are stupid and cannot remember. Whereas he moves surely and smoothly and successfully in the path of knowledge and inquiry, always making progress, like the noiseless flow of a river of oil; at his age, it is just wonderful. — Theaetetus, 144.

Youth is the time of learning. — Cratylus, 440.

We are resolved to take the greatest care of the youths, and not let them run about as they like, which is too often the way with the young, when they are no longer children. — Laches, 179.

Good youths often appear to be simple, and are easily victimized by the evil, because they have no samples of evil in their own souls. — Republic, III, 409.

The young of every creature has the triangles new, and may be compared to the keel of a vessel which is just off the stocks; they are locked closely together and yet the entire frame is soft and delicate, as if freshly formed of marrow and nurtured on milk. — Timaeus, 81.

Z

Zeal. Your zeal is invaluable, if a right one; but if wrong, the greater the zeal the greater the evil. — Crito, 46.

Zeno. Zeno was [at the time of the great Panathenaea] nearly forty years of age, of a noble figure and fair aspect; and in the days of his youth he was reported to have been beloved of Parmenides. — Parmenides, 127.

Zeus. Zeus, the god of gods, rules with law. — Critias, 120. What would you say to the tale of Zeus, who, while other gods and men were asleep, lay devising plans, but forgot them all in a moment through his lust, and was so completely overcome at the sight of Hera that he would not even go into the tent, but wanted to lie with her on the ground, declaring that he had never been in such a state of rapture before? — Republic, III, 390.